THE
OFFICIAL
FA AND
ENGLAND
YEARBOOK

1998-99

THE OFFICIAL FA AND ENGLAND YEARBOOK

1998-99

PAN BOOKS

This edition published 1997 by Pan Books

an imprint of Macmillan Publishers Limited
25 Eccleston Place, London SW1W 9NF
and Basingstoke

Associated companies throughout the world

ISBN 0 330 34583 4

1 3 5 7 9 8 6 4 2

A CIP catalogue record for this book is available from
the British Library.

Typeset by The Florence Group, Stoodleigh
Printed and bound in Great Britain by
The Bath Press, Bath

CONTENTS

1 ● FRANCE 98

A REPORT BY THE CHIEF EXECUTIVE

The World Cup Finals of 1998 was a mammoth event. A cumulative total of 475 million people in Britain watched live. The average audience, 8.5 million, a million more than in 1990. The figure for England's second round match against Argentina, shown on ITV, touched 26 million, approaching the figure for the semi-final against Germany in 1990, which was transmitted live on both terrestrial channels.

In France, too, tickets for all the matches were sold, the television coverage was immense and interest in all the host cities was high.

The atmosphere at all the matches was vibrant and colourful, though Paris came late to the party, with the French players complaining about the lack of passion in the semi-final against Croatia at St. Denis. Passion joined fashion when the hosts reached the final, however.

The support for the England team from the travelling fans at all their matches was tremendous, both in their numbers and their volume. Unfortunately, to achieve that, many were forced to pay over the odds for tickets. They certainly contributed hugely to the event.

The Scottish fans were, as always, marvellously barmy. For the first time in his life, surely the only time, the Chief Executive of The Football Association wore a Scottish scarf to a match.

FIFA's ban on the tackle likely to endanger the safety of an opponent proved much less controversial than other aspects of refereeing, particularly the problems increasingly caused by players' dramatics.

It may be that 1998 produced few truly memorable matches, though I would pick out a few worthy of mention. The 2–2 draws between Morocco and Norway and Chile and Italy were highlights at the start of Groups A and B, whilst Nigeria's 3–2 victory over Spain equally well kicked off Group D. And who could forget Iran's dramatic 2–1 defeat of USA?

England's dramatic match against Argentina was clearly the match of the Second Round, if not of the whole tournament.

The goal of the year was scored by Dennis Bergkamp, eliminating Argentina in the 90th minute of Holland's quarter-final match, but he could not repeat his brilliantly deadly technique in the semi-final against Brazil, who clinically despatched their penalties to go through to the final.

For me, the notable star performers included Chilavert, Paraguay's goalkeeper, who demonstrated his powerful dead-ball skill. In the Dutch side, Frank de Boer carried on the traditions of Koeman in the best possible way and Davids deserved to grace the final – all left foot and artistry. Our own Michael Owen exploded onto the world scene, surprising absolutely no one in the F.A. Technical Department, whilst Ince and Campbell were giants. Suker deservedly took the Golden Boot and his contribution epitomised the emergence of Croatia as a World force. Finally, for the host nation and ultimate Champions, Zidane purred through the French midfield and snatched the trophy with his two goals and Petit was a powerhouse, showing many of the skills we saw last season in the English Premiership.

So, all in all, a wonderful month of football in the last World Cup of this Millennium. And an inspiring incentive to match the hospitality of our friendly hosts by succeeding in out bid to stage the first European finals of the next millennium in England in 2006.

Graham Kelly

2 ● WORLD CUP FINALS 1930–1998

Year	Venue	Winner		Runner-up	Result
1930	Montevideo	Uruguay	v	Argentina	4 – 2
1934	Rome	Italy	v	Czechoslovakia	2 – 1 *
1938	Paris	Italy	v	Hungary	4 – 2
1950	Rio de Janeiro	Uruguay	v	Brazil	2 – 1
1954	Berne	West Germany	v	Hungary	3 – 2
1958	Stockholm	Brazil	v	Sweden	5 – 2
1962	Santiago	Brazil	v	Czechoslovakia	3 – 1
1966	Wembley	England	v	West Germany	4 – 2 *
1970	Mexico City	Brazil	v	Italy	4 – 1
1974	Munich	West Germany	v	Holland	2 – 1
1978	Buenos Aires	Argentina	v	Holland	3 – 1 *
1982	Madrid	Italy	v	West Germany	3 – 1
1986	Mexico City	Argentina	v	West Germany	3 – 2
1990	Rome	West Germany	v	Argentina	1 – 0
1994	Los Angeles	Brazil	v	Italy	0 – 0 †
1998	Paris	France	v	Brazil	3 – 0

*after extra time
†won on penalty-kicks

3 ● EUROPEAN CHAMPIONSHIP FINALS 1960–1996

Year	Venue	Winner		Runner-up	Result
1960	Paris	USSR	v	Yugoslavia	2 – 1
1964	Madrid	Spain	v	USSR	2 – 1
1968	Rome	Italy	v	Yugoslavia	2 – 0†
1972	Brussels	West Germany	v	USSR	3 – 0
1976	Belgrade	Czechoslovakia	v	West Germany	2 – 2 ‡
1980	Rome	West Germany	v	Belgium	2 – 1
1984	Paris	France	v	Spain	2 – 0
1988	Munich	Holland	v	USSR	2 – 0
1992	Gothenburg	Denmark	v	Germany	2 – 0
1996	Wembley	Germany	v	Czech Republic	2 – 1 *

†*after 1–1 draw*
‡*won on penalty-kicks*
won with "golden goal"

4 ● EUROPEAN CHAMPION CLUBS' CUP WINNERS 1956–1998

Year	Venue	Winner		Runners-up	Result
1956	Paris	Real Madrid	v	Stade de Rheims	4 – 3
1957	Madrid	Real Madrid	v	AC Fiorentina	2 – 0
1958	Brussels	Real Madrid	v	AC Milan	3 – 2 *
1959	Stuttgart	Real Madrid	v	Stace de Rheims	2 – 0
1960	Glasgow	Real Madrid	v	Eintracht Frankfurt	7 – 3
1961	Berne	Benfica	v	Barcelona	3 – 2
1962	Amsterdam	Benfica	v	Real Madrid	5 – 3
1963	Wembley	AC Milan	v	Benfica	2 – 1
1964	Vienna	Inter-Milan	v	Real Madrid	3 – 1
1965	Madrid	Inter-Milan	v	Benfica	1 – 0
1966	Brussels	Real Madrid	v	Partizan Belgrade	2 – 1
1967	Lisbon	Celtic	v	Inter-Milan	2 – 1
1968	Wembley	Manchester United	v	Benfica	4 – 1 *
1969	Madrid	AC Milan	v	Ajax Amsterdam	4 – 1
1970	Milan	Feyenoord	v	Celtic	2 – 1 *
1971	Wembley	Ajax Amsterdam	v	Panathinaikos	2 – 0
1972	Rotterdam	Ajax Amsterdam	v	Inter-Milan	2 – 0
1973	Belgrade	Ajax Amsterdam	v	Juventus	1 – 0
1974	Brussels	Bayern Munich	v	Atletico Madrid	1 – 1
	Brussels	*Bayern Munich*	*v*	*Atletico Madrid*	*4 – 0*
1975	Paris	Bayern Munich	v	Leeds United	2 – 0
1976	Glasgow	Bayern Munich	v	St Etienne	1 – 0
1977	Rome	Liverpool	v	Borussia Mönchengladbach	3 – 1
1978	Wembley	Liverpool	v	FC Bruges	1 – 0
1979	Munich	Nottingham Forest	v	Malmö	1 – 0
1980	Madrid	Nottingham Forest	v	Hamburg	1 – 0
1981	Paris	Liverpool	v	Real Madrid	1 – 0
1982	Rotterdam	Aston Villa	v	Bayern Munich	1 – 0
1983	Athens	Hamburg	v	Juventus	1 – 0
1984	Rome	Liverpool	v	Roma	1 – 1 **
1985	Brussels	Juventus	v	Liverpool	1 – 0
1986	Seville	Steaua Bucharest	v	Barcelona	0 – 0 **
1987	Vienna	Porto	v	Bayern Munich	2 – 1
1988	Stuttgart	PSV Eindhoven	v	Benfica	0 – 0 **
1989	Barcelona	AC Milan	v	Steaua Bucharest	4 – 0
1990	Vienna	AC Milan	v	Benfica	1 – 0
1991	Bari	Red Star Belgrade	v	Marseille	0 – 0 **
1992	Wembley	Barcelona	v	Sampdoria	1 – 0 *
1993	Munich	Marseille	v	AC Milan	1 – 0
1994	Athens	AC Milan	v	Barcelona	4 – 0
1995	Vienna	Ajax Amsterdam	v	AC Milan	1 – 0
1996	Rome	Juventus	v	Ajax Amsterdam	1 – 1 **
1997	Munich	Borussia Dortmund	v	Juventus	3 – 1
1998	Amsterdam	Real Madrid	v	Juventus	1 – 0

*after extra time
**won on penalty-kicks

5 ● EUROPEAN CUP WINNERS' CUP WINNERS 1961–1998

Year	Venue	Winner		Runners-up	Result
1961		AC Fiorentina	v	Glasgow Rangers	4 – 1 †
1962	Glasgow	Atletico Madrid	v	AC Fiorentina	1 – 1
	Stuttgart	Atletico Madrid	v	AC Fiorentina	3 – 0
1963	Rotterdam	Tottenham Hotspur	v	Atletico Madrid	5 – 1
1964	Brussels	Sporting Lisbon	v	MTK Budapest	3 – 3 *
	Antwerp	Sporting Lisbon	v	MTK Budapest	1 – 0
1965	Wembley	West Ham United	v	Munich 1860	2 – 0
1966	Glasgow	Borussia Dortmund	v	Liverpool	2 – 1 *
1967	Nuremberg	Bayern Munich	v	Rangers	1 – 0 *
1968	Rotterdam	AC Milan	v	Hamburg	2 – 0
1969	Basle	Slovan Bratislava	v	Barcelona	3 – 2
1970	Vienna	Manchester City	v	Gornik Zabrze	2 – 1
1971	Athens	Chelsea	v	Real Madrid	1 – 1 *
	Athens	Chelsea	v	Real Madrid	2 – 1
1972	Barcelona	Glasgow Rangers	v	Moscow Dynamo	3 – 2
1973	Salonika	AC Milan	v	Leeds United	1 – 0
1974	Rotterdam	Magdeburg	v	AC Milan	2 – 0
1975	Basle	Dynamo Kiev	v	Ferencvaros	3 – 0
1976	Brussels	Anderlecht	v	West Ham United	4 – 2
1977	Amsterdam	Hamburg	v	Anderlecht	2 – 0
1978	Paris	Anderlecht	v	Austria Vienna	4 – 0
1979	Basle	Barcelona	v	Fortuna Düsseldorf	4 – 3 *
1980	Brussels	Valencia	v	Arsenal	0 – 0 **
1981	Düsseldorf	Dynamo Tbilisi	v	Carl Zeiss Jena	2 – 1
1982	Barcelona	Barcelona	v	Standard Liège	2 – 1
1983	Gothenburg	Aberdeen	v	Real Madrid	2 – 1 *
1984	Basle	Juventus	v	Porto	2 – 1
1985	Rotterdam	Everton	v	Rapid Vienna	3 – 1
1986	Lyon	Dynamo Kiev	v	Atletico Madrid	3 – 0
1987	Athens	Ajax Amsterdam	v	Lokomotiv Leipzig	1 – 0
1988	Strasbourg	Mechelen	v	Ajax Amsterdam	1 – 0
1989	Berne	Barcelona	v	Sampdoria	2 – 0
1990	Gothenburg	Sampdoria	v	Anderlecht	2 – 0
1991	Rotterdam	Manchester United	v	Barcelona	2 – 1
1992	Lisbon	Werder Bremen	v	Monaco	2 – 0
1993	Wembley	Parma	v	Royal Antwerp	3 – 1
1994	Copenhagen	Arsenal	v	Parma	1 – 0
1995	Paris	Real Zaragoza	v	Arsenal	2 – 1 *
1996	Brussels	Paris St-Germain	v	Rapid Vienna	1 – 0
1997	Rotterdam	Barcelona	v	Paris St-Germain	1 – 0
1998	Stockholm	Chelsea	v	VfB Stuttgart	1 – 0

†aggregate over two legs
*after extra time
**won on penalty-kicks

● 5

6 ● UEFA CUP WINNERS 1958–1998

Known also as the Inter Cities Fairs' Cup until 1971. Two-leg finals except in 1964, 1965 and 1998. Aggregate scores.

Year	Winner		Runners-up	Result
1958	Barcelona	v	London	8 – 2
1960	Barcelona	v	Birmingham	4 – 1
1961	Roma	v	Birmingham	4 – 2
1962	Valencia	v	Barcelona	7 – 3
1963	Valencia	v	Dynamo Zagreb	4 – 1
1964	Real Zaragoza	v	Valencia	2 – 1
1965	Ferencvaros	v	Juventus	1 – 0
1966	Barcelona	v	Real Zaragoza	4 – 3
1967	Dynamo Zagreb	v	Leeds United	2 – 0
1968	Leeds United	v	Ferencvaros	1 – 0
1969	Newcastle United	v	Ujpest Dozsa	6 – 2
1970	Arsenal	v	Anderlecht	4 – 3
1971	Leeds United	v	Juventus	3 – 3 *
1972	Tottenham Hotspur	v	Wolverhampton Wanderers	3 – 2
1973	Liverpool	v	Borussia Mönchengladbach	3 – 2
1974	Feyenoord	v	Tottenham Hotspur	4 – 2
1975	Borussia Mönchengladbach	v	Twente Enschede	5 – 1
1976	Liverpool	v	FC Bruges	4 – 3
1977	Juventus	v	Bilbao	2 – 2 *
1978	PSV Eindhoven	v	Bastia	3 – 0
1979	Borussia Mönchengladbach	v	Red Star Belgrade	2 – 1
1980	Eintracht Frankfurt	v	Borussia Mönchengladbach	3 – 3 *
1981	Ipswich Town	v	AZ 67 Alkmaar	5 – 4
1982	IFK Gothenburg	v	Hamburg	4 – 0
1983	Anderlecht	v	Benfica	2 – 1
1984	Tottenham Hotspur	v	Anderlecht	2 – 2 †
1985	Real Madrid	v	Videoton	3 – 1
1986	Real Madrid	v	Cologne	5 – 3
1987	IFK Gothenburg	v	Dundee United	2 – 1
1988	Bayer Leverkusen	v	Espanol	3 – 3 †
1989	Napoli	v	Stuttgart	5 – 4
1990	Juventus	v	AC Fiorentina	3 – 1
1991	Inter-Milan	v	Roma	2 – 1
1992	Ajax Amsterdam	v	Torino	2 – 2 *
1993	Juventus	v	Borussia Dortmund	6 – 1
1994	Inter-Milan	v	Casino Salzburg	2 – 0
1995	Parma	v	Juventus	2 – 1
1996	Bayern Munich	v	Bordeaux	5 – 1
1997	Schalke	v	Inter-Milan	1 – 1 †
1998	Inter-Milan	v	Lazio	3 – 0

*won on away goals rule
†won on penalty-kicks 3–0

7 ● GLORY DAYS FOR CHELSEA

REVIEW OF THE EUROPEAN SEASON
1997–98

Almost thirty years ago Chelsea achieved a special "double" of FA Cup and Cup Winners' Cup in successive seasons. Now the glory days were definitely back as a cosmopolitan Blues team overcame VfB Stuttgart in Stockholm on 13 May, twelve months after beating Middlesbrough at Wembley. But in their European semi-final with Vicenza, the position looked desperate after the Serie A outfit had gone into a 2 – 0 aggregate lead during the second leg at the Bridge. Chelsea were then obliged to score three without reply, which they managed courtesy of Poyet, Zola and Hughes.

Following a frustrating series of defeats against German sides in recent years – notably at Italia 90 and Euro 96 and in Manchester United's European Cup semi-final in '97 – Chelsea finally turned the tables. Their match-winning hero in the Rasunda Stadium was Gianfranco Zola, who didn't even enter the fray until 19 minutes from time. The stocky Italian international had struggled for nine months to recapture the form that had made him one of the most feared players in England. Champing at the bit on the touchline, Chelsea coach Graham Rix finally threw Zola into the action and within a minute he had run onto Wise's through-ball and hit a half-volley high into Wohlfahrt's goal. It was a piece of brilliance that could well have boosted his chances of being included in Maldini's World Cup squad.

Italian giants Juventus must have had a sense of deja vu after their Champions' Cup Final with Real Madrid in the Amsterdam Arena on 20 May. For the second successive season they had gone into the final as clear favourites and ended up losing. A legendary set of Real players - including the likes of Di Stefano, Puskas and Kopa - had won the first five European Cups and established the status of the competition. Now, most observers thought, a poor imitation would not make an impact this time. The portents were not good: Real had lost three of their last six matches, had not won away from Madrid since the previous November and had finished a miserable (for them) fourth in the League. There were so many world-class players on view in Amsterdam that there were eight internationals on the benches! Pedrag Mijatovic, a Yugoslav, scored an opportunist goal on 66 minutes and it was enough for Real to put their name on the Cup for the first time since 1966.

Inter-Milan, last year's beaten finalists in the UEFA Cup, won the trophy for the third time in the 1990s in a one-off match in Paris's Parc des Princes against Lazio on 6 May. So, impressively, three Serie A clubs made it to European finals, though there were plenty of non-Italians in their line-ups. Gazza's old club Lazio, essentially one without a "history" in Europe, could hardly have made a worse start to their first final, the Chilean Zamorano speeding clear of a static defence to blast Inter in front after only four minutes. Lazio were still in contention at the break but were blown away in the second half as Zanetti and Ronaldo added further goals. In a meaningless last few minutes West (Inter) and Almeyda (Lazio) were red-carded by the Spanish referee.

Seven English clubs enjoyed mixed fortunes in Europe. Chelsea became the third English side to lift the Cup Winners' Cup in eight seasons. Manchester United (Champions' Cup) and Aston Villa (UEFA Cup) were quarter-finalists, losing to Monaco and Atletico Madrid respectively. United won five out of six matches at the League stage and mighty Juventus were humbled on one of those magical European nights at Old Trafford.

Newcastle United were our other representative in the Champions' Cup, the Premiership runners-up now allowed in by UEFA, and there was an Asprilla-inspired 3 – 2 victory against Barcelona at St. James' Park to live in the memory. But they ultimately failed to progress beyond Group C. Our other three teams in the UEFA Cup had undistinguished campaigns: Arsenal (v PAOK Salonika) and Leicester City (v Atletico Madrid) went out in the first round and Liverpool (v Strasbourg, despite a thrilling Anfield fight back) in the second.

8 ● FIFA WORLD CUP FINALS – FRANCE 1998

GROUP MATCHES

GROUP A

10.06.98   St. Denis   80,000
Brazil 2   Cesar Sempaio, Boyd o.g.
Scotland 1   Collins (pen.)

10.06.98   Montpellier   29,750
Morocco 2   Hadji, Hadda
Norway 2   Chippo o.g., Eggen

16.06.98   Bordeaux   30,236
Scotland 1   Burley
Norway 1   Flo H

16.06.98   Nantes   33,236
Brazil 3   Ronaldo, Rivaldo, Bebeto
Morocco 0

23.06.98   St. Etienne   35,500
Scotland 0
Morocco 3   Bassir 2, Hadda

23.06.98   Marseille   55,000
Brazil 1   Bebeto
Norway 2   Flo T., Rekdal (pen.)

	P	W	D	L	F	A	Pts
Brazil	3	2	0	1	6	3	6
Norway	3	1	2	0	5	4	5
Morocco	3	1	1	1	5	5	4
Scotland	3	0	1	2	2	6	1

Brazil and Norway qualify for the Round of 16

GROUP B

11.06.98   Bordeaux   31,800
Italy 2   Vieri, Baggio R. (pen.)
Chile 2   Salas 2

11.06.98   Toulouse   33,460
Cameroon 1   Njanka
Austria 1   Polster

17.06.98   St. Etienne   30,392
Chile 1   Salas
Austria 1   Vastic

Holland's Overmars sprints through the Belgian defence in the Stade de France.

17.06.98   Montpellier   35,500
Italy 3   Di Biagio, Vieri 2
Cameroon 0

23.06.98   St. Denis   75,000
Italy 2   Vieri, Baggio R.
Austria 1   Herzog (pen.)

23.06.98   Nantes   39,000
Chile 1   Sierra
Cameroon 1   Mboma

	P	W	D	L	F	A	Pts
Italy	3	2	1	0	7	3	7
Chile	3	0	3	0	4	4	3
Austria	3	0	2	1	3	4	2
Cameroon	3	0	2	1	2	5	2

Italy and Chile qualify for the Round of 16

GROUP C

12.06.98   Lens   38,140
Saudi Arabia 0
Denmark 1   Rieper

12.06.98   Marseille   55,077
France 3   Dugarry, Issa o.g., Henry
South Africa 0

18.06.98   Toulouse   36,500
South Africa 1   McCarthy
Denmark 1   Nielsen

18.06.98   St. Denis   75,000
France 4   Henry 2, Trezeguet, Lizarazu
Saudi Arabia 0

24.06.98   Lyon   43,500
France 2   Djorkaeff (pen.), Petit
Denmark 1   Laudrup M. (pen.)

24.06.98   Bordeaux   34,500
South Africa 2   Bartlett 2 (1 pen.)
Saudi Arabia 2   Al-Jaber (pen.), Al-Thynayan (pen.)

	P	W	D	L	F	A	Pts
France	3	3	0	0	9	1	9
Denmark	3	1	1	1	3	3	4
South Africa	3	0	2	1	3	6	2
Saudi Arabia	3	0	1	2	2	7	1

France and Denmark qualify for the Round of 16

GROUP D

12.06.98   Montpellier   27,650
Paraguay 0
Bulgaria 0

13.06.98   Nantes   33,257
Spain 2   Hierro, Raul
Nigeria 3   Adepoju, Zubizarreta o.g., Oliseh

19.06.98   Paris   48,500
Nigeria 1   Ikpeba
Bulgaria 0

Paul Scholes shoots England into a 2–0 lead against Tunisia in Marseille.

19.06.98   St. Etienne   35,300
Spain 0
Paraguay 0

24.06.98   Lens   40,500
Spain 6   Hierro (pen.), Luis Enrique, Morientes 2,
          Kiko 2
Bulgaria 1   Kostadinov

24.06.98   Toulouse   36,500
Nigeria 1   Oruma
Paraguay 3   Ayala, Benitez, Cardoso

	P	W	D	L	F	A	Pts
Nigeria	3	2	0	1	5	5	6
Paraguay	3	1	2	0	3	1	5
Spain	3	1	1	1	8	4	4
Bulgaria	3	0	1	2	1	7	1

Nigeria and Paraguay qualify for the Round of 16

GROUP E

13.06.98   Lyon   37,588
South Korea 1   Ha Seok-Ju
Mexico 3   Pelaez, Hernandez 2

13.06.98   St. Denis   75,000
Holland 0
Belgium 0

20.06.98   Bordeaux   34,750
Belgium 2   Wilmots 2
Mexico 2   Garcia Aspe (pen.), Blanco

20.06.98   Marseille   55,000
Holland 5   Cocu, Overmars, Bergkamp, Van
            Hooijdonk, de Boer R.
South Korea 0

25.6.98   Paris   48,500
Belgium 1   Nilis
South Korea 1   Yoo Sang-Chul

25.06.98   St. Etienne   35,500
Holland 2   Cocu, de Boer R.
Mexico 2   Pelaez, Hernandez

	P	W	D	L	F	A	Pts
Holland	3	1	2	0	7	2	5
Mexico	3	1	2	0	7	5	5
Belgium	3	0	3	0	3	3	3
South Korea	3	0	1	2	2	9	1

Holland and Mexico qualify for the Round of 16

GROUP F

14.06.98   St. Etienne   30,392
Yugoslavia 1   Mihajlovic
Iran 0

15.06.98   Paris   43,815
Germany 2   Moller, Klinsmann
USA 0

21.06.98   Lens   40,775
Germany 2   Mihajlovic o.g., Bierhoff
Yugoslavia 2   Mijatovic, Stojkovic

21.06.98   Lyon   43,500
USA 1   McBride
Iran 2   Estili, Mahdavikia

25.06.98   Montpellier   35,000
Germany 2   Bierhoff, Klinsmann
Iran 0

25.06.98   Nantes   39,000
USA 0
Yugoslavia 1   Komljenovic

	P	W	D	L	F	A	Pts
Germany	3	2	1	0	6	2	7
Yugoslavia	3	2	1	0	4	2	7
Iran	3	1	0	2	2	4	3
USA	3	0	0	3	1	5	0

Germany and Yugoslavia qualify for the Round of 16

GROUP G

15.06.98   Marseille   54,587
England 2   Shearer, Scholes
Tunisia 0

15.06.98   Lyon   37,572
Romania 1   Ilie
Colombia 0

22.06.98   Montpellier   35,000
Colombia 1   Preciado
Tunisia 0

22.06.98   Toulouse   36,500
Romania 2   Moldovan, Petrescu
England 1   Owen

26.06.98   St. Denis   80,000
Romania 1   Moldovan
Tunisia 1   Souayah (pen.)

26.06.98   Lens   41,275
Colombia 0
England 2   Anderton, Beckham

	P	W	D	L	F	A	Pts
Romania	3	2	1	0	4	2	7
England	3	2	0	1	5	2	6
Colombia	3	1	0	2	1	3	3
Tunisia	3	0	1	2	1	4	1

Romania and England qualify for the Round of 16

GROUP H

14.06.98   Toulouse   33,400
Argentina 1   Batistuta
Japan 0

14.06.98   Lens   38,058
Jamaica 1   Earle
Croatia 3   Stanic, Prosinecki, Suker

20.06.98   Nantes   39,000
Japan 0
Croatia 1   Suker

21.06.98   Paris   48,500
Argentina 5   Ortega 2, Batistuta 3 (1 pen.)
Jamaica 0

26.06.98   Lyon   43,500
Japan 1   Nakayama
Jamaica 2   Whitmore 2

26.06.98   Bordeaux   35,000
Argentina 1   Pineda
Croatia 0

	P	W	D	L	F	A	Pts
Argentina	3	3	0	0	7	0	9
Croatia	3	2	0	1	4	2	6
Jamaica	3	1	0	2	3	9	3
Japan	3	0	0	3	1	4	0

Argentina and Croatia qualify for the Round of 16

ROUND OF 16

27.06.98   Marseille   59,500
Italy 1   Vieri
Norway 0

27.06.98   Paris   48,500
Brazil 4   Cesar Sempaio 2, Ronaldo 2 (1 pen.)
Chile 1   Salas

28.06.98   Lens   41,275
France 1   Blanc
Paraguay 0
(France won with a 'golden goal')

28.06.98   St. Denis   79,500
Nigeria 1   Babangida
Demark   Moller, Laudrup B., Sand, Helveg

29.06.98   Montpellier   35,000
Germany 2   Klinsmann, Bierhoff
Mexico 1   Hernandez

29.06.98   Toulouse   36,500
Holland 2   Bergkamp, Davids
Yugoslavia 1   Komljenovic

30.06.98   Bordeaux   34,700
Romania 0
Croatia 1   Suker (pen.)

30.06.98   St. Etienne   30,600
Argentina 2   Batistuta (pen.), Zanetti
England 2   Shearer (pen.), Owen
Argentina won 4–3 on penalties

QUARTER FINALS

03.07.98   St. Denis   77,000
Italy 0
France 0
France won 4–3 on penalties

03.07.98   Nantes   35,500
Brazil 3   Bebeto, Rivaldo 2
Denmark 2   Jorgensen, Laudrup 8

04.07.98   Marseille   55,000
Holland 2   Kluivert, Bergkamp
Argentina 1   Lopez

04.07.98   Lyon   39,100
Germany 0
Croatia 3   Jarni, Vlaovic, Suker

SEMI FINALS

07.07.98   Marseille   54,000
Brazil 1   Ronaldo
Holland 1   Kluivert
Brazil won 4–2 on penalties

08.07.98   St. Denis   76,000
France 2   Thurman 2
Croatia 1   Suker

Match for Third Place

11.07.98   Paris   45,500
Holland 1   Zenden
Croatia 2   Prosinecki, Suker

FINAL

12.07.98   St. Denis   75,000
Brazil 0
France 3   Zidane 2, Petit

9 ● EUROPEAN CHAMPIONSHIP 2000

QUALIFYING COMPETITION

GROUP 1

(Italy, Denmark, Switzerland, Wales, Belarus)

05.09.98	Wales – Italy
05.09.98	Belarus – Denmark
10.10.98	Denmark – Wales
10.10.98	Italy – Switzerland
14.10.98	Wales – Belarus
14.10.98	Switzerland – Denmark
27.03.99	Denmark – Italy
27.03.99	Belarus – Switzerland
31.03.99	Italy – Belarus
31.03.99	Switzerland – Wales
05.06.99	Denmark – Belarus
05.06.99	Italy – Wales
09.06.99	Wales – Denmark
09.06.99	Switzerland – Italy
04.09.99	Denmark – Switzerland
04.09.99	Belarus – Wales
08.09.99	Italy – Denmark
08.09.99	Switzerland – Belarus
09.10.99	Wales – Switzerland
09.10.99	Belarus – Italy

GROUP 2

(Norway, Greece, Georgia, Latvia, Slovenia, Albania)

05.09.98	Georgia – Albania
06.09.98	Greece – Slovenia
06.09.98	Norway – Latvia
10.10.98	Albania – Greece
10.10.98	Slovenia – Norway
10.10.98	Latvia – Georgia
14.10.98	Norway – Albania
14.10.98	Greece – Georgia
14.10.98	Slovenia – Latvia
27.03.99	Greece – Norway
27.03.99	Georgia – Slovenia
31.03.99	Slovenia – Albania
31.03.99	Latvia – Greece
28.04.99	Albania – Latvia
28.04.99	Georgia – Norway
30.05.99	Norway – Georgia
05.06.99	Albania – Norway
05.06.99	Georgia – Greece
05.06.99	Latvia – Slovenia
09.06.99	Albania – Slovenia
09.06.99	Greece – Latvia
04.09.99	Norway – Greece
04.09.99	Latvia – Albania
04.09.99	Slovenia – Georgia

08.09.99	Greece – Albania
08.09.99	Norway – Slovenia
08.09.99	Georgia – Latvia
09.10.99	Albania – Georgia
09.10.99	Slovenia – Greece
09.10.99	Latvia – Norway

GROUP 3

(Germany, Turkey, Finland, Northern Ireland, Moldova)

05.09.98	Finland – Moldova
05.09.98	Turkey – Northern Ireland
10.10.98	Turkey – Germany
10.10.98	Northern Ireland – Finland
14.10.98	Moldova – Germany
14.10.98	Turkey – Finland
18.11.98	Northern Ireland – Moldova
27.03.99	Northern Ireland – Germany
27.03.99	Turkey – Moldova
31.03.99	Germany – Finland
31.03.99	Moldova – Northern Ireland
04.06.99	Germany – Moldova
05.06.99	Finland – Turkey
09.06.99	Moldova – Finland
04.09.99	Finland – Germany
04.09.99	Northern Ireland – Turkey
08.09.99	Germany – Northern Ireland
08.09.99	Moldova – Turkey
09.10.99	Germany – Turkey
09.10.99	Finland – Northern Ireland

GROUP 4

(Russia, France, Ukraine, Iceland, Armenia, Andorra)

05.09.98	Armenia – Andorra
05.09.98	Ukraine – Russia
05.09.98	Iceland – France
10.10.98	Andorra – Ukraine
10.10.98	Russia – France
10.10.98	Armenia – Iceland
14.10.98	Ukraine – Armenia
14.10.98	France – Andorra
14.10.98	Iceland – Russia
27.03.99	Andorra – Iceland
27.03.99	France – Ukraine
27.03.99	Armenia – Russia
31.03.99	Ukraine – Iceland
31.03.99	Russia – Andorra
31.03.99	France – Armenia
05.06.99	Ukraine – Andorra
05.06.99	France – Russia

05.06.99	Iceland – Armenia	08.09.99	Israel – San Marino
09.06.99	Andorra – France	08.09.99	Spain – Cyprus
09.06.99	Russia – Iceland	09.10.99	Spain – Israel
09.06.99	Armenia – Ukraine	10.10.99	Austria – Cyprus
04.09.99	Ukraine – France		
04.09.99	Iceland – Andorra		
04.09.99	Russia – Armenia		
08.09.99	Andorra – Russia		
08.09.99	Iceland – Ukraine		
08.09.99	Armenia – France		
09.10.99	France – Iceland		
09.10.99	Russia – Ukraine		
09.10.99	Andorra – Armenia		

GROUP 7

(Romania, Portugal, Slovakia, Hungary, Liechtenstein, Azerbaijan)

02.09.98	Romania – Liechtenstein
05.09.98	Slovakia – Azerbaijan
06.09.98	Hungary – Portugal
10.10.98	Portugal – Romania
10.10.98	Liechtenstein – Slovakia
10.10.98	Azerbaijan – Hungary
14.10.98	Liechtenstein – Azerbaijan
14.10.98	Hungary – Romania
14.10.98	Slovakia – Portugal
26.03.99	Portugal – Azerbaijan
27.03.99	Hungary – Liechtenstein
27.03.99	Romania – Slovakia
31.03.99	Liechtenstein – Portugal
31.03.99	Azerbaijan – Romania
31.03.99	Slovakia – Hungary
05.06.99	Portugal – Slovakia
05.06.99	Azerbaijan – Liechtenstein
05.06.99	Romania – Hungary
09.06.99	Portugal – Liechtenstein
09.06.99	Hungary – Slovakia
09.06.99	Romania – Azerbaijan
03.09.99	Azerbaijan – Portugal
04.09.99	Liechtenstein – Hungary
04.09.99	Slovakia – Romania
08.09.99	Hungary – Azerbaijan
08.09.99	Romania – Portugal
08.09.99	Slovakia – Liechtenstein
09.10.99	Liechtenstein – Romania
09.10.99	Azerbaijan – Slovakia
10.10.99	Portugal – Hungary

GROUP 5

(England, Bulgaria, Sweden, Poland, Luxembourg)

05.09.98	Sweden – England
06.09.98	Bulgaria – Poland
10.10.98	Poland – Luxembourg
10.10.98	England – Bulgaria
14.10.98	Luxembourg – England
14.10.98	Bulgaria – Sweden
27.03.99	Sweden – Luxembourg
27.03.99	England – Poland
31.03.99	Poland – Sweden
31.03.99	Luxembourg – Bulgaria
05.06.99	Poland – Bulgaria
05.06.99	England – Sweden
09.06.99	Luxembourg – Poland
09.06.99	Bulgaria – England
04.09.99	England – Luxembourg
05.09.99	Sweden – Bulgaria
08.09.99	Poland – England
08.09.99	Luxembourg – Sweden
09.10.99	Sweden – Poland
10.10.99	Bulgaria – Luxembourg

GROUP 6

(Spain, Austria, Israel, Cyprus, San Marino)

05.09.98	Austria – Israel
05.09.98	Cyprus – Spain
10.10.98	Cyprus – Austria
10.10.98	San Marino – Israel
14.10.98	San Marino – Austria
14.10.98	Israel – Spain
18.11.98	San Marino – Cyprus
10.02.99	Cyprus – San Marino
27.03.99	Spain – Austria
28.03.99	Israel – Cyprus
31.03.99	San Marino – Spain
28.04.99	Austria – San Marino
05.06.99	Spain – San Marino
06.06.99	Israel – Austria
04.09.99	Austria – Spain
05.09.99	Cyprus – Israel

GROUP 8

(Yugoslavia, Croatia, Rep. of Ireland, FYR Macedonia, Malta)

05.09.98	Rep. of Ireland – Croatia
06.09.98	FYR Macedonia – Malta
10.10.98	Malta – Croatia
10.10.98	Yugoslavia – Rep. of Ireland
14.10.98	Rep. of Ireland – Malta
14.10.98	Croatia – FYR Macedonia
18.11.98	Malta – FYR Macedonia
10.02.99	Malta – Yugoslavia
27.03.99	FYR Macedonia – Rep. of Ireland
27.03.99	Yugoslavia – Croatia
31.03.99	Croatia – Malta
31.03.99	Yugoslavia – FYR Macedonia
05.06.99	FYR Macedonia – Croatia

05.06.99	Rep. of Ireland – Yugoslavia
09.06.99	Yugoslavia – Malta
04.09.99	Croatia – Rep. of Ireland
08.09.99	Malta – Rep. of Ireland
08.09.99	FYR Macedonia – Yugoslavia
10.10.99	Croatia – Yugoslavia
10.10.99	Rep. of Ireland – FYR Macedonia

GROUP 9

(Scotland, Czech Republic, Lithuania, Bosnia-Herzegovina, Faroe Islands, Estonia)

04.06.98	Estonia – Faroe Islands 5–0
19.08.98	Bosnia-Herzegovina – Faroe Islands
05.09.98	Bosnia-Herzegovina – Estonia
05.09.98	Lithuania – Scotland
06.09.98	Faroe Islands – Czech Republic
10.10.98	Bosnia-Herzegovina – Czech Republic
10.10.98	Lithuania – Faroe Islands
10.10.98	Scotland – Estonia
14.10.98	Lithuania – Bosnia-Herzegovina

14.10.98	Scotland – Faroe Islands
14.10.98	Czech Republic – Estonia
27.03.99	Czech Republic – Lithuania
27.03.99	Scotland – Bosnia-Herzegovina
31.03.99	Lithuania – Estonia
31.03.99	Scotland – Czech Republic
05.06.99	Bosnia-Herzegovina – Lithuania
05.06.99	Estonia – Czech Republic
05.06.99	Faroe Islands – Scotland
09.06.99	Estonia – Lithuania
09.06.99	Faroe Islands – Bosnia-Herzegovina
09.06.99	Czech Republic – Scotland
04.09.99	Bosnia-Herzegovina – Scotland
04.09.99	Faroe Islands – Estonia
04.09.99	Lithuania – Czech Republic
08.09.99	Czech Republic – Bosnia- Herzegovina
08.09.99	Faroe Islands – Lithuania
08.09.99	Estonia – Scotland
09.10.99	Estonia – Bosnia-Herzegovina
09.10.99	Czech Republic – Faroe Islands
09.10.99	Scotland – Lithuania

10 ● ENGLAND'S FULL INTERNATIONAL RECORD 1872–1998

(Up to and including 1st July 1998)

	HOME						*AWAY*					
	P	W	D	L	F	A	P	W	D	L	F	A
Albania	1	1	0	0	5	0	1	1	0	0	2	0
Argentina	5	3	2	0	10	6	6	1	3	2	7	7
Australia	–	–	–	–	–	–	5	3	2	0	5	2
Austria	5	3	1	1	18	9	10	5	2	3	36	16
Belgium	4	3	1	0	17	3	15	10	4	1	50	21
Bohemia	–	–	–	–	–	–	1	1	0	0	4	0
Brazil	8	2	4	2	10	10	11	1	3	7	6	16
Bulgaria	3	2	1	0	4	1	3	2	1	0	4	0
Cameroon	2	2	0	0	4	0	1	1	0	0	3	2
Canada	–	–	–	–	–	–	1	1	0	0	1	0
Chile	2	0	1	1	0	2	3	2	1	0	4	1
China	–	–	–	–	–	–	1	1	0	0	3	0
Colombia	2	0	2	0	1	1	2	2	0	0	6	0
Croatia	1	0	1	0	0	0	–	–	–	–	–	–
Cyprus	1	1	0	0	5	0	1	1	0	0	1	0
Czechoslovakia	5	4	1	0	13	6	7	3	2	2	12	9
Denmark	6	5	0	1	9	3	8	4	4	0	18	8
Ecuador	–	–	–	–	–	–	1	1	0	0	2	0
Egypt	–	–	–	–	–	–	2	2	0	0	5	0
FIFA	1	0	1	0	4	4	–	–	–	–	–	–
Finland	2	2	0	0	7	1	7	6	1	0	27	5
France	8	6	2	0	23	4	15	10	1	4	40	23
Georgia	1	1	0	0	2	0	1	1	0	0	2	0
Germany, East	2	2	0	0	4	1	2	1	1	0	3	2
Germany (and West)	9	5	1	3	16	10	13	4	4	5	22	19
Greece	3	2	1	0	8	0	3	3	0	0	7	1
Holland	7	3	3	1	18	9	6	2	2	2	4	6
Hungary	8	7	0	1	21	9	11	6	1	4	29	18
Iceland	–	–	–	–	–	–	1	0	1	0	1	1
Ireland, Northern	49	40	6	3	169	36	47	34	10	3	150	44
Ireland, Republic of	6	3	2	1	11	6	7	2	4	1	8	6
Israel	–	–	–	–	–	–	2	1	1	0	2	1
Italy	7	3	2	2	9	6	13	4	4	5	18	17
Japan	1	1	0	0	2	1	–	–	–	–	–	–
Kuwait	–	–	–	–	–	–	1	1	0	0	1	0
Luxembourg	3	3	0	0	18	1	4	4	0	0	20	2
Malaysia	–	–	–	–	–	–	1	1	0	0	4	2
Malta	1	1	0	0	5	0	1	1	0	0	1	0
Mexico	3	3	0	0	12	0	4	1	1	2	4	3
Moldova	1	1	0	0	4	0	1	1	0	0	3	0
Morocco	–	–	–	–	–	–	2	1	1	0	1	0
New Zealand	–	–	–	–	–	–	2	2	0	0	3	0
Nigeria	1	1	0	0	1	0	–	–	–	–	–	–
Norway	4	2	2	0	9	1	6	3	1	2	17	6
Paraguay	–	–	–	–	–	–	1	1	0	0	3	0

	HOME						AWAY					
	P	W	D	L	F	A	P	W	D	L	F	A
Peru	–	–	–	–	–	–	2	1	0	1	5	4
Poland	6	4	2	0	12	3	7	3	3	1	8	4
Portugal	8	6	2	0	16	5	9	3	4	2	23	13
Rest of Europe	1	1	0	0	3	0	–	–	–	–	–	–
Rest of the World	1	1	0	0	2	1	–	–	–	–	–	–
Romania	4	0	4	0	3	3	6	2	2	2	5	4
San Marino	1	1	0	0	6	0	1	1	0	0	7	1
Saudi Arabia	1	0	1	0	0	0	1	0	1	0	1	1
Scotland	54	26	11	17	117	87	54	18	13	23	73	81
South Africa	1	1	0	0	2	1	–	–	–	–	–	–
Spain	7	5	1	1	19	6	11	5	2	4	16	14
Sweden	5	2	2	1	12	9	10	4	3	3	15	10
Switzerland	7	4	3	0	16	5	11	7	1	3	26	10
Tunisia	–	–	–	–	–	–	2	1	1	0	3	1
Turkey	4	4	0	0	18	0	4	3	1	0	11	0
USA	1	1	0	0	2	0	6	4	0	2	29	7
USSR (and CIS)	4	2	1	1	10	5	8	3	3	2	11	10
Uruguay	4	1	2	1	3	3	5	1	1	3	5	9
Wales	49	32	9	8	126	46	48	30	12	6	113	44
Yugoslavia	7	4	3	0	15	7	7	1	2	4	8	13
TOTAL	328	208	75	45	821	311	421	218	104	99	898	464

GRAND TOTAL

Played	Won	Drawn	Lost	Goals For	Goals Against
749	426	179	144	1719	775

The England squad pictured in 1998.

11 ● ENGLAND'S GOALSCORERS 1946–1998

(Up to and including 1st July 1998)

49	Charlton, R	6	Mullen	2	Broadbent
48	Lineker	6	Rowley	2	Brooks
44	Greaves	6	Waddle	2	Cowans
30	Finney	5	Atyeo	2	Eastham
30	Lofthouse	5	Baily	2	Fowler
27	Platt	5	Brooking	2	Froggatt, J
26	Robson, B	5	Carter	2	Froggatt, R
24	Hurst	5	Edwards	2	Haines
27	Mortensen	5	Ferdinand	2	Hancocks
21	Channon	5	Hitchens	2	Hunter
21	Keegan	5	Latchford	2	Ince
20	Peters	5	Neal	2	Lee, R
20	Shearer	5	Pearce	2	Lee, S
18	Haynes	5	Pearson, S C (Stan)	2	Merson
18	Hunt, R	5	Pearson, J S (Stuart)	2	Moore
16	Lawton	5	Pickering, F	2	Perry
16	Taylor, T	4	Adams	2	Pointer
16	Woodcock	4	Barnes, P	2	Royle
13	Chivers	4	Bull	2	Smith, A
13	Mariner	4	Dixon, K	2	Stone
13	Smith, R	4	Hassall	2	Taylor, P
12	Francis, T	4	Revie	2	Tueart
11	Douglas	4	Robson, R	2	Wignall
11	Mannion	4	Scholes	2	Worthington
11	Barnes, J	4	Steven	1	A'Court
10	Clarke, A	4	Watson, D	1	Astall
10	Flowers, R	4	Webb	1	Beattie
10	Gascoigne	3	Baker	1	Beckham
10	Lee, F	3	Barmby	1	Bowels
10	Milburn	3	Blissett	1	Bradford
10	Wilshaw	3	Butcher	1	Bridges
9	Beardsley	3	Currie	1	Chamberlain
9	Bell	3	Elliott	1	Crawford
9	Bentley	3	Francis, G	1	Dixon, L
9	Hateley	3	Grainger	1	Goddard
9	Sheringham	3	Kennedy, R	1	Hirst
9	Wright, I	3	McDermott	1	Hughes, E
8	Ball	3	Matthews, S	1	Kay
8	Broadis	3	Morris	1	Keown
8	Byrne, J	3	O'Grady	1	Kidd
8	Hoddle	3	Owen	1	Langton
8	Kevan	3	Peacock	1	Lawler
7	Connelly	3	Ramsey	1	Lee, J
7	Coppell	3	Sewell	1	Le Saux
7	Paine	3	Wilkins	1	Mabbutt
6	Anderton	3	Wright, W	1	Marsh
6	Charlton, J	2	Allen, R	1	Medley
6	Johnson	2	Anderson	1	Melia
6	Macdonald	2	Bradley	1	Mullery

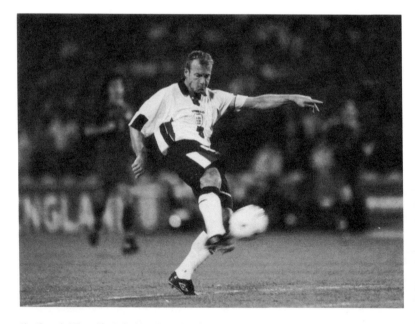

Alan Shearer's 18th goal for England is on its way into the net.

12 ● ENGLAND CAPS 1872–1998

(Up to and including 1st July 1998)

1	Abbott W (Everton)
5	A'Court A (Liverpool)
55	Adams T (Arsenal)
5	Adcock H (Leicester City)
1	Alcock C (Wanderers)
1	Alderson J (C Palace)
2	Aldridge A (WBA, Walsall Town Swifts)
3	Allen A (Stoke)
1	Allen A (Aston Villa)
5	Allen C (QPR, Spurs)
5	Allen H (Wolves)
2	Allen J (Portsmouth)
5	Allen R (WBA)
1	Alsford W (Spurs)
2	Amos A (Old Carthusians)
1	Anderson R (Old Etonians)
2	Anderson S (Sunderland)
30	Anderson V (Nottm Forest, Arsenal, Man Utd)
22	Anderton D (Spurs)
1	Angus J (Burnley)
43	Armfield J (Blackpool)
1	Armitage G (Charlton)
3	Armstrong D (Middlesbrough, Southampton)
1	Armstrong K (Chelsea)
1	Arnold J (Fulham)
7	Arthur J (Blackburn)
3	Ashcroft J (Woolwich Arsenal)
1	Ashmore G (WBA)
1	Ashton C (Corinthians)
5	Ashurst W (Notts County)
2	Astall G (Birmingham)
5	Astle J (WBA)
17	Aston J (Man Utd)
12	Athersmith W (Aston Villa)
6	Atyeo J (Bristol City)
1	Austin S (Man Utd)
1	Bach P (Sunderland)
7	Bache J (Aston Villa)
5	Baddeley T (Wolves)
1	Bagshaw J (Derby County)
2	Bailey G (Man Utd)
5	Bailey H (Leicester Fosse)
2	Bailey M (Charlton)
19	Bailey N (Clapham Rovers)
9	Baily E (Spurs)
1	Bain J (Oxford Univ)
1	Baker A (Arsenal)
2	Baker B (Everton, Chelsea)
8	Baker J (Hibernian, Arsenal)
72	Ball A (Blackpool, Everton, Arsenal)

1	Ball J (Bury)
1	Palmer W (Everton)
1	Bamber J (Liverpool)
3	Bambridge A (Swifts)
18	Bambridge E C (Swifts)
1	Bambridge E H (Swifts)
73	Banks G (Leicester, Stoke)
1	Banks H (Millwall)
6	Banks T (Bolton)
2	Bannister W (Burnley, Bolton)
3	Barclay R (Sheff Wed)
2	Bardsley D (QPR)
2	Barham M (Norwich City)
5	Barkas S (Man City)
11	Barker J (Derby County)
1	Barker R (Herts Rangers)
1	Barker R R (Casuals)
1	Barlow R (WBA)
10	Barmby N (Spurs, Middlesbrough, Everton)
79	Barnes J (Watford, Liverpool)
22	Barnes P (Man City, WBA, Leeds Utd)
1	Barnet H (Royal Engineers)
3	Barrass M (Bolton)
1	Barrett A (Fulham)
3	Barrett E (Oldham, Aston Villa)
1	Barrett J (West Ham Utd)
5	Barry L (Leicester City)
1	Barson F (Aston Villa)
1	Barton J (Blackburn)
7	Barton P (Birmingham)
3	Barton W (Wimbledon, Newcastle)
16	Bassett W (WBA)
1	Bastard S (Upton Park)
21	Bastin C (Arsenal)
35	Batty D (Leeds Utd, Blackburn, Newcastle)
2	Baugh R (Stafford Road, Wolves)
1	Bayliss A (WBA)
3	Baynham R (Luton)
59	Beardsley P (Newcastle, Liverpool)
2	Beasant D (Chelsea)
1	Beasley A (Huddersfield)
2	Beats W (Wolves)
9	Beattie K (Ipswich)
18	Beckham D (Man Utd)
2	Becton F (Preston, Liverpool)
2	Bedford H, (Blackpool)
48	Bell C (Man City)
2	Bennett W (Sheff Utd)
1	Benson R (Sheff Utd)
12	Bentley R (Chelsea)
1	Beresford J (Aston villa)
1	Berry A (Oxford Univ)

4 Berry J (Man Utd)	3 Brown A (Aston Villa)
1 Bestall J (Grimsby)	2 Brown A S (Sheff Utd)
1 Betmead H (Grimsby)	9 Brown G (Huddersfield, Aston Villa)
1 Betts M (Old Harrovians)	5 Brown J (Blackburn)
1 Betts W (Sheff Wed)	6 Brown J H (Sheff Wed)
3 Beverley J (Blackburn)	1 Brown K (West Ham)
1 Birkett R H (Clapham Rovers)	1 Brown T (WBA)
1 Birkett R (Middlesbrough)	1 Brown W (West Ham)
2 Birley F (Oxford Univ, Wanderers)	3 Bruton J (Burnley)
3 Birtles G (Nottm Forest)	1 Bryant W (Clapton)
4 Bishop S (Leicester City)	6 Buchan C (Sunderland)
3 Blackburn F (Blackburn)	1 Buchanan W (Clapham Rovers)
1 Blackburn G (Aston Villa)	1 Buckley F C (Derby County)
26 Blenkinsop E (Sheff Wed)	13 Bull S (Wolves)
1 Bliss H (Spurs)	1 Bullock F E (Huddersfield)
14 Blissett L (Watford)	3 Bullock N (Bury)
1 Blockley J (Arsenal)	4 Burgess H (Man City)
23 Bloomer S (Derby County, Middlesbrough)	4 Burgess H (Sheff Wed)
5 Blunstone F (Chelsea)	1 Burnup C (Cambridge Univ)
8 Bond R (Preston, Bradford City)	3 Burrows H (Sheff Wed)
7 Bonetti P (Chelsea)	1 Burton F E (Nottm Forest)
2 Bonsor A (Wanderers)	2 Bury L (Cambridge Univ, Old Etonians)
1 Booth F (Man City)	77 Butcher T (Ipswich, Rangers)
2 Booth T (Blackburn, Everton)	1 Butler J (Arsenal)
2 Bould S (Arsenal)	1 Butler W (Bolton)
6 Bowden E (Arsenal)	6 Butt N (Man Utd)
5 Bower A (Corinthians)	2 Byrne G (Liverpool)
3 Bowers J (Derby County)	11 Byrne J J (C Palace, West Ham)
5 Bowles S (QPR)	33 Byrne R (Man Utd)
1 Bowser S (WBA)	
1 Boyer P (Norwich)	4 Callaghan I (Liverpool)
3 Boyes W (WBA, Everton)	1 Calvey J (Nottm Forest)
1 Boyle T (Burnley)	8 Campbell A (Blackburn, Huddersfield)
3 Bradbrook P (Chelsea)	20 Campbell S (Spurs)
3 Bracewell P (Everton)	9 Camsell G (Middlesbrough)
1 Bradford G (Bristol Rovers)	1 Capes A (Stoke)
12 Bradford J (Birmingham)	2 Carr J (Middlesbrough)
3 Bradley W (Man Utd)	2 Carr J (Newcastle)
1 Bradshaw F (Sheff Wed)	1 Carr W H (Owlerton)
1 Bradshaw T (Liverpool)	13 Carter H S (Sunderland, Derby County)
4 Bradshaw W (Blackburn)	3 Carter J H (WBA)
3 Brann G (Swifts)	5 Catlin A E (Sheff Wed)
2 Brawn W (Aston Villa)	2 Chadwick A (Southampton)
6 Bray J (Man City)	7 Chadwick E (Everton)
1 Brayshaw E (Sheff Wed)	8 Chamberlain M (Stoke)
4 Bridges B (Chelsea)	8 Chambers H (Liverpool)
11 Bridgett A (Sunderland)	46 Channon M (Southampton, Man City)
2 Brindle T (Darwen)	2 Charles G (Nottm Forest)
5 Brittleton J (Sheff Wed)	35 Charlton J (Leeds Utd)
9 Britton C (Everton)	106 Charlton R (Man Utd)
7 Broadbent P (Wolves)	1 Charnley R (Blackpool)
14 Broadis I (Man City, Newcastle)	1 Charnsley C (Small Heath)
1 Brockbank J (Cambridge Univ)	8 Chedgzoy S (Everton)
3 Brodie JB (Wolves)	3 Chenery C (C Palace)
5 Bromilow T G (Liverpool)	27 Cherry T (Leeds Utd)
2 Bromley-Davenport W E (Oxford Univ)	2 Chilton A (Man Utd)
18 Brook E (Man City)	1 Chippendale H (Blackburn)
47 Brooking T (West Ham)	24 Chivers M (Spurs)
3 Brooks J (Spurs)	1 Christian E (Old Etonians)
7 Broome F H (Aston Villa)	4 Clamp E (Wolves)

1	Clapton D (Arsenal)
4	Clare T (Stoke)
19	Clarke A (Leeds Utd)
1	Clarke H (Spurs)
4	Clay T (Spurs)
35	Clayton R (Blackburn)
1	Clegg J (Sheff Wed)
2	Clegg W (Sheff Wed, Sheff Albion)
61	Clemence R (Liverpool, Spurs)
5	Clement D (QPR)
2	Clough B (Middlesbrough)
14	Clough N (Nottm Forest)
4	Coates R (Burnley, Spurs)
9	Cobbold W (Cambridge Univ, Old Carthusians)
2	Cock J (Huddersfield, Chelsea)
13	Cockburn H (Man Utd)
37	Cohen G (Fulham)
1	Colclough H (C Palace)
2	Cole A (Man Utd)
1	Coleman E (Dulwich Hamlet)
1	Coleman J (Woolwich Arsenal)
3	Collymore S (Nottm Forest, Aston Villa)
3	Common A (Sheff Utd, Middlesbrough)
2	Compton L H (Arsenal)
1	Conlin J (Bradford City)
20	Connelly J (Burnley, Man Utd)
1	Cook T E (Brighton)
2	Cooper C (Nottm Forest)
1	Cooper N C (Cambridge Univ)
15	Cooper T (Derby County)
20	Cooper T (Leeds Utd)
42	Coppell S Man Utd)
20	Copping W (Leeds Utd, Arsenal)
1	Corbett B (Corinthians)
1	Corbett R (Old Malvernians)
3	Corbett W (Birmingham)
9	Corrigan J (Man City)
7	Cottee A (West Ham, Everton)
4	Cotterill G (Cambridge Univ, Old Brightonians)
1	Cottle J (Bristol City)
3	Cowans S (Man City)
10	Cowns G (Aston Villa, Bari)
1	Cowell A (Blackburn)
3	Cox J (Liverpool)
1	Cox J D (Derby County)
14	Crabtree J (Burnley, Aston Villa)
1	Crawford JF (Chelsea)
2	Crawford R (Ipswich)
10	Crawshaw T (Sheff Wed)
8	Crayston W (Arsenal)
1	Creek N (Corinthians)
7	Cresswell W (South Shields, Sunderland, Everton)
41	Crompton R (Blackburn)
26	Crooks S (Derby County)
1	Crowe C (Wolves)
2	Cuggy F (Sunderland)
12	Cullis S (Wolves)
2	Cunliffe A (Blackburn)
1	Cunliffe D (Portsmouth)

1	Cunliffe J (Everton)
6	Cunningham L (WBA, Real Madrid)
3	Curle K (Man City)
2	Currey E (Oxford Univ)
17	Currie A (Sheff Utd, Leeds Utd)
6	Cursham A (Notts County)
8	Cursham H (Notts County)
5	Daft H (Notts County)
7	Daley A (Aston Villa)
1	Danks T (Nottm Forest)
2	Davenport J (Bolton)
1	Davenport P (Nottm Forest)
2	Davis G (Derby County)
3	Davis H (Sheff Wed)
1	Davidson J (Sheff Wed)
2	Dawson J (Burnley)
3	Day S (Old Malvernians)
16	Dean W (Everton)
3	Deane B (Sheffield Utd)
2	Deeley N (Wolves)
2	Devey J (Aston Villa)
8	Devonshire A (West Ham)
9	Dewhurst F (Preston)
1	Dewhurst G (Liverpool Ramblers)
48	Dickinson J (Portsmouth)
3	Dimmock J (Spurs)
6	Ditchburn E (Spurs)
1	Dix R (Derby County)
1	Dixon J (Notts County)
8	Dixon K (Chelsea)
21	Dixon L (Arsenal)
4	Dobson A (Notts County)
1	Dobson C (Notts County)
5	Dobson M (Burnley, Everton)
1	Doggart A (Corinthians)
15	Dorigo T (Chelsea, Leeds Utd)
4	Dorrell A (Aston Villa)
36	Douglas B (Blackburn)
1	Downs R (Everton)
5	Doyle M (Man City)
5	Drake E (Arsenal)
3	Dublin D (Coventry)
6	Ducat J (Woolwich Arsenal, Aston Villa)
4	Dunn A T (Cambridge Univ, Old Etonians)
10	Duxbury M (Man Utd)
2	Earle S (Clapton, West Ham)
19	Eastham G (Arsenal)
1	Eastham G R (Bolton)
17	Eckersley W (Blackburn)
18	Edwards D (Man Utd)
1	Edwards J (Shropshire Wanderers)
16	Edwards W (Leeds Utd)
1	Ehiogu U (Aston Villa)
2	Ellerington W (Southampton)
3	Elliott G (Middlesbrough)
5	Elliott W (Burnley)
4	Evans R (Sheff Utd)
2	Ewer F (Casuals)

1 Fairclough P (Old Foresters)	1 Gosnell A (Newcastle)
1 Fairhurst D (Newcastle)	1 Gough H (Sheff Utd)
1 Fantham J (Sheff Wed)	14 Goulden L (West Ham)
2 Fashanu J (Wimbledon)	2 Graham L (Millwall)
1 Felton W (Sheff Wed)	2 Graham T (Nottm Forest)
1 Fenton M (Middlesbrough)	7 Grainger C (Sheff Utd, Sunderland)
20 Fenwick T (QPR, Spurs)	1 Gray A (Crystal Palace)
20 Ferdinand L (QPR, Newcastle, Tottenham)	57 Greaves J (Chelsea, Spurs)
3 Ferdinand R (West Ham)	8 Green G (Sheff Utd)
2 Field E (Clapham Rovers)	1 Green T (Wanderers)
76 Finney T (Preston)	2 Greenhalgh E (Notts County)
11 Fleming H (Swindon)	18 Greenhoff B (Man Utd, Leeds Utd)
2 Fletcher A (Wolves)	2 Greenwood D (Blackburn)
49 Flowers R (Wolves)	6 Gregory J (QPR)
11 Flowers T (Southampton, Blackburn)	6 Grimsdell A (Spurs)
9 Forman F (Nottm Forest)	3 Grosvenor A (Birmingham)
3 Forman F R (Nottm Forest)	2 Gunn W (Notts County)
11 Forest J (Blackburn)	1 Gurney R (Sunderland)
1 Fort J (Millwall)	
5 Foster R (Oxford Univ, Corinthians)	3 Hacking J (Oldham)
3 Foster S (Brighton & Hove Albion)	1 Hadley N (WBA)
1 Foulke W (Sheff Utd)	1 Hagan J (Sheff Utd)
1 Foulkes W (Man Utd)	1 Haines J (WBA)
7 Fowler, R (Liverpool)	1 Hall A (Aston Villa)
1 Fox F (Gillingham)	10 Hall G (Spurs)
12 Francis G (QPR)	17 Hall J (Birmingham)
52 Francis T (Birmingham, Nottm Forest,	1 Halse H (Man Utd)
Man City, Sampdoria)	1 Hammond H (Oxford Univ)
27 Franklin C (Stoke)	3 Hampson J (Blackpool)
5 Freeman B (Everton, Burnley)	4 Hampton H (Aston Villa)
13 Froggatt J (Portsmouth)	3 Hancocks J (Wolves)
4 Froggatt R (Sheff Wed)	30 Hapgood E (Arsenal)
1 Fry C (Corinthians)	1 Harding H (Sheff Utd)
1 Furness W (Leeds Utd)	4 Hardman H (Everton)
	13 Hardwick G (Middlesbrough)
2 Galley T (Wolves)	1 Hardy H (Stockport County)
2 Gardner T (Aston Villa)	21 Hardy S (Liverpool, Aston Villa)
1 Garfield B (WBA)	2 Harford M (Luton Town)
1 Garratty W (Aston Villa)	3 Hargreaves F (Blackburn)
3 Garrett T (Blackpool)	2 Hargreaves J (Blackburn)
57 Gascoigne P (Spurs, Lazio, Rangers, M'brough)	1 Harper E (Blackburn)
2 Gates E (Ipswich)	1 Harris G (Burnley)
3 Gay L (Cambridge Univ, Old Brightonians)	2 Harris P (Portsmouth)
2 Geary F (Everton)	6 Harris S (Cambridge Univ, Old Westminsters)
1 Geaves R (Clapham Rovers)	2 Harrison A (Old Westminsters)
3 Gee C (Everton)	2 Harrison G (Everton)
4 Geldard A (Everton)	2 Harrow J (Chelsea)
1 George C (Derby County)	8 Hart E (Leeds Utd)
3 George W (Aston Villa)	1 Hartley F (Oxford City)
2 Gibbins W (Clapton)	1 Harvey A (Wednesbury Strollers)
1 Gidman J (Aston Villa)	1 Harvey C (Everton)
3 Gillard I (QPR)	5 Hassall H (Huddersfield, Bolton)
1 Gilliat W (Old Carthusians)	32 Hateley M (Portsmouth, AC Milan, Monaco,
1 Goddard P (West Ham)	Rangers)
25 Goodall F (Huddersfield)	5 Hawkes R (Luton)
14 Goodall J (Preston, Derby County)	5 Haworth G (Accrington)
3 Goodhart H (Old Etonians)	2 Hawtrey J (Old Etonians)
1 Goodwyn A (Royal Engineers)	1 Haygarth E (Swifts)
1 Goodyer A (Nottm Forest)	56 Haynes J (Fulham)
5 Gosling R (Old Etonians)	2 Healless H (Blackburn)

2	Hector K (Derby County)
1	Hedley G (Sheff Utd)
4	Hegan K (Corinthians)
2	Hellawell M (Birmingham)
5	Henfrey A (Cambridge Univ, Corinthians)
1	Henry R (Spurs)
1	Heron F (Wanderers)
5	Heron G (Uxbridge, Wanderers)
1	Hibbert W (Bury)
25	Hibbs H (Birmingham)
2	Hill F (Bolton)
6	Hill G (Man Utd)
11	Hill J (Burnley)
3	Hill R (Luton)
1	Hill R H (Milwall)
1	Hillman J (Burnley)
1	Hills A (Old Harrovians)
8	Hilsdon G (Chelsea)
6	Hinchcliffe A (Everton, Sheff Wed)
6	Hine E (Leicester City)
3	Hinton A (Wolves, Nottm Forest)
3	Hirst D (Sheff Wed)
7	Hitchens G (Aston Villa, Inter-Milan)
2	Hobbis H (Charlton)
53	Hoddle G (Spurs, Monaco)
24	Hodge S (Aston Villa, Spurs, Nottm Forest)
6	Hodgetts D (Aston Villa)
5	Hodgkinson A (Sheff Utd)
3	Hodgson G (Liverpool)
3	Hodkinson J (Blackburn)
3	Hogg W (Sunderland)
2	Holdcroft G (Preston)
5	Holden A (Bolton)
4	Holden G (Wednesbury OA)
2	Holden-White C (Corinthians)
1	Holford T (Stoke)
10	Holley G (Sunderland)
3	Holliday E (Middlesbrough)
1	Hollins J (Chelsea)
7	Holmes R (Preston)
10	Holt J (Everton, Reading)
14	Hopkinson E (Bolton)
2	Hossack A (Corinthians)
7	Houghton W (Aston Villa)
5	Houlker A (Blackburn, Portsmouth, Southampton)
5	Howarth R (Preston, Everton)
23	Howe D (WBA)
3	Howe J (Derby)
1	Howell L (Wanderers)
2	Howell R (Sheff Utd, Liverpool)
4	Howey S (Newcastle)
2	Hudson A (Stoke)
1	Hudson J (Sheffield)
1	Hudspeth F (Newcastle)
6	Hufton A (West Ham)
62	Hughes E (Liverpool, Wolves)
3	Hughes L (Liverpool)
9	Hulme J (Arsenal)
1	Humphreys P (Notts County)

3	Hunt G (Spurs)
2	Hunt Rev. K (Leyton)
34	Hunt R (Liverpool)
2	Hunt S (WBA)
7	Hunter J (Sheff Heeley)
28	Hunter N (Leeds Utd)
49	Hurst G (West Ham)
43	Ince P (Man Utd, Inter-Milan, Liverpool)
2	Iremonger J (Nottm Forest)
9	Jack D (Bolton, Arsenal)
1	Jackson E (Oxford Univ)
1	James D (Liverpool)
3	Jarrett B (Cambridge Univ)
2	Jefferis F (Everton)
2	Jezzard B (Fulham)
8	Johnson D (Ipswich, Liverpool)
2	Johnson E (Saltley Coll, Stoke)
5	Johnson J (Stoke)
5	Johnson T (Man City, Everton)
6	Johnson W (Sheff Utd)
10	Johnston N (Blackpool)
3	Jones A (Walsall Swifts, Great Lever)
6	Jones H (Blackburn)
1	Jones H (Nottm Forest)
3	Jones M (Sheff Utd, Leeds Utd)
8	Jones R (Liverpool)
1	Jones W (Bristol City)
2	Jones W (Liverpool)
1	Joy B (Casuals)
3	Kail E (Dulwich Hamlet)
1	Kay T (Everton)
9	Kean F (Sheff Wed, Bolton)
63	Keegan K (Liverpool, SV Hamburg, Southampton)
4	Keen E (Derby County)
14	Kelly R (Burnley, Sunderland, Huddersfield)
2	Kennedy A (Liverpool)
17	Kennedy R (Liverpool)
1	Kenyon-Slaney W (Wanderers)
18	Keown M (Everton, Arsenal)
14	Kevan D (WBA)
2	Kidd B (Man Utd)
1	King R (Oxford Univ)
1	Kingsford R (Wanderers)
1	Kinsley M (Newcastle)
4	Kinsey G (Wolves, Derby County)
3	Kirchen A (Arsenal)
1	Kirton W (Aston Villa)
1	Knight A (Portsmouth)
4	Knowles C (Spurs)
26	Labone B (Everton)
2	Lampard F (West Ham)
3	Langey J (Fulham)
11	Langton R (Blackburn, Preston, Bolton)
12	Latchford R (Everton)
2	Latheron E (Blackburn)

4 Lawler C (Liverpool)	2 Marshall T (Darwen)
23 Lawton T (Everton, Chelsea, Notts County)	17 Martin A (West Ham)
2 Leach T (Sheff Wed)	1 Martin H (Sunderland)
5 Leake A (Aston Villa)	7 Martyn N (Crystal Palace, Leeds Utd)
1 Lee E (Southampton)	1 Marwood B (Arsenal)
27 Lee F (Man City)	1 Maskrey H (Derby County)
1 Lee J (Derby)	3 Mason C (Wolves)
18 Lee R (Newcastle)	5 Matthews R (Coventry)
14 Lee S (Liverpool)	54 Matthews S (Stoke, Blackpool)
1 Leighton J (Nottm Forest)	2 Matthews V (Sheff Utd)
29 Le Saux G (Blackburn, Chelsea)	2 Maynard W (1st Surrey Rifles)
8 Le Tissier M (Southampton)	1 Meadows J (Man City)
1 Lilley H (Sheff Utd)	6 Medley L (Spurs)
2 Linacre H (Nottm Forest)	1 Meehan T (Chelsea)
13 Lindley T (Cambridge Univ, Nottm Forest)	2 Melia J (Liverpool)
4 Lindsay A (Liverpool)	2 Mercer D (Sheff Utd)
1 Lindsay W (Wanderers)	5 Mercer J (Everton)
80 Lineker G (Leicester, Everton, Barcelona, Spurs)	23 Merrick G (Birmingham)
7 Lintott E (QPR, Bradford City)	19 Merson P (Arsenal, Middlesbrough)
1 Lipsham H (Sheff Utd)	2 Metcalfe V (Huddersfield)
1 Little B (Aston Villa)	1 Mew J (Man Utd)
4 Lloyd L (Liverpool, Nottm Forest)	1 Middleditch B (Corinthians)
1 Lockett A (Stoke)	13 Milburn J (Newcastle)
5 Lodge L (Cambridge Univ, Corinthians)	1 Miller B (Burnley)
7 Lofthouse J (Blackburn, Accrington)	1 Miller H (Charlton)
33 Lofthouse N (Bolton)	3 Mills G (Chelsea)
5 Longworth E (Liverpool)	42 Mills M (Ipswich)
1 Lowder A (Wolves)	14 Milne G (Liverpool)
3 Lowe E (Aston Villa)	1 Milton A (Arsenal)
3 Lucas T (Liverpool)	4 Milward A (Everton)
2 Luntley E (Nottm Forest)	5 Mitchell C (Upton Park)
1 Lyttelton Hon A (Cambridge Univ)	1 Mitchell J (Man City)
1 Lyttelton Hon E (Cambridge Univ)	1 Moffatt H (Oldham)
	4 Molyneux G (Southampton)
16 Mabbutt G (Spurs)	7 Moon W (Old Westminsters)
1 Macauley R (Cambridge Univ)	2 Moore H (Notts County)
14 Macdonald M (Newcastle)	1 Moore J (Derby County)
6 Macrae S (Notts County)	108 Moore R (West Ham)
5 McCall J (Preston)	1 Moore W (West Ham)
25 McDermott T (Liverpool)	2 Mordue J (Sunderland)
8 McDonald C (Burnley)	1 Morice C (Barnes)
28 McFarland R (Derby County)	6 Morley A (Aston Villa)
4 McGarry W (Huddersfield)	1 Morley H (Notts County)
2 McGuinness W (Man Utd)	1 Morren T (Sheff Utd)
1 McInroy A (Sunderland)	2 Morris F (WBA)
17 McMahon A (Liverpool)	3 Morris J (Derby)
22 McManaman S (Liverpool)	3 Morris W (Wolves)
4 McNab R (Arsenal)	1 Morse H (Notts County)
2 McNeal R (WBA)	3 Mort T (Aston Villa)
9 McNeil M (Middlesbrough)	1 Morten A (C Palace)
1 Maddison F (Oxford Univ)	25 Mortensen S (Blackpool)
24 Madeley P (Leeds Utd)	1 Morton J (West Ham)
5 Magee T (WBA)	9 Mosforth W (Sheff Wed,
4 Makepeace H (Everton)	Sheff Albion)
19 Male G (Arsenal)	4 Moss F (Arsenal)
26 Mannion W (Middlesbrough)	5 Moss F (Aston Villa)
35 Mariner P (Ipswich, Arsenal)	2 Mosscrop E (Burnley)
1 Marsden J (Darwen)	3 Mozley B (Derby)
3 Marsden W (Sheff Wed)	12 Mullen J (Wolves)
9 Marsh R (QPR, Man City)	35 Mullery A (Spurs)

50 Neal P (Liverpool)
16 Needham E (Sheff Utd)
30 Neville G (Man Utd)
12 Neville P (Man Utd)
27 Newton K (Blackburn, Everton)
 2 Nicholls J (WBA)
 1 Nicholson W (Spurs)
 5 Nish D (Derby)
23 Norman M (Spurs)
 3 Nuttall H (Bolton)

16 Oakley W (Oxford Univ, Corinthians)
 3 O'Dowd J (Chelsea)
 2 O'Grady M (Huddersfield, Leeds Utd)
 1 Ogilvie R (Clapham Rovers)
 1 Oliver L (Fulham)
 2 Olney B (Aston Villa)
 4 Osborne F (Fulham, Spurs)
 1 Osborne R (Leicester City)
 4 Osgood P (Chelsea)
11 Osman R (Ipswich)
 2 Ottaway C (Oxford Univ)
 1 Owen J (Sheffield)
 9 Owen M (Liverpool)
 3 Owen S (Luton)

 7 Page L (Burnley)
19 Paine T (Southampton)
22 Pallister G (Middlesbrough, Man Utd)
18 Palmer C (Sheff Wed)
 1 Panting H (Sheff Utd)
 3 Paravacini P J de (Cambridge Univ)
19 Parker P (QPR, Man Utd)
 1 Parker T (Southampton)
 1 Parkes P (QPR)
 2 Parkinson J (Liverpool)
 1 Parr P (Oxford Univ)
 3 Parry E (Old Carthusians)
 2 Parry R (Bolton)
 2 Patchitt B (Corinthians)
 2 Pawson F (Cambridge Univ, Swifts)
 1 Payne J (Luton)
 6 Peacock A (Middlesbrough, Leeds Utd)
 3 Peacock J (Middlesbrough)
76 Pearce S (Nottm Forest)
 1 Pearson H (WBA)
 1 Pearson J H (Crewe)
15 Pearson J S (Stuart) (Man Utd)
 8 Pearson S C (Stan) (Man Utd)
 1 Pease W (Middlesbrough)
 1 Pegg D (Man Utd)
 4 Pejic M (Stoke)
 3 Pelly F (Old Foresters)
25 Pennington J (WBA)
 5 Pentland F (Middlesbrough)
 3 Perry C (WBA)
 1 Perry T (WBA)
 3 Perry W (Blackpool)
 1 Perryman S (Spurs)
67 Peters M (West Ham, Spurs)

 1 Phelan M (Man Utd)
 3 Phillips L (Portsmouth)
 3 Pickering F (Everton)
 1 Pickering J (Sheff Utd)
 1 Pickering N (Sunderland)
 1 Pike T (Cambridge Univ)
 1 Pilkington B (Burnley)
 1 Plant J (Bury)
62 Platt D (Aston Villa, Bari, Juventus, Sampdoria, Arsenal)
 1 Plum S (Charlton)
 3 Pointer R (Burnley)
 1 Porteous T (Sunderland)
 1 Priest A (Sheff Utd)
 1 Prinsep J (Clapham Rovers)
 2 Puddefoot S (Blackburn)
 1 Pye J (Wolves)
 3 Pym R (Bolton)

 4 Quantrill A (Derby County)
 5 Quixall A (Sheff Wed)

 2 Radford J (Arsenal)
 4 Raikes G (Oxford Univ)
32 Ramsey A (Southampton, Spurs)
 1 Rawlings A (Preston)
 2 Rawlings W (Southampton)
 1 Rawlinson J (Cambridge Univ)
 1 Rawson H (Royal Engineers)
 2 Rawson W (Oxford Univ)
 1 Read A (Tufnell Park)
 1 Reader J (WBA)
 3 Reaney P (Leeds Utd)
 8 Redknapp J (Liverpool)
 2 Reeves K (Norwich, Man City)
 5 Regis C (WBA, Coventry)
13 Reid P (Everton)
 6 Revie D (Man City)
 8 Reynolds J (WBA, Aston Villa)
 1 Richards C (Nottm Forest)
 1 Richards G (Derby County)
 1 Richards J (Wolves)
 2 Richardson J (Newcastle)
 1 Richardson K (Aston Villa)
 1 Richardson W (WBA)
 1 Rickaby S (WBA)
 5 Rigby A (Blackburn)
 4 Rimmer E (Sheff Wed)
 1 Rimmer J (Arsenal)
 2 Ripley S (Blackburn)
17 Rix G (Arsenal)
 1 Robb G (Spurs)
 3 Roberts C (Man Utd)
 4 Roberts F (Man City)
 6 Roberts G (Spurs)
 1 Roberts H (Arsenal)
 1 Roberts H (Millwall)
 3 Roberts R (WBA)
 2 Roberts W (Preston)
 4 Robinson J (Sheff Wed)

11 Robinson J W (Derby County, New Brighton Tower, Southampton)
90 Robson B (WBA, Man Utd)
20 Robson R (WBA)
14 Rocastle D (Arsenal)
 5 Rose W (Wolves, Preston)
 2 Rostron T (Darwen)
 1 Rowe A (Spurs)
 6 Rowley J (Man Utd)
 2 Rowley W (Stoke)
 6 Royle J (Everton, Man City)
 3 Ruddlesdin H (Sheff Wed)
 1 Ruddock N (Liverpool)
 6 Ruffell J (West Ham)
 1 Russell B (Royal Engineers)
11 Rutherford J (Newcastle)

 4 Sadler D (Man Utd)
 2 Sagar C (Bury)
 4 Sagar E (Everton)
 5 Salako J (Crystal Palace)
 1 Sandford E (WBA)
 5 Sandilands R (Old Westminsters)
 1 Sands J (Nottm Forest)
86 Sansom K (C Palace, Arsenal)
 1 Saunders F (Swifts)
 1 Savage A (C Palace)
 1 Sayer J (Stoke)
 3 Scales J (Liverpool)
 1 Scattergood E (Derby County)
 3 Schofield J (Stoke)
11 Scholes P (Man Utd)
17 Scott L (Arsenal)
 1 Scott W (Brentford)
44 Seaman D (QPR, Arsenal)
 6 Seddon J (Bolton)
 5 Seed J (Spurs)
 6 Settle J (Bury, Everton)
 6 Sewell J (Sheff Wed)
 1 Sewell W (Blackburn)
 5 Shackleton L (Sunderland)
 2 Sharp J (Everton)
 8 Sharpe L (Man Utd)
 1 Shaw G E (WBA)
 5 Shaw G L (Sheff Utd)
 2 Shea D (Blackburn)
43 Shearer A (Southampton, Blackburn, Newcastle)
 1 Shellito K (Chelsea)
 6 Stelton A (Notts County)
 1 Shelton C (Notts Rangers)
 2 Shepherd A (Bolton, Newcastle)
35 Sheringham T (Spurs, Man Utd)
125 Shilton P (Leicester, Stoke, Nottm Forest, Southampton, Derby County)
 1 Shimwell E (Blackpool)
 1 Shutt G (Stoke)
 3 Silcock J (Man Utd)
 3 Sillett P (Chelsea)
 1 Simms E (Luton)
 8 Simpson J (Blackburn)

12 Sinton A (QPR)
12 Slater W (Wolves)
 1 Smalley T (Wolves)
 5 Smart T (Aston Villa)
 3 Smith A (Nottm Forest)
 1 Smith A K (Oxford Univ)
13 Smith A M (Arsenal)
 2 Smith B (Spurs)
 1 Smith C E (C Palace)
20 Smith G O (Oxford Univ, Old Carthusians, Corinthians)
 4 Smith H (Reading)
 2 Smith J (WBA)
 5 Smith Joe (Bolton)
 2 Smith J C R (Millwall)
 3 Smith J W (Portsmouth)
 1 Smith Leslie (Brentford)
 6 Smith Lionel (Arsenal)
15 Smith R A (Spurs)
 1 Smith S (Aston Villa)
 1 Smith S C (Leicester City)
 2 Smith T (Birmingham)
 1 Smith T (Liverpool)
 3 Smith W H (Huddersfield)
 1 Sorby T (Thursday Wanderers)
27 Southgate G (Aston Villa)
 3 Southworth J (Blackburn)
 3 Sparks F (Herts Rangers, Clapham Rovers)
 2 Spence J (Man Utd)
 2 Spence R (Chelsea)
 2 Spencer C (Newcastle)
 6 Spencer H (Aston Villa)
 7 Spiksley F (Sheff Wed)
 3 Spilsbury B (Cambridge Univ)
 1 Spink N (Aston Villa)
 1 Spouncer W (Nottm Forest)
33 Springett R (Sheff Wed)
11 Sproston B (Leeds Utd, Spurs, Man City)
 3 Squire R (Cambridge Univ)
 1 Stanbrough M (Old Carthusians)
 8 Stanoforth R (Huddersfield)
 2 Starling R (Sheff Wed, Aston Villa)
 3 Statham D (WBA)
 6 Steele F (Stoke)
 1 Stein B (Luton)
 1 Stephenson C (Huddersfield)
 3 Stephenson G (Derby County, Sheff Wed)
 2 Stephenson J (Leeds Utd)
 1 Stepney A (Man Utd)
 1 Sterland M (Sheff Wed)
36 Steven T (Everton, Rangers, Marseille)
 7 Stevens G A (Spurs)
46 Stevens G (Everton, Rangers)
 3 Stewart J (Sheff Wed, Newcastle)
 3 Stewart P (Spurs)
28 Stiles N (Man Utd)
 3 Stoker J (Birmingham)
 9 Stone S (Nottm Forest)
 2 Storer H (Derby County)
19 Storey P (Arsenal)

1	Storey-Moore I (Nottm Forest)
20	Strange A (Sheff Wed)
1	Stratford A (Wanderers)
1	Streten B (Luton)
2	Sturgess A (Sheff Utd)
8	Summerbee M (Man City)
1	Sunderland A (Arsenal)
5	Sutcliffe J (Bolton, Millwall)
1	Sutton C (Blackburn)
19	Swan P (Sheff Wed)
6	Swepstone H (Pilgrims)
19	Swift F (Man City)
1	Tait G (Birmingham Excelsior)
6	Talbot B (Ipswich, Arsenal)
3	Tambling R (Chelsea)
3	Tate J (Aston Villa)
1	Taylor E (Blackpool)
8	Taylor E J (Huddersfield)
2	Taylor J (Fulham)
3	Taylor P H (Liverpool)
4	Taylor P J (C Palace)
19	Taylor T (Man Utd)
1	Temple D (Everton)
2	Thickett H (Sheff Utd)
2	Thomas D (Coventry)
8	Thomas D (QPR)
9	Thomas G (Crystal Palace)
2	Thomas M (Arsenal)
16	Thompson P (Peter) (Liverpool)
42	Thompson P (Phil) (Liverpool)
2	Thompson T (Aston Villa, Preston)
8	Thomson R (Wolves)
4	Thornewell G (Derby County)
1	Thornley I (Man City)
4	Tilson S (Man City)
2	Titmuss F (Southampton)
27	Todd C (Derby)
2	Toone G (Notts County)
1	Topham A (Casuals)
2	Topham R (Wolves, Casuals)
3	Towers A (Sunderland)
2	Townley W (Blackburn)
2	Townrow J (Clapton Orient)
1	Tremelling D (Birmingham)
2	Tresadern J (West Ham)
6	Tueart D (Man City)
7	Tunstall F (Sheff Utd)
1	Turnbull R (Bradford City)
2	Turner A (Southampton)
2	Turner H (Huddersfield)
3	Turner J (Bolton, Stoke, Derby County)
1	Tweedy G (Grimsby)
1	Ufton D (Charlton)
2	Underwood A (Stoke)
1	Unsworth D (Everton)
4	Urwin T (Middlesbrough, Newcastle)
1	Utley G (Barnsley)

5	Vaughton O (Aston Villa)
6	Veitch C (Newcastle)
1	Veitch J (Old Westminsters)
2	Venables T (Chelsea)
2	Venison B (Newcastle)
1	Vidal R (Oxford Univ)
2	Viljoen C (Ipswich)
2	Viollet D (Man Utd)
2	Von Donop P (Royal Engineers)
3	Wace H (Wanderers)
62	Waddle C (Newcastle, Spurs, Marseille)
9	Wadsworth S (Huddersfield)
1	Wainscoat W (Leeds Utd)
5	Waiters A (Blackpool)
2	Walden F (Spurs)
59	Walker D (Nottm Forest, Sampdoria, Sheff Wed)
3	Walker I (Spurs)
18	Walker W (Aston Villa)
7	Wall G (Man Utd)
3	Wallace C (Aston Villa)
1	Wallace D (Southampton)
5	Walsh P (Luton)
9	Walters A (Cambridge Univ, Old Carthusians)
1	Walters M (Rangers)
13	Walters P (Oxford Univ, Old Carthusians)
1	Walton N (Blackburn)
1	Ward J (Blackburn Olympic)
1	Ward P (Brighton and Hove Albion)
2	Ward T (Derby County)
5	Waring A (Aston Villa)
1	Warner C (Upton Park)
22	Warren B (Derby County, Chelsea)
1	Waterfield G (Burnley)
12	Watson D (Norwich, Everton)
65	Watson D (Sunderland, Man City, Werder Bremen, Southampton, Stoke)
5	Watson V (West Ham)
3	Watson W (Burnley)
4	Watson W (Sunderland)
3	Weaver S (Newcastle)
2	Webb G (West Ham)
26	Webb N (Nottm Forest, Man Utd)
3	Webster M (Middlesbrough)
26	Wedlock W (Bristol City)
2	Weir D (Bolton)
2	Welch R de C (Wanderers, Harrow Chequers)
4	Weller K (Leicester)
3	Welsh D (Charlton)
3	West G (Everton)
6	Westwood R (Bolton)
2	Whateley O (Aston Villa)
1	Wheeler J (Bolton)
4	Wheldon G (Aston Villa)
1	White D (Man City)
1	White T (Everton)
2	Whitehead J (Accrington, Blackburn)
1	Whitfield H (Old Etonians)
1	Whitham M (Sheff Utd)
7	Whitworth S (Leicester)

1	Whymark T (Ipswich)	4	Wollaston C (Wanderers)
1	Widdowson S (Nottm Forest)	3	Wolstenholme S (Everton, Blackburn)
2	Wignall F (Nottm Forest)	3	Wood H (Wolves)
1	Wilcox J (Blackburn)	3	Wood R (Man Utd)
5	Wilkes A (Aston Villa)	42	Woodcock T (Nottm Forest, Cologne, Arsenal)
84	Wilkins R (Chelsea, Man Utd, AC Milan)		
1	Wilkinson B (Sheff Utd)	1	Woodger G (Oldham)
1	Wilkinson L (Oxford Univ)	2	Woodhall G (WBA)
24	Williams B (Wolves)	19	Woodley V (Chelsea)
2	Williams O (Clapton Orient)	43	Woods C (Norwich, Rangers, Shef Wed)
6	Williams S (Southampton)	23	Woodward V (Spurs, Chelsea)
6	Williams W (WBA)	1	Woosnam M (Man City)
2	Williamson E (Arsenal)	2	Worrall F (Portsmouth)
7	Williamson R (Middlesbrough)	8	Worthington F (Leicester City)
12	Willingham C (Huddersfield)	4	Wreford-Brown C (Oxford Univ, Old Carthusians)
1	Willis A (Spurs)		
12	Wilshaw D (Wolves)	1	Wright E (Cambridge Univ)
2	Wilson C P (Hendon)	31	Wright I (C Palace, Arsenal)
2	Wilson C W (Oxford Univ)	1	Wright J (Newcastle)
12	Wilson G (Sheff Wed)	45	Wright M (Southampton, Derby County, Liverpool)
2	Wilson G P (Corinthians)		
63	Wilson R (Huddersfield, Everton)	11	Wright T (Everton)
1	Wilson T (Huddersfield)	105	Wright W (Wolves)
2	Winckworth W (Old Westminsters)	1	Wylie J (Wanderers)
8	Windridge J (Chelsea)		
1	Wingfield-Straford C (Royal Engineers)	1	Yates J (Burnley)
2	Winterburn N (Arsenal)	2	York R (Aston Villa)
12	Wise D (Chelsea)	9	Young A (Huddersfield)
11	Withe P (Aston Villa)	1	Young G (Sheff Wed)

13 ● ENGLAND SENIOR CAPS 1997–1998

	Moldova	Italy	Cameroon	Chile	Switzerland	Portugal	Saudi Arabia	Morocco	Belgium	Tunisia	Romania	Colombia	Argentina
D. Seaman (Arsenal)	1	1				1	1			1	1	1	1
G. Neville (Manchester United)	2		2			2	2		2		2	2	2
P. Neville (Manchester United)	3		3	6		2*	3*		3				
D. Batty (Newcastle United)	4	11		4	8*	8	4			8	8	4*	8*
S. Campbell (Tottenham Hotspur)	5	2	2	3			6	5	5	2	6	6	6
G. Southgate (Aston Villa)	6	6	5		5		6	6		6			3*
D. Beckham (Manchester United)	7	7	7			7	7		8*		4*	7	7
P. Gascoigne (Rangers and Middlesbrough)	8	8	8				9	7*	8	8			
L. Ferdinand (Tottenham Hotspur)	9						9*	9*	9				
I. Wright (Arsenal)	10	9						10*	10				
P. Scholes (Manchester United)	11		10			11	11			11	11	11	11
S. Ripley (Blackburn Rovers)	7*												
N. Butt (Manchester United)	7**	8*		8*					4				
S. Collymore (Aston Villa)	9*												
G. Le Saux (Chelsea)			3	6*		3		3	11	3	3	3	3
P. Ince (Liverpool)		4	4	4*	4	4			4	4	4	4	4
T. Adams (Arsenal)		5	5			5	5			5	5	5	5
T. Sheringham (Manchester United)		10	10		10*	10	10				10	10	
N. Martyn (Leeds United)			1	1						1			
A. Hinchcliffe (Everton and Sheffield Wednesday)			6		3			3					
R. Fowler (Liverpool)			9										
S. McManaman (Liverpool)		11			7				11			11*	
R. Ferdinand (West Ham United)		5*			6				2*				
R. Lee (Newcastle United)		8*		7	11				7			8*	
C. Sutton (Blackburn Rovers)		10*											
D. Dublin (Coventry City)				9				9	5*				
M. Owen (Liverpool)				11		10	10*	10*	3*	10*	10*	10	10
A. Shearer (Newcastle United)		10*				9	9	9		9	9	9	9
T. Flowers (Blackburn Rovers)						1			1				
M. Keown (Arsenal)						2			2	6			
P. Merson (Middlesbrough)						8	7*			10		11*	
D. Anderton (Tottenham Hotspur)							8	7		7	7	8	8

*substitute

● 29

14 ● ENGLAND UNDER-21 CAPS 1997–1998

	Moldova	Italy	Greece	Greece	Switzerland	France	South Africa	Argentina
R.Wright (Ipswich Town)	1	1	1	1			1	1
K. Dyer (Ipswich Town)	2	2	2		2		2	2
D. Granville (Chelsea)	3	10*						
M. Duberry (Chelsea)	4			4				
R. Scimeca (Aston Villa)	5	4	5	2				
M. Hall (Coventry City)	6		6	6				
D. Murphy (Liverpool)	7		2*					
N. Quashie (QPR)	8		8		8			
B. Dyer (Crystal Palace)	9		9					
L. Bowyer (Leeds United)	10							
S. Hughes (Arsenal)	11	11	11		6*			
L. Bradbury (Man. City)	10*	9*						
W. Quinn (Sheffield Utd)	3*	3						
J. Carragher (Liverpool)	7*	8		7	8*	7	7	7
R. Ferdinand (West Ham Utd)		5		5				
B. Thatcher (Wimbledon)		6						
P. Murray (QPR)		7			11			
E. Heskey (Leicester City)		9	10	9	9	10	10	10
D. Eadie (Norwich City)		10						
J. Curtis (Man. United)		11*	4		4	2	5	5
C. Serrant (Oldham Ath)			3	3				
F. Lampard (West Ham Utd)			7	8	7	8	8	8
A. Moses (Barnsley)			9*					
K. Davies (Southampton)			10*					
M. Owen (Liverpool)				10				
J. Scowcroft (Ipswich T)				3*				
M. Bullock (Barnsley)				4*				
S. Hislop (Newcastle Utd)					1			
S. Guppy (Leicester City)					3			
J. Redknapp (Liverpool)					5			
D. Matteo (Liverpool)					6			
N. Barmby (Everton)					10			
T. Sinclair (West Ham Utd)					11			
D. Holloway (Sunderland)					5*			
L. Hendrie (Aston Villa)					7*			
D. Williams (Sunderland)					9*			
S. Simonsen (Tranmere Rov)						1		
A. Rogers (Nottm Forest)						3	3	3
D. Purse (Birmingham City)						4	4	
S. Marsh (Oxford United)						5		
R. Kozluk (Derby County)						6		11*
M. Oakley (Southampton)						9	9	9
J. Euell (Wimbledon)						11		4*
S. Elliott (Derby County)						5*	6	6
M. Clegg (Man. United)						6*	7*	
R. Allen (Tottenham H)						11*	11	6*
M. Bent (Crystal Palace)							10*	11
E. Howe (Bournemouth)							11*	4

*substitute

15 ● ENGLAND UNDER-21 INTERNATIONAL MATCHES 1976–1998

UQ   UEFA Competition Qualifier
UF   UEFA Competition Finals

v Albania

| 1989 | 7/3 | Shkoder | W | 2 – 1 | UQ |
| 1989 | 25/4 | Ipswich | W | 2 – 0 | UQ |

v Angola

| 1995 | 10/6 | La Seyne | W | 1 – 0 | |
| 1996 | 28/5 | Cuers | L | 0 – 2 | |

v Argentina

| 1998 | 18/5 | Manosque | L | 0 – 2 | |

v Austria

| 1994 | 11/10 | Kapfenberg | W | 3 – 1 | UQ |
| 1995 | 14/11 | Middlesbrough | W | 2 – 1 | UQ |

v Belgium

| 1994 | 5/6 | Berre | W | 2 – 1 | |
| 1996 | 24/5 | Toulon | W | 1 – 0 | |

v Brazil

1993	11/6	Draguignan	D	0 – 0	
1995	6/6	Toulon	L	0 – 2	
1996	1/6	Toulon	L	1 – 2	

v Bulgaria

1979	5/6	Pernik	W	3 – 1	UQ
1979	20/11	Leicester	W	5 – 0	UQ
1989	5/6	Toulon	L	2 – 3	

v Croatia

| 1996 | 23/4 | Sunderland | L | 0 – 1 | |

v Czech Republic

| 1993 | 9/6 | Saint Cyr | D | 1 – 1 | |

v Czechoslovakia

| 1990 | 27/4 | Toulon | W | 2 – 1 | |
| 1992 | 26/5 | Toulon | L | 1 – 2 | |

v Denmark

1978	19/9	Hvidovre	W	2 – 1	UQ
1979	11/9	Watford	W	1 – 0	UQ
1982	21/9	Hvidovre	W	4 – 1	UQ
1983	20/9	Norwich	W	4 – 1	UQ
1986	12/3	Copenhagen	W	1 – 0	UF
1986	26/3	Manchester City	D	1 – 1	UF
1988	13/9	Watford	D	0 – 0	
1994	8/3	Brentford	W	1 – 0	

v Finland

1977	26/5	Helsinki	W	1 – 0	UQ
1977	12/10	Hull	W	8 – 1	UQ
1984	16/10	Southampton	W	2 – 0	UQ
1985	21/5	Mikkeli	L	1 – 3	UQ

v France

1984	28/2	Sheffield Wed	W	6 – 1	UF
1984	28/3	Rouen	W	1 – 0	UF
1987	11/6	Toulon	L	0 – 2	
1988	13/4	Besançon	L	2 – 4	UF
1988	27/4	Arsenal	D	2 – 2	UF
1988	12/6	Toulon	L	2 – 4	
1990	23/5	Aix en Provence	W	7 – 3	
1991	3/6	Toulon	W	1 – 0	
1992	28/5	Aubagne	D	0 – 0	
1993	15/6	Toulon	W	1 – 0	
1994	31/5	Aubagne	L	0 – 3	
1995	12/6	Cannes	L	0 – 2	
1998	14/5	Nimes	D	1 – 1	

v Georgia

| 1996 | 8/11 | Batumi | W | 1 – 0 | UQ |
| 1997 | 29/4 | Charlton | D | 0 – 0 | UQ |

v East Germany

| 1980 | 16/4 | Sheffield Wed | L | 1 – 2 | UF |
| 1980 | 23/4 | Jena | L | 0 – 1 | UF |

v West Germany

1982	21/9	Sheffield United	W	3 – 1	UF
1982	12/10	Bremen	L	2 – 3	UF
1987	8/9	Lüdenscheid	L	0 – 2	

v Germany

| 1991 | 10/9 | Scunthorpe | W | 2 – 1 | |

v Greece

| 1982 | 16/11 | Piraeus | L | 1 – 0 | UQ |

● 31

1983	29/3	Portsmouth	W	2 – 1	UQ
1989	7/2	Patras	L	0 – 1	
1997	13/11	Heraklion	L	0 – 2	UQ
1997	17/12	Norwich	W	4 – 2	UQ

v Holland

1993	27/4	Portsmouth	W	3 – 0	UQ
1993	12/10	Utrecht	D	1 – 1	UQ

v Hungary

1981	5/6	Keszthely	W	2 – 1	UQ
1981	17/11	Nottingham	W	2 – 0	UQ
1983	26/4	Newcastle	W	1 – 0	UQ
1983	11/10	Nyiregyhaza	W	2 – 0	UQ
1990	11/9	Southampton	W	3 – 1	
1992	12/5	Vac	D	2 – 2	

v Israel

1985	27/2	Tel Aviv	W	2 – 1	

v Italy

1978	8/3	Manchester City	W	2 – 1	UF
1978	5/4	Rome	D	0 – 0	UF
1984	18/4	Manchester City	W	3 – 1	UF
1984	2/5	Florence	L	0 – 1	UF
1986	9/4	Pisa	L	0 – 2	UF
1986	23/4	Swindon	D	1 – 1	UF
1997	12/2	Bristol	W	1 – 0	UQ
1997	10/10	Rieti	W	1 – 0	UQ

v Latvia

1995	25/4	Riga	W	1 – 0	UQ
1995	7/6	Burnley	W	4 – 0	UQ

v Malaysia

1995	8/6	Six-Fours	W	2 – 0	

v Mexico

1988	5/6	Toulon	W	2 – 1	
1991	29/5	Vitrolles	W	6 – 0	
1992	24/5	Six-Fours	D	1 – 1	

v Moldova

1996	31/8	Chisinau	W	2 – 0	UQ
1997	9/9	Wycombe	W	1 – 0	UQ

v Morocco

1987	7/6	Toulon	W	2 – 0	
1988	9/6	Toulon	W	1 – 0	

v Norway

1977	1/6	Bergen	W	2 – 1	UQ
1977	6/9	Brighton	W	6 – 0	UQ
1980	9/9	Southampton	W	3 – 0	
1981	8/9	Drammen	D	0 – 0	
1992	13/10	Peterborough	L	0 – 2	UQ

1993	1/6	Stavanger	D	1 – 1	UQ
1995	10/10	Stavanger	D	2 – 2	

v Poland

1982	17/3	Warsaw	W	2 – 1	UF
1982	7/4	West Ham	D	2 – 2	UF
1989	2/6	Plymouth	W	2 – 1	UQ
1989	10/10	Jastrzebie Zdroj	W	3 – 1	UQ
1990	16/10	Tottenham	L	0 – 1	UQ
1991	12/11	Pila	L	1 – 2	UQ
1993	28/5	Jastrzebie Zdroj	W	4 – 1	UQ
1993	7/9	Millwall	L	1 – 2	UQ
1996	8/10	Wolverhampton	D	0 – 0	UQ
1997	30/5	Katowice	D	1 – 1	UQ

v Portugal

1987	13/6	Sollies-Pont	D	0 – 0	
1990	21/5	Six-Fours	L	0 – 1	
1993	7/6	Miramas	W	2 – 0	
1994	7/6	Toulon	W	2 – 0	
1994	6/9	Leicester	D	0 – 0	UQ
1995	2/9	Santa Maria	L	0 – 2	UQ
1996	30/5	Arles	L	1 – 3	

v Republic of Ireland

1981	25/2	Liverpool	W	1 – 0	
1985	25/3	Portsmouth	W	3 – 2	
1989	9/6	Six-Fours	D	0 – 0	
1990	13/11	Cork	W	3 – 0	UQ
1991	26/3	Brentford	W	3 – 0	UQ
1994	15/11	Newcastle	W	1 – 0	UQ
1995	27/3	Dublin	W	2 – 0	UQ

v Romania

1980	14/10	Ploesti	L	0 – 4	UQ
1981	28/4	Swindon	W	3 – 0	UQ
1985	30/4	Brasov	D	0 – 0	UQ
1985	9/9	Ipswich	W	3 – 0	UQ

v Russia

1994	29/5	Bandol	W	2 – 0	

v San Marino

1993	16/2	Luton	W	6 – 0	UQ
1993	17/11	San Marino	W	4 – 0	UQ

v Scotland

1977	27/4	Sheffield United	W	1 – 0	
1980	12/2	Coventry	W	2 – 1	UF
1980	4/3	Aberdeen	D	0 – 0	UF
1982	19/4	Glasgow	W	1 – 0	UF
1982	28/4	Manchester City	D	1 – 1	UF
1988	16/2	Aberdeen	W	1 – 0	UF
1989	22/3	Nottingham	W	1 – 0	UF
1993	13/6	La Ciotat	W	1 – 0	

v Senegal

1989	7/6	Sainte-Maxime	W	6 – 1	
1991	27/5	Arles	W	2 – 1	

v South Africa

1998	16/5	Aubagne	W	3 – 1	

v Spain

1984	17/5	Seville	W	1 – 0	UF
1984	24/5	Sheffield United	W	2 – 0	UF
1987	18/2	Burgos	W	2 – 1	
1992	8/9	Burgos	W	1 – 0	

v Sweden

1979	9/6	Vasteras	W	2 – 1	
1986	9/9	Oestersund	D	1 – 1	
1988	18/10	Coventry	D	1 – 1	UQ
1989	5/9	Uppsala	L	0 – 1	UQ

v Switzerland

1980	18/11	Ipswich	W	5 – 0	UQ
1981	31/5	Neuenburg	D	0 – 0	UQ
1988	28/5	Lausanne	D	1 – 1	
1997	1/4	Swindon	D	0 – 0	
1998	24/3	Aarau	L	0 – 2	

v Turkey

1984	13/11	Bursa	D	0 – 0	UQ

1985	15/10	Bristol	W	3 – 0	UQ
1987	28/4	Izmir	D	0 – 0	UQ
1987	13/10	Sheffield	D	1 – 1	UQ
1991	30/4	Izmir	D	2 – 2	UQ
1991	15/10	Reading	W	2 – 0	UQ
1992	17/11	Leyton	L	0 – 1	UQ
1993	30/3	Izmir	D	0 – 0	UQ

v USA

1989	11/6	Toulon	L	0 – 2	
1994	2/6	Arles	W	3 – 0	

v USSR

1987	9/6	La Ciotat	D	0 – 0	
1988	7/6	Six-Fours	W	1 – 0	
1990	25/5	Toulon	W	2 – 1	
1991	31/5	Aix-en-Provence	W	2 – 1	

v Wales

1976	15/12	Wolverhampton	D	0 – 0	
1979	6/2	Swansea	W	1 – 0	
1990	5/12	Tranmere	D	0 – 0	

v Yugoslavia

1978	19/4	Novi Sad	L	1 – 2	UF
1978	2/5	Manchester City	D	1 – 1	UF
1986	11/11	Peterborough	D	1 – 1	UQ
1987	10/11	Zemun	W	5 – 1	UQ

16 ● ENGLAND UNDER-21 CAPS 1976–1998

(Up to and including 1st July 1998)

1   Ablett G (Liverpool)
1   Adams N (Everton)
5   Adams T (Arsenal)
8   Allen B (QPR)
2   Allen C (Oxford Utd)
3   Allen C (QPR, C Palace)
2   Allen M (QPR)
3   Allen P (West Ham, Spurs)
3   Allen R (Spurs)
1   Anderson V (Nottm Forest)
12   Anderton D (Spurs)
1   Andrews I (Leicester City)
10   Ardley N (Wimbledon)
6   Atkinson B (Sunderland)
1   Atherton P (Coventry City)
9   Awford A (Portsmouth)

14   Bailey G (Man Utd)
2   Baker G (Southampton)
1   Bannister G (Sheff Wed)
4   Barker S (Blackburn)
4   Barmby N (Spurs, Everton)
2   Barnes J (Watford)
9   Barnes P (Man City)
4   Barrett E (Oldham)
16   Bart-Williams C (Sheff Wed, Nottm Forest)
7   Batty D (Leeds Utd)
1   Bazeley D (Watford)
2   Beagrie P (Sheff Utd)
5   Beardsmore R (Man Utd)
9   Beckham D (Man Utd)
1   Beeston C (Stoke)
2   Bent M (C Palace)
3   Bertschin K (Birmingham)
2   Birtles G (Nottm Forest)
6   Blackwell D (Wimbledon)
8   Blake M (Aston Villa)
4   Blissett L (Watford)
3   Booth A (Huddersfield)
9   Bowyer L (Charlton, Leeds Utd)
13   Bracewell P (Stoke, Sunderland, Everton)
3   Bradbury L (Portsmouth, Man City)
4   Bradshaw P (Wolves)
2   Branch M (Everton)
2   Breacker T (Luton Town)
5   Brennan M (Ipswich)
1   Bridges M (Sunderland)
4   Brightwell I (Man City)
5   Briscoe L (Sheff Wed)

4   Brock K (Oxford Utd)
2   Broomes M (Blackburn)
4   Brown M (Man City)
5   Bull S (Wolves)
1   Bullock M (Barnsley)
7   Burrows D (WBA, Liverpool)
7   Butcher T (Ipswich)
7   Butt N (Man Utd)
3   Butters G (Spurs)
8   Butterworth I (Coventry City, Nottm Forest)

3   Caesar G (Arsenal)
9   Callaghan N (Watford)
4   Campbell K (Arsenal)
11   Campbell S (Spurs)
4   Carbon M (Derby)
1   Carr C (Fulham)
9   Carr F (Nottm Forest)
11   Carragher J (Liverpool)
1   Casper C (Man Utd)
14   Caton T (Man City, Arsenal)
2   Challis T (QPR)
4   Chamberlain M (Stoke)
1   Chapman L (Stoke City)
4   Charles G (Nottm Forest)
12   Chettle S (Nottm Forest)
11   Clark L (Newcastle)   ✓
2   Clegg M (Man Utd)
15   Clough N (Nottm Forest)
8   Cole A (Arsenal, Bristol City, Newcastle)
4   Coney D (Fulham)
1   Connor T (Brighton & Hove Albion)
1   Cooke R (Spurs)
4   Cooke T (Man United)
8   Cooper C (Middlesbrough)
3   Corrigan J (Man City)
8   Cottee T (West Ham)
3   Couzens A (Leeds Utd)
5   Cowans G (Aston Villa)
6   Cox N (Aston Villa)
5   Cranson I (Ipswich)
4   Croft G (Grimsby)
4   Crooks G (Stoke City)
3   Crossley M (Nottm Forest)
3   Cundy J (Chelsea)
6   Cunningham L (WBA)
1   Curbishley A (Birmingham)
6   Curtis J (Man Utd)

7	Daniel P (Hull City)
1	Davies K (Southampton)
2	Davis K (Luton)
11	Davis P (Arsenal)
2	D'Avray M (Ipswich)
6	Day C (Spurs)
7	Deehan J (Aston Villa)
3	Dennis M (Birmingham)
1	Dichio D (QPR)
1	Dickens A (West Ham)
4	Dicks J (West Ham)
5	Digby F (Swindon)
1	Dillon K (Birmingham)
1	Dixon K (Chelsea)
4	Dobson T (Coventry City)
8	Dodd J (Southampton)
3	Donowa L (Norwich City)
11	Dorigo T (Aston Villa)
9	Dozzell J (Ipswich)
3	Draper M (Notts County)
5	Duberry M (Chelsea)
7	Duxbury M (Man Utd)
11	Dyer B (C Palace)
6	Dyer K (Ipswich)
4	Dyson P (Coventry City)
7	Eadie D (Norwich)
14	Ebbrell J (Everton)
3	Edghill R (Man City)
15	Ehiogu U (Aston Villa)
3	Elliott P (Luton, Aston Villa)
2	Elliott R (Newcastle)
3	Elliott S (Derby)
2	Euell J (Wimbledon)
7	Fairclough C (Nottm Forest, Spurs)
1	Fairclough D (Liverpool)
11	Fashanu Justin (Norwich, Nottm Forest)
3	Fear P (Wimbledon)
1	Fenton G (Aston Villa)
11	Fenwick T (QPR)
4	Ferdinand R (West Ham)
5	Fereday W (QPR)
10	Flitcroft G (Man City)
3	Flowers T (Southampton)
2	Ford M (Leeds)
4	Foster N (Brentford)
1	Forsyth M (Derby County)
1	Foster S (Brighton & Hove Albion)
8	Fowler R (Liverpool)
2	Froggatt S (Aston Villa)
11	Futcher P (Luton, Man City)
2	Gabbiadini M (Sunderland)
1	Gale T (Fulham)
4	Gallen K (QPR)
13	Gascoigne P (Newcastle)
3	Gayle H (Birmingham)
18	Gerrard P (Oldham)
1	Gernon I (Ipswich)

5	Gibbs N (Watford)
1	Gibson C (Aston Villa)
11	Gilbert W (C Palace)
8	Goddard P (West Ham)
13	Gordon D (C Palace)
4	Gordon D (Norwich)
4	Granville D (Chelsea)
2	Gray A (Aston Villa)
1	Guppy S (Leicester)
1	Haigh P (Hull)
8	Hall M (Coventry City)
11	Hall R (Southampton)
1	Hamilton D (Newcastle)
2	Hardyman P (Portsmouth)
10	Hateley M (Coventry City, Portsmouth)
3	Hayes M (Arsenal)
1	Hazell R (Wolves)
6	Heaney N (Arsenal)
8	Heath A (Stoke, Everton)
7	Hendon I (Spurs)
2	Hendrie L (Aston Villa)
7	Hesford I (Blackpool)
12	Heskey E (Leicester)
9	Hilaire V (C Palace)
4	Hill D (Spurs)
1	Hillier D (Arsenal)
1	Hinchcliffe A (Man City)
2	Hinshelwood P (C Palace)
7	Hirst D (Sheff Wed)
1	Hislop S (Newcastle)
12	Hoddle G (Spurs)
8	Hodge S (Nottm Forest, Aston Villa)
7	Hodgson D (Middlesbrough, Liverpool)
1	Holdsworth D (Watford)
10	Holland C (Newcastle)
4	Holland P (Mansfield)
1	Holloway D (Sunderland)
5	Horne B (Millwall)
2	Howe E (Bournemouth)
2	Hucker P (QPR)
4	Huckerby D (Coventry City)
8	Hughes S (Arsenal)
3	Humphreys R (Sheff Wed)
1	Impey A (QPR)
2	Ince P (West Ham)
10	Jackson M (Everton)
10	James D (Watford)
2	James J (Luton)
1	Jemson N (Nottm Forest)
9	Joachim J (Leicester)
7	Johnson T (Notts County, Derby)
2	Johnston C (Middlesbrough)
1	Jones C (Spurs)
1	Jones D (Everton)
2	Jones R (Liverpool)
1	Keegan G (Oldham)

1 Kenny W (Everton)	4 Newell M (Luton Town)
8 Keown M (Aston Villa)	4 Newton E (Chelsea)
1 Kerslake D (QPR)	3 Newton S (Charlton)
2 Kilcline B (Notts County)	1 Nicholls A (Plymouth)
2 King A (Everton)	
7 Kitson P (Leicester, Derby)	7 Oakes M (Aston Villa)
2 Knight A (Portsmouth)	4 Oakley M (Southampton)
2 Knight I (Sheff Wed)	3 O'Connor J (Everton)
2 Kozluk R (Derby)	1 Oldfield D (Luton)
	10 Olney I (Aston Villa)
5 Lake P (Man City)	3 Ord R (Sunderland)
6 Lampard F (West Ham)	7 Osman R (Ipswich)
1 Langley T (Chelsea)	22 Owen G (Man City, WBA)
10 Lee D (Chelsea)	1 Owen M (Liverpool)
2 Lee R (Charlton)	
6 Lee S (Liverpool)	1 Painter I (Stoke)
4 Le Saux G (Chelsea)	4 Palmer C (Sheff Wed)
2 Lowe D (Ipswich)	6 Parker G (Hull, Nottm Forest)
7 Lukic J (Leeds Utd)	8 Parker P (Fulham)
3 Lund G (Grimsby)	1 Parkes P (QPR)
	5 Parkin S (Stoke City)
7 Mabbutt G (Bristol Rovers, Spurs)	12 Parlour R (Arsenal)
6 McCall S (Ipswich)	6 Peach D (Southampton)
5 McDonald N (Newcastle)	1 Peake A (Leicester City)
1 McGrath L (Coventry City)	3 Pearce I (Blackburn)
3 Mackenzie S (WBA)	1 Pearce S (Nottm Forest)
1 McLeary A (Millwall)	15 Pickering N (Sunderland, Coventry City)
6 McMahon S (Everton, Aston Villa)	3 Platt D (Aston Villa)
7 McManaman S (Liverpool)	5 Plummer C (QPR)
5 Makin C (Oldham)	3 Pollock J (Middlesbrough)
1 Marriott A (Nottm Forest)	12 Porter G (Watford)
1 Marsh S (Oxford)	1 Potter G (Southampton)
4 Marshall A (Norwich)	1 Pressman K (Sheff Wed)
2 Martin L (Man Utd)	4 Proctor M (Middlesbrough, Nottm Forest)
11 Martyn N (Bristol Rovers)	2 Purse D (Birmingham)
4 Matteo D (Liverpool)	
9 Matthew D (Chelsea)	4 Quashie N (QPR)
1 May A (Man City)	2 Quinn W (Sheff Utd)
4 Merson P (Arsenal)	
3 Middleton J (Nottm Forest, Derby County)	3 Ramage C (Derby County)
4 Miller A (Arsenal)	10 Ranson R (Man City)
2 Mills G (Nottm Forest)	19 Redknapp J (Liverpool)
3 Mimms R (Rotherham, Everton)	14 Redmond S (Man City)
6 Minto S (Charlton)	10 Reeves K (Norwich, Man City)
7 Moore I (Tranmere, Nottm Forest)	6 Regis C (WBA)
2 Moran S (Southampton)	6 Reid N (Man City)
2 Morgan S (Leicester)	6 Reid P (Bolton)
3 Morris J (Chelsea)	4 Richards D (Wolves)
2 Mortimer P (Charlton)	2 Richards J (Wolves)
2 Moses A (Barnsley)	5 Rideout P (Aston Villa, Bari)
8 Moses R (WBA, Man Utd)	8 Ripley S (Middlesbrough)
1 Mountfield D (Everton)	1 Ritchie A (Brighton & Hove Albion)
1 Muggleton C (Leicester City)	7 Rix G (Arsenal)
2 Murphy D (Liverpool)	5 Roberts A (Millwall, C Palace)
4 Murray P (QPR)	1 Roberts B (Middlesbrough)
1 Mutch A (Wolves)	6 Robins M (Man City)
4 Myers A (Chelsea)	7 Robson B (WBA)
	6 Robson S (Arsenal, West Ham)
8 Nethercott S (Spurs)	14 Rocastle D (Arsenal)
7 Neville P (Man Utd)	4 Rodger G (Coventry City)

3	Rogers A (Nottm Forest)	1	Talbot B (Ipswich)
4	Rosario R (Norwich)	4	Thatcher B (Millwall, Wimbledon)
2	Rose M (Arsenal)	7	Thomas D (Coventry City, Spurs)
1	Rowell G (Sunderland)	12	Thomas M (Arsenal)
4	Ruddock N (Southampton)	3	Thomas M (Luton)
6	Rufus R (Charlton)	1	Thomas R (Watford)
1	Ryan J (Oldham Athletic)	2	Thompson A (Bolton)
3	Ryder S (Walsall)	2	Thompson D (Liverpool)
		6	Thompson G (Coventry City)
5	Samways V (Spurs)	5	Thorn A (Wimbledon)
8	Sansom K (Crystal Palace)	3	Thornley B (Man Utd)
9	Scimeca R (Aston Villa)	13	Tiler C (Barnsley, Nottm Forest)
5	Scowcroft J (Ipswich)		
10	Seaman D (Birmingham)	7	Unsworth D (Everton)
11	Sedgley S (Coventry City, Spurs)		
3	Sellars S (Blackburn)	10	Venison B (Sunderland)
3	Selley I (Arsenal)	12	Vinnicombe C (Rangers)
2	Serrant C (Oldham)		
8	Sharpe L (Man Utd)	1	Waddle C (Newcastle)
7	Shaw G (Aston Villa)	7	Walker D (Nottm Forest)
11	Shearer A (Southampton)	9	Walker I (Spurs)
1	Shelton G (Sheff Wed)	14	Wallace D (Southampton)
1	Sheringham T (Millwall)	4	Wallace Ray (Southampton)
16	Sheron M (Man City)	11	Wallace Rod (Southampton)
4	Sherwood T (Norwich City)	2	Walsh G (Man Utd)
7	Shipperley N (Chelsea, Southampton)	4	Walsh P (Luton Town)
1	Simonsen S (Tranmere)	9	Walters M (Aston Villa)
5	Simpson P (Man City)	2	Ward P (Brighton & Hove Albion)
10	Sims S (Leicester City)	8	Warhurst P (Oldham, Sheff Wed)
14	Sinclair T (QPR, West Ham)	5	Watson D (Barnsley)
1	Sinnott L (Watford)	7	Watson D (Norwich)
4	Slade S (Spurs)	2	Watson G (Sheff Wed)
3	Slater S (West Ham)	13	Watson S (Newcastle)
12	Small B (Aston Villa)	3	Webb N (Portsmouth, Nottm Forest)
10	Smith D (Coventry City)	2	Whelan N (Leeds Utd)
5	Smith M (Sheff Wed)	3	Whelan P (Ipswich)
1	Smith M (Sunderland)	6	White D (Man City)
4	Snodin I (Doncaster)	4	Whyte C (Arsenal)
3	Statham B (Spurs)	1	Wicks S (QPR)
6	Statham D (WBA)	1	Wilkins R (Chelsea)
3	Stein B (Luton)	4	Wilkinson P (Grimsby, Everton)
7	Sterland M (Sheff Wed)	1	Williams D (Sunderland)
2	Steven T (Everton)	4	Williams P (Charlton)
1	Stevens G (Everton)	6	Williams P (Derby County)
7	Stevens G (Brighton & Hove Albion, Spurs)	14	Williams S (Southampton)
		1	Winterburn N (Wimbledon)
1	Stewart P (Man City)	1	Wise D (Wimbledon)
5	Stuart G (Chelsea)	2	Woodcock A (Nottm Forest)
4	Stuart J (Charlton)	6	Woods C (Nottm Forest, QPR, Norwich)
10	Suckling P (Coventry City, Man City, C Palace)	2	Wright A (Blackburn)
3	Summerbee N (Swindon)	2	Wright M (Southampton)
1	Sunderland A (Wolves)	8	Wright R (Ipswich)
4	Sutch D (Norwich)	6	Wright W (Everton)
13	Sutton C (Norwich)		
1	Swindlehurst D (C Palace)	5	Yates D (Notts County)

17 ● ENGLAND B INTERNATIONAL MATCHES 1949–1998

v Algeria

1990	11/12	Algiers	D	0 – 0

v Australia

1980	17/11	Birmingham	W	1 – 0

v Chile

1998	10/2	West Bromwich	L	1 – 2

v CIS

1992	28/4	Moscow	D	1 – 1

v Czechoslovakia

1978	28/11	Prague	W	1 – 0
1990	24/4	Sunderland	W	2 – 0
1992	24/3	Ceske Budejovice	W	1 – 0

v Finland

1949	15/5	Helsinki	W	4 – 0

v France

1952	22/5	Le Havre	L	1 – 7
1992	18/2	QPR	W	3 – 0

v West Germany

1954	24/3	Gelsenkirchen	W	4 – 0
1955	23/3	Sheffield	D	1 – 1
1978	21/2	Augsburg	W	2 – 1

v Holland

1949	18/5	Amsterdam	W	4 – 0
1950	22/2	Newcastle	W	1 – 0
1950	17/5	Amsterdam	L	0 – 3
1952	26/3	Amsterdam	W	1 – 0

v Iceland

1989	19/5	Reykjavik	W	2 – 0
1991	27/4	Watford	W	1 – 0

v Italy

1950	11/5	Milan	L	0 – 5
1989	14/11	Brighton	D	1 – 1

v Luxembourg

1950	21/5	Luxembourg	W	2 – 1

v Malaysia

1978	30/5	Kuala Lumpur	D	1 – 1

v Malta

1987	14/10	Ta'Qali	W	2 – 0

v New Zealand

1978	7/6	Christchurch	W	4 – 0
1978	11/6	Wellington	W	3 – 1
1978	14/6	Auckland	W	4 – 0
1979	15/10	Leyton Orient	W	4 – 1
1984	13/11	Nottingham Forest	W	2 – 0

v Northern Ireland

1994	10/5	Sheffield	W	4 – 2

v Norway

1989	22/5	Stavanger	W	1 – 0

v Republic of Ireland

1990	27/3	Cork	L	1 – 4
1994	13/12	Liverpool	W	2 – 0

v Russia

1998	21/4	QPR	W	4 – 1

v Scotland

1953	11/3	Edinburgh	D	2 – 2
1954	3/3	Sunderland	D	1 – 1
1956	29/2	Dundee	D	2 – 2
1957	6/2	Birmingham	W	4 – 1

v Singapore

1978	18/6	Singapore	W	8 – 0

v Spain

1980	26/3	Sunderland	W	1 – 0
1981	25/3	Granada	L	2 – 3
1991	18/12	Castellon	W	1 – 0

v Switzerland

1950	18/1	Sheffield	W	5 – 0
1954	22/5	Basle	L	0 – 2
1956	21/3	Southampton	W	4 – 1
1989	16/5	Winterthur	W	2 – 0
1991	20/5	Walsall	W	2 – 1

v USA

1980	14/10	Manchester	W	1 – 0

v Wales

1991	5/2	Swansea	W	1 – 0

v Yugoslavia

1954	16/5	Ljubljana	L	1 – 2
1955	19/10	Manchester	W	5 – 1
1989	12/12	Millwall	W	2 – 1

18 ● ENGLAND B CAPS 1978–1998

(Up to and including 1st July 1998)

1 Ablett G (Liverpool)
4 Adams T (Arsenal)
7 Anderson V (Nottingham Forest)
1 Anderton D (Tottenham)
1 Armstrong C (Crystal Palace)
2 Armstrong D (Middlesbrough)
1 Atkinson D (Sheffield Wednesday)
2 Bailey G (Manchester United)
1 Bailey J (Everton)
2 Barmby N (Tottenham and Everton))
1 Barnes P (WBA)
4 Barrett E (Oldham Athletic)
3 Barton W (Wimbledon)
1 Bart-Williams C (Sheffield Wednesday)
2 Batson B (WBA)
5 Batty D (Leeds United)
2 Beagrie P (Eveton)
2 Beardsley P (Liverpool)
7 Beasant D (Wimbledon)
2 Beresford J (Newcastle)
1 Birtles G (Nottingham Forest)
1 Bishop I (West Ham United)
1 Blissett L (Watford)
2 Bond K (Norwich and Manchester City)
1 Borrows B (Coventry City)
1 Bould S (Arsenal)
1 Brock K (QPR)
1 Bruce S (Norwich City)
5 Bull S (Wolves)
3 Burrows D (Liverpool)
1 Butcher T (Ipswich Town)
1 Callaghan N (Watford)
1 Campbell K (Arsenal)
1 Campbell S (Tottenham)
2 Carragher J (Liverpool)
1 Chapman L (Leeds United)
3 Clough N (Nottingham Forest)
1 Cole A (Newcastle)
10 Corrigan J (Manchester City)
2 Coton T (Manchester City)
2 Cowans G (Aston Villa)
1 Crook I (Norwich City)
1 Cunningham L (WBA)
1 Curle K (Wimbledon and Manchester City)
1 Curtis J (Manchester United)
6 Daley S (Wolves)
1 Daley T (Aston Villa)
1 Davenport P (Nottingham Forest)
1 Davis P (Arsenal)
3 Deane B (Sheffield United)
1 Devonshire A (West Ham United)
2 Dicks J (West Ham)

4 Dixon L (Arsenal)
7 Dorigo T (Chelsea, Leeds United)
2 Dyer K (Ipswich Town)
1 Ebbrell J (Everton)
1 Edghill R (Manchester City)
1 Ehiogu U (Aston Villa)
1 Elliott P (Celtic)
3 Elliott S (Sunderland)
3 Eves M (Wolves)
1 Fairclough C (Tottenham)
1 Fairclough D (Liverpool)
1 Fashanu J (Nottingham Forest)
1 Ferdinand L (Tottenham)
3 Flanagan M (Charlton and
  Crystal Palace)
3 Ford T (WBA)
1 Forsyth M (Derby County)
1 Fowler R (Liverpool)
2 Fox R (Newcastle)
1 Gabbiadini M (Sunderland)
1 Gallagher J (Birmingham)
4 Gascoigne P (Tottenham)
1 Geddis D (Ipswich Town)
1 Gibson C (Aston Villa)
1 Gidman J (Aston Villa)
1 Goddard P (West Ham United)
1 Gordon D (Norwich City)
1 Greenhoff B (Manchester United)
1 Guppy S (Leicester City)
1 Hall M (Coventry City)
1 Harford M (Luton Town)
1 Hazell R (Wolves)
1 Heath A (Everton)
1 Hendrie L (Aston Villa)
1 Heskey E (Leicester City)
1 Hilaire V (Crystal Palace)
6 Hill G (Manchester Utd and
  Derby County)
3 Hirst D (Sheffield Wednesday)
2 Hoddle G (Tottenham)
2 Hodge S (Nottingham Forest)
1 Holdsworth D (Wimbledon)
5 Hollins J (QPR)
1 Huckerby D (Coventry City)
3 Hurlock T (Millwall)
1 Ince P (Manchester United)
1 James D (Liverpool)
2 Jobson R (Oldham)
1 Johnson D (Ipswich Town)
1 Johnston C (Liverpool)
2 Joseph R (Wimbledon)
7 Kennedy A (Liverpool)

● 39

1 Keown M (Everton)	3 Rix G (Arsenal)
1 King P (Sheffield Wednesday)	1 Roberts G (Tottenham)
1 Lake P (Manchester City)	3 Robson B (WBA, Manchester United)
1 Lampard F (West Ham United)	2 Rocastle D (Arsenal)
3 Langley T (Chelsea)	5 Roeder G (Orient and QPR)
1 Laws B (Nottingham Forest)	1 Ruddock N (Liverpool)
1 Lee R (Newcastle)	2 Sansom K (Crystal Palace)
2 Le Saux G (Chelsea)	2 Scales J (Wimbledon, Liverpool)
6 Le Tissier M (Southampton)	1 Scimeca R (Aston Villa)
1 Lineker G (Leicester City)	6 Seaman D (QPR)
4 Linighan A (Norwich City)	1 Serrant C (Oldham Athletic)
1 Lukic J (Leeds United)	1 Sharpe L (Manchester United)
1 Lyons M (Everton)	1 Shearer A (Southampton)
1 McCall S (Ipswich Town)	1 Sherwood T (Blackburn)
1 McDermott T (Liverpool)	1 Sims S (Leicester City)
3 McLeary A (Millwall)	1 Sinclair T (West Ham United)
2 McMahon S (Aston Villa and Liverpool)	3 Sinton A (QPR)
9 Mabbutt G (Tottenham)	2 Slater S (West Ham United)
3 Mckenzie S (Manchester City and Charlton)	4 Smith A (Arsenal)
7 Mariner P (Ipswich Town)	2 Snodin I (Everton)
2 Martin A (West Ham United)	4 Speight M (Sheffield United)
6 Martyn N (Bristol Rovers and C Palace)	2 Spink N (Aston Villa)
1 Matteo D (Liverpool)	2 Statham D (WBA)
4 Merson P (Arsenal and Middlesbrough)	3 Sterland M (Sheffield Wednesday, Leeds)
1 Money R (Liverpool)	1 Stevens G (Everton)
2 Morley T (Aston Villa)	5 Stewart P (Tottenham)
3 Mortimer D (Aston Villa)	1 Stubbs A (Bolton)
1 Mountfield D (Everton)	1 Summerbee N (Swindon)
3 Mowbray T (Middlesbrough)	7 Sunderland A (Arsenal)
1 Murray P (QPR)	2 Sutton C (Norwich, Blackburn)
3 Mutch A (Wolves)	8 Talbot B (Ipswich and Arsenal)
3 Naylor S (WBA)	3 Thomas G (Crystal Palace)
6 Needham D (Nottingham Forest)	5 Thomas M (Liverpool)
2 Newell M (Everton)	1 Thomas M (Tottenham Hotspur)
2 Osman R (Ipswich Town)	1 Thompson P (Liverpool)
7 Owen G (Manchester City)	1 Waldron M (Southampton)
9 Pallister G (Middlesbrough, Manchester Utd)	1 Walker I (Tottenham)
5 Palmer C (Sheffield Wednesday)	1 Wallace D (Manchester United)
1 Parker G (Nottingham Forest)	1 Wallace R (Southampton)
3 Parker P (QPR)	1 Walters M (Rangers)
2 Parkes P (West Ham United)	2 Ward P (Nottingham Forest)
1 Parlour R (Arsenal)	1 Watson S (Newcastle United)
1 Peach D (Southampton)	4 Webb N (Manchester United)
1 Phillips K (Sunderland)	1 White D (Manchester City)
3 Platt D (Aston Villa)	2 Wilcox J (Blackburn)
1 Power P (Manchester City)	1 Williams D (Sunderland)
3 Preece D (Luton Town)	3 Williams P (Charlton Athletic)
3 Pressman K (Sheffield Wednesday)	4 Williams S (Southampton)
1 Quashie N (QPR)	3 Winterburn N (Arsenal)
1 Quinn W (Sheffield United)	3 Wise D (Wimbledon)
1 Redknapp J (Liverpool)	1 Woodcock T (Cologne)
3 Reeves K (Manchester City)	2 Woods C (Norwich, Rangers)
3 Regis C (WBA)	2 Wright B (Everton)
3 Richards J (Wolves)	3 Wright I (Crystal Palace)

19 ● ENGLAND'S INTERNATIONAL MATCHES 1997–1998

FULL INTERNATIONALS

England 4   Moldova 0

10 September 1997, Wembley

There was some encouraging news from Tbilisi - Italy had only managed a 0–0 draw in their penultimate World Cup qualifier – and a moving tribute to Diana, Princess of Wales, before England set about the task of achieving three points against first-time visitors Moldova. Against a team whose ambition was clearly to keep the score down to a respectable level, Glenn Hoddle's game-plan was simple: to release Gascoigne through the middle or to create some crossing opportunities.

Beckham was taking corners from both sides with his right foot, causing all kinds of mayhem in Moldova's box. On 29 minutes Roumanenco elected to punch a Beckham inswinger from the left and the ball immediately found its way back to the Manchester United midfielder. He picked out United team-mate Scholes and a diving header put England in front.

The home side were clearly in the mood to make their superiority count with more goals after the break. The devastation that Gascoigne had been hinting at finally arrived within moments of the resumption. Collecting the ball from Wright about 40 yards from goal, he went on a long swaying run forward before sliding it through for Wright to beat the goal-keeper at his near post. Now the points were secure.

Blackburn's Stuart Ripley, winning his second cap as a 67th-minute substitute for Beckham, provided some dash down the right flank and Gascoigne hit a post from one of his crosses. Sadly, Ripley was off with a hamstring injury within eight minutes of his entry. Wright and Gascoigne then combined to telling effect once again with ten minutes to go, the latter scoring after a high-speed exchange of passes. Wright raced onto Collymore's pass to make it 4–0 in the last minute and "Are you watching Italy?" rang around Wembley.

England: Seaman, Neville G., Neville P., Batty, Campbell, Southgate, Beckham (Ripley) (Butt), Gascoigne, Ferdinand L. (Collymore), Wright, Scholes.

Moldova: Roumanenco, Fistican, Tistimitstanu, Culibaba (Suharev), Spinu, Stroenco, Curtean, Shishkin (Popovici), Miterev, Rebetadj, Rogaciov (Cibotari).

Referee: K-E. Nilsson (Sweden)

Attendance: 74,102

Italy 0   England 0

11 October 1997, Rome

England were on their way to the World Cup Finals for the first time in eight years after a battling draw in the Olympic Stadium. The precious qualifying point achieved in difficult circumstances condemned the Italians, as Group runners-up, to the ordeal of a tense two-legged play-off with Russia for a place at France 98. The hosts had previously won all of their fifteen World Cup matches in the capital city and had felt even more confident after beating England at Wembley eight months before.

A spiky, resolute England side, characterised by David Batty, a snapping bulldog in midfield, gave the Italians very few opportunities to break them down. Zola and Inzaghi, strangely ineffective, were both substituted and as the home side lost their way, they started losing their tempers too. They had five players booked and Di Livio went off on 76 minutes following an outrageous foul on Sol Campbell.

There was some heart-stopping action in the last couple of minutes. England might well have won the match, as Ian Wright got round the goalkeeper but struck the outside of a post from a difficult angle. Almost immediately Del Piero, "The Magician" merely a late substitute, put in an inviting cross from the left from which Vieri directed a free header inches wide of Seaman's right-hand post. England's goalkeeper said afterwards that he had no fears that the ball was going in. Still, automatic qualification for the World Cup had been obtained with inches to spare.

Italy began the match knowing that only a victory would guarantee that automatic place, so Maldini plumped for a 4-3-3 formation which had Vieri and Inzaghi providing the pace and power to complement the talismanic Zola. But it all went wrong for the "Azzurri" and Hoddle's brave team survived a very competitive match with their goal intact – and their credibility considerably enhanced.

Italy: Peruzzi, Nesta, Maldini (Benarrivo), Albertini, Cannavaro, Costacurta, Di Livio, Baggio D., Vieri, Zola (Del Piero), Inzaghi (Chiesa).

England: Seaman, Campbell, Le Saux, Ince, Adams, Southgate, Beckham, Gascoigne (Butt), Wright, Sheringham, Batty.

Referee: M. Van Der Ende (Holland)

Attendance: 80,000

● **41**

Ian Wright rifles in a shot against Moldova.

Paul Gascoigne slots home the third goal against Moldova.

Albertini clears from Teddy Sheringham in Rome.

Beckham, Ince and Gascoigne in euphoric mood after helping England to qualify for World Cup 98.

England 2   Cameroon 0

15 November 1997, Wembley

After the drama and excitement of Rome, England easily won a more mundane Wembley friendly against a disappointing Cameroon team which would surely struggle to make an impact in the World Cup. This was the first of five warm-up matches, plus the tournament in Morocco, in which England's Head Coach could prepare or experiment before France 98. The team facing the "Indomitable Lions" had to be experimental to a degree, following the withdrawal through injury of regulars like Adams, Le Saux and Sheringham. Alan Shearer, of course, was still months away from fitness.

For most of the first half the exchanges were distinctly low-key, with Cameroon 'keeper Ongandzi called into action only intermittently. He made a mess of trying to deal with Andy Hinchcliffe's left-wing cross but redeemed himself with an impressive save from Robbie Fowler's low shot from the edge of the box. As the first period went into the stoppage time added for the Southgate injury that allowed West Ham's Rio Ferdinand to make his England debut at 19, England suddenly put two goals past Ongandzi in a couple of minutes.

For the first Paul Gascoigne surged through the middle, taking on and beating three defenders before threading a short pass through for Paul Scholes. Two Cameroon players lunged in to avert the danger but only made it easier for the Manchester United prodigy to lift the ball expertly over the advancing 'keeper. Then David Beckham curved in one of his measured crosses from the right and Fowler scored with a simple downward header from close in.

Scholes almost netted a third early in the second half after McManaman's through pass had given him enough space for a hard, low shot. Fowler, now more confident after his goal, had a long-range effort blocked. With Cameroon showing little inclination to mount attacks themselves, they were on the back foot again near the end as Ince clipped the bar with a spectacular volley.

England: Martyn, Campbell, Neville P. Ince, Southgate (Ferdinand R.), Hinchcliffe, Beckham, Gascoigne (Lee), Fowler, Scholes (Sutton), McManaman.

Cameroon: Ongandzi, Song, Wome, Mimboe, Kalla, Job, Mboma (Njitap), Etchi, Etame (Olembe), Foe, Ipouta.

Referee: T. Hauge (Norway)
Attendance: 46,176

England 0   Chile 2

11 February 1998, Wembley

Another team which had qualified for the World Cup provided England's next Wembley opposition. When Chile came for a Rous Cup fixture in 1989, the result was a sterile 0–0 draw. Now the Chileans had Marcelo Salas, a striker who would be moving to Lazio at the end of the season for £13 million. His stunning volley close

to half-time, plus a penalty-kick after Campbell had tripped him, condemned England to their first defeat since Le Tournoi.

A home striker was making history. Liverpool's Michael Owen, at 18 years 59 days, became England's youngest debutant of the twentieth century. The scorer of 29 goals in 28 Internationals at youth level started the match and did well in difficult circumstances. As well as Shearer, other absentees from the starting line-up included Gascoigne, Beckham and Ince. England struggled to penetrate the Chilean rearguard, despite playing with a three-man attack of Owen, Dion Dublin (another debut) and Sheringham.

The kick-off had been delayed for fifteen minutes with many fans held up on the London Underground and some may still have missed an early piece of action involving the precocious Owen. On six minutes Nicky Butt burst down the right flank, Dublin laid back his cross and Owen hit the ball first time with the outside of his right foot to bring an excellent one-handed stop from Tapia in Chile's goal.

Midfielder Jose Luis Sierra had impressed as a passer in the opening half and struck a beauty to Salas from all of fifty yards as the interval approached. The ball just cleared Batty's head outside the box and the lurking Chilean hit-man controlled it briefly on his thigh before lashing a shot past Martyn. It was finishing of the highest international quality and Wembley gasped.

Graeme Le Saux produced another good save from Tapia with a half-volley and then Alan Shearer, playing again well before schedule, was brought on for Sheringham for the last half-hour. England pressed hard for an equaliser but it was that man Salas who was the tormentor once again. Campbell lunged at his twisting, turning frame and the result was a penalty, which Salas converted himself with minimal fuss.

England: Martyn, Neville G., Campbell, Batty (Ince), Adams, Neville P. (Le Saux), Lee, Butt, Dublin, Sheringham (Shearer), Owen.

Chile: Tapia, Villarroel, Reyes, Fuentes, Margas, Rojas, Parraguez, Acuna, Sierra (Valenzuela), Barrera (Carreno), Salas.

Referee: R. Wojcik (Poland)
Attendance: 65,228

Switzerland 1   England 1

25 March 1998, Berne

England took on the Swiss in a cold Wankdorf Stadium with another team depleted by injury. No Manchester United player started the match. England went into it having only lost once to their opponents in fifty years, but for a while it did not look as though they were going to keep the record intact. As England struggled to keep possession on a difficult surface, any kind of rhythm went out the window and the Swiss noticeably grew in confidence as they could see the possibility of a shock result.

The disjointed nature of the match was emphasised at a Swiss free-kick out on the left. Fournier touched the ball sideways to Wicky and then realised that he was passing to empty space because his team-mate had already turned his back and made a run. Then the home side stunned England with a goal on 38 minutes, Tottenham defender Ramon Vega glancing Chapuisat's centre past Flowers.

England clearly improved in the second half, with more support afforded to Alan Shearer up front. Paul Merson, in his first international start for nearly four years, began to see more of the ball and drove a shot just over the top on the hour. Ten minutes later Corminboeuf inadvertently made a present of the ball to Shearer and he slipped it across to the far post where an unmarked Merson had time to measure a right-footer inside the near post. After the boost of an equaliser England played like a proper unit again and Shearer could even have grabbed a winner. But that, perhaps, would have been too flattering.

Switzerland: Corminboeuf, Vega, Yakin, Henchoz, Vogel, Sforza, Wicky (Lonfat), Fournier, Sesa (Kunz), Grassi, Chapuisat.

England: Flowers, Keown, Hinchcliffe, Ince, Southgate, Ferdinand R., McManaman, Merson (Batty), Shearer, Owen (Sheringham), Lee.

Referee: P. Garibian (France)

Attendance: 17,100

England 3   Portugal 0

22 April 1998, Wembley

Alan Shearer, with two goals on the night, looked to be back to his best form as England got back in the groove at Wembley. Glenn Hoddle observed afterwards that scoring chances at the top level were getting slimmer and slimmer and that, with a player like Shearer, England had someone capable of winning a match. David Seaman had a rock-steady game in goal with plenty to do as Portuguese stars Luis Figo, Joao Pinto and Paulo Sousa flowed forward - and Michael Owen had an eventful last thirteen minutes as a substitute for Sheringham in which he could have had two goals and a penalty.

From the start England prospered when they managed to get the ball forward quickly. The first goal came after just minutes, Shearer creating space for himself at the far post to score with a straightforward header from Le Saux's accurate cross. Portugal then confirmed their status as arguably the best team not to have qualified for France 98 as they confidently built up moves and threatened Seaman's goal. If they had had a striker of Shearer's calibre, providing a cutting edge to all their creativity around the box, the visitors would surely have registered a goal or two.

As the first period came a close, Seaman rescued England by spreading himself to block Joao Pinto's shot after defensive confusion allowed him a clear sight of goal. Portugal continued to exert more pressure after the break, but it was the home side who increased their lead. It was an odd goal, Ince's pass deflecting off the Spanish

referee and into the path of Sheringham who quickly lifted the ball gently over the advancing Vitor Baia.

A scintillating move on 65 minutes brought a third England goal. The ball was transferred swiftly from Scholes to Le Saux and then to Batty who hooked it across to Shearer near the "D". Most players would have taken the ball on a couple of strides, but the Newcastle man simply let it bounce once before crashing a shot high into the net. The crowd loved that.

England: Seaman, Neville G. (Neville P.), Le Saux, Ince, Adams, Campbell, Beckham (Merson), Batty, Shearer, Sheringham (Owen), Scholes.

Portugal: Vitor Baia, Abel Xavier, Dimas (Pedro Barbosa), Beto, Fernando Couto, Paulo Sousa (Oceano), Figo, Joao Pinto (Capucho), Calado, Paulinho Santos, Cadete.

Referee: M. Vega (Spain)

Attendance: 63,463

England 0   Saudi Arabia 0

23 May 1998, Wembley

Eighteen days before the World Cup kicked-off in the Stade de France, England played their last home warm-up match against Saudi Arabia. The first-time visitors to Wembley – the countries had only met once before, drawing 1–1 in Riyadh in 1988 - had also qualified for France 98 and were now managed by Carlos Alberto Parreira, Brazil's World Cup-winning boss from 1994. England would have looked for a convincing performance, and a victory, for their send-off. But the Saudis had obviously not read the script.

Without Paul Gascoigne, not match fit, and the stricken Jamie Redknapp (he would miss the World Cup), England fielded Beckham alongside Batty in the centre, with Scholes on the left and Anderton working down the right touchline as a wing-back. It all looked promising early on as England put together some enterprising moves, particularly down a cluttered right side, with chances being fashioned for Hinchcliffe, Sheringham and Shearer.

Having survived the onslaught, the Saudis came out of their shell and played with a lot more belief in their ability to achieve a result. There was some attractive interpassing as they worked their way forward and only a desperate saving challenge from Gareth Southgate prevented Saeed Al-Owairan from turning in Al-Jaber's low centre. The Wembley crowd, or parts of it, implored England's Head Coach to introduce "Gazza" into the action and he did enter the fray, with Ian Wright, on the hour.

Both newcomers made an impact. Gascoigne got past players in central midfield, though he did give the ball away a few times, and Wright rushed all over the place in an effort to impress enough for inclusion in the World Cup 22. "Wrighty" nearly won the match eight minutes from the end, shooting against the 'keeper's legs. Then, with virtually the last kick, the Saudis almost snatched it. Al-Shahrani had a clear sight of Seaman's goal with the ball at his feet inside the box, but his shot was well wide.

Paul Ince fends off Calado's challenge in the match with Portugal.

Alan Shearer crashes an unstoppable shot into the Portuguese net. 3–0 to England.

Shearer, back to top form after injury, celebrates another successful strike.

Gascoigne, head bandaged, occupies the attention of the Belgian midfield for England.

England: Seaman, Neville G., Hinchcliffe (Neville P.), Batty, Adams, Southgate, Beckham (Gascoigne), Anderton, Shearer (Ferdinand L.), Sheringham (Wright), Scholes.

Saudi Arabia: Al-Daye, Al-Jahni, Al-Khlaiwi, Zebramawi, Amin (Al-Dosary), Al-Shahrani, Al-Jaber, Al-Owairan S. (Al-Temiyat), Solaimani, Al-Muwalid, Al-Owairan K.

Referee: D. Jol (Holland)
Attendance: 63,733

Morocco 0   England 1

27 May 1998, Casablanca

England's last bit of fine-tuning before the World Cup involved two matches in the King Hassan II International Cup in Morocco. The host country, whom England met in the tournament's opening fixture in the Mohammed V Stadium, were thought to play in a similar style to Tunisia, England's first World Cup opposition in Marseille. There were many pleasing aspects in a victory in a match that was always going to be a useful exercise: England won in front of an 80,000 crowd, weathering an early storm before subduing the masses with some forceful attacking play in the second half.

Michael Owen, England's youngest player this century when he was chosen to start against Chile three months earlier, set another record. Winning his fourth cap as a 25th-minute substitute for Wright, the Liverpool starlet became the youngest player ever to score for England on 59 minutes. McManaman played the ball up to him a few yards inside the Moroccan half and after cleverly shinning the ball past the last defender, Owen set off on a scorching run that ended with a nerveless piece of finishing. He was 18 years and 164 days old.

In a way Owen had been fortunate to survive the first half physically intact. He was involved in a shuddering collision with the Moroccan 'keeper nine minutes after coming on, in which something hard connected with his jaw. He was briefly unconscious and team-mates gestured frantically for a stretcher to be brought on. The brave youngster staggered to his feet and asked to be allowed to continue. Not quite so lucky was Ian Wright, who may have torn a hamstring.

It had been tough for England in the early stages of the match as the partisan crowd roared their encouragement. Saber's free-kick missed by inches in the third minute and there were several misplaced English passes on a strange, spongy surface. Gascoigne held it all together in a deeper role and McManaman, having his best game for a while, was a creative influence in the second half.

Morocco: Benzakri, Saber, Rossi, Neqrouz, Hadrioui, Chiba (Amzine), Tahar, Chippo, Ouakili, Bassir, Rokki (El Khattabi).

England: Flowers, Keown, Le Saux, Ince, Campbell, Southgate, Anderton, Gascoigne, Dublin (Ferdinand L.), Wright (Owen), McManaman.

Referee: M. Ghani (Tunisia)
Attendance: 80,000

Belgium 0   England 0
(Belgium won 4–3 on penalty-kicks)

29 May 1998, Casablanca

Cornishman Nigel Martyn, one of four goalkeepers under consideration for places in England's World Cup 22 to be announced in two days' time, did his chances of inclusion no harm at all with a very safe display in the last of the warm-up fixtures. He played for the whole ninety minutes, keeping England's seventh clean sheet in nine Internationals from September and impressing with his clean handling of the ball as well as a string of important stops.

The big Leeds United 'keeper's work began in earnest on 20 minutes when he advanced quickly from his goal to beat away a blistering shot from Emile Mpenza after the ball had fallen kindly for him from the right knee of Sol Campbell, now England's youngest skipper since Bobby Moore. Belgium then stepped up the pressure in a bid to land their first win against England for 62 years and Martyn had to win his personal duel with the star Belgian striker to keep England in the match. But the best save of all came five minutes from the whistle, as midfield maestro Enzo Scifo struck a rascal of a shot from twenty yards that swerved all over the place before a flying Martyn palmed it over at the last split-second.

England had a lot fewer goal attempts than Belgium, though Paul Merson had a memorable snap-shot in the second half that cleared the bar by a couple of inches. The match finished goalless and in accordance with the rules of the competition, a penalty shoot-out ensued. Rob Lee's first kick was comfortably pushed away. Then Owen, Beckham and Merson were successful. Belgian 'keeper Van de Walle, a bit of a specialist taker too, scored efficiently himself and then got enough on Les Ferdinand's effort to turn the ball against his left-hand post and away to safety. By that time the unhappy Tottenham striker had been wearing the captain's armband, Campbell having been forced to go off on 75 minutes with a "dead leg".

Belgium: Van de Walle, Deflandre, Van Meir, Verstraeten, Borkelmans, De Boeck, Verheyen (Claessens), Mpenza E., Goossens (Mpenza M.), Scifo, Boffin.

England: Martyn, Neville G. (Ferdinand R.), Neville P. (Owen), Butt, Campbell (Dublin), Keown, Lee, Gascoigne (Beckham), Ferdinand L., Merson, Le Saux.

Referee: E. Arjoune (Morocco)
Attendance: 18,000

France 98
England's World Cup Adventure

For the first time 32 countries took part in the World Cup Finals. The original entry had been 172, again the most ever. France were hosts for the first time since 1938 and there were 2.5 million seats available in ten different

grounds, including the 80,000-capacity Stade de France, built specially for the tournament. It was there in St. Denis that Brazil, Cup winners in 1994, met Scotland in the opening fixture on 10 June. Ominously, Cesar Sempaio headed the holders and clear favourites into the lead after just four minutes.

England, based throughout at La Baule, entered the action five days later in Marseille's Stade Velodrome. Tunisia were considered to be the weakest team in Group G and the poorest of the five African representatives in the finals, but the effective way in which England despatched them suggested that they were playing well within themselves. Souayah had taken too long with an early chance as England were suddenly exposed; then Glenn Hoddle's team proceeded to dominate the rest of the half. Scholes was twice close, a thumping Sheringham volley was tipped over and nerves were settled as Shearer nodded Le Saux's free-kick firmly beyond El-Ouaer on 42 minutes for England's opening goal of the World Cup. Another looked likely in the second period and it finally came two minutes from time, after Owen had substituted for Sheringham to become England's youngest ever World Cup player. Scholes curled a clever shot into the top corner from near the edge of the box.

England: Seaman, Campbell, Le Saux, Ince, Adams, Southgate, Anderton, Batty, Shearer, Sheringham (Owen), Scholes.

Tunisia: El-Ouaer, Badra, Boukadida, Trabelsi S., Trabelsi H. (Thabet), Chihi, Souayah (Beya), Godhbane, Clayton, Sellimi, Ben Slimane (Ben Younes).

Referee: M. Okada (Japan)

Attendance: 54,587

After their brave display against the Brazilians, Scotland held Norway to a draw in Bordeaux on 16 June to keep alive their hopes of qualifying for the second phase for the first time in their history. On the following weekend, as Belgium drew with Mexico after being two goals ahead, Bordeaux's Stade Lescure had a recorded temperature of 37 degrees centigrade. Fortunately England's next match, against seeded Romania, would be played late in the evening of the 22nd in Toulouse. It had been a case of 'so far, so good' after Tunisia were comprehensively beaten in Marseille and England were confident of more points as they faced up to the World Cup 94 quarter-finalists.

It turned out to be a desperately disappointing match for England, with Chelsea star Petrescu consigning them to a last-minute defeat. Ceding the Group G initiative to Romania now meant that Argentina were the most likely opposition in the second round. England had enjoyed some promising possession, though Shearer looked isolated in attack. Romania were able to celebrate two goals by Premiership players and England were left to rue two moments of poor defending which ultimately cost them dear. Close to half-time Hagi lifted the ball across the box from the right, Adams struggled to cope as it bounced in front of him, and Coventry City striker Modovan chested it down before slamming a shot past an exposed Seaman. England supporters

implored the England coach to bring on the livewire Owen and he duly bounded on with 17 minutes left. Within six minutes he had equalised, a typically opportunist effort from close in after Shearer had cut the ball back behind Scholes. But elation turned to despair as Petrescu held off Le Saux's belated challenge to flick the ball between Seaman's legs. England were doing things the hard way now.

England: Seaman, Neville G., Le Saux, Ince (Beckham), Adams, Campbell, Anderton, Batty, Shearer, Sheringham (Owen), Scholes.

Romania: Stelea, Petrescu, Ciobotariu, Popescu Gh., Filipescu, Munteanu, Hagi (Stanga) (Marinescu), Glaca, Popescu Ga., Moldovan (Lacatus), Ilie.

Referee: M. Batta (France)

Attendance: 36,500

So England needed a point from their last Group G fixture with Colombia on 26 June to make it into the second round. 24 million TV viewers at home and several thousand England fans inside the Stade Felix-Bollaert in Lens were on the edge of their seats. Fortunately it was "alright on the night" as attack-minded England put on their best performance of the World Cup. There were two goals to savour in the first half-hour and for several minutes after Beckham's wonderful free-kick there was joy unconfined as fans danced the conga along the front of the stands.

After two exciting substitute appearances, Owen started this time and certainly didn't let his coach or his country down. Both Anderton and Beckham had been making good ground down the right flank in the first twenty minutes; then suddenly it was Owen's turn as he speared a cross into the middle. Colombia's Bermudez, otherwise a towering presence, could only direct his headed clearance to Anderton who struck a rising shot that flew past the 'keeper's left hand. Nine minutes later a foul by Preciado on Ince presented Beckham with a mouth-watering free-kick some 25 yards out. A shot of power and placement cleared the Colombian "wall" and was in the back of the net before Mondragon could scamper across. 2–0 to England, and in the end it could have been six.

England: Seaman, Neville G., Le Saux, Ince (Batty), Adams, Campbell, Beckham, Anderton (Lee), Shearer, Owen, Scholes (McManaman).

Colombia: Mondragon, Cabrera, Bermudez, Palacios, Moreiro, Rincon, Serna (Aristizabal), Lozano, Valderrama, Preciado (Valencia), De Avila (Ricard).

Referee: A. Brizio Carter (Mexico)

Attendance: 41,275

The 48 group matches having been completed, sixteen teams were on their way home as the other sixteen prepared for the first knockout stage. France scraped through against Paraguay with Blanc's "golden goal" and Germany were late winners after going a goal down to Mexico in the second half. The fancied Africans, Nigeria, were brushed aside by Denmark – but France 98 had still not produced a big surprise. On the afternoon

of 30 June a team of blonds had no fun against Croatia; then in the evening England clashed with old World Cup adversaries Argentina in St. Etienne for the last available place in the quarter finals.

History repeated itself as for the third time in the 1990s England went out of a major tournament in a heartbreaking penalty shootout. After Beckham had been shown the red card for a petulant assault on Simeone a minute into the second half, England's ten men produced a defensive display of heroic propor-tions. Against one of the favourites for the World Cup, Hoddle's defiant team kept Argentina at bay for almost 75 minutes. Hopes were high as the shoot-out commenced, with England believing they had the better goalkeeper. Seaman did manage to block Argentina's second kick from Crespo, but misses by Ince and Batty ruined England's chances of avenging their famous "Hand of God" defeat twelve years before.

England had a terrible start to the match, Argentinian captain Simeone plunging to the turf after minimal contact with Seaman. Batistuta blasted in the spot-kick and England were behind within four minutes of the start. Owen then won the penalty which allowed Shearer to shoot high into the net for an equaliser six minutes later. The excitement continued as Owen scored the goal of the tournament on 16 minutes to put England in front. The incredibly talented youngster received the ball from Beckham's delicate chip and set off on a determined run that took him swiftly around Chamot and Ayala before a rifled shot left Roa clutching at thin air. What a start – but there was significantly more drama to come.

Argentina were clearly on the back foot as England poured forward. Another blistering run from Owen was halted illegally by Chamot, an Ince volley missed the goal by a foot or so and Scholes was even closer as he burst into the box to get on the end of Shearer's downward header. Then a rampant England team was knocked out of its stride by two unfortunate incidents either side of the break. With the first half in injury time Adams and Campbell combined to force the ball from under Lopez a yard outside the penalty area and Argentina's cleverly-worked free-kick had Zanetti peeling off the "wall" and slapping a rising left-footer beyond Seaman. But there was worse to come: Beckham was fouled by Simeone and, from a prone position, flicked out his right leg to kick the Argentinian and saw a red card being waved in his face as a consequence. The course of the match was changed irretrievably; now it was "backs to the wall".

England: Seaman, Neville G., Le Saux (Southgate), Ince, Adams, Campbell, Beckham, Anderton (Batty), Shearer, Owen, Scholes (Merson).

Argentina: Roa, Chamot, Ayala, Vivas, Zanetti, Almeyda, Simeone (Berti), Veron, Ortega, Batistuta (Crespo), Lopez (Gallardo).

Referee: K; Nielsen (Demark)
Attendance: 30,600

"B" MATCHES

England 1   Chile 2

10 February 1998, West Bromwich

Paul Merson, England's captain on the night, was one player who did himself justice before the watching Glenn Hoddle. If injury should claim the likes of Sheringham and Scholes this side of France 98, the England Head Coach knew he could call on the lively Middlesbrough forward. The few first-half moments of note came from Merson, operating alongside Huckerby and just behind Heskey.

England created openings but it was the South American visitors who showed them how to finish. When Valenzuela slipped the ball through a square home defence, the unmarked Neira raced through to place it neatly to one side of the advancing Pressman. Navia set up another goal eight minutes later with a break down the right. Neira tricked his way past Scimeca before confidently shooting in. As the crowd drifted away near the end, Heskey halved the deficit after good work by Huckerby.

England: Pressman, Dyer (Guppy), Wilcox (Carragher), Scimeca, Matteo, Hall, Huckerby, Quashie (Lampard), Heskey, Merson, Parlour (Murray).

Chile: Tejas, Gonzales, Rojas, Fuentes, Munoz, Pena (Cornejo), Mirosevic (Vivar), Gomez (Olarra), Cortes (Valenzuela), Neira, Rozental (Navia).

Referee: T. Mikulski (Poland)
Attendance: 13,917

England 4   Russia 1

21 April 1998, Queens Park Rangers

This was Le Tissier's match, admittedly against fairly lightweight opposition. After a quiet start the mercurial Southampton midfielder clicked into gear after sweeping in England's second goal on 13 minutes – Les Ferdinand, England's captain, had headed them in front five minutes earlier – and finished with a splendid hat-trick. He went through his full repertoire of party tricks, leaving Russian defenders looking clumsy and embarrassed, and an unfurled banner low down in the Ellerslie Road stand read: "Please Hod. Pick Le God".

Anderton, missing from the full England line-up since Euro 96 because of a numbing series of injuries, was busy rushing around in midfield with the odd telling pass or tackle. Ferdinand and Sunderland youngster Darren Williams impressed too – but it was Le Tissier, who also struck the woodwork twice, whose showing was bound to dominate the headlines. The player himself accepted that he was still an outsider for the World Cup. At Loftus Road he had the added boost of ending the match as England's captain, following the substitution of Ferdinand and then Anderton.

England: Walker, Watson (Curtis), Serrant, Williams, Quinn, Carragher, Le Tissier, Sinclair (Dyer), Ferdinand L. (Johnson), Barmby (Phillips), Anderton (Hendrie).

Russia: Kharine M., Davydov (Temrioukov), Berketrov, Evseev, Ossinov, Solomatine, Golovskoi (Krivov), Choukov (Bourtchenkov), Titov, Bakharev, Bouznikine.

Referee: A. Douden-Ibanez (Spain)

Attendance: 5,105

UNDER-21 MATCHES

England 1   Moldova 0

9 September 1997, Wycombe Wanderers

A narrow win against the group minnows took Peter Taylor's England team four points clear at the top. But they had found it hard-going against Moldova's multi-layered defence and ultimately it was fitting that a defender should score the decisive goal, given the England attack's struggle to create chances themselves. Under pressure from Michael Duberry, Moldovan 'keeper Hiuaruc failed to deal with Jamie Carragher's left-wing corner and Coventry's Marcus Hall rammed home his first goal in senior football.

Until Hall's timely intervention, on 72 minutes, Moldova had looked livelier in possession and Sosnovsehi particularly impressed as a sweeper who could strike accurate 40-yard passes at will. The goal boosted England's confidence and Wayne Quinn, a substitute, struck the bar with two minutes to go. So England enjoyed an upbeat finish and knew that they were very much in pole position in Group 2.

England: Wright, Dyer, Granville (Quinn), Duberry, Scimeca, Hall, Murphy (Carragher), Quashie, Dyer, Bowyer (Bradbury), Hughes.

Moldova: Hiuaruc, Gilca, Platon, Sosnovsehi, Lungu (Soiv), Bursuc, Catinsus, Stratulat (Arlet), Boret, Barburos, Comledwoc (Berco).

Referee: C. Larsen (Denmark)

Attendance: 5,534

Italy 0   England 1

10 October 1997, Rieti

Peter Taylor's young England side overcame the controversial dismissal of Wimbledon defender Ben Thatcher in the first half to achieve a brave victory against Italy, previously unbeaten at home for twelve years at Under-21 level. It meant that England finished top of their qualifying group – although, somewhat bizarrely, they still needed France to slip up in Group 3 because only the seven group winners with the best records would automatically go through to the finals.

Thatcher's red card on 28 minutes was slightly mysterious. Italian striker Totti went down after minimal contact and the England player was adjudged to have prevented a clear scoring opportunity. But England then regrouped, switched to a flat back-four and left substitute Lee Bradbury more or less

on his own up front. Ipswich 'keeper Wright dealt brilliantly with everything the hosts could throw at him and, considerably encouraged by that, England charged forward to try for maximum points. They got them with two minutes remaining, when Kieron Dyer volleyed in from Eadie's left-wing cross.

Italy: Buffon, Innocenti, Rivalta, Mezzano, Amoroso (Foglio), Longo, Fiore (Lucarelli), De Ascentis, Frezza, Totti, Bellucci.

England: Wright, Dyer, Quinn, Scimeca, Ferdinand R., Thatcher, Murray, Carragher, Heskey (Bradbury), Eadie (Granville), Hughes (Curtis).

Referee: H-J. Weber (Germany)

Attendance: 8,800

Greece 2   England 0

13 November 1997, Heraklion

England found themselves having to tackle Greece in a two-legged play-off for a place in the finals and went down to a disappointing defeat in the first leg on Crete. A team missing several players through injury, suspension and senior call-ups conceded two late goals and that left them with a difficult task in the second leg at Carrow Road. To make matters worse, another England player got a red card.

A strong wind and a bumpy pitch were less than perfect conditions for an England side which had won its qualifying group without losing a match and with only one in the "goals against" column. Manchester United's John Curtis tested Limperopoulos with a header in the first half before the Greeks took command. Dellas, the Greek defender signed earlier in the season by Sheffield United, beat Wright with a deflected shot on 78 minutes and the other Limperopoulos scored a second with an injury-time penalty. Curtis went off for two bookable offences.

Greece: Limperopoulos S., Dellas, Antzas, Goumas, Lakis, Kiassos, Mavrogenidis, Dermitzakis, Stoltidis, Konstantinidis (Kostoulas), Limperopoulos N.

England: Wright, Dyer K. (Murphy), Serrant, Curtis, Scimeca, Hall, Lampard, Quashie, Dyer B. (Moses), Heskey (Davies), Hughes.

Referee: F. Marin (Spain)

Attendance: 1,500

England 4   Greece 2

17 December 1997, Norwich

England went desperately close to changing things around at Carrow Road but in the end they went out of the Championship on the away goals' rule after a stirring second leg. The good work begun by Emile Heskey, heading England in front from Serrant's free-kick on 21 minutes, was undone in a crazy two-minute period later in the half when the Greeks twice took advantage of some defensive indiscipline. Konstantinidis shot home the first and Marcus Hall turned the ball past Wright for the second as he attempted to clear for a corner.

But, inspired by Heskey and debutant Michael Owen, England clawed their way back into the tie and almost succeeded in scoring the requisite number of goals for an aggregate victory. Heskey headed his second from Lampard's centre on 33 minutes and Owen netted from close range on the hour. With eleven minutes on the clock Hall atoned for his earlier indiscretion by cracking in a fierce shot that brought the sides level at 4–4. Taylor's team pushed hard for the winner but the Greeks held on.

England: Wright, Scimeca, Serrant (Scowcroft), Duberry (Bullock), Ferdinand R., Hall, Carragher, Lampard, Heskey, Owen, Murray.

Greece: Limperopoulos S., Mavrogenidis, Dermitzakis (Katsouris), Alexopoulos (Basinas), Antzas, Goumas, Karagounis (Koulakiotis), Kiassos, Konstantinidis, Limperopoulos N., Stoltidis.

Referee: E. Blareau (Belgium)

Attendance: 14,114

Switzerland 2   England 0

24 March 1998, Aarau

After a break of three months England's Under-21s were in action again for a friendly fixture in Switzerland and an interesting feature was the experiment of playing Jamie Redknapp in a sweeper role. The Liverpool youngster insisted afterwards that he had enjoyed the role, though his start was a nervous one and included playing the ball across his own box to the feet of Pizzinat who shot just wide.

The Swiss kept probing an English defence that was struggling to cope and took the lead after four minutes. Hislop and Heskey both failed to deal effectively with Tarone's left-wing corner and Haas reacted quickly to knock the ball in from ten yards. Then Curtis robbed Thurre but Matteo was slow to get to the loose ball and Di Napoli was on the spot to make it 2-0. England certainly improved after the break, with Redknapp spraying some of his trademark passes around.

Switzerland: Benito, Zellweger, Smiljanic, Haas, Berner, Tarone, Pizzinat (Sutter), Celestini (Seoane), Di Jorio, Di Napoli, Thurre (Huber).

England: Hislop, Dyer K., Guppy, Curtis, Redknapp (Holloway), Matteo (Hughes), Lampard (Hendrie), Quashie (Carragher), Heskey (Williams), Barmby, Sinclair.

Referee: H. Albrecht (Germany)

Attendance: 1,300

Toulon Tournament

France 1   England 1

14 May 1998, Nimes

England got off to an excellent start in the first match of the annual Toulon Under-21 tournament with Emile Heskey on target within nine minutes against the host country. Six players in England's starting line-up were making their debuts at this level, yet the team showed few signs of nerves and they were a goal to the good from virtually their first serious attack. Frank Lampard fed Jason Euell and Heskey stabbed the ball home from the latter's first-time cross.

England could have quickly built on the lead when Euell went clear of the French defence, but his tame shot was saved easily by Landreau. Louis Saha was brought on for the second half and the pacy forward immediately caused England problems as the home side camped in their half. Heroics by the Tranmere 'keeper and his defenders kept the French out until Saha wriggled his way through with eleven minutes to go to strike a low shot under the advancing Simonsen. Two minutes later Heskey saw his shot thud against the bar.

France: Landreau, Domi, Silvestre, Camara, Henin (Saha), Hendani, Cisse, Dabo (Jager), Mouret, Kanoute (Proment), Moreira.

England: Simonsen, Curtis, Rogers, Purse, Marsh (Elliott), Kozluk (Clegg), Carragher, Lampard, Oakley, Heskey, Euell (Allen).

Referee: M. Albrecht (Germany)

England 3   South Africa 1

16 May 1998, Aubagne

After drawing with the hosts in the opening fixture, England needed maximum points against unfancied South Africa to have a chance of progressing in the tournament. Leicester's Emile Heskey, surely not too far from the full England squad, scored a brace and Frank Lampard sealed a comprehensive win. The always improving Heskey showed glimpses of his strength and pace in the early minutes, but it was Lampard the skipper who hit a low shot past Baron to put England in front.

Some very direct play twice paid dividends for England after that. Close to the interval Heskey picked up a long clearance, outran the South African defence and gently lobbed the ball over the 'keeper for 2–0. Then, fifteen minutes into the second period, Heskey slotted in England's third after pouncing onto Wright's boot upfield. There were substitutions in the humid conditions and Salmon netted a consolation strike for the South Africans.

England: Wright, Dyer, Rogers, Purse, Curtis, Elliott, Carragher (Clegg), Lampard, Oakley, Heskey (Bent), Allen (Howe).

South Africa: Baron, Matombo, Booth (Motale), Mokoena, Makhanya, Fredericks (Salmon), Mbuthu, De Weber, Carnell, Matsau, August.

Referee: M. Vitkovic (Croatia)

England 0 Argentina 2

18 May 1998, Manosque

England's Under-21s were eliminated from the tournament after a disappointing performance in the Stade A

Gilly against the Argentinians. England had only required a draw to qualify for the semi-finals, but the match was effectively over when two goals were conceded in the first sixteen minutes. Quintina fired past Wright from just inside the box in the sixth minute and Guerrero gratefully shot in from close range after Heskey had made a hash of trying to chest the ball down from an Argentinian corner-kick.

Lampard, captain again, tested Bizarri with a well-struck free-kick and that was England's best effort in the first half. Manager Peter Taylor used the maximum three substitutes after the break in an attempt to salvage something from the match and Rory Allen, on for Elliott, managed a couple of efforts that went close. But it was all to no avail.

England: Wright, Dyer, Rogers, Howe (Euell), Curtis, Elliott (Allen), Carragher, Lampard, Oakley, Heskey, Bent (Kozluk).

Argentina: Bizarri, Quiroga, Rivarola, Cufra, Samuel, Diaz (Guinazu), Riquelme, Markic, Quintana, Scalon (Cupero), Guerrero.

Referee: M. Wegereef (Holland)

20 ● ENGLAND'S FULL INTERNATIONAL TEAMS 1946–1998

(Up to and including 1st July 1998)

*captain   †own goal   Small numerals goals scored   Numbers after sub player replaced

Versus	Venue	Result	1	2	3	4	5
1946–47							
Northern Ireland	A	7 – 2	Swift	Scott	Hardwick*	W Wright	Franklin
Republic of Ireland	A	1 – 0	Swift	Scott	Hardwick*	W Wright	Franklin
Wales	H	3 – 0	Swift	Scott	Hardwick*	W Wright	Franklin
Holland	H	8 – 2	Swift	Scott	Hardwick*	W Wright	Franklin
Scotland	H	1 – 1	Swift	Scott	Hardwick*	W Wright	Franklin
France	H	3 – 0	Swift	Scott	Hardwick*	W Wright	Franklin
Switzerland	A	0 – 1	Swift	Scott	Hardwick*	W Wright	Franklin
Portugal	A	10 – 0	Swift	Scott	Hardwick*	W Wright	Franklin
1947–48							
Belgium	A	5 – 2	Swift	Scott	Hardwick*	Ward	Franklin
Wales	A	3 – 0	Swift	Scott	Hardwick*	P Taylor	Franklin
Northern Ireland	H	2 – 2	Swift	Scott	Hardwick*	P Taylor	Franklin
Sweden	H	4 – 2	Swift	Scott	Hardwick*	P Taylor	Franklin
Scotland	A	2 – 0	Swift	Scott	Hardwick*	W Wright	Franklin
Italy	A	4 – 0	Swift*	Scott	J Howe	W Wright	Franklin
1948–49							
Denmark	A	0 – 0	Swift*	Scott	Aston	W Wright	Franklin
Ireland	A	6 – 2	Swift	Scott	J Howe	W Wright*	Franklin
Wales	H	1 – 0	Swift	Scott	Aston	Ward	Franklin
Switzerland	H	6 – 0	Ditchburn	Ramsey	Aston	W Wright*	Franklin
Scotland	H	1 – 3	Swift	Aston	J Howe	W Wright*	Franklin
Sweden	A	1 – 3	Ditchburn	Shimwell	Aston	W Wright*	Franklin
Norway	A	4 – 1	Swift	Ellerington	Aston	W Wright	Franklin
France	A	3 – 1	Williams	Ellerington	Aston	W Wright*	Franklin
1949–50							
Republic of Ireland	H	0 – 2	Williams	Mozley	Aston	W Wright*	Franklin
Wales	A	4 – 1	Williams	Mozley	Aston	W Wright*	Franklin
Northern Ireland	H	9 – 2	Streten	Mozley	Aston	Watson	Franklin
Italy	H	2 – 0	Williams	Ramsey	Aston	Watson	Franklin
Scotland	A	1 – 0	Williams	Ramsey	Aston	W Wright*	Franklin
Portugal	A	5 – 3	Williams	Ramsey	Aston	W Wright	WH Jones
Belgium	A	4 – 1	Williams	Ramsey	Aston	W Wright*	WH Jones
Chile	N	2 – 0	Williams	Ramsey	Aston	W Wright*	L Hughes
USA	N	0 – 1	Williams	Ramsey	Aston	W Wright*	L Hughes
Spain	N	0 – 1	Williams	Ramsey	Eckersley	W Wright*	L Hughes
1950–51							
Northern Ireland	A	4 – 1	Williams	Ramsey	Aston	W Wright*†	Chilton
Wales	H	4 – 2	Williams	Ramsey*	L Smith	Watson	L Compton
Yugoslavia	H	2 – 2	Williams	Ramsey*	Eckersley	Watson	L Compton
Scotland	H	2 – 3	Williams	Ramsey	Eckersley	Johnston	J Froggatt

6	7	8	9	10	11	Substitutes
Cockburn	Finney[1]	Carter[1]	Lawton[1]	Mannion[1]	Langton[1]	
Cockburn	Finney[1]	Carter	Lawton	Mannion	Langton	
Cockburn	Finney	Carter	Lawton[1]	Mannion[2]	Langton	
Johnston	Finney[1]	Carter[2]	Lawton[4]	Mannion[1]	Langton	
Johnston	S Matthews	Carter[1]	Lawton	Mannion	Mullen	
Lowe	Finney[1]	Carter[1]	Lawton	Mannion[1]	Langton	
Lowe	S Matthews	Carter	Lawton	Mannion	Langton	
Lowe	S Matthews[1]	Mortensen[4]	Lawton[4]	Mannion	Finney[1]	
W Wright	S Matthews	Mortensen[1]	Lawton[2]	Mannion	Finney[2]	
W Wright	S Matthews	Mortensen[1]	Lawton[1]	Mannion	Finney[1]	
W Wright	S Matthews	Mortensen	Lawton[1]	Mannion[1]	Finney	
W Wright	Finney	Mortensen[3]	Lawton[1]	Mannion	Langton	
Cockburn	S Matthews	Mortensen[1]	Lawton	Pearson	Finney[1]	
Cockburn	S Matthews	Mortensen[1]	Lawton[1]	Mannion	Finney[2]	
Cockburn	S Matthews	Hagan	Lawton	Shackleton	Langton	
Cockburn	S Matthews[1]	Mortensen[3]	Milburn[1]	Pearson[1]	Finney	
W Wright*	S Matthews	Mortensen	Milburn	Shackleton	Finney[1]	
Cockburn	S Matthews	J Rowley[1]	Milburn[1]	Haines[2]	Hancocks[2]	
Cockburn	S Matthews	Mortensen	Milburn[1]	Pearson	Finney	
Cockburn	Finney[1]	Mortensen	Bentley	J Rowley	Langton	
Dickinson	Finney[1]	Morris[1]	Mortensen	Mannion	Mullen[1†]	
Dickinson	Finney	Morris[2]	J Rowley[1]	Mannion	Mullen	
Dickinson	P Harris	Morris	Pye	Mannion	Finney	
Dickinson	Finney	Mortensen[1]	Milburn[3]	Shackleton	Hancocks	
W Wright*	Finney	Mortensen[2]	J Rowley[4]	Pearson[2]	J Froggatt[1]	
W Wright*[1]	Finney	Mortensen	J Rowley[1]	Pearson	J Froggatt	
Dickinson	Finney	Mannion	Mortensen	Bentley[1]	Langton	
Dickinson	Milburn	Mortensen[1]	Bentley	Mannion	Finney[4]	
Dickinson	Milburn	Mortensen[1]	Bentley[1]	Mannion[1]	Finney	Mullen 7[1]
Dickinson	Finney	Mannion[1]	Bentley	Mortensen[1]	Mullen	
Dickinson	Finney	Mannion	Bentley	Mortensen	Mullen	
Dickinson	S Matthews	Mortensen	Milburn	E Baily	Finney	
Dickinson	S Matthews	Mannion	J Lee[1]	E Baily[2]	Langton	
Dickinson	Finney	Mannion[1]	Milburn[1]	E Baily[2]	Medley	
Dickinson	Hancocks	Mannion	Lofthouse[2]	E Baily	Medley	
W Wright*	S Matthews	Mannion	Mortensen	Hassall[1]	Finney[1]	

Versus	Venue	Result	1	2	3	4	5
Argentina	H	2 – 1	Williams	Ramsey	Eckersley	W Wright*	J Taylor
Portugal	H	5 – 2	Williams	Ramsey*	Eckersley	Nicholson[1]	J Taylor

1951–52

Versus	Venue	Result	1	2	3	4	5
France	H	2 – 2	Williams	Ramsey	Willis	W Wright*	Chilton
Wales	A	1 – 1	Williams	Ramsey	L Smith	W Wright*	Barrass
Northern Ireland	H	2 – 0	Merrick	Ramsey	L Smith	W Wright*	Barrass
Austria	H	2 – 2	Merrick	Ramsey[1]	Eckersley	W Wright*	J Froggatt
Scotland	A	2 – 1	Merrick	Ramsey	Garrett	W Wright*	J Froggatt
Italy	A	1 – 1	Merrick	Ramsey	Garrett	W Wright*	J Froggatt
Austria	A	3 – 2	Merrick	Ramsey	Eckersley	W Wright*	J Froggatt
Switzerland	A	3 – 0	Merrick	Ramsey	Eckersley	W Wright*	J Froggatt

1952–53

Versus	Venue	Result	1	2	3	4	5
Northern Ireland	A	2 – 2	Merrick	Ramsey	Eckersley	W Wright*	J Froggatt
Wales	H	5 – 2	Merrick	Ramsey	L Smith	W Wright*	J Froggatt[1]
Belgium	H	5 – 0	Merrick	Ramsey	L Smith	W Wright*	J Froggatt
Scotland	H	2 – 2	Merrick	Ramsey	L Smith	W Wright*	Barrass
Argentina	A	0 – 0	Merrick	Ramsey	Eckersley	W Wright*	Johnston
Chile	A	2 – 1	Merrick	Ramsey	Eckersley	W Wright*	Johnston
Uruguay	A	1 – 2	Merrick	Ramsey	Eckersley	W Wright*	Johnson
USA	A	6 – 3	Ditchburn	Ramsey	Eckersley	W Wright*	Johnston

1953–54

Versus	Venue	Result	1	2	3	4	5
Wales	A	4 – 1	Merrick	Garrett	Eckersley	W Wright*	Johnston
FIFA	H	4 – 4	Merrick	Ramsey[1]	Eckersley	W Wright*	Ufton
Ireland	H	3 – 1	Merrick	Rickaby	Eckersley	W Wright*	Johnston
Hungary	H	3 – 6	Merrick	Ramsey[1]	Eckersley	W Wright*	Johnston
Scotland	A	4 – 2	Merrick	Staniforth	R Byrne	W Wright*	H Clarke
Yugoslavia	A	0 – 1	Merrick	Staniforth	R Byrne	W Wright*	Owen
Hungary	A	1 – 7	Merrick	Staniforth	R Byrne	W Wright*	Owen
Belgium	N	4 – 4	Merrick	Staniforth	R Byrne	W Wright*	Owen
Switzerland	N	2 – 0	Merrick	Staniforth	R Byrne	McGarry	W Wright*
Uruguay	N	2 – 4	Merrick	Staniforth	R Byrne	McGarry	W Wright*

1954–55

Versus	Venue	Result	1	2	3	4	5
Northern Ireland	A	2 – 0	Wood	Foulkes	R Byrne	Wheeler	W Wright*
Wales	H	3 – 2	Wood	Staniforth	R Byrne	Phillips	W Wright
West Germany	H	3 – 1	Williams	Staniforth	R Byrne	Phillips	W Wright*
Scotland	H	7 – 2	Williams	Meadows	R Byrne	Armstrong	W Wright*
France	A	0 – 1	Williams	P Sillett	R Byrne	Flowers	W Wright*
Spain	A	1 – 1	Williams	P Sillett	R Byrne	Dickinson	W Wright*
Portugal	A	1 – 3	Williams	P Sillett	R Byrne	Dickinson	W Wright*

1955–56

Versus	Venue	Result	1	2	3	4	5
Denmark	A	5 – 1	Baynham	Hall	R Byrne	McGarry	W Wright*
Wales	A	1 – 2	Williams	Hall	R Byrne	McGarry	W Wright*
Northern Ireland	H	3 – 0	Baynham	Hall	R Byrne	Clayton	W Wright*
Spain	H	4 – 1	Baynham	Hall	R Byrne	Clayton	W Wright*
Scotland	A	1 – 1	R Matthews	Hall	R Byrne	Dickinson	W Wright*
Brazil	H	4 – 2	R Matthews	Hall	R Byrne	Clayton	W Wright*
Sweden	A	0 – 0	R Matthews	Hall	R Byrne	Clayton	W Wright*
Finland	A	5 – 1	Wood	Hall	R Byrne	Clayton	W Wright*
West Germany	A	3 – 1	R Matthews	Hall	R Byrne	Clayton	W Wright*

6	7	8	9	10	11	Substitutes
Cockburn	Finney	Mortensen[1]	Milburn[1]	Hassall	Metcalfe	
Cockburn	Finney[1]	Pearson	Milburn[2]	Hassall[1]	Metcalfe	
Cockburn	Finney	Mannion	Milburn	Hassall	Medley[1]	†
Dickinson	Finney	T Thompson	Lofthouse	E Baily[1]	Medley	
Dickinson	Finney	Sewell	Lofthouse[2]	Phillips	Medley	
Dickinson	Milton	Broadis	Lofthouse[1]	E Baily	Medley	
Dickinson	Finney	Broadis	Lofthouse	Pearson[2]	J Rowley	
Dickinson	Finney	Broadis[1]	Lofthouse	Pearson	Elliott	
Dickinson	Finney	Sewell[1]	Lofthouse[2]	E Baily	Elliott	
Dickinson	R Allen	Sewell[1]	Lofthouse[2]	E Baily	Finney	
Dickinson	Finney	Sewell	Lofthouse[1]	E Baily	Elliott[1]	
Dickinson	Finney[1]	R Froggatt	Lofthouse[2]	Bentley[1]	Elliott	
Dickinson	Finney	Bentley	Lofthouse[2]	R Froggatt[1]	Elliott[2]	
Dickinson	Finney	Broadis[2]	Lofthouse	R Froggatt	J Froggatt	
Dickinson	Finney	Broadis	Lofthouse	T Taylor	Berry	
Dickinson	Finney	Broadis	Lofthouse[1]	T Taylor[1]	Berry	
Dickinson	Finney	Broadis	Lofthouse	T Taylor[1]	Berry	
Dickinson	Finney[2]	Broadis[1]	Lofthouse[2]	R Froggatt[1]	J Froggatt	
Dickinson	Finney	Quixall	Lofthouse[2]	Wilshaw[2]	Mullen	
Dickinson	S Matthews	Mortensen[1]	Lofthouse	Quixall	Mullen[2]	
Dickinson	S Matthews	Quixall	Lofthouse[1]	Hassall[2]	Mullen	
Dickinson	S Matthews	E Taylor	Mortensen[1]	Sewell[1]	Robb	
Dickinson	Finney	Broadis[1]	R Allen[1]	Nicholls[1]	Mullen[1]	
Dickinson	Finney	Broadis	R Allen	Nicholls	Mullen	
Dickinson	P Harris	Sewell	Jezzard	Broadis[1]	Finney	
Dickinson	S Matthews	Broadis[2]	Lofthouse[2]	T Taylor	Finney	
Dickinson	Finney	Broadis	T Taylor	Wilshaw[1]	Mullen[1]	
Dickinson	S Matthews	Broadis	Lofthouse[1]	Wilshaw	Finney[1]	
Barlow	S Matthews	Revie[1]	Lofthouse	Haynes[1]	Pilkington	
Slater	S Matthews	Bentley[3]	R Allen	Shackleton	Blunstone	
Slater	S Matthews	Bentley[1]	R Allen[1]	Shackleton[1]	Finney	
Edwards	S Matthews	Revie[1]	Lofthouse[2]	Wilshaw[4]	Blunstone	
Edwards	S Matthews	Revie	Lofthouse	Wilshaw	Blunstone	
Edwards	S Matthews	Bentley[1]	Lofthouse	Quixall	Wilshaw	
Edwards	S Matthews	Bentley[1]	Lofthouse	Wilshaw	Blunstone	Quixall 9
Dickinson	Milburn	Revie[2]	Lofthouse[2]	Bradford[1]	Finney	
Dickinson	S Matthews	Revie	Lofthouse	Wilshaw	Finney	†
Dickinson	Finney[1]	Haynes	Jezzard	Wilshaw[2]	Perry	
Dickinson	Finney[1]	Atyeo[1]	Lofthouse	Haynes	Perry[2]	
Edwards	Finney	T Taylor	Lofthouse	Haynes[1]	Perry	
Edwards	S Matthews	Atyeo	T Taylor[2]	Haynes	Grainger[2]	
Edwards	Berry	Atyeo	T Taylor	Haynes	Grainger	
Edwards	Astall[1]	Haynes[1]	T Taylor	Wilshaw[1]	Grainger	Lofthouse 9[2]
Edwards[1]	Astall	Haynes[1]	T Taylor	Wilshaw	Grainger[1]	

Versus	Venue	Result	1	2	3	4	5
1956–57							
Northern Ireland	A	1 – 1	R Matthews	Hall	R Byrne	Clayton	W Wright*
Wales	H	3 – 1	Ditchburn	Hall	R Byrne	Clayton	W Wright*
Yugoslavia	H	3 – 0	Ditchburn	Hall	R Byrne	Clayton	W Wright*
Denmark	H	5 – 2	Ditchburn	Hall	R Byrne	Clayton	W Wright*
Scotland	H	2 – 1	Hodgkinson	Hall	R Byrne	Clayton	W Wright*
Republic of Ireland	H	5 – 1	Hodgkinson	Hall	R Byrne	Clayton	W Wright*
Denmark	A	4 – 1	Hodgkinson	Hall	R Byrne	Clayton	W Wright*
Republic of Ireland	A	1 – 1	Hodgkinson	Hall	R Byrne	Clayton	W Wright*
1957–58							
Wales	A	4 – 0	Hopkinson	D Howe	R Byrne	Clayton	W Wright*
Northern Ireland	H	2 – 3	Hopkinson	D Howe	R Byrne	Clayton	W Wright*
France	H	4 – 0	Hopkinson	D Howe	R Byrne	Clayton	W Wright*
Scotland	A	4 – 0	Hopkinson	D Howe	Langley	Clayton	W Wright*
Portugal	H	2 – 1	Hopkinson	D Howe	Langley	Clayton	W Wright*
Yugoslavia	A	0 – 5	Hopkinson	D Howe	Langley	Clayton	W Wright*
USSR	A	1 – 1	McDonald	D Howe	T Banks	Clamp	W Wright*
USSR	N	2 – 2	McDonald	D Howe	T Banks	Clamp	W Wright*
Brazil	N	0 – 0	McDonald	D Howe	T Banks	Clamp	W Wright*
Austria	N	2 – 2	McDonald	D Howe	T Banks	Clamp	W Wright*
USSR	N	0 – 1	McDonald	D Howe	T Banks	Clamp	W Wright*
1958–59							
Northern Ireland	A	3 – 3	McDonald	D Howe	T Banks	Clamp	W Wright*
USSR	H	5 – 0	McDonald	D Howe	G Shaw	Clamp	W Wright*
Wales	H	2 – 2	McDonald	D Howe	G Shaw	Clamp	W Wright*
Scotland	H	1 – 0	Hopkinson	D Howe	G Shaw	Clamp	W Wright*
Italy	H	2 – 2	Hopkinson	D Howe	G Shaw	Clamp	W Wright*
Brazil	A	0 – 2	Hopkinson	D Howe	Armfield	Clamp	W Wright*
Peru	A	1 – 4	Hopkinson	D Howe	Armfield	Clamp	W Wright*
Mexico	A	1 – 2	Hopkinson	D Howe	Armfield	Clamp	W Wright*
USA	A	8 – 1	Hopkinson	D Howe	Armfield	Clamp	W Wright*
1959–60							
Wales	A	1 – 1	Hopkinson	D Howe	A Allen	Clayton*	T Smith
Sweden	H	2 – 3	Hopkinson	D Howe	A Allen	Clayton*	T Smith
Northern Ireland	H	2 – 1	R Springett	D Howe	A Allen	Clayton*	Brown
Scotland	A	1 – 1	R Springett	Armfield	Wilson	Clayton*	Slater
Yugoslavia	H	3 – 3	R Springett	Armfield	Wilson	Clayton*	Swan
Spain	A	0 – 3	R Springett	Armfield	Wilson	R Robson	Swan
Hungary	A	0 – 2	R Springett	Armfield	Wilson	R Robson	Swan
1960–61							
Northern Ireland	A	5 – 2	R Springett	Armfield	McNeil	R Robson	Swan
Luxembourg	A	9 – 0	R Springett	Armfield	McNeil	R Robson	Swan
Spain	H	4 – 2	R Springett	Armfield	McNeil	R Robson	Swan
Wales	H	5 – 1	Hodgkinson	Armfield	McNeil	R Robson	Swan
Scotland	H	9 – 3	R Springett	Armfield	McNeil	R Robson[1]	Swan
Mexico	H	8 – 0	R Springett	Armfield	McNeil	R Robson[1]	Swan
Portugal	A	1 – 1	R Springett	Armfield	McNeil	R Robson	Swan
Italy	A	3 – 2	R Springett	Armfield	McNeil	R Robson	Swan
Austria	A	1 – 3	R Springett	Armfield	Angus	Miller	Swan
1961–62							
Luxembourg	H	4 – 1	R Springett	Armfield*	McNeil	R Robson	Swan

6	7	8	9	10	11	Substitutes
Edwards	S Matthews[1]	Revie	T Taylor	Wilshaw	Grainger	
Dickinson	S Matthews	Brooks[1]	Finney[1]	Haynes[1]	Grainger	
Dickinson	S Matthews	Brooks[1]	Finney	Haynes	Blunstone	T Taylor 10[2]
Dickinson	S Matthews	Brooks	T Taylor[1]	Edwards[2]	Finney	
Edwards[1]	S Matthews	T Thompson	Finney	Kevan[1]	Grainger	
Edwards	S Matthews	Atyeo[2]	T Taylor[3]	Haynes	Finney	
Edwards	S Matthews	Atyeo[1]	T Taylor[2]	Haynes[1]	Finney	
Edwards	Finney	Atyeo[1]	T Taylor	Haynes	Pegg	
Edwards	Douglas	Kevan	T Taylor	Haynes[2]	Finney[1]	†
Edwards[1]	Douglas	Kevan	T Taylor	Haynes	A'Court[1]	
Edwards	Douglas	R Robson[2]	T Taylor[2]	Haynes	Finney	
Slater	Douglas[1]	R Charlton[1]	Kevan[2]	Haynes	Finney	
Slater	Douglas	R Charlton[2]	Kevan	Haynes	Finney	
Slater	Douglas	R Charlton	Kevan	Haynes	Finney	
Slater	Douglas	R Robson	Kevan[1]	Haynes	Finney	
Slater	Douglas	R Robson	Kevan[1]	Haynes	Finney[1]	
Slater	Douglas	R Robson	Kevan	Haynes	A'Court	
Slater	Douglas	R Robson	Kevan[1]	Haynes[1]	A'Court	
Slater	Brabrook	Broadbent	Kevan	Haynes	A'Court	
McGuinness	Brabrook	Broadbent	R Charlton[2]	Haynes	Finney[1]	
Slater	Douglas	R Charlton[1]	Lofthouse[1]	Haynes[3]	Finney	
Flowers	Clapton	Broadbent[2]	Lofthouse	Haynes	A'Court	
Flowers	Douglas	Broadbent	R Charlton[1]	Haynes	Holden	
Flowers	Bradley[1]	Broadbent	R Charlton[1]	Haynes	Holden	
Flowers	Deeley	Broadbent	R Charlton	Haynes	Holden	
Flowers	Deeley	Greaves[1]	R Charlton	Haynes	Holden	
McGuinness	Holden	Greaves	Kevan[1]	Haynes	R Charlton	Flowers 6, Bradley 7
Flowers[2]	Bradley[1]	Greaves	Kevan[1]	Haynes[1]	R Charlton[3]	
Flowers	Connelly	Greaves[1]	Clough	R Charlton	Holliday	
Flowers	Connelly[1]	Greaves	Clough	R Charlton[1]	Holliday	
Flowers	Connelly	Haynes	Baker[1]	Parry[1]	Holliday	
Flowers	Connelly	Broadbent	Baker	Parry	R Charlton[1]	
Flowers	Douglas[1]	Haynes[1]	Baker	Greaves[1]	R Charlton	
Flowers	Brabrook	Haynes	Baker	Greaves	R Charlton	
Flowers	Douglas	Haynes*	Baker	Viollet	R Charlton	
Flowers	Douglas[1]	Greaves[2]	R Smith[1]	Haynes*	R Charlton[1]	
Flowers	Douglas	Greaves[3]	R Smith[2]	Haynes*[1]	R Charlton[3]	
Flowers	Douglas[1]	Greaves[1]	R Smith[2]	Haynes*	R Charlton	
Flowers	Douglas	Greaves[2]	R Smith[1]	Haynes*[1]	R Charlton[1]	
Flowers	Douglas[1]	Greaves[3]	R Smith[2]	Haynes*[2]	R Charlton	
Flowers[1]	Douglas[2]	Kevan	Hitchens[1]	Haynes*	R Charlton[3]	
Flowers[1]	Douglas	Greaves	R Smith	Haynes*	R Charlton	
Flowers	Douglas	Greaves[1]	Hitchens[2]	Haynes*	R Charlton	
Flowers	Douglas	Greaves[1]	Hitchens	Haynes*	R Charlton	
Flowers	Douglas	Fantham	Pointer[1]	Viollet[1]	R Charlton[2]	

Versus	Venue	Result	1	2	3	4	5
Wales	A	1 – 1	R Springett	Armfield	Wilson	R Robson	Swan
Portugal	H	2 – 0	R Springett	Armfield	Wilson	R Robson	Swan
Northern Ireland	H	1 – 1	R Springett	Armfield	Wilson	Robson	Swan
Austria	H	3 – 1	R Springett	Armfield	Wilson	Anderson	Swan
Scotland	A	0 – 2	R Springett	Armfield	Wilson	Anderson	Swan
Switzerland	H	3 – 1	R Springett	Armfield	Wilson	R Robson	Swan
Peru	A	4 – 0	R Springett	Armfield	Wilson	Moore	Norman
Hungary	N	1 – 2	R Springett	Armfield	Wilson	Moore	Norman
Argentina	N	3 – 1	R Springett	Armfield	Wilson	Moore	Norman
Bulgaria	N	0 – 0	R Springett	Armfield	Wilson	Moore	Norman
Brazil	N	1 – 3	R Springett	Armfield	Wilson	Moore	Norman

1962–63

Versus	Venue	Result	1	2	3	4	5
France	H	1 – 1	R Springett	Armfield*	Wilson	Moore	Norman
Northern Ireland	A	3 – 1	R Springett	Armfield*	Wilson	Moore	Labone
Wales	H	4 – 0	R Springett	Armfield*	G Shaw	Moore	Labone
France	A	2 – 5	R Springett	Armfield*	Henry	Moore	Labone
Scotland	H	1 – 2	G Banks	Armfield*	G Byrne	Moore	Norman
Brazil	H	1 – 1	G Banks	Armfield*	Wilson	Milne	Norman
Czechoslovakia	A	4 – 2	G Banks	Shellito	Wilson	Milne	Norman
East Germany	A	2 – 1	G Banks	Armfield*	Wilson	Milne	Norman
Switzerland	A	8 – 1	R Springett	Armfield*	Wilson	Kay[1]	Moore

1963–64

Versus	Venue	Result	1	2	3	4	5
Wales	A	4 – 0	G Banks	Armfield*	Wilson	Milne	Norman
Rest of the World	H	2 – 1	G Banks	Armfield*	Wilson	Milne	Norman
Northern Ireland	H	8 – 3	G Banks	Armfield*	R Thomson	Milne	Norman
Scotland	A	0 – 1	G Banks	Armfield*	Wilson	Milne	Norman
Uruguay	H	2 – 1	G Banks	Cohen	Wilson	Milne	Norman
Portugal	A	4 – 3	G Banks	Cohen	Wilson	Milne	Norman
Republic of Ireland	A	3 – 1	Waiters	Cohen	Wilson	Milne	Flowers
USA	A	10 – 0	G Banks	Cohen	R Thomson	M Bailey	Norman
Brazil	A	1 – 5	Waiters	Cohen	Wilson	Milne	Norman
Portugal	N	1 – 1	G Banks	R Thomson	Wilson	Flowers	Norman
Argentina	N	0 – 1	G Banks	R Thomson	Wilson	Milne	Norman

1964–65

Versus	Venue	Result	1	2	3	4	5
Northern Ireland	A	4 – 3	G Banks	Cohen	R Thomson	Milne	Norman
Belgium	H	2 – 2	Waiters	Cohen	R Thomson	Milne	Norman
Wales	H	2 – 1	Waiters	Cohen	R Thomson	M Bailey	Flowers*
Holland	A	1 – 1	Waiters	Cohen	R Thomson	Mullery	Norman
Scotland	H	2 – 2	G Banks	Cohen	Wilson	Stiles	J Charlton
Hungary	H	1 – 0	G Banks	Cohen	Wilson	Stiles	J Charlton
Yugoslavia	A	1 – 1	G Banks	Cohen	Wilson	Stiles	J Charlton
West Germany	A	2 – 1	G Banks	Cohen	Wilson	Flowers	J Charlton
Sweden	A	2 – 1	G Banks	Cohen	Wilson	Stiles	J Charlton

1965–66

Versus	Venue	Result	1	2	3	4	5
Wales	A	0 – 0	R Springett	Cohen	Wilson	Stiles	J Charlton
Austria	H	2 – 3	R Springett	Cohen	Wilson	Stiles	J Charlton
Northern Ireland	H	2 – 1	G Banks	Cohen	Wilson	Stiles	J Charlton
Spain	A	2 – 0	G Banks	Cohen	Wilson	Stiles	J Charlton
Poland	H	1 – 1	G Banks	Cohen	Wilson	Stiles	J Charlton
West Germany	H	1 – 0	G Banks	Cohen	K Newton	Moore*	J Charlton
Scotland	A	4 – 3	G Banks	Cohen	K Newton	Stiles	J Charlton
Yugoslavia	H	2 – 0	G Banks	Armfield*	Wilson	Peters	J Charlton

6	7	8	9	10	11	Substitutes
Flowers	Connelly	Douglas[1]	Pointer	Haynes*	R Charlton	
Flowers	Connelly[1]	Douglas	Pointer[1]	Haynes*	R Charlton	
Flowers	Douglas	J Byrne	Crawford	Haynes*	R Charlton[1]	
Flowers[1]	Connelly	Hunt[1]	Crawford[1]	Haynes*	R Charlton	
Flowers	Douglas	Greaves	R Smith	Haynes*	R Charlton	
Flowers[1]	Connelly[1]	Greaves	Hitchens[1]	Haynes*	R Charlton	
Flowers[1]	Douglas	Greaves[3]	Hitchens	Haynes*	R Charlton	
Flowers[1]	Douglas	Greaves	Hitchens	Haynes*	R Charlton	
Flowers[1]	Douglas	Greaves[1]	Peacock	Haynes*	R Charlton[1]	
Flowers	Douglas	Greaves	Peacock	Haynes*	R Charlton	
Flowers	Douglas	Greaves	Hitchens[1]	Haynes*	R Charlton	
Flowers[1]	Hellawell	Crowe	Charnley	Greaves	A Hinton	
Flowers	Hellawell	F Hill	Peacock	Greaves[1]	O'Grady[2]	
Flowers	Connelly[1]	F Hill	Peacock[2]	Greaves[1]	Tambling	
Flowers	Connelly	Tambling[1]	R Smith[1]	Greaves	R Charlton	
Flowers	Douglas[1]	Greaves	R Smith	Melia	R Charlton	
Moore	Douglas[1]	Greaves	R Smith	Eastham	R Charlton	
Moore*	Paine	Greaves[2]	R Smith[1]	Eastham	R Charlton[1]	
Moore	Paine	Hunt[1]	R Smith	Eastham	R Charlton[1]	
Flowers	Douglas[1]	Greaves	J Byrne[2]	Melia[1]	R Charlton[3]	
Moore	Paine	Greaves[1]	R Smith[2]	Eastham	R Charlton[1]	
Moore	Paine[1]	Greaves[1]	R Smith	Eastham	R Charlton	
Moore	Paine[3]	Greaves[4]	R Smith[1]	Eastham	R Charlton	
Moore	Paine	Hunt	J Byrne	Eastham	R Charlton	
Moore*	Paine	Greaves	J Byrne[2]	Eastham	R Charlton	
Moore*	P Thompson	Greaves	J Byrne[3]	Eastham	R Charlton[1]	
Moore*	P Thompson	Greaves[1]	J Byrne[1]	Eastham[1]	R Charlton	
Flowers*	Paine[2]	Hunt[4]	Pickering[3]	Eastham	P Thompson	R Charlton 10[1]
Moore*	P Thompson	Greaves[1]	J Byrne	Eastham	R Charlton	
Moore*	Paine	Greaves	J Byrne	Hunt[1]	P Thompson	
Moore*	P Thompson	Greaves*	J Byrne	Eastham	R Charlton	
Moore*	Paine	Greaves[3]	Pickering[1]	R Charlton	P Thompson	
Moore*	P Thompson	Greaves	Pickering[1]	Venables	A Hinton[†]	
Young	P Thompson	Hunt	Wignall[2]	J Byrne	A Hinton	
Flowers*	P Thompson	Greaves[1]	Wignall	Venables	R Charlton	
Moore*	P Thompson	Greaves[1]	Bridges	J Byrne	R Charlton[1]	
Moore*	Paine	Greaves[1]	Bridges	Eastham	Connelly	
Moore*	Paine	Greaves	Bridges[1]	Ball	Connelly	
Moore*	Paine[1]	Ball	M Jones	Eastham	Temple	
Moore*	Paine	Ball[1]	M Jones	Eastham	Connelly[1]	
Moore*	Paine	Greaves	Peacock	R Charlton	Connelly	
Moore*	Paine	Greaves	Bridges	R Charlton[1]	Connelly[1]	
Moore*	P Thompson	Baker[1]	Peacock[1]	R Charlton	Connelly	
Moore*	Ball	Hunt[1]	Baker[1]	Eastham	R Charlton	Hunter 9
Moore*[1]	Ball	Hunt	Baker	Eastham	G Harris	
Hunter	Ball	Hunt	Stiles[1]	G Hurst	R Charlton	Wilson 3
Moore*	Ball	Hunt[2]	R Charlton[1]	G Hurst[1]	Connelly	
Hunter	Paine	Greaves[1]	R Charlton[1]	G Hurst	Tambling	

Versus	Venue	Result	1	2	3	4	5
Finland	A	3 – 0	G Banks	Armfield*	Wilson	Peters[1]	J Charlton[1]
Norway	A	6 – 1	R Springett	Cohen	G Byrne	Stiles	Flowers
Denmark	A	2 – 0	Bonetti	Cohen	Wilson	Stiles	J Charlton[1]
Poland	A	1 – 0	G Banks	Cohen	Wilson	Stiles	J Charlton
Uruguay	H	0 – 0	G Banks	Cohen	Wilson	Stiles	J Charlton
Mexico	H	2 – 0	G Banks	Cohen	Wilson	Stiles	J Charlton
France	H	2 – 0	G Banks	Cohen	Wilson	Stiles	J Charlton
Argentina	H	1 – 0	G Banks	Cohen	Wilson	Stiles	J Charlton
Portugal	H	2 – 1	G Banks	Cohen	Wilson	Stiles	J Charlton
West Germany	H	4 – 2	G Banks	Cohen	Wilson	Stiles	J Charlton

1966–67

Versus	Venue	Result	1	2	3	4	5
Northern Ireland	A	2 – 0	G Banks	Cohen	Wilson	Stiles	J Charlton
Czechoslovakia	H	0 – 0	G Banks	Cohen	Wilson	Stiles	J Charlton
Wales	H	5 – 1	G Banks	Cohen	Wilson	Stiles	J Charlton[1]
Scotland	H	2 – 3	G Banks	Cohen	Wilson	Stiles	J Charlton[1]
Spain	H	2 – 0	Bonetti	Cohen	K Newton	Mullery	Labone
Austria	A	1 – 0	Bonetti	K Newton	Wilson	Mullery	Labone

1967–68

Versus	Venue	Result	1	2	3	4	5
Wales	A	3 – 0	G Banks	Cohen	K Newton	Mullery	J Charlton
Northern Ireland	H	2 – 0	G Banks	Cohen	Wilson	Mullery	Sadler
USSR	H	2 – 2	G Banks	C Knowles	Wilson	Mullery	Sadler
Scotland	A	1 – 1	G Banks	K Newton	Wilson	Mullery	Labone
Spain	H	1 – 0	G Banks	C Knowles	Wilson	Mullery	J Charlton
Spain	A	2 – 1	Bonetti	K Newton	Wilson	Mullery	Labone
Sweden	H	3 – 1	Stepney	K Newton	C Knowles	Mullery	Labone
West Germany	A	0 – 1	G Banks	K Newton	C Knowles	Hunter	Labone
Yugoslavia	N	0 – 1	G Banks	K Newton	Wilson	Mullery	Labone
USSR	N	2 – 0	LG Banks	T Wright	Wilson	Stiles	Labone

1968–69

Versus	Venue	Result	1	2	3	4	5
Romania	A	0 – 0	G Banks	T Wright	K Newton	Mullery	Labone
Bulgaria	H	1 – 1	West	K Newton	McNab	Mullery	Labone
Romania	H	1 – 1	G Banks	T Wright	McNab	Stiles	J Charlton[1]
France	H	5 – 0	G Banks	K Newton	Cooper	Mullery	J Charlton
Northern Ireland	A	3 – 1	G Banks	K Newton	McNab	Mullery	Labone
Wales	H	2 – 1	West	K Newton	Cooper	Moore*	J Charlton
Scotland	H	4 – 1	G Banks	K Newton	Cooper	Mullery	Labone
Mexico	A	0 – 0	West	K Newton	Cooper	Mullery	Labone
Uruguay	A	2 – 1	G Banks	T Wright	K Newton	Mullery	Labone
Brazil	A	1 – 2	G Banks	T Wright	K Newton	Mullery	Labone

1969–70

Versus	Venue	Result	1	2	3	4	5
Holland	A	1 – 0	Bonetti	T Wright	E Hughes	Mullery	J Charlton
Portugal	H	1 – 0	Bonetti	Reaney	E Hughes	Mullery	J Charlton[1]
Holland	H	0 – 0	G Banks	K Newton	Cooper	Peters	J Charlton
Belgium	A	3 – 1	G Banks	T Wright	Cooper	Moore*	Labone
Wales	A	1 – 1	G Banks	T Wright	E Hughes	Mullery	Labone
Northern Ireland	H	3 – 1	G Banks	K Newton	E Hughes	Mullery	Moore*
Scotland	A	0 – 0	G Banks	K Newton	E Hughes	Stiles	Labone
Colombia	A	4 – 0	G Banks	K Newton	Cooper	Mullery	Labone
Ecuador	A	2 – 0	G Banks	K Newton	Cooper	Mullery	Labone
Romania	N	1 – 0	G Banks	K Newton	Cooper	Mullery	Labone
Brazil	N	0 – 1	G Banks	T Wright	Cooper	Mullery	Labone
Czechoslovakia	N	1 – 0	G Banks	K Newton	Cooper	Mullery	J Charlton

6	7	8	9	10	11	*Substitutes*
Hunter	Callaghan	Hunt[1]	R Charlton	G Hurst	Ball	
Moore*[1]	Paine	Greaves[4]	R Charlton	Hunt	Connelly[1]	
Moore*	Ball	Greaves	G Hurst	Eastham[1]	Connelly	
Moore*	Ball	Greaves	R Charlton	Hunt[1]	Peters	
Moore*	Ball	Greaves	R Charlton	Hunt	Connelly	
Moore*	Paine	Greaves	R Charlton[1]	Hunt[1]	Peters	
Moore*	Callaghan	Greaves	R Charlton	Hunt[2]	Peters	
Moore*	Ball	G Hurst[1]	R Charlton	Hunt	Peters	
Moore*	Ball	G Hurst	R Charlton[2]	Hunt	Peters	
Moore*	Ball	G Hurst[3]	R Charlton	Hunt	Peters[1]	
Moore*	Ball	G Hurst	R Charlton	Hunt[1]	Peters[1]	
Moore*	Ball	G Hurst	R Charlton	Hunt	Peters	
Moore*	Ball	G Hurst[2]	R Charlton[1]	Hunt	Peters	†
Moore*	Ball	Greaves	R Charlton[1]	G Hurst[1]	Peters	
Moore*	Ball	Graves[1]	G Hurst	Hunt[1]	Hollins	
Moore*	Ball[1]	Greaves	G Hurst	Hunt	Hunter	
Moore*	Ball[1]	Hunt	R Charlton[1]	G Hurst	Peters[1]	
Moore*	P Thompson	Hunt	R Charlton[1]	G Hurst[1]	Peters	
Moore*	Ball[1]	Hunt	R Charlton	G Hurst	Peters[1]	
Moore*	Ball	G Hurst	Summerbee	R Charlton	Peters[1]	
Moore*	Ball	Hunt	Summerbee	R Charlton[1]	Peters	
Moore*	Ball	Peters[1]	R Charlton	Hunt	Hunter[1]	
Moore*	Bell	Peters[1]	R Charlton[1]	Hunt[1]	Hunter	G Hurst 9
Moore*	Ball	Bell	Summerbee	G Hurst	P Thompson	
Moore*	Ball	Peters	R Charlton	Hunt	Hunter	
Moore*	Hunter	Hunt	R Charlton[1]	G Hurst[1]	Peters	
Moore*	Ball	Hunt	R Charlton	G Hurst	Peters	McNab 2
Moore*	F Lee	Ball	R Charlton	G Hurst[1]	Peters	Reaney 2
Hunter	Radford	Hunt	R Charlton*	G Hurst	Ball	
Moore*	F Lee[1]	Bell	G Hurst[3]	Peters	O'Grady[1]	
Moore*	Ball	F Lee[1]	R Charlton	G Hurst[1]	Peters[1]	
Hunter	F Lee[1]	Bell	Astle	R Charlton[1]	Ball	
Moore*	F Lee	Ball	R Charlton	G Hurst[2]	Peters[2]	
Moore*	F Lee	Ball	R Charlton	G Hurst	Peters	T Wright 2
Moore*	F Lee[1]	Bell	G Hurst[1]	Ball	Peters	
Moore*	Ball	Bell[1]	R Charlton	G Hurst	Peters	
Moore*	F Lee	Bell[1]	R Charlton	G Hurst	Peters	P Thompson 7
Moore*	F Lee	Bell	Astle	R Charlton	Ball	Peters 8
Hunter	F Lee	Bell	M Jones	R Charlton*	Storey-Moore	Mullery 7, G Hurst 9
E Hughes	F Lee	Ball[2]	Osgood	G Hurst[1]	Peters	
Moore*	F Lee[1]	Ball	R Charlton	G Hurst	Peters	
Stiles	Coates	Kidd	R Charlton[1]	G Hurst[1]	Peters[1]	Bell 2
Moore*	P Thompson	Ball	Astle	G Hurst	Peters	Mullery 7
Moore*	F Lee	Ball[1]	R Charlton[1]	G Hurst	Peters[2]	
Moore*	F Lee[1]	Ball	R Charlton	G Hurst	Peters	Kidd 7[1], Sadler 9
Moore*	F Lee	Ball	R Charlton	G Hurst[1]	Peters	T Wright 2, Osgood 7
Moore*	F Lee	Ball	R Charlton	G Hurst	Peters	Astle 7, Bell 9
Moore*	Bell	R Charlton	Astle	A Clarke[1]	Peters	Ball 8, Osgood 10

Versus	Venue	Result	1	2	3	4	5
West Germany	N	2 – 3	Bonetti	K Newton	Cooper	Mullery[1]	Labone
1970–71							
East Germany	H	3 – 1	Shilton	E Hughes	Cooper	Mullery	Sadler
Malta	A	1 – 0	G Banks	Reaney	E Hughes	Mullery*	McFarland
Greece	H	3 – 0	G Banks	Storey	E Hughes	Mullery	McFarland
Malta	H	5 – 0	G Banks	Lawler[1]	Cooper	Moore*	McFarland
Northern Ireland	A	1 – 0	G Banks	Madeley	Cooper	Storey	McFarland
Wales	H	0 – 0	Shilton	Lawler	Cooper	T Smith	Lloyd
Scotland	H	3 – 1	G Banks	Lawler	Cooper	Storey	McFarland
1971–72							
Switzerland	A	3 – 2	G Banks	Lawler	Cooper	Mullery	McFarland
Switzerland	H	1 – 1	Shilton	Madeley	Cooper	Storey	Lloyd
Greece	A	2 – 0	G Banks	Madeley	E Hughes	Bell	McFarland
West Germany	H	1 – 3	G Banks	Madeley	E Hughes	Bell	Moore*
West Germany	A	0 – 0	G Banks	Madeley	E Hughes	Storey	McFarland
Wales	A	3 – 0	G Banks	Madeley	E Hughes[1]	Storey	McFarland
Northern Ireland	H	0 – 1	Shilton	Todd	E Hughes	Storey	Lloyd
Scotland	A	1 – 0	G Banks	Madeley	E Hughes	Storey	McFarland
1972–73							
Yugoslavia	H	1 – 1	Shilton	M Mills	Lampard	Storey	Blockley
Wales	A	1 – 0	Clemence	Storey	E Hughes	Hunter	McFarland
Wales	H	1 – 1	Clemence	Storey	E Hughes	Hunter[1]	McFarland
Scotland	A	5 – 0	Shilton	Storey	E Hughes	Bell	Madeley
Northern Ireland	A	2 – 1	Shilton	Storey	Nish	Bell	McFarland
Wales	H	3 – 0	Shilton	Storey	E Hughes	Bell	McFarland
Scotland	H	1 – 0	Shilton	Storey	E Hughes	Bell	McFarland
Czechoslovakia	A	1 – 1	Shilton	Madeley	Storey	Bell	McFarland
Poland	A	0 – 2	Shilton	Madeley	E Hughes	Storey	McFarland
USSR	A	2 – 1	Shilton	Madeley	E Hughes	Storey	McFarland
Italy	A	0 – 2	Shilton	Madeley	E Hughes	Storey	McFarland
1973– 74							
Austria	H	7 – 0	Shilton	Madeley	E Hughes	Bell[1]	McFarland
Poland	H	1 – 1	Shilton	Madeley	E Hughes	Bell	McFarland
Italy	H	0 – 1	Shilton	Madeley	E Hughes	Bell	McFarland
Portugal	A	0 – 0	Parkes	Nish	Pejic	Dobson	Watson
Wales	A	2 – 0	Shilton	Nish	Pejic	E Hughes*	McFarland
Northern Ireland	H	1 – 0	Shilton	Nish	Pejic	E Hughes*	McFarland
Scotland	A	0 – 2	Shilton	Nish	Pejic	E Hughes*	Hunter
Argentina	H	2 – 2	Shilton	E Hughes*	Lindsay	Todd	Watson
East Germany	A	1 – 1	Clemence	E Hughes*	Lindsay	Todd	Watson
Bulgaria	A	1 – 0	Clemence	E Hughes*	Todd	Watson	Lindsay
Yugoslavia	A	2 – 2	Clemence	E Hughes*	Lindsay	Todd	Watson
1974–75							
Czechoslovakia	H	3 – 0	Clemence	Madeley	E Hughes*	Dobson	Watson
Portugal	H	0 – 0	Clemence	Madeley	Watson	E Hughes*	Cooper
West Germany	H	2 – 0	Clemence	Whitworth	Gillard	Bell[1]	Watson
Cyprus	H	5 – 0	Shilton	Madeley	Watson	Todd	Beattie
Cyprus	A	1 – 0	Clemence	Whitworth	Beattie	Watson	Todd
Northern Ireland	A	0 – 0	Clemence	Whitworth	E Hughes	Bell	Watson
Wales	H	2 – 2	Clemence	Whitworth	Gillard	G Francis	Watson

6	7	8	9	10	11	Substitutes
Moore*	F Lee	Ball	R Charlton	G Hurst	Peters[1]	Bell 9, Hunter 11
Moore*	F Lee[1]	Ball	G Hurst	A Clarke[1]	Peters[1]	
Hunter	Ball	Chivers	Royle	Harvey	Peters[1]	
Moore*	F Lee[1]	Ball	Chivers[1]	G Hurst[1]	Peters	Coates 8
E Hughes	F Lee[1]	Coates	Chivers[2]	A Clarke[1]	Peters	Ball 11
Moore*	F Lee	Ball	Chivers	A Clarke[1]	Peters	
E Hughes	F Lee	Coates	G Hurst	Coates	Peters*	A Clarke 8
Moore*	F Lee	Ball	Chivers[2]	G Hurst	Peters[1]	A Clarke 7
Moore*	F Lee	Madeley	Chivers[1]	G Hurst[1]	Peters[†]	Radford 10
Moore*	Summerbee[1]	Ball	G Hurst	F Lee	E Hughes	Chivers 7, Marsh 10
Moore*	F Lee	Ball	Chivers[1]	G Hurst[1]	Peters	
Hunter	F Lee[1]	Ball	Chivers	G Hurst	Peters	Marsh 10
Moore*	Ball	Bell	Chivers	Marsh	Hunter	Summerbee 10, Peters 11
Moore*	Summerbee	Bell[1]	MacDonald	Marsh[1]	Hunter	
Hunter	Summerbee	Bell*	MacDonald	Marsh	Currie	Chivers 9, Peters 11
Moore*	Ball[1]	Bell	Chivers	Marsh	Hunter	MacDonald 10
Moore*	Ball	Channon	Royle[1]	Bell	Marsh	
Moore*	Keegan	Chivers	Marsh	Bell[1]	Ball	
Moore*	Keegan	Bell	Chivers	Marsh	Ball	
Moore*	Ball	Channon[1]	Chivers[1]	A Clarke[2]	Peters[†]	
Moore*	Ball	Channon	Chivers[2]	Richards	Peters	
Moore*	Ball	Channon[1]	A Clarke	Peters[1]		
Moore*	Ball	Cannon	Chivers	A Clarke	Peters[1]	
Moore*	Ball	Channon	Chivers	A Clarke[1]	Peters	
Moore*	Ball	Bell	Chivers	A Clarke	Peters	
Moore*	Currie	Channon	Chivers[1]	A Clarke	Peters[†]	MacDonald 10,
Moore*	Currie	Channon	Chivers	A Clarke	Peters	Hunter 11, Summerbee 8
Hunter	Currie[1]	Channon[2]	Chivers[1]	A Clarke[2]	Peters*	
Hunter	Currie	Channon	Chivers	A Clarke[1]	Peters*	Hector 9
Moore*	Currie	Channon	Osgood	A Clarke	Peters	Hector 10
Todd	Bowles	Channon	MacDonald	Brooking	Peters*	Ball 9
Todd	Keegan[1]	Bell	Channon	Weller	Bowles[1]	
Todd	Keegan	Weller[1]	Channon	Bell	Bowles	Hunter 5, Worthington 11
Todd	Channon	Bell	Worthington	Weller	Peters	Watson 5, MacDonald 9
Bell	Keegan	Channon[1]	Worthington[1]	Weller	Brooking	
Dobson	Keegan	Channon[1]	Worthington	Bell	Brooking	
Dobson	Brooking	Bell	Keegan	Channon	Worthington[1]	
Dobson	Keegan[1]	Channon[1]	Worthington	Bell	Brooking	MacDonald 9
Hunter	Bell[2]	G Francis	Worthington	Channon[1]	Keegan	Brooking 4, Thomas 9
Brooking	G Francis	Bell	Thomas	Channon	A Clarke	Todd 5, Worthington 11
Todd	Ball*	MacDonald[1]	Channon	Hudson	Keegan	
Bell	Ball	Hudson	Channon	MacDonald[5]	Keegan	Thomas 9
Bell	Thomas	Ball*	Channon	MacDonald	Keegan[1]	E Hughes 3, Tuert 11
Todd	Ball*	Viljoen	MacDonald	Keegan	Tueart	Channon 9
Todd	Ball*	Channon	Johnson[2]	Viljoen	Thomas	Little 8

Versus	Venue	Result	1	2	3	4	5
Scotland	H	5 – 1	Clemence	Whitworth	Beattie[1]	Bell[1]	Watson
1975–76							
Switzerland	A	2 – 1	Clemence	Whitworth	Todd	Watson	Beattie
Czechoslovakia	A	1 – 2	Clemence	Madeley	Gillard	G Francis*	McFarland
Portugal	A	1 – 1	Clemence	Whitworth	Beattie	G Francis*	Watson
Wales	A	2 – 1	Clemence	Cherry	M Mills	Neal	P Thompson
Wales	A	1 – 0	Clemence	Clement	M Mills	Towers	B Greenhoff
Northern Ireland	H	4 – 0	Clemence	Todd	M Mills	P Thompson	B Greenhoff
Scotland	A	1 – 2	Clemence	Todd	M Mills	P Thompson	McFarland
Brazil	N	0 – 1	Clemence	Todd	Doyle	P Thompson	Doyle
Italy	N	3 – 2	Rimmer	Clement	Neal	P Thompson[1]	Doyle
Finland	A	4 – 1	Clemence	Todd	M Mills	P Thompson	Madeley
1976–77							
Republic of Ireland	H	1 – 1	Clemence	Todd	Madeley	Cherry	McFarland
Finland	H	2 – 1	Clemence	Todd	Beattie	P Thompson	Greenhoff
Italy	A	0 – 2	Clemence	Clement	M Mills	B Greenhoff	McFarland
Holland	H	0 – 2	Clemence	Clement	Beattie	Doyle	Watson
Luxembourg	H	5 – 0	Clemence	Gidman	Cherry	Kennedy[1]	Watson
Northern Ireland	A	2 – 1	Shilton	Cherry	M Mills	Greenhoff	Watson
Wales	H	0 – 1	Shilton	Neal	M Mills	Greenhoff	Watson
Scotland	H	1 – 2	Clemence	Neal	M Mills	Greenhoff	Watson
Brazil	A	0 – 0	Clemence	Neal	Cherry	B Greenhoff	Watson
Argentina	A	1 – 1	Clemence	Neal	Cherry	B Greenhoff	Watson
Uruguay	A	0 – 0	Clemence	Neal	Cherry	B Greenhoff	Watson
1977–78							
Switzerland	H	0 – 0	Clemence	Neal	Cherry	McDermott	Watson
Luxembourg	A	2 – 0	Clemence	Cherry	Watson	E Hughes*	R Kennedy[1]
Italy	H	2 – 0	Clemence	Neal	Cherry	Wilkins	Watson
West Germany	A	1 – 2	Clemence	Neal	M Mills	Wilkins	Watson
Brazil	H	1 – 1	Corrigan	M Mills	Cherry	B Greenhoff	Watson
Wales	A	3 – 1	Shilton	M Mills*	Cherry	B Greenhoff	Watson
Northern Ireland	H	1 – 0	Clemence	Neal[1]	M Mills	Wilkins	Watson
Scotland	A	1 – 0	Clemence	Neal	M Mills	Currie	Watson
Hungary	H	4 – 1	Shilton	Neal[1]	M Mills	Wilkins	Watson
1978–79							
Denmark	A	4 – 3	Clemence	Neal[1]	M Mills	Wilkins	Watson
Republic of Ireland	A	1 – 1	Clemence	Neal	M Mills	Wilkins	Watson
Czechoslovakia	H	1 – 0	Shilton	Anderson	Cherry	P Thompson	Watson
Northern Ireland	H	4 – 0	Clemence	Neal	M Mills	Currie	Watson[1]
Northern Ireland	A	2 – 0	Clemence	Neal	M Mills*	P Thompson	Watson[1]
Wales	H	0 – 0	Corrigan	Cherry	Sansom	Wilkins	Watson
Scotland	H	3 – 1	Clemence	Neal	M Mills	P Thompson	Watson
Bulgaria	A	3 – 0	Clemence	Neal	M Mills	P Thompson	Watson[1]
Sweden	A	0 – 0	Shilton	Anderson	Cherry	McDermott	Watson
Austria	A	3 – 4	Shilton	Neal	M Mills	P Thompson	Watson
1979– 80							
Denmark	H	1 – 0	Clemence	Neal	M Mills	P Thompson	Watson
Northern Ireland	A	5 – 1	Shilton	Neal	M Mills	P Thompson	Watson
Bulgaria	H	2 – 0	Clemence	Anderson	Sansom	P Thompson*	Watson[1]
Republic of Ireland	H	2 – 0	Clemence	Cherry	Sansom	P Thompson	Watson

6	7	8	9	10	11	Substitutes
Todd	Ball*	Channon	Johnson[1]	G Francis[2]	Keegan	Thomas 11
Bell	Currie	G Francis*	Channon[1]	Johnson	Keegan[1]	MacDonald 10
Todd	Keegan	Channon[1]	MacDonald	A Clarke	Bell	Watson 5, Thomas 8
Todd	Keegan	Channon[1]	MacDonald	Brooking	Madeley	A Clarke 11, Thomas 9
Doyle	Keegan*	Channon	Boyer	Brooking	Kennedy[1]	Clement 2, P Taylor 8[1]
P Thompson	Keegan	G Francis*	Pearson	Kennedy	P Taylor[1]	
R Kennedy	Keegan	G Francis*[1]	Pearson[1]	Channon[2]	P Taylor	Towers 11, Royle 7
R Kennedy	Keegan	G Francis*	Pearson	Channon[1]	P Taylor	Cherry 9, Doyle 5
G Francis*	Cherry	Brooking	Keegan	Pearson	Channon	
Towers	Wilkins	Brooking	Royle	Channon*[2]	Hill	Corrigan 1, M Mills 3
Cherry	Keegan[2]	Channon[1]	Pearson[1]	Brooking	G Francis*	
Greenhoff	Keegan*	Wilkins	Pearson[1]	Brooking	George	Hill 11
Wilkins	Keegan*	Channon	Royle[1]	Brooking	Tueart[1]	M Mills 10, Hill 11
E Hughes	Keegan*	Channon	Bowles	Cherry	Brooking	Beattie 2
Madeley	Keegan*	Greenhoff	T Francis	Bowles	Brooking	Todd 8, S Pearson 6
E Hughes[1]	Keegan*[1]	Channon	Royle	T Francis[1]	Hill	Mariner 9
Todd	Wilkins	Channon*[1]	Mariner	Brooking	Tueart[1]	Talbot 7
E Hughes	Keegan*	Channon	Pearson	Brooking	R Kennedy	Tueart 10
E Hughes	T Francis	Channon[1]	Pearson	Talbot	R Kennery	Cherry 4, Tueart 11
E Hughes	Keegan*	T Francis	Pearson	Wilkins	Talbot	Channon 9, Kennedy 10
E Hughes	Keegan*	Channon	Pearson[1]	Wilkins	Talbot	R Kennedy 4
E Hughes	Keegan*	Channon	Pearson	Wilkins	Talbot	
E Hughes*	Keegan	Channon	T Francis	R Kennedy	Callaghan	Hill 8, Wilkins 11
Callaghan	McDermott	Wilkins	T Francis	Mariner[1]	G Hill	Whymark 7, Beattie 3
E Hughes*	Keegan[1]	Coppell	R Latchford	Brooking[1]	P Barnes	Pearson 9, T Francis 7
E Hughes*	Kegan	Coppell	S Pearson[1]	Brooking	P Barnes	T Francis 7
Currie	Keegan*[1]	Coppell	R Latchford	T Francis	P Barnes	
Wilkins	Coppell	T Francis	R Latchford[1]	Brooking	P Barnes[1]	Currie 3[1]1, Mariner 9
E Hughes*	Currie	Coppell	Pearson	Woodcock	B Greenhoff	
E Hughes*	Wilkins	Coppell[1]	Mariner	T Francis	P Barnes	B Greenhoff 6, Booking 9
E Hughes*	Keegan	Coppell	T Francis[1]	Brooking	P Barnes[1]	B Greenhoff 5, Currie 8[1]
E Hughes*	Keegan[2]	Coppell	Latchford[1]	Brooking	P Barnes	
E Hughes*	Keegan	Coppell	Latchford[1]	Brooking	P Barnes	P Thompson 5, Woodcock 11
Wilkins	Keegan*	Coppell[1]	Woodcock	Currie	P Barnes	Latchford 9
E Hughes*	Keegan[1]	Coppell	Latchford[2]	Brooking	P Barnes	
Wilkins	Coppell[1]	Wilkins	Latchford	Currie	P Barnes	
E Hughes*	Keegan	Wilkins	Latchford	McDermott	Cunningham	Coppell 7, Brooking 4
Wilkins	Keegan*[1]	Coppell[1]	Latchford	Brooking	P Barnes[1]	
Wilkins	Keegan*[1]	Coppell	Latchford	Brooking	P Barnes[1]	T Francis 9, Woodcock 11
E Hughes*	Keegan	T Francis	T Francis	Woodcock	Cunningham	Wilkins 4, Brooking 8
Wilkins[1]	Keegan*[1]	Coppell[1]	Latchford	Brooking	P Barnes	Clemence 1, T Francis 9 Cunningham 11
Wilkins	Coppell	McDermott	Keegan*[1]	Brooking	P Barnes	
Wilkins	Keegan*	Coppell	T Francis[2]	Brooking	Woodcock[2]	[†]McDermott 10
Wilkins	Reeves	Hoddle[1]	T Francis	Kennedy	Woodcock	
Robson	Keegan*[2]	McDermott	Johnson	Woodcock	Cunningham	Coppell 9

● 67

Versus	Venue	Result	1	2	3	4	5
Spain	A	2 – 0	Shilton	Neal	M Mills	P Thompson	Watson
Argentina	H	3 – 1	Clemence	Neal	Sansom	P Thompson	Watson
Wales	A	1 – 4	Clemence	Neal	Cherry	P Thompson*	Lloyd
Northern Ireland	H	1 – 1	Corrigan	Cherry	Sansom	E Hughes*	Watson
Scotland	A	2 – 0	Clemence	Cherry	Sansom	P Thompson*	Watson
Australia	A	2 – 1	Corrigan	Cherry*	Lampard	Talbot	Osman
Belgium	N	1 – 1	Clemence	Neal	Sansom	P Thompson	Watson
Italy	A	0 – 1	Shilton	Neal	Sansom	P Thompson	Watson
Spain	N	2 – 1	Clemence	Anderson	M Mills	P Thompson	Watson

1980–81

Versus	Venue	Result	1	2	3	4	5
Norway	H	4 – 0	Shilton	Anderson	Sansom	P Thompson*	Watson
Romania	A	1 – 2	Clemence	Neal	Sansom	P Thompson*	Watson
Switzerland	H	2 – 1	Shilton	Neal	Sansom	Robson	Watson
Spain	H	1 – 2	Clemence	Neal	Sansom	Robson	Butcher
Romania	H	0 – 0	Shilton	Anderson	Sansom	Robson	Watson*
Brazil	H	0 – 1	Clemence*	Neal	Sansom	Robson	Martin
Wales	H	0 – 0	Corrigan	Anderson	Sansom	Robson	Watson*
Scotland	H	0 – 1	Corrigan	Anderson	Sansom	Wilkins	Watson*
Switzerland	A	1 – 2	Clemence	M Mills	Sansom	Wilkins	Watson
Hungary	A	3 – 1	Clemence	Neal	M Mills	P Thompson	Watson

1981–82

Versus	Venue	Result	1	2	3	4	5
Norway	A	1 – 2	Clemence	Neal	M Mills	P Thompson	Osman
Hungary	H	1 – 0	Shilton	Neal	M Mills	P Thompson	Martin
Northern Ireland	H	4 – 0	Clemence	Anderson	Sansom	Wilkins[1]	Watson
Wales	A	1 – 0	Corrigan	Neal	Sansom	P Thompson*	Butcher
Holland	H	2 – 0	Shilton*	Neal	Sansom	P Thompson	Foster
Scotland	A	1 – 0	Shilton	N Mills	Sansom	P Thompson	Butcher
Iceland	A	1 – 1	Corrigan	Anderson	Neal*	Watson	Osman
Finland	A	4 – 1	Clemence	M Mills	Sansom	P Thompson	Martin
France	N	3 – 1	Shilton	M Mills*	Sansom	P Thompson	Butcher
Czechoslovakia	N	2 – 0	Shilton	M Mills*	Sansom	P Thompson	Butcher
Kuwait	N	1 – 0	Shilton	Neal	M Mills*	P Thompson	Foster
West Germany	N	0 – 0	Shilton	M Mills*	Sansom	P Thompson	Butcher
Spain	A	0 – 0	Shilton	M Mills*	Sansom	P Thompson	Butcher

6	7	8	9	10	11	Substitutes
Wilkins	Keegan*	Coppell	T Francis[1]	R Kennedy	Woodcock[1]	E Hughes, 2 Cunningham
Wilkins	Keegan*[1]	Coppell	Johnson[2]	Woodcock	R Kennedy	Cherry 2, Birtles 9, Brooking 11
R Kennedy	Coppell	Hoddle	Mariner[1]	Brooking	Barnes	Sansom 2, Wilkins 5
Wilkins	Reeves	Wilkins	Johnson[1]	Brooking	Devonshire	Mariner 7
Wilkins	Coppell[1]	McDermott	Johnson	Mariner	Brooking[1]	E Hughes 10
Butcher	Robson	Sunderland	Mariner[1]	Hoddle[1]	Armstrong	B Greenhoff 7, Ward 10 Devonshire 11
Wilkins	Keegan*	Coppell	Johnson	Woodcock	Brooking	McDermott 8, R Kennedy
Wilkins	Keegan*	Coppell	Birtles	R Kennedy	Woodcock	Mariner 9
Wilkins	McDermott	Hoddle	Keegan*	Woodcock[1]	Brooking[1]	Cherry 3, Mariner 8
Robson	Gates	McDermott[2]	Mariner[1]	Woodcock[1]	Rix	
Robson	Rix	McDermott	Birtles	Woodcock[1]	Gates	Cunningham 9, Coppell 11
M Mills*	Coppell	McDermott	Mariner[1]	Brooking	Woodcock	[†] Rix 10
Osman	Keegan*	T Francis	Mariner	Brooking	Hoddle[1]	P Barnes 8, Wilkins 10
Osman	Wilkins	Brooking	Coppell	T Francis	Woodcock	McDermott 11
Wilkins	Coppell	McDermott	Withe	Rix	P Barnes	
Wilkins	Coppell	Hoddle	Withe	Rix	P Barnes	Woodcock 9
Robson	Coppell	Hoddle	Withe	Rix	Woodcock	Martin 5, T Francis 11
Osman	Keegan*	Robson	Coppell	Mariner	T Francis	McDermott 1[1], P Barnes 5
Robson	Keegan*[1]	McDermott	Mariner	Brooking[2]	Coppell	Wilkins 10
Robson[1]	Keegan*	T Francis	Mariner	Hoddle	McDermott	Withe 9, P Barnes 10
Robson	Keegan*	Coppell	Mariner[1]	Brooking	McDermott	Morley 8
Foster	Keegan*[1]	Robson[1]	T Francis	Hoddle[1]	Morley	Regis 9, Woodcock 11
Robson	Wilkins	T Francis[1]	Withe	Hoddle	Morley	McDermott 8, Regis 10
Robson	Wilkins	Devonshire	Mariner[1]	McDermott	Woodcock[1]	Rix 8, Barnes 9
Robson	Keegan*	Coppell	Mariner[1]	Brooking	Wilkins	McDermott 7, T Francis 9,
McDermott	Hoddle	Devonshire	Withe	Regis	Morley	Perryman 8, Goddard 10[†]
Robson[2]	Keegan*	Coppell	Mariner[2]	Brooking	Wilkins	Rix 6, T Francis 8 Woodcock 10
Robson[2]	Coppell	T Francis	Mariner[1]	Rix	Wilkins	Neal 3
Robson	Coppell	T Francis[1]	Mariner	Rix	Wilkins	[†] Hoddle 6
Hoddle	Coppell	T Francis[1]	Mariner	Rix	Wilkins	
Robson	Coppell	T Francis	Mariner	Rix	Wilkins	Woodcock 8
Robson	Rix	T Francis	Mariner	Woodcock	Wilkins	Brooking 7, Keegan 10

Versus	Venue	Result	1	2	3	4	5
1982–83							
Denmark	A	2 – 2	Shilton	Neal	Sansom	Wilkins*	Osman
West Germany	H	1 – 2	Shilton	Mabbutt	Sansom	P Thompson	Butcher
Greece	A	3 – 0	Shilton	Neal	Sansom	P Thompson	Martin
Luxembourg	H	9 – 0	Clemence	Neal[1]	Sansom	Robson*	Martin
Wales	H	2 – 1	Shilton*	Neal[1]	Statham	S Lee	Martin
Greece	H	0 – 0	Shilton*	Neal	Sansom	S Lee	Martin
Hungary	H	2 – 0	Shilton*	Neal	Sansom	S Lee	Martin
Northern Ireland	A	0 – 0	Shilton*	Neal	Sansom	Hoddle	Roberts
Scotland	H	2 – 0	Shilton	Neal	Sansom	S Lee	Roberts
Australia	A	0 – 0	Shilton*	Thomas	Statham	Williams	Osman
Australia	A	1 – 0	Shilton*	Neal	Statham	Barham	Osman
Australia	A	1 – 1	Shilton*	Neal	Pickering	S Lee	Osman
1983–84							
Denmark	H	0 – 1	Shilton	Neal	Sanson	S Lee	Osman
Hungary	A	3 – 0	Shilton	Gregory	Sansom	S Lee[1]	Martin
Luxembourg	A	4 – 0	Clemence	Duxbury	Sansom	S Lee	Martin
France	A	0 – 2	Shilton	Duxbury	Sansom	S Lee	Roberts
Northern Ireland	H	1 – 0	Shilton	Anderson	A Kennedy	S Lee	Roberts
Wales	A	0 – 1	Shilton	Duxbury	A Kennedy	S Lee	Martin
Scotland	A	1 – 1	Shilton	Duxbury	Sansom	Wilkins	Roberts
USSR	H	0 – 2	Shilton	Duxbury	Sansom	Wilkins	Roberts
Brazil	A	2 – 0	Shilton	Duxbury	Sansom	Wilkins	Watson
Uruguay	A	0 – 2	Shilton	Duxbury	Sansom	Wilkins	Watson
Chile	A	0 – 0	Shilton	Duxbury	Sansom	Wilkins	Watson
1984–85							
East Germany	H	1 – 0	Shilton	Duxbury	Sansom	Williams	Wright
Finland	H	5 – 0	Shilton	Duxbury	Sansom[1]	Williams	Wright
Turkey	A	8 – 0	Shilton	Anderson[1]	Sansom	Williams	Wright
Northern Ireland	A	1 – 0	Shilton	Anderson	Sansom	Steven	Martin
Republic of Ireland	H	2 – 1	Bailey	Anderson	Sansom	Steven[1]	Wright
Romania	A	0 – 0	Shilton	Anderson	Sansom	Steven	Wright

6	7	8	9	10	11	Substitutes
Butcher	Morley	Robson	Mariner	T Francis[2]	Rix	Hill 7
Wilkins*	R Hill	Regis	Mariner	Armstrong	Devonshire	Woodcock 8[1], Blissett 9, Rix 10
Robson*	S Lee[1]	Mabbutt	Mariner	Woodcock[2]	Morley	
Butcher	Coppell[1]	S Lee	Woodcock[1]	Blissett[3]	Mabbutt	[†]Chamberlain 7[1], Hoddle 11[1]
Butcher[1]	Mabbutt	Blissett	Mariner	Cowans	Devonshire	
Butcher	Coppell	Mabbutt	T Francis	Woodcock	Devonshire	Blissett 10, Rix 11
Butcher	Mabbutt	T Francis[1]	Withe[1]	Blissett	Cowans	
Butcher	Mabbutt	T Francis	Withe	Blissett	Cowans	J Barnes 10
Butcher	Robson*[1]	T Francis	Withe	Hoddle	Cowans[1]	Mabbutt 7, Blissett 9
Butcher	Barham	Gregory	Blissett	T Francis	Cowans	J Barnes 3, Walsh 9
Butcher	Gregory	T Francis	Walsh[1]	Cowans	J Barnes	Williams 3
Butcher	Gregory	T Francis[1]	Walsh	Cowans	J Barnes	Spink 1, Thomas 2, Blissett 9
Butcher	Wilkins*	Gregory	Mariner	T Francis	J Barnes	Blissett 4, Chamberlain 11
Butcher	Robson*	Hoddle[1]	Mariner[1]	Blissett	Mabbutt	Withe 10
Butcher[1]	Robson*[2]	Hoddle	Mariner[1]	Woodcock	Devonshire	J Barnes 10
Butcher	Robson*	Stein	Walsh	Hoddle	Williams	J Barnes 4, Woodcock 8
Butcher	Robson*	Wilkins	Woodcock[1]	T Francis	Rix	Fenwick 5, Blissett 11
Wright	Wilkins*	Gregory	Walsh	Woodcock	Armstrong	
Fenwick	Chamberlain	Robson*	Woodcock[1]	Blissett	J Barnes	Hunt 7, Lineker 9
Fenwick	Chamberlain	Robson*	T Francis	Blissett	J Barnes	Hateley 9, Hunt 11
Fenwick	Robson*	Chamberlain	Hateley[1]	Woodcock	J Barnes[1]	Allen 10
Fenwick	Robson*	Chamberlain	Hateley	Allen	J Barnes	Woodcock 10
Fenwick	Robson*	Chanberlain	Hateley	Allen	J Barnes	S Lee 8
Butcher	Robson*[1]	Wilkins	Mariner	Woodcock	J Barnes	Hateley 9, T Francis 10
Butcher	Robson*[1]	Wilkins	Hateley[2]	Woodcock[1]	J Barnes	GA Stevens 2, Chamberlain 7
Butcher	Robson*[3]	Wilkins	Withe	Woodcock[2]	J Barnes[2]	GA Stevens 4, Francis 10
Butcher	Steven	Wilkins*	Hateley[1]	Woodcock	J Barnes	T Francis 10
Butcher	Robson*	Wilkins	Hateley	Lineker[1]	Waddle	Hoddle 7, Davenport 9
Butcher	Robson*	Wilkins	Mariner	T Francis	J Barnes	Lineker 9, Waddle 11

Versus	Venue	Result	1	2	3	4	5
Finland	A	1 – 1	Shilton	Anderson	Sansom	Steven	Fenwick
Scotland	A	0 – 1	Shilton	Anderson	Sansom	Hoddle	Fenwick
Italy	N	1 – 2	Shilton	Stevens	Sansom	Steven	Wright
Mexico	A	0 – 1	Bailey	Anderson	Sansom	Hoddle	Fenwick
West Germany	N	3 – 0	Shilton	Stevens	Sansom	Hoddle	Wright
USA	A	5 – 0	Woods	Anderson	Sansom	Hoddle	Fenwick

1985–86

Versus	Venue	Result	1	2	3	4	5
Romania	H	1 – 1	Shilton	Stevens	Sansom	Reid	Wright
Turkey	H	5 – 0	Shilton	Stevens	Sansom	Hoddle	Wright
Northern Ireland	H	0 – 0	Shilton	GA Stevens	Sansom	Hoddle	Wright
Egypt	A	4 – 0	Shilton	Stevens	Sansom	Cowans[1]	Wright
Israel	A	2 – 1	Shilton	Stevens	Sansom	Hoddle	Martin
USSR	A	1 – 0	Shilton	Anderson	Sansom	Hoddle	Wright
Scotland	H	2 – 1	Shilton	Stevens	Sansom	Hoddle[1]	Watson
Mexico	N	3 – 0	Shilton	Anderson	Sansom	Hoddle	Fenwick
Canada	A	1 – 0	Shilton	Stevens	Sansom	Hoddle	Martin
Portugal	N	0 – 1	Shilton	Stevens	Sansom	Hoddle	Fenwick
Morocco	N	0 – 0	Shilton	Stevens	Sansom	Hoddle	Fenwick
Poland	N	3 – 0	Shilton*	Stevens	Sansom	Hoddle	Fenwick
Paraguay	N	3 – 0	Shilton*	Stevens	Sansom	Hoddle	Martin
Argentina	N	1 – 2	Shilton*	Stevens	Sansom	Hoddle	Fenwick

1986–87

Versus	Venue	Result	1	2	3	4	5
Sweden	A	0 – 1	Shilton*	Anderson	Sansom	Hoddle	Martin
Northern Ireland	H	3 – 0	Shilton	Anderson	Sansom	Hoddle	Watson
Yugoslavia	H	2 – 0	Woods	Anderson[1]	Sansom	Hoddle	Wright

6	7	8	9	10	11	Substitutes
Butcher	Robson*	Wilkins	Hateley[1]	T Francis	J Barnes	Waddle 4
Butcher	Robson*	Wilkins	Hateley	T Francis	J Barnes	Lineker 4, Waddle 11
Butcher	Robson*	Wilkins	Hateley[1]	T Francis	Waddle	Hoddle 4, Lineker 10, J Barnes 11
Watson	Robson*	Wilkins	Hateley	T Francis	J Barnes	K Dixon 4, Reid 8, Waddle 11
Butcher	Robson*[1]	Reid	K Dixon[2]	Lineker	Waddle	Bracewell 7, J Barnes 10
Butcher	Robson*	Bracewell	K Dixon[2]	Lineker[2]	Waddle	Watson 3, Steven 4[1], Reid 7, J Barnes 11
Fenwick	Robson*	Hoddle[1]	Hateley	Lineker	Waddle	Woodcock 10, J Barnes 11
Fenwick	Robson*[1]	Wilkins	Hateley	Lineker[3]	Waddle[1]	Steven 7, Woodcock 9
Fenwick	Bracewell	Wilkins*	K Dixon	Lineker	Waddle	
Fenwick	Steven[1]	Wilkins*	Hateley	Lineker	Wallace[1]	[†]Woods 1, Hill 7, Beardsley 10
Butcher	Robson*[2]	Wilkins	Dixon	Beardsley	Waddle	Woods 1, Woodcock 9, J Barnes 10
Butcher	Cowans	Wilkins*	Beardsley	Lineker	Waddle[1]	Hodge 7, Steven 11
Butcher[1]	Wilkins*	T Francis	Hateley	Hodge	Waddle	Reid 7, GA Stevens 10
Butcher	Robson*	Wilkins	Hateley[2]	Beardsley[1]	Waddle	GA Stevens 7, Steven 8, K Dixon 9
Butcher	Hodge	Wilkins*	Hateley[1]	Lineker	Waddle	Woods 1, Reid 8, Beardsley 10, J Barnes 11
Butcher	Robson*	Wilkins	Hateley	Lineker	Waddle	Hodge 7, Beardsley 11
Butcher	Robson*	Wilkins	Hateley	Lineker	Waddle	Horde 7, GA Stevens 9
Butcher	Hodge	Reid	Beardsley	Lineker[3]	Steven	Waddle 9, K Dixon 10
Butcher	Hodge	Reid	Beardsley[1]	Lineker[2]	Steven	GA Stevens 8, Hateley 9
Butcher	Hodge	Reid	Beardsley	Lineker[1]	Steven	Waddle 8, J Barnes 11
Butcher	Steven	Wilkins	K Dixon	Hodge	J Barnes	Cottee 7, Waddle 11
Butcher	Robson*	Hodge	Beardsley	Lineker[2]	Waddle[1]	Cottee 9
Butcher*	Mabbutt[1]	Hodge	Beardsley	Lineker	Waddle	Wilkins 8, Steven 11

● 73

Versus	Venue	Result	1	2	3	4	5
Spain	A	4 – 2	Shilton	Anderson	Sansom	Hoddle	Adams
Northern Ireland	A	2 – 0	Shilton	Anderson	Sansom	Mabbutt	Wright
Turkey	A	0 – 0	Woods	Anderson	Sansom	Hoddle	Adams
Brazil	H	1 – 1	Shilton	Stevens	Pearce	Reid	Adams
Scotland	A	0 – 0	Woods	Stevens	Pearce	Hoddle	Wright

1987–88

Versus	Venue	Result	1	2	3	4	5
West Germany	A	1 – 3	Shilton*	Anderson	Sansom	Hoddle	Adams
Turkey	H	8 – 0	Shilton	Stevens	Sansom	Steven	Adams
Yugoslavia	A	4 – 1	Shilton	Stevens	Sansom	Steven	Adams[1]
Israel	A	0 – 0	Woods	Stevens	Pearce	Webb	Watson
Holland	H	2 – 2	Shilton	Stevens	Sansom	Steven	Adams[1]
Hungary	A	0 – 0	Woods	Anderson	Pearce	Steven	Adams
Scotland	H	1 – 0	Shilton	Stevens	Sansom	Webb	Watson
Colombia	H	1 – 1	Shilton	Anderson	Sansom	McMahon	Wright
Switzerland	A	1 – 0	Shilton	Stevens	Sansom	Webb	Wright
Republic of Ireland	N	0 – 1	Shilton	Stevens	Sansom	Webb	Wright
Holland	N	1 – 3	Shilton	Stevens	Sansom	Hoddle	Wright
USSR	N	1 – 3	Woods	Stevens	Sansom	Hoddle	Watson

1988–89

Versus	Venue	Result	1	2	3	4	5
Denmark	H	1 – 0	Shilton	Stevens	Pearce	Rocastle	Adams
Sweden	H	0 – 0	Shilton	Stevens	Pearce	Webb	Adams
Saudi Arabia	A	1 – 1	Seaman	Sterland	Pearce	M Thomas	Adams[1]
Greece	A	2 – 1	Shilton	Stevens	Pearce	Webb	Walker
Albania	A	2 – 0	Shilton	Stevens	Pearce	Webb	Walker
Albania	H	5 – 0	Shilton	Stevens	Pearce	Webb	Walker
Chile	H	0 – 0	Shilton	Parker	Pearce	Webb	Walker

6	7	8	9	10	11	Substitutes
Butcher	Robson*	Hodge	Beardsley	Lineker[4]	Waddle	Woods 1, Steven 11
Butcher	Robson*[1]	Hodge	Beardsley	Lineker	Waddle[1]	Woods 1
Mabbutt	Robson*	Hodge	Allen	Lineker	Waddle	J Barnes 8, Hateley 9
Butcher	Robson*	J Barnes	Beardsley	Lineker[1]	Waddle	Hateley 10
Butcher	Robson*	Hodge	Beardsley	Hateley	Waddle	
Mabbutt	Reid	J Barnes	Beardsley	Lineker[1]	Waddle	Pearce 3, Webb 4, Hateley 11
Butcher	Robson*[1]	Webb[1]	Beardsley[1]	Lineker[3]	J Barnes[2]	Hoddle 4, Regis 9
Butcher	Robson*[1]	Webb	Beardsley[1]	Lineker	J Barnes[1]	Reid 7, Hoddle 8
Wright	Allen	McMahon	Beardsley*	J Barnes	Waddle	Fenwick 6, Harford 7
Watson	Robson*	Webb	Beardsley	Lineker[1]	J Barnes	Wright 6, Hoddle 8, Hateley 9
Pallister	Robson*	McMahon	Beardsley	Lineker	Waddle	Stevens 3, Hateley 9, Cottee 10, Hoddle 11
Adams	Robson*	Steven	Beardsley[1]	Lineker	J Barnes	Waddle 8
Adams	Robson*	Steven	Beardsley	Lineker[1]	J Barnes	Hoddle 8, Hateley 9,
Adams	Robson*	Steven	Beardsley	Lineker	J Barnes	Woods 1, Watson 7, Reid 7, Waddle 8
Adams	Robson*	Waddle	Beardsley	Lineker	J Barnes	Hoddle 4, Hateley 9
Adams	Robson*[1]	Steven	Beardsley	Lineker	J Barnes	Waddle 8, Hateley 9
Adams[1]	Robson*1	Steven	McMahon	Lineker	J Barnes	Webb 9, Hateley 10
Butcher	Robson*	Webb[1]	Harford	Beardsley	Hodge	Woods 1, Walker 5, Cottee 9, Gascoigne 10
Butcher	Robson*	Beardsley	Waddle	Lineker	J Barnes	Walker 5, Cottee 11
Pallister	Robson*	Rocastle	Beardsley	Lineker	Waddle	Gascoigne 4, A Smith, Marwood 11
Butcher	Robson*[1]	Rocastle	A Smith	Lineker	J Barnes[1]	Beardsley 9
Butcher	Robson*[1]	Rocastle	Waddle	Lineker	J Barnes[1]	Beardsley 9, A Smith 10
Butcher	Robson*[1]	Rocastle	Beardsley[2]	Lineker[1]	Waddle[1]	Parker 2, Gascoigne 8[1]
Butcher	Robson*	Gascoigne	Clough	Fashanu	Waddle	Cottee 10

Versus	Venue	Result	1	2	3	4	5
Scotland	A	2 – 0	Shilton	Stevens	Pearce	Webb	Walker
Poland	H	3 – 0	Shilton	Stevens	Pearce	Webb[1]	Walker
Denmark	A	1 – 1	Shilton	Parker	Pearce	Webb	Walker
1989–90							
Sweden	A	0 – 0	Shilton	Stevens	Pearce	Webb	Walker
Poland	A	0 – 0	Shilton	Stevens	Pearce	McMahon	Walker
Italy	H	0 – 0	Shilton	Stevens	Pearce	McMahon	Walker
Yugoslavia	H	2 – 1	Shilton	Parker	Pearce	M Thomas	Walker
Brazil	H	1 – 0	Shilton	Stevens	Pearce	McMahon	Walker
Czechoslovakia	H	4 – 2	Shilton	Dixon	Pearce[1]	Steven	Walker
Denmark	H	1 – 0	Shilton	Stevens	Pearce	McMahon	Walker
Uruguay	H	1 – 2	Shilton	Parker	Pearce	Hodge	Walker
Tunisia	A	1 – 1	Shilton	Stevens	Pearce	Hodge	Walker
Republic of Ireland	N	1 – 1	Shilton	Stevens	Pearce	Gascoigne	Walker
Holland	N	0 – 0	Shilton	Parker	Pearce	Wright	Walker
Egypt	N	1 – 0	Shilton	Parker	Pearce	Gascoigne	Walker
Belgium	N	1 – 0	Shilton	Parker	Pearce	Wright	Walker
Cameroon	N	3 – 2	Shilton	Parker	Pearce	Wright	Walker
West Germany	N	1 – 1	Shilton	Parker	Pearce	Wright	
Italy	A	1 – 2	Shilton*	Stevens	Dorigo	Parker	Walker
1990–91							
Hungary	H	1 – 0	Woods	Dixon	Pearce	Parker	Walker
Poland	H	2 – 0	Woods	Dixon	Pearce	Parker	Walker
Republic of Ireland	A	1 – 1	Woods	Dixon	Pearce	Adams	Walker
Cameroon	H	2 – 0	Seaman	Dixon	Pearce	Steven	Walker

6	7	8	9	10	11	Substitutes
Butcher	Robson*	Steven	Fashanu	Cottee	Waddle[1]	Bull 9[1], Gascoigne 10
Butcher	Robson*	Waddle	Beardsley	Lineker[1]	J Barnes[1]	Rocastle 8, A Smith 9
Butcher	Robson*	Rocastle	Beardsley	Lineker[1]	J Barnes	Seaman 1, McMahon 4, Bull 9, Waddle 11
Butcher*	Beardsley	McMahon	Waddle	Lineker	J Barnes	Gascoigne 4, Rocastle 11
Butcher	Robson*	Rocastle	Beardsley	Lineker	Waddle	
Butcher	Robson*	Waddle	Beardsley	Lineker	J Barnes	Beasant 1, Winterburn 3, Hodge 4, Phelan 7, Platt 9
Butcher*	Platt	Waddle	Beardsley	Lineker[1]	J Barnes	Woods 1, Gascoigne 9
Butcher	Robson*	Gascoigne[1]	Bull[2]	Lineker	Hodge	Seaman 1, Dorigo 3, Wright 5, McMahon 7
Butcher*	Hodge	Gascoigne	Waddle	Lineker[1]	J Barnes	Woods 1, Dorigo 3, Platt 4, Rocastle 9, Bull 10
Butcher	Robson*	Gascoigne	Waddle	Lineker	J Barnes[1]	Beardsley 4, Bull 10
Butcher	Robson*	Waddle	Gascoigne	Lineker	J Barnes	Beardsley 4, Wright 6, Platt 8, Bull 10[1]
Butcher	Waddle	Robson*	Beardsley	Lineker[1]	J Barnes	McMahon 9, Bull 10
Butcher	Robson*	Waddle	Gascoigne	Lineker	J Barnes	Platt 7, Bull 8
Wright[1]	McMahon	Waddle	Bull	Lineker	J Barnes	Platt 8, Beardsley 9
Butcher*	McMahon	Waddle	Gascoigne	Lineker	J Barnes	Platt 7[1], Bull 11
Butcher*	Platt[1]	Waddle	Gascoigne	Lineker[2]	J Barnes	Steven 6, Beardsley 11
Butcher*	Platt	Waddle	Gascoigne	Lineker[1]	Beardsley	Steven 6
Wright	Platt[1]	Steven	McMahon	Lineker	Beardsley	Waddle 6, Webb
Wright	Platt	Gascoigne	Bull	Lineker*[1]	J Barnes	Dorigo 3, Waddle 9
Wright	Platt	Gascoigne	Bull	Lineker*[1]	J Barnes	Beardsley 9[1], Waddle 10
Wright	Platt[1]	Cowans	Beardsley	Lineker*	McMahon	
Wright	Robson	Gascoigne	I Wright	Lineker*[2]	J Barnes	Pallister 7, Hodge 8

Versus	Venue	Result	1	2	3	4	5
Republic of Ireland	H	1 – 1	Seaman	Dixon[1]	Pearce	Adams	Walker
Turkey	A	1 – 0	Seaman	Dixon	Pearce	Wise[1]	Walker
USSR	H	3 – 1	Woods	Stevens	Dorigo	Wise	Parker
Argentina	H	2 – 2	Seaman	Dixon	Pearce	Batty	Walker
Australia	A	1 – 0	Woods	Parker	Pearce	Batty	Walker
New Zealand	A	1 – 0	Woods	Parker	Pearce	Batty	Walker
New Zealand	A	2 – 0	Woods	Charles	Pearce*[1]	Wise	Walker
Malaysia	A	4 – 2	Woods	Charles	Pearce	Batty	Walker
1991 – 92							
Germany	H	0 – 1	Woods	Dixon	Dorigo	Batty	Pallister
Turkey	H	1 – 0	Woods	Dixon	Pearce	Batty	Walker
Poland	A	1 – 1	Woods	Dixon	Pearce	Gray	Walker
France	H	2 – 0	Woods	R Jones	Pearce*	Keown	Walker
Czechoslovakia	A	2 – 2	Seaman	Keown[1]	Pearce*	Rocastle	Walker
CIS	A	2 – 2	Woods	Stevens	Sinton	Palmer	Walker
Hungary	A	1 – 0	Martyn	Stevens	Dorigo	Curle	Walker
Brazil	H	1 – 1	Woods	Stevens	Dorigo	Palmer	Walker
Finland	A	2 – 1	Woods	Stevens	Pearce	Keown	Walker
Denmark	N	0 – 0	Woods	Curle	Pearce	Palmer	Walker
France	N	0 – 0	Woods	Batty	Pearce	Palmer	Walker
Sweden	A	1 – 2	Woods	Batty	Pearce	Keown	Walker
1992 – 93							
Spain	A	0 – 1	Woods	Dixon	Pearce*	Ince	Walker
Norway	H	1 – 1	Woods	Dixon	Pearce*	Batty	Walker
Turkey	H	4 – 0	Woods	Dixon	Pearce*[1]	Palmer	Walker
San Marino	H	6 – 0	Woods	Dixon	Dorigo	Palmer[1]	Walker
Turkey	A	2 – 0	Woods	Dixon	Sinton	Palmer	Walker

6	7	8	9	10	11	*Substitutes*
Wright	Robson	Platt	Beardsley	Lineker*	J Barnes	Sharpe 4, I Wright 10
Pallister	Platt	G Thomas	A Smith	Lineker*	J Barnes	Hodge 8
Wright*	Platt[2]	G Thomas	A Smith[1]	I Wright	J Barnes	Batty 4, Beardsley 10
Wright	Platt[1]	G Thomas	A Smith	Lineker*[1]	J Barnes	Clough 11
Wright	Platt	G Thomas	Clough	Lineker*	Hirst	[†]Wise 10, Salako 11
Barrett	Platt	G Thomas	Wise	Lineker*[1]	Walters	Deane 4, Salako 11
Wright	Platt	G Thomas	Deane	I Wright	Salako	Hirst 9[1]
Wright	Platt	G Thomas	Clough	Lineker*[4]	Salako	
Parker	Platt	Steven	A Smith	Lineker*	Salako	Stewart 8, Merson 11
Mabbutt	Robson	Platt	A Smith[1]	Lineker*	Waddle	
Mabbutt	Platt	G Thomas	Rocastle	Lineker*[1]	Sinton	A Smith 4, Daley 11
Wright	Webb	G Thomas	Clough	Shearer[1]	Hirst	Lineker 11[1]
Mabbutt	Platt	Merson[1]	Clough	Hateley	J Barnes	Dixon 4, Lineker 6 Stewart 9, Dorigo 11
Keown	Platt	Steven[1]	Shearer	Lineker*[1]	Daley	Martyn 1, Curle 3, Stewart 8, Clough 9
Keown	Webb[1]	Palmer	Merson	Lineker*	Daley	Seaman 1, Sinton 4, Batty 7, A Smith 9, I Wright 10
Keown	Daley	Steven	Platt[1]	Lineker*	Sinton	Pearce 3, Merson 7, Webb 8, Rocastle 11
Wright	Platt[2]	Steven	Webb	Lineker	J Barnes	Palmer 2, Daley 8, Merson 11
Keown	Platt	Steven	A Smith	Lineker*	Merson	Daley 2, Webb 11
Keown	Platt	Steven	Shearer	Lineker*	Palmer	
Palmer	Platt[1]	Webb	Sinton	Lineker*	Daley	Merson 9, A Smith 10
Wright	White	Platt	Clough	Shearer	Sinton	Beardsley 2, Palmer 2, Merson 7, Deane 11
Adams	Platt[1]	Gascoigne	Shearer	I Wright	Ince	
Adams	Platt	Gascoigne[2]	Shearer[1]	I Wright	Ince	
Adams	Platt*[4]	Gascoigne	Ferdinand[1]	J Barnes	Batty	
Adams	Platt*[1]	Gascoigne[1]	J Barnes	I Wright	Ince	Clough 2, Sharpe 10

Versus	*Venue*	*Result*	*1*	*2*	*3*	*4*	*5*
Holland	H	2 – 2	Woods	Dixon	Keown	Palmer	Walker
Poland	A	1 – 1	Woods	Beardsley	Dorigo	Palmer	Walker
Norway	A	0 – 2	Woods	Dixon	Pallister	Palmer	Walker
United States	A	0 – 2	Woods	Dixon	Dorigo	Palmer	Pallister
Brazil	N	1 – 1	Flowers	Barrett	Dorigo	Walker	Pallister
Germany	N	1 – 2	Martyn	Barrett	Sinton	Walker	Pallister
1993–94							
Poland	H	3 – 0	Seaman	Jones	Pearce*[1]	Ince	Pallister
Holland	A	0 – 2	Seaman	Parker	Dorigo	Ince	Pallister
San Marino	A	7 – 1	Seaman	Dixon	Pearce*	Ince[2]	Pallister
Denmark	H	1 – 0	Seaman	Parker	Le Saux	Ince	Adams
Greece	H	5 – 0	Flowers	Jones	Le Saux	Richardson	Bould
Norway	H	0 – 0	Seaman	Jones	Le Saux	Ince	Bould
1994–95							
United States	H	2 – 0	Seaman	Jones	Le Saux	Vehison	Adams
Romania	H	1 – 1	Seaman	Jones	Le Saux	Ince	Adams*
Nigeria	H	1 – 0	Flowers	Jones	Le Saux	Lee	Howey
Rep. of Ireland	A	0 – 1[§§]	Seaman	Barton	Le Saux	Ince	Adams
Uruguay	H	0 – 0	Flowers	Jones	Le Saux	Venison	Adams
Japan	H	2 – 1	Flowers	Neville	Pearce	Batty	Scales
Sweden	H	3 – 3	Flowers	Barton	Le Saux	Barnes	Cooper
Brazil	H	1 – 3	Flowers	Neville	Pearce	Batty	Cooper
1995–96							
Colombia	H	0 – 0	Seaman	G Neville	Le Saux	Redknapp	Adams*
Norway	A	0 – 0	Seaman	G Neville	Pearce	Redknapp	Adams*

[§§]*Match abandoned after 27 minutes*

6	7	8	9	10	11	*Substitutes*
Adams	Platt*[1]	Gascoigne	Ferdinand	J Barnes[1]	Ince	Merson 8
Adams	Platt*	Gascoigne	Sheringham	J Barnes	Ince	I Wright 4[1], Clough 8
Adams	Platt*	Gascoigne	Ferdinand	Sheringham	Sharpe	Clough 5, I Wright 10
Batty	Ince*	Clough	Sharpe	Ferdinand	J Barnes	Walker 4, I Wright 10
Batty	Ince*	Clough	I Wright	Sinton	Sharpe	Platt 6[1], Palmer 7, Merson 8
Ince	Platt*[1]	Clough	Sharpe	J Barnes	Merson	Keown 5, I Wright 8, Winterburn 9
Adams	Platt	Gascoigne[1]	Ferdinand[1]	Wright	Sharpe	
Adams	Platt*	Palmer	Shearer	Merson	Sharpe	Sinton 8, I Wright 10
Walker	Platt	Ripley	Ferdinand[1]	I Wright[4]	Sinton	
Pallister	Platt*[1]	Gascoigne	Shearer	Beardsley	Anderton	Batty 4, Le Tissier 8
Adams	Platt*[2]	Merson	Shearer[1]	Beardsley[1]	Anderton[1]	Pearce 2, I Wright 10, Le Tissier 11
Adams	Platt*	Wise	Shearer	Beardsley	Anderton	Le Tissier 4, Wright 11
Pallister	Platt*	Barnes	Shearer[2]	Sheringham	Anderton	Ferdinand 9, Wright 10
Pallister	Lee[1]	Wright	Shearer	Barnes	Le Tissier	Pearce 2, Wise 7, Sheringham 8
Ruddock	Platt*[1]	Beardsley	Shearer	Barnes	Wise	McManaman 4, Le Tissier 8, Sheringham 9
Pallister	Platt*	Beardsley	Shearer	Le Tissier	Anderton	
Pallister	Platt*	Beardsley	Sheringham	Barnes	Anderton	McManaman 3, Barmby 8, Cole 9
Unsworth	Platt*[1]	Beardsley	Shearer	Collymore	Anderton[1]	McManaman 4, Gascoigne 8, Sheringham 10
Pallister	Platt*[1]	Beardsley	Shearer	Sheringham[1]	Anderton[1]	Gascoigne 4, Scales 6, Barmby 8
Scales	Platt*	Le Saux[1]	Shearer	Sheringham	Anderton	Gascoigne 4, Barton 6, Collymore 10
Howey	Barmby	Gascoigne	Shearer	McManaman	Wise	Lee 4, Barnes 8, Sheringham 9
Pallister	Barmby	Lee	Shearer	McManaman	Wise	Sheringham 7, Stone 11

Versus	Venue	Result	1	2	3	4	5
Switzerland	H	3 – 1	Seaman	G Neville	Pearce†	Redknapp	Adams*
Portugal	H	1 – 1	Seaman	G Neville	Pearce	Wise	Adams*
Bulgaria	H	1 – 0	Seaman	G Neville	Pearce*	Ince	Southgate
Croatia	H	0 – 0	Seaman	G Neville	Pearce	Ince	Wright
Hungary	H	3 – 0	Seaman	G Neville	Pearce	Ince	Wright
China	A	3 – 0	Flowers	G Neville	P Neville	Redknapp	Adams*
Switzerland	H	1 – 1	Seaman	G Neville	Pearce	Ince	Adams*
Scotland	H	2 – 0	Seaman	G Neville	Pearce	Ince	Adams*
Holland	H	4 – 1	Seaman	G Neville	Pearce	Ince	Adams*
Spain	H	0 – 0¶	Seaman	G Neville	Pearce	McManaman	Adams*
Germany	H	1 – 1‖	Seaman	McManaman	Pearce	Ince	Adams
1996–97							
Moldova	A	3 – 0	Seaman	G Neville	Pearce	Ince	Pallister
Poland	H	2 – 1	Seaman	G Neville	Pearce	Ince	Southgate
Georgia	A	2 – 0	Seaman	Campbell	Hinchcliffe	Ince	Adams*
Italy	H	0 – 1	Walker	G Neville	Pearce	Ince	Campbell
Mexico	H	2 – 0	James	Keown	Pearce	Batty	Southgate
Georgia	H	2 – 0	Seaman	G Neville	Campbell	Batty	Adams
South Africa	H	2 – 1	Martyn	P Neville	Pearce*	Keown	Southgate
Poland	A	2 – 0	Seaman	G Neville	Campbell	Ince	Southgate
Italy	N	2 – 0	Flowers	P Neville	Pearce	Keown	Southgate

¶*England won 4–2 on penalties*   ‖*Germany won 6–5 on penalties*

6	7	8	9	10	11	Substitutes
Pallister	Lee	Gascoigne	Shearer	Sheringham[1]	McManaman	Stone 4[1]
Howey	Barmby	Gascoigne	Shearer	Ferdinand	Stone[1]	Le Saux 3, Southgate 4, McManaman 7, Beardsley 10
Howey	McManaman	Gascoigne	Ferdinand[1]	Sheringham	Stone	Lee 8, Fowler 9, Platt 10
McManaman	Platt*	Gascoigne	Fowler	Sheringham	Stone	Walker 1, Campbell 4, Southgate 5, Wise 7, Shearer 8
Lee	Platt*[1]	Wilcox	Ferdinand	Sheringham	Anderton[2]	
Southgate	Barmby[2]	Gascoigne[1]	Shearer	McManaman	Anderton	Walker 1, Ehiogu 5, Beardsley 7, Fowler 9, Stone 10
Southgate	McManaman	Gascoigne	Shearer[1]	Sheringham	Anderton	Stone 7, Platt 8, Barmby 10
Southgate	McManaman	Gascoigne	Shearer[1]	Sheringham	Anderton	Redknapp 3, Campbell 3, Stone 4
Southgate	McManaman	Gascoigne	Shearer[1]	Sheringham	Anderton	Platt 4, Fowler 9, Barmby 10
Southgate	Platt	Gascoigne	Shearer	Sheringham	Anderton	Barmby 4, Stone 10, Fowler 11
Southgate	Platt	Gascoigne	Shearer[1]	Anderton		
Southgate	Beckham	Gascoigne[1]	Shearer*[1]	Barmby[1]	Hinchcliffe	Batty 8, Le Tissier 10
Hinchcliffe	Beckham	Gascoigne	Shearer*[2]	Ferdinand	McManaman	Pallister 5
Southgate	Beckham	Gascoigne	Ferdinand[1]	Sheringham[1]	Batty	Wright 9
Le Saux	Beckham	Batty	Shearer*	Le Tissier	McManaman	Wright 8, Ferdinand 10, Merson 11
Le Saux	Lee	Ince*	Fowler[1]	Sheringham[1]	McManaman	Redknapp 4, Wright 10, Butt 11
Le Saux	Beckham	Ince	Shearer*[1]	Sheringham[1]	Lee	Southgate 5, Redknapp 8
Le Saux	Redknapp	Gascoigne	Wright[1]	Sheringham	Lee[1]	Beckham 6, Batty 7, Campbell 8, Scholes 10, Butt 11
Le Saux	Beckham	Gascoigne	Shearer*[1]	Sheringham[1]	Lee	P Neville 7, Batty 8
Le Saux	Beckham	Ince*	Wright[1]	Sheringham	Scholes[1]	G Neville 6, Cole 9, Gascoigne 10

Versus	Venue	Result	1	2	3	4	5
France	A	1–0	Seaman	G Neville	Campbell	P Neville	Southgate
Brazil	N	0–1	Seaman	Keown	Campbell	Ince	Southgate

1997–98

Versus	Venue	Result	1	2	3	4	5
Moldova	H	4–0	Seaman*	G. Neville	P. Neville	Batty	Campbell
Italy	A	0–0	Seaman	Campbell	Le Saux	Ince	Adams*
Cameroon	H	2–0	Martyn	Campbell	P. Neville	Ince*	Southgate
Chile	H	0–2	Martyn	G. Neville	Campbell	Batty	Adams*
Switzerland	A	1–1	Flowers	Keown	Hinchcliffe	Ince	Southgate
Portugal	H	3–0	Seaman	G. Neville	Le Saux	Ince	Adams
Saudi Arabia	H	0–0	Seaman	G. Neville	Hinchcliffe	Batty	Adams
Morocco	A	1–0	Flowers	Keown	Le Saux	Ince*	Campbell
Belgium†	N	0–0	Martyn	G. Neville	P. Neville	Butt	Campbell*
Tunisia	N	2–0	Seaman	Campbell	Le Saux	Ince	Adams
Romania	N	1–2	Seaman	G. Neville	Le Saux	Ince	Adams
Colombia	N	2–0	Seaman	G. Neville	Le Saux	Ince	Adams
Argentina*	N	2–2	Seaman	G. Neville	Le Saux	Ince	Adams

6	7	8	9	10	11	Substitutes
Le Saux	Beckham	Gascoigne	Shearer*[1]	Wright	Batty	Lee 7, Sheringham 10, Ince 11
Le Saux	P Neville	Gascoigne	Shearer*	Sheringham	Scholes	G Neville 2, Wright 20, Lee 11
Southgate	Beckham	Gascoigne[1]	L. Ferdinand	Wright[2]	Scholes[1]	Ripley 7, Butt 7, Collymore 9
Southgate	Beckham	Gascoigne	Wright	Sheringham	Batty	Butt 8
Hinchcliffe	Beckham	Gascoigne	Fowler[1]	Scholes[1]	McManaman	R. Ferdinand 5, Lee 8, Sutton 10
P. Neville	Lee	Butt	Dublin	Sheringham	Owen	Ince 4, Le Saux 6, Shearer 10
R. Ferdinand	McManaman	Merson[1]	Shearer*	Owen	Lee	Batty 8, Sheringham 10
Campbell	Beckham	Batty	Shearer*[2]	Sheringham[1]	Scholes	P. Neville 2, Merson 7, Owen 10
Southgate	Beckham	Anderton	Shearer*	Sheringham	Scholes	P. Neville 3, Gascoigne 7, L. Ferdinand 9, Wright 10
Southgate	Anderton	Gascoigne	Dublin	Wright	McManaman	L. Ferdinand 9, Owen 10[1]
Keown	Lee	Gascoigne	L. Ferdinand	Merson	Le Saux	R.Ferdinand 2, Owen 3, Dublin 5, Beckham 8
Southgate	Anderton	Batty	Shearer*[1]	Sheringham	Scholes	Owen 10
Campbell	Anderton	Batty	Shearer*	Sheringham	Scholes	Beckham 4, Owen 10[1]
Campbell	Beckham[1]	Anderton[1]	Shearer*	Owen	Scholes	Batty 4, Lee 8, McManaman 11
Campbell	Beckham	Anderton	Shearer*[1]	Owen[1]	Scholes	Southgate 3, Batty 8, Merson 11

[†]Belgium won 4–3 on penalties
[*]Argentina won 4–3 on penalties

21 ● ENGLAND'S INTERNATIONAL MATCHES 1872–1998

WCQ	World Cup Qualifer			
WCF	World Cup Finals			
ECQ	European Championship Qualifier			
ECF	European Championship Finals			
RC	Rous Cup			
BJT	Brazilian Jubilee Tournament			
USBT	US Bicentennial Tournament			
USC	US Cup			
TDF	Tournoi de France			
KHC	King Hassan II Cup			

v Albania

| 1989 | 8/3 | Tirana | W | 2 – 0 WCO |
| 1989 | 26/4 | Wembley | W | 5 – 0 WCQ |

v Argentina

1951	9/5	Wembley	W	2 – 1
1953	17/5	Buenos Aires	D	0 – 0 *
1961	2/6	Rancagua	W	3 – 1 WCF
1964	6/6	Rio de Janeiro	L	0 – 1 BJT
1966	23/7	Wembley	W	1 – 0 WCF
1974	22/5	Wembley	D	2 – 2
1977	12/6	Buenos Aires	D	1 – 1
1980	13/5	Wembley	W	3 – 1
1986	22/6	Mexico City	L	1 – 2 WCF
1991	25/5	Wembley	D	2 – 2
1998	30/6	St Etienne	D	2 – 2⁺ WCF

P 11, W 4, D 5, L 2, F 17, A 13

*Abandoned after 21 minutes
⁺After extra time (England lost 4–3 on penalties)

v Australia

1980	31/5	Sydney	W	2 – 1
1983	12/6	Sydney	D	0 – 0
1983	15/6	Brisbane	W	1 – 0
1983	19/6	Melbourne	D	1 – 1
1991	1/6	Sydney	W	1 – 0

P 5, W 4, D 2, L 0, F 5, A 2

v Austria

1908	6/6	Vienna	W	6 – 1
1908	8/6	Vienna	W	11 – 1
1909	1/6	Vienna	W	8 – 1
1930	14/5	Vienna	D	0 – 0
1932	7/12	Chelsea	W	4 – 3
1936	6/5	Vienna	L	1 – 2
1951	28/11	Wembley	D	2 – 2
1952	25/5	Vienna	W	3 – 2
1958	15/6	Boras	D	2 – 2 WCF

1961	27/5	Vienna	L	1 – 3
1962	4/4	Wembley	W	3 – 1
1965	20/10	Wembley	L	2 – 3
1967	27/5	Vienna	W	1 – 0
1973	26/9	Wembley	W	7 – 0
1979	13/6	Vienna	L	3 – 4

P 15, W 8, D 3, L 4, F 54, A 25

v Belgium

1921	21/5	Brussels	W	2 – 0
1923	19/3	Arsenal	W	6 – 1
1923	1/11	Antwerp	D	2 – 2
1924	8/12	West Bromwich	W	4 – 0
1926	24/5	Antwerp	W	5 – 3
1927	11/5	Brussels	W	5 – 1
1928	19/5	Antwerp	W	3 – 1
1929	11/5	Brussels	W	5 – 1
1931	16/5	Brussels	W	4 – 1
1936	9/5	Brussels	L	2 – 3
1947	21/9	Brussels	W	5 – 2
1950	18/5	Brussels	W	4 – 1
1952	26/11	Wembley	W	5 – 0
1954	17/6	Basle	D	4 – 4 WCE
1964	21/10	Wembley	D	2 – 2
1970	25/2	Brussels	W	3 – 1
1980	12/6	Turin	D	1 – 1 ECF
1990	26/6	Bologna	W	1 – 0 WCF
1998	29/5	Casablanca	D	0 – 0*KHC

P 19, W 13, D 5, L 1, F 67, A 24

*England lost 4–3 on penalties

v Bohemia

| 1908 | 13/6 | Prague | W | 4 – 0 |

P 1, W 1, D 0, L 0, F 4, A 0

v Brazil

1956	9/5	Wembley	W	4 – 2
1958	11/6	Gothenburg	D	0 – 0 WCF
1959	13/5	Rio de Janeiro	L	0 – 2
1962	10/6	Vina del Mar	L	1 – 3 WCF
1963	8/5	Wembley	D	1 – 1
1964	30/5	Rio de Janeiro	L	1 – 5 BJT
1969	12/6	Rio de Janeiro	L	1 – 2
1970	7/6	Guadalajara	L	0 – 1 WCF
1976	23/5	Los Angeles	L	0 – 1 USBT
1977	8/6	Rio de Janeiro	D	0 – 0
1978	19/4	Wembley	D	1 – 1
1981	12/5	Wembley	L	0 – 1
1984	10/6	Rio de Janeiro	W	2 – 0
1987	19/5	Wembley	D	1 – 1 RC
1990	28/3	Wembley	W	1 – 0

1992	17/5	Wembley	D	1 – 1
1993	13/6	Washington	D	1 – 1 USC
1995	11/6	Wembley	L	1 – 3
1997	10/6	Paris	L	0 – 1 TDF

P 19, W 3, D 7, L 9, F 16, A 26

v Bulgaria

1962	7/6	Rancagua	D	0 – 0 WCF
1968	11/12	Wembley	D	1 – 1
1974	1/6	Sofia	W	1 – 0
1979	6/6	Sofia	W	3 – 0 ECQ
1979	22/11	Wembley	W	2 – 0 ECQ
1996	27/3	Wembley	W	1 – 0

P 6, W 4, D 2, L 0, F 8, A 1

v Cameroon

1990	1/7	Naples	W	3 – 2 WCF
1991	6/2	Wembley	W	2 – 0
1997	15/11	Wembley	W	2 – 0

P 3, W 3, D 0, L 0, F 7, A 2

v Canada

| 1986 | 24/5 | Vancouver | w | 1 – 0 |

P 1, W 1, D 0, L 0, F 1, A 0

v Chile

1950	25/6	Rio de Janeiro	W	2 – 0 WCF
1953	24/5	Santiago	W	2 – 1
1984	17/6	Santiago	D	0 – 0
1989	23/5	Wembley	D	0 – 0 RC
1998	11/2	Wembley	L	0 – 2

P 5, W 2, D 2, L 1, F 4, A 3

v China

| 1996 | 23/5 | Beijing | W | 3 – 0 |

P 1, W 1, D 0, L 0, F 3, A 0

v CIS

| 1992 | 29/4 | Moscow | W | 2 – 2 |

P 1, W 0, D 1, L 0, F 2, A 2

v Colombia

1970	20/5	Bogota	W	4 – 0
1988	24/5	Wembley	D	1 – 1 RC
1995	6/9	Wembley	D	0 – 0
1998	26/6	Lens	W	2 – 0 WCF

P 4, W 2, D 2, L 0, F 7, A 1

v Croatia

| 1996 | 24/4 | Wembley | D | 0 – 0 |

P 1, W 0, D 1, L 0, F 0, A 0

v Cyprus

| 1975 | 16/4 | Wembley | W | 5 – 0 ECQ |
| 1975 | 11/5 | Limassol | W | 1 – 0 ECQ |

P 2, W 2, D 0, L 0, F 6, A 0

v Czechoslovakia

1934	16/5	Prague	L	1 – 2
1937	1/12	Tottenham	W	5 – 4
1963	29/5	Bratislava	W	4 – 2
1966	2/11	Wembley	D	0 – 0
1970	11/6	Guadalajara	W	1 – 0 WCF
1973	27/5	Prague	D	1 – 1
1974	30/10	Wembley	W	3 – 0 ECQ
1975	30/10	Bratislava	L	1 – 2 ECQ
1978	29/11	Wembley	W	1 – 0
1982	20/6	Bilbao	W	2 – 0 WCF
1990	25/4	Wembley	W	4 – 2
1992	25/3	Prague	D	2 – 2

P 12, W 7, D 3, L 2, F 25, A 15

v Denmark

1948	26/9	Copenhagen	D	0 – 0
1955	2/10	Copenhagen	W	5 – 1
1956	5/12	Wolverhampton	W	5 – 2 WCQ
1957	15/5	Copenhagen	W	4 – 1 WCQ
1966	3/7	Copenhagen	W	2 – 0
1978	20/9	Copenhagen	W	4 – 3 ECQ
1979	12/9	Wembley	W	1 – 0 ECQ
1982	22/9	Copenhagen	D	2 – 2 ECQ
1983	21/9	Wembley	L	0 – 1 ECQ
1988	14/9	Wembley	W	1 – 0
1989	7/6	Copenhagen	D	1 – 1
1990	15/5	Wembley	W	1 – 0
1992	11/6	Malmö	D	0 – 0 ECF
1994	9/3	Wembley	W	1 – 0

P 14, W 9, D 4, L 1, F 27, A 11

v Ecuador

| 1970 | 24/5 | Quito | W | 2 – 0 |

P 1, W 1, D 0, L 0, F 2, A 0

v Egypt

| 1986 | 29/1 | Cairo | W | 4 – 0 |
| 1990 | 21/6 | Cagliari | W | 1 – 0 WCF |

P 2, W 2, D 0, L 0, F 5, A 0

v FIFA

| 1953 | 21/10 | Wembley | D | 4 – 4 |

P 1, W 0, D 1, L 0, F 4, A 4

v Finland

| 1937 | 20/5 | Helsinki | W | 8 – 0 |
| 1956 | 20/5 | Helsinki | W | 5 – 1 |

● 87

1966	26/6	Helsinki	W	3 – 0	
1976	13/6	Helsinki	W	4 – 1	WCQ
1976	13/10	Wembley	W	2 – 1	WCQ
1982	3/6	Helsinki	W	4 – 1	
1984	17/10	Wembley	W	5 – 0	WCQ
1985	22/5	Helsinki	D	1 – 1	WCQ
1992	3/6	Helsinki	W	2 – 1	

P 9, W 8, D 1, L 0, F 34, A 6

v France

1923	10/5	Paris	W	4 – 1	
1924	17/5	Paris	W	3 – 1	
1925	21/5	Paris	W	3 – 2	
1927	26/5	Paris	W	6 – 0	
1928	17/5	Paris	W	5 – 1	
1929	9/5	Paris	W	4 – 1	
1931	14/5	Paris	L	2 – 5	
1933	6/12	Tottenham	W	4 – 1	
1938	26/5	Paris	W	4 – 2	
1947	3/5	Arsenal	W	3 – 0	
1949	22/5	Paris	W	3 – 1	
1951	3/10	Arsenal	D	2 – 2	
1955	15/5	Paris	L	0 – 1	
1957	27/11	Wembley	W	4 – 0	
1962	3/10	Sheffield	D	1 – 1	ECQ
1963	27/2	Paris	L	2 – 5	ECQ
1966	20/7	Wembley	W	2 – 0	WCF
1969	12/3	Wembley	W	5 – 0	
1982	16/6	Bilbao	W	3 – 1	WCF
1984	29/2	Paris	L	0 – 2	
1992	19/2	Wembley	W	2 – 0	
1992	14/6	Malmö	D	0 – 0	ECF
1997	7/6	Montpellier	W	1 – 0	TDF

P 24, W 16, D 4, L 4, F 63, A 27

v Georgia

1996	9/11	Tbilisi	W	2 – 0	WCQ
1997	30/4	Wembley	W	2 – 0	WCQ

P 2, W 2, D 0, L 0, F 4, A 0

v East Germany

1963	2/6	Leipzig	W	2 – 1
1970	25/11	Wembley	W	3 – 1
1974	29/5	Leipzig	D	1 – 1
1984	12/9	Wembley	W	1 – 0

P 4, W 3, D 1, L 0, F 7, A 3

v West Germany

1930	10/5	Berlin	D	3 – 3 †	
1935	4/12	Tottenham	W	3 – 0 †	
1938	14/5	Berlin	W	6 – 3 †	
1954	1/12	Wembley	W	3 – 1	
1956	26/5	Berlin	W	3 – 1	
1965	12/5	Nuremberg	W	1 – 0	
1966	23/2	Wembley	W	1 – 0	WCF
1966	30/7	Wembley	W	4 – 2	
1968	1/6	Hanover	L	0 – 1	
1970	14/6	Leon	L	2 – 3	WCF
1972	29/4	Wembley	L	1 – 3	ECQ
1972	13/5	Berlin	D	0 – 0	ECQ
1975	12/3	Wembley	W	2 – 0	
1978	22/2	Munich	L	1 – 2	
1982	29/6	Madrid	D	0 – 0	ECF
1982	13/10	Wembley	L	1 – 2	
1985	12/6	Mexico City	W	3 – 0	
1987	9/9	Düsseldorf	L	1 – 3	
1990	4/7	Turin	D	1 – 1*	WCF

P 19, W 9, D 4, L 6, F 36, A 25

* *After extra time (England lost 4–3 on penalties)*
† *as Germany*

v Germany

1991	11/9	Wembley	L	0 – 1	
1993	19/6	Detroit	L	1 – 2	USC
1996	26/6	Wembley	D	1 – 1	*ECF

P 3, W 0, D 1, L 2, F 2, A 4

* *After extra time (England lost 6–5 on penalties)*

v Greece

1971	21/4	Wembley	W	3 – 0	ECQ
1971	1/12	Athens	W	2 – 0	ECQ
1982	17/11	Salonika	W	3 – 0	ECQ
1983	30/3	Wembley	D	0 – 0	ECQ
1989	8/2	Athens	W	2 – 1	
1994	17/5	Wembley	W	5 – 0	

P 6, W 5, D 1, L 0, F 15, A 1

v Hungary

1935	18/5	Amsterdam	W	1 – 0	
1946	27/11	Huddersfield	W	8 – 2	
1964	9/12	Amsterdam	D	1 – 1	
1969	5/11	Amsterdam	W	1 – 0	
1970	14/1	Wembley	D	0 – 0	
1977	9/2	Wembley	L	0 – 2	
1982	25/5	Wembley	W	2 – 0	
1988	23/3	Wembley	D	2 – 2	
1988	15/6	Düsseldorf	L	1 – 3	ECF
1990	16/6	Cagliari	D	0 – 0	WCF
1993	28/4	Wembley	D	2 – 2	WCQ
1993	13/10	Rotterdam	L	0 – 2	WCQ
1996	18/6	Wembley	W	4 – 1	ECF

P 13, W 5, D 5, L 3, F 22, A 15

v Hungary

1908	10/6	Budapest	W	7 – 0
1909	29/5	Budapest	W	4 – 2
1909	31/5	Budapest	W	8 – 2
1934	10/5	Budapest	L	1 – 2
1936	2/12	Arsenal	W	6 – 2
1953	25/11	Wembley	L	3 – 6

1954	23/5	Budapest	L	1 – 7	
1960	22/5	Budapest	L	0 – 2	
1962	31/5	Rancagua	L	1 – 2	WCF
1965	5/5	Wembley	W	1 – 0	
1978	24/5	Wembley	W	4 – 1	
1981	6/6	Budapest	W	3 – 1	WCQ
1981	18/11	Wembley	W	1 – 0	WCQ
1983	27/4	Wembley	W	2 – 0	ECQ
1983	12/10	Budapest	W	3 – 0	ECQ
1988	27/4	Budapest	D	0 – 0	
1990	12/9	Wembley	W	1 – 0	
1992	12/5	Budapest	W	1 – 0	
1996	18/5	Wembley	W	3 – 0	

P 19, W 13, D 1, L 5, F 50, A 27

v Iceland

1982	2/6	Reykjavik	D	1 – 1

P 1, W 0, D 1, L 0, F 1, A 1

v Ireland

1882	18/2	Belfast	W	13 – 0	
1883	24/2	Liverpool	W	7 – 0	
1884	23/2	Belfast	2	8 – 1	
1885	28/2	Manchester	W	4 – 0	
1886	13/3	Belfast	W	6 – 1	
1887	5/2	Sheffield	W	7 – 0	
1888	31/3	Belfast	W	5 – 1	
1889	2/3	Everton	W	6 – 1	
1890	15/3	Belfast	W	9 – 1	
1891	7/3	Wolverhampton	W	6 – 1	
1892	5/3	Belfast	W	2 – 0	
1893	25/2	Birmingham	W	6 – 1	
1894	3/3	Belfast	D	2 – 2	
1895	9/3	Derby	W	9 – 0	
1896	7/3	Belfast	W	2 – 0	
1897	20/2	Nottingham	W	6 – 0	
1898	5/3	Belfast	W	3 – 2	
1899	18/2	Sunderland	W	13 – 2	
1900	17/3	Dublin	W	2 – 0	
1901	9/3	Southampton	W	3 – 0	
1902	22/3	Belfast	W	1 – 0	
1903	14/2	Wolverhampton	W	4 – 0	
1904	12/3	Belfast	W	3 – 1	
1905	25/2	Middlesbrough	D	1 – 1	
1906	17/2	Belfast	W	5 – 0	
1907	16/2	Everton	W	1 – 0	
1908	15/2	Belfast	W	3 – 1	
1909	13/2	Bradford	W	4 – 0	
1910	12/3	Belfast	D	1 – 1	
1911	11/2	Derby	W	2 – 1	
1912	10/2	Dublin	W	6 – 1	
1913	15/2	Belfast	L	1 – 2	
1914	14/2	Middlesbrough	L	0 – 3	
1919	25/10	Belfast	D	1 – 1	
1920	23/10	Sunderland	W	2 – 0	
1921	22/10	Belfast	D	1 – 1	
1922	21/10	West Bromwich	W	2 – 0	
1923	20/10	Belfast	L	1 – 2	
1924	22/10	Everton	W	3 – 1	
1925	24/10	Belfast	D	0 – 0	
1926	20/10	Liverpool	D	3 – 3	
1927	22/10	Belfast	L	0 – 2	
1928	22/10	Everton	W	2 – 1	
1929	19/10	Belfast	W	3 – 0	
1930	20/10	Sheffield	W	5 – 1	
1931	17/10	Belfast	W	6 – 2	
1932	17/10	Blackpool	W	1 – 0	
1933	14/10	Belfast	W	3 – 0	
1935	6/2	Everton	W	2 – 1	
1935	19/10	Belfast	W	3 – 1	
1936	18/11	Stoke	W	3 – 1	
1937	23/10	Belfast	W	5 – 1	
1938	16/11	Manchester	W	7 – 0	
1946	28/9	Belfast	W	7 – 2	
1947	5/11	Everton	D	2 – 2	
1948	9/10	Belfast	W	6 – 2	
1949	16/11	Manchester	W	9 – 2	WCQ
1950	7/10	Belfast	W	4 – 1	
1951	14/11	Aston Villa	W	2 – 0	
1952	4/10	Belfast	D	2 – 2	
1953	11/11	Everton	W	3 – 1	WCQ
1954	2/10	Belfast	W	2 – 0	
1955	2/11	Wembley	W	3 – 0	
1956	6/10	Belfast	D	1 – 1	
1957	6/11	Wembley	L	2 – 3	
1958	4/10	Belfast	D	3 – 3	
1959	18/11	Wembley	W	2 – 1	
1950	8/10	Belfast	W	5 – 2	
1961	22/11	Wembley	D	1 – 1	
1962	20/10	Belfast	W	3 – 1	
1963	20/11	Wembley	W	8 – 3	
1964	3/10	Belfast	W	4 – 3	
1965	10/11	Wembley	W	2 – 1	
1966	20/10	Belfast	W	2 – 0	ECQ
1967	22/11	Wembley	W	2 – 0	ECQ
1969	3/5	Belfast	W	3 – 1	
1970	21/4	Wembley	W	3 – 1	
1971	15/5	Belfast	W	1 – 0	
1972	23/5	Wembley	L	0 – 1	
1973	12/5	Everton	W	2 – 1	
1974	15/5	Wembley	W	1 – 0	
1975	17/5	Belfast	D	0 – 0	
1976	11/5	Wembley	W	4 – 0	
1977	28/5	Belfast	W	2 – 1	
1978	16/5	Wembley	W	1 – 0	
1979	7/2	Wembley	W	4 – 0	ECQ
1979	19/5	Belfast	W	2 – 0	
1979	17/10	Belfast	W	5 – 1	ECQ
1980	20/5	Wembley	D	1 – 1	
1982	23/2	Wembley	W	4 – 0	
1983	28/5	Belfast	D	0 – 0	
1984	4/4	Wembley	W	1 – 0	
1985	27/2	Belfast	W	1 – 0	WCQ
1985	13/11	Wembley	D	0 – 0	WCQ
1986	15/10	Wembley	W	3 – 0	ECQ
1987	1/4	Belfast	W	2 – 0	ECQ

P 96, W 74, D 16, L 6, F 319, A 80

v Israel

1986	26/2	Tel Aviv	W	2 – 1
1988	17/2	Tel Aviv	D	0 – 0

P 2, W 1, D 1, L 0, F 2, A 1

v Italy

1933	13/5	Rome	D	1 – 1	
1934	14/11	Arsenal	W	3 – 2	
1939	13/5	Milan	D	2 – 2	
1948	16/5	Turin	W	4 – 0	
1949	30/11	Tottenham	W	2 – 0	
1953	18/5	Florence	D	1 – 1	
1959	6/5	Wembley	D	2 – 2	
1961	24/5	Rome	W	3 – 2	
1973	14/6	Turin	L	0 – 2	
1973	14/11	Wembley	L	0 – 1	
1976	28/5	New York	W	3 – 2	USBT
1976	17/11	Rome	L	0 – 2	WCQ
1977	16/11	Wembley	W	2 – 0	WCQ
1980	15/6	Turin	L	0 – 1	ECF
1985	6/6	Mexico City	L	1 – 2	
1989	15/11	Wembley	D	0 – 0	
1990	7/7	Bari	L	1 – 2	WCF
1997	12/2	Wembley	L	0 – 1	WCQ
1997	4/6	Nantes	W	2 – 0	TDF
1997	11/10	Rome	D	0 – 0	WCQ

P 20, W 7, D 6, L 7, F 27, A 23

v Japan

1995	3/6	Wembley	W	2 – 1

P 1, W 1, D 0, L 0, F 2, A 1

v Kuwait

1982	25/6	Bilbao	W	1 – 0	WCF

P 1, W 1, D 0, L 0, F 1, A 0

v Luxembourg

1927	21/5	Luxembourg	W	5 – 2	
1960	19/10	Luxembourg	W	9 – 0	WCQ
1961	28/9	Arsenal	W	4 – 1	WCQ
1977	30/3	Wembley	W	5 – 0	WCQ
1977	12/10	Luxembourg	W	2 – 0	WCQ
1982	15/12	Wembley	W	9 – 0	ECQ
1983	16/11	Luxembourg	W	4 – 0	ECQ

P 7, W 7, D 0, L 0, F 38, A 3

v Malaysia

1991	12/6	Kuala Lumpur	W	4 – 2

P 1, W 1, D 0, L 0, F 4, A 2

v Malta

1971	3/2	Valletta	W	1 – 0	ECQ
1971	12/5	Wembley	W	5 – 0	ECQ

P 2, W 2, D 0, L 0, F 6, A 0

v Mexico

1959	24/5	Mexico City	L	1 – 2	
1961	10/5	Wembley	W	8 – 0	
1966	16/7	Wembley	W	2 – 0	WCF
1997	29/3	Wembley	W	2 – 0	
1969	1/6	Mexico City	D	0 – 0	
1985	9/6	Mexico City	L	0 – 1	
1986	17/5	Los Angeles	W	3 – 0	
1997	29/3	Wembley	W	2 – 0	

P 6, W 3, D 1, L 2, F 14, A 3

v Moldova

1996	1/9	Chisinau	W	3 – 0	WCQ
1997	10/9	Wembley	W	4 – 0	WCQ

P 2, W 2, D 0, L 0, F 7, A 0

v Morocco

1986	6/6	Monterrey	D	0 – 0	WCF
1998	27/5	Casablanca	W	1 – 0	KHC

P 2, W 1, D 1, L 0, F 1, A 0

v New Zealand

1991	3/6	Auckland	W	1 – 0
1991	8/6	Wellington	W	2 – 0

P 2, W 2, D 0, L 0, F 3, A 0

v Nigeria

1994	16/11	Wembley	W	1 – 0

P 1, W 1, D 0, L 0, F 1, A 0

v Northern Ireland (see Ireland)

v Norway

1937	14/5	Oslo	W	6 – 0	
1938	9/11	Newcastle	W	4 – 0	
1949	18/5	Oslo	W	4 – 1	
1966	29/6	Oslo	W	6 – 1	
1980	10/9	Wembley	W	4 – 0	WCQ
1981	9/9	Oslo	L	1 – 2	WCQ
1992	14/10	Wembley	D	1 – 1	WCQ
1993	2/6	Oslo	L	0 – 2	WCQ
1994	22/5	Wembley	D	0 – 0	
1995	11/10	Oslo	D	0 – 0	

P 10, W 5, D 3, L 2, F 26, A 7

v Paraguay

1986	18/6	Mexico City	W	3 – 0	WCQ

P 1, W 1, D 0, L 0, F 3, A 0

v Peru

1959	17/5	Lima	L	1 – 4
1962	20/5	Lima	W	4 – 0

P 2, W 1, D 0, L 1, F 5, A 4

Poland

1966	5/1	Everton	D	1 – 1	
1966	5/7	Chorzow	W	1 – 0	
1973	6/6	Chorzow	L	0 – 2	WCQ
1973	17/10	Wembley	D	1 – 1	WCQ
1986	11/6	Monterrey	W	3 – 0	WCF
1989	3/6	Wembley	W	3 – 0	WCQ
1989	11/10	Katowice	D	0 – 0	WCQ
1990	17/10	Wembley	W	2 – 0	ECQ
1991	13/11	Poznan	D	1 – 1	ECQ
1993	29/5	Katowice	D	1 – 1	WCQ
1993	8/9	Wembley	W	3 – 0	ECQ
1996	9/10	Wembley	W	2 – 1	WCQ
1997	31/5	Chorzow	W	2 – 0	WCQ

P 13, W 7, D 5, L 1, F 20, A 7

Portugal

1947	25/5	Lisbon	W	10 – 0	
1950	14/5	Lisbon	W	5 – 3	
1951	19/5	Everton	W	5 – 2	
1955	22/5	Oporto	L	1 – 3	
1958	7/5	Wembley	W	2 – 1	
1961	21/5	Lisbon	D	1 – 1	WCQ
1961	25/10	Wembley	W	2 – 0	WCQ
1964	17/5	Lisbon	W	4 – 3	
1964	4/6	São Paolo	D	1 – 1	BJT
1966	26/7	Wembley	W	2 – 1	WCF
1969	10/12	Wembley	W	1 – 0	
1974	3/4	Lisbon	D	0 – 0	
1974	20/11	Wembley	D	0 – 0	ECQ
1975	19/11	Lisbon	D	1 – 1	ECQ
1986	3/6	Monterrey	L	0 – 1	WCF
1995	12/12	Wembley	D	1 – 1	
1998	22/4	Wembley	W	3 – 0	

P 17, W 9, D 6, L 2, F 39, A 18

Republic of Ireland

1946	30/9	Dublin	W	1 – 0	
1949	21/9	Everton	L	0 – 2	
1957	8/5	Wembley	W	5 – 1	WCQ
1957	19/5	Dublin	D	1 – 1	WCQ
1964	24/5	Dublin	W	3 – 1	
1976	8/9	Wembley	D	1 – 1	
1978	25/10	Dublin	D	1 – 1	ECQ
1980	6/2	Wembley	W	2 – 0	ECQ
1985	26/3	Wembley	W	2 – 1	
1988	121/6	Stuttgart	L	0 – 1	ECF
1990	11/6	Cagliari	D	1 – 1	WCF
1990	14/11	Dublin	D	1 – 1	ECQ
1991	27/3	Wembley	D	1 – 1	ECQ

P 13, W 5, D 6, L 2, F 19, A 12

Rest of Europe

1938	26/10	Arsenal	W	3 – 0	

P 1, W 1, D 0, L 0, F 3, A 0

v Rest of the World

1963	23/10	Wembley	W	2 – 1

P 1, W 1, D 0, L 0, F 2, A 1

v Romania

1939	24/5	Bucharest	W	2 – 0	
1968	6/11	Bucharest	D	0 – 0	
1969	15/1	Wembley	D	1 – 1	
1970	2/6	Guadalajara	W	1 – 0	WCF
1980	15/10	Bucharest	l	1 – 2	WCQ
1981	29/4	Wembley	D	0 – 0	WCQ
1985	1/5	Bucharest	D	0 – 0	WCQ
1985	11/9	Wembley	D	1 – 1	WCQ
1994	12/10	Wembley	D	1 – 1	
1998	22/6	Toulouse	L	1 – 2	WCF

P 10, W 2, D 6, L 2, F 8, A 7

v San Marino

1993	17/2	Wembley	W	6 – 0	WCQ
1993	17/11	Bologna	W	7 – 1	WCQ

P 2, W 2, D 0, L 0, F 13, A 1

v Saudi Arabia

1988	16/11	Riyadh	D	1 – 1
1998	23/5	Wembley	D	0 – 0

P 2, W 0, D 2, L 0, F 1, A 1

v Scotland

1872	30/11	Glasgow	D	0 – 0
1873	8/3	Kennington	W	4 – 2
1874	7/3	Glasgow	L	1 – 2
1875	6/3	Kennington	D	2 – 2
1876	4/3	Glasgow	L	0 – 3
1877	3/3	Kennington	L	1 – 3
1878	2/3	Glasgow	L	2 – 7
1879	5/4	Kennington	W	5 – 4
1880	13/3	Glasgow	L	4 – 5
1881	12/3	Kennington	L	1 – 6
1882	11/3	Glasgow	L	1 – 5
1883	10/3	Sheffield	L	2 – 3
1884	15/3	Glasgow	L	0 – 1
1885	21/3	Kennington	D	1 – 1
1886	31/3	Glasgow	D	1 – 1
1887	19/3	Blackburn	L	2 – 3
1888	17/3	Glasgow	W	5 – 0
1889	13/4	Kennington	L	2 – 3
1890	5/4	Glasgow	D	1 – 1
1891	6/4	Blackburn	W	2 – 1
1892	2/4	Glasgow	W	4 – 1
1893	1/4	Richmond	W	5 – 2
1894	7/4	Glasgow	D	2 – 2
1895	6/4	Everton	W	3 – 0
1896	4/4	Glasgow	L	1 – 2
1897	3/4	Crystal Palace	L	1 – 2

1898	2/4	Glasgow	W	3 – 1
1899	8/4	Birmingham	W	2 – 1
1900	7/4	Glasgow	L	1 – 4
1901	30/3	Cyrstal Palace	D	2 – 2
1902	3/3	Birmingham	D	2 – 2
1903	4/4	Sheffield	L	1 – 2
1904	9/4	Glasgow	W	1 – 0
1905	1/4	Crystal Palace	W	1 – 0
1906	7/4	Glasgow	L	1 – 2
1907	6/4	Newcastle	D	1 – 1
1908	4/4	Glasgow	D	1 – 1
1909	3/4	Crystal Palace	W	2 – 0
1910	2/4	Glasgow	L	0 – 2
1911	1/4	Everton	D	1 – 1
1912	23/3	Glasgow	D	1 – 1
1913	5/4	Chelsea	W	1 – 0
1914	14/4	Glasgow	L	1 – 3
1920	10/4	Sheffield	W	5 – 4
1921	9/4	Glasgow	L	0 – 3
1922	8/4	Aston Villa	L	0 – 1
1923	14/4	Glasgow	D	2 – 2
1924	12/4	Wembley	D	1 – 1
1925	4/4	Glasgow	L	0 – 2
1926	17/4	Manchester	L	0 – 1
1927	2/4	Glasgow	W	2 – 1
1928	31/3	Wembley	L	1 – 5
1929	13/4	Glasgow	L	0 – 1
1930	5/4	Wembley	W	5 – 2
1931	28/3	Glasgow	L	0 – 2
1932	9/4	Wembley	W	3 – 0
1933	1/4	Glasgow	L	1 – 2
1934	14/4	Wembley	W	3 – 0
1935	6/4	Glasgow	L	0 – 2
1936	4/4	Wembley	D	1 – 1
1937	17/4	Glasgow	L	1 – 3
1938	9/4	Wembley	L	0 – 1
1939	15/4	Glasgow	W	2 – 1
1947	12/4	Wembley	D	1 – 1
1948	10/4	Glasgow	W	2 – 0
1949	9/4	Wembley	L	1 – 3
1950	15/4	Glasgow	W	1 – 0 WCQ
1951	14/4	Wembley	L	2 – 3
1952	5/4	Glasgow	W	2 – 1
1953	18/4	Wembley	D	2 – 2
1954	3/4	Glasgow	W	4 – 2 WCQ
1955	2/4	Wembley	W	7 – 2
1956	14/4	Glasgow	D	1 – 1
1957	6/4	Wembley	W	2 – 1
1958	19/4	Glasgow	W	4 – 0
1959	11/4	Wembley	W	1 – 0
1960	19/4	Glasgow	D	1 – 1
1961	15/4	Wembley	W	9 – 3
1962	14/4	Glasgow	L	0 – 2
1963	6/4	Wembley	L	1 – 2
1964	11/4	Glasgow	L	0 – 1
1965	10/4	Wembley	D	2 – 2
1966	2/4	Glasgow	W	4 – 3
1967	15/4	Wembley	L	2 – 3 ECQ
1968	24/2	Glasgow	D	1 – 1 ECQ
1969	10/5	Wembley	W	4 – 1

1970	25/4	Glasgow	D	0 – 0
1971	22/5	Wembley	W	3 – 1
1972	27/5	Glasgow	W	1 – 0
1973	14/2	Glasgow	W	5 – 0
1973	19/5	Wembley	W	1 – 0
1974	18/5	Glasgow	L	0 – 2
1975	24/5	Wembley	W	5 – 1
1976	15/5	Glasgow	L	1 – 2
1977	4/6	Wembley	L	1 – 2
1978	20/5	Glasgow	W	1 – 0
1979	26/5	Wembley	W	3 – 1
1980	24/5	Glasgow	W	2 – 0
1981	23/5	Wembley	L	0 – 1
1982	29/5	Glasgow	W	1 – 0
1983	1/6	Wembley	W	2 – 0
1984	26/5	Glasgow	D	1 – 1
1985	25/5	Glasgow	L	0 – 1 RC
1986	23/4	Wembley	W	2 – 1 RC
1987	23/5	Glasgow	D	0 – 0 RC
1988	21/5	Wembley	W	1 – 0 RC
1989	27/5	Glasgow	W	2 – 0 RC
1996	15/6	Wembley	W	2 – 0 ECF

P 108, W 44, D 24, L 40, F 190, A 168

v South Africa

1997	24/5	Old Trafford	W	2 – 1

P 1, W 1, D 0, L 0, F 2, A 1

v Spain

1929	15/5	Madrid	L	3 – 4
1931	9/12	Arsenal	W	7 – 1
1950	2/7	Rio de Janeiro	L	0 – 1 WCF
1955	18/5	Madrid	D	1 – 1
1955	30/11	Wembley	W	4 – 1
1960	15/5	Madrid	L	0 – 3
1960	26/10	Wembley	W	4 – 2
1965	8/12	Madrid	W	2 – 0
1967	24/5	Wembley	W	2 – 0
1968	3/4	Wembley	W	1 – 0 ECQ
1968	8/5	Madrid	W	2 – 1 ECQ
1980	26/3	Barcelona	W	2 – 0
1980	18/6	Naples	W	2 – 1 ECF
1981	25/3	Wembley	L	1 – 2
1982	5/7	Madrid	D	0 – 0 WCF
1987	18/2	Madrid	W	4 – 2
1992	9/9	Santander	L	0 – 1
1996	22/6	Wembley	D	0 – 0 *ECF

P 18, W 10, D 3, L 5, F 35, A 20
*After extra time (England won 4–2 on penalties)

v Sweden

1923	21/5	Stockholm	W	4 – 2
1923	24/5	Stockholm	W	3 – 1
1937	17/5	Stockholm	W	4 – 0
1947	19/11	Arsenal	W	4 – 2
1949	13/5	Stockholm	L	1 – 3
1956	16/5	Stockholm	D	0 – 0

1959	28/10	Wembley	L	2 – 3	
1965	16/5	Gothenburg	W	2 – 1	
1968	22/5	Wembley	W	3 – 1	
1979	10/6	Stockholm	D	0 – 0	
1986	10/9	Stockholm	L	0 – 1	
1988	19/10	Wembley	D	0 – 0	WCQ
1989	6/9	Stockholm	D	0 – 0	WCQ
1992	17/6	Stockholm	L	1 – 2	ECF
1995	8/6	Leeds	D	3 – 3	

15, W 6, D 5, L 4, F 27, A 19

Switzerland

1933	29/5	Berne	W	4 – 0	
1938	21/5	Zurich	L	1 – 2	
1947	18/5	Zurich	L	0 – 1	
1948	2/12	Arsenal	W	6 – 0	
1952	28/5	Zurich	W	3 – 0	
1954	20/6	Berne	W	2 – 0	WCF
1962	9/5	Wembley	W	3 – 1	
1963	5/6	Basle	W	8 – 1	
1971	13/10	Basle	W	3 – 2	ECQ
1971	10/11	Wembley	D	1 – 1	ECQ
1975	3/9	Basle	W	2 – 1	
1977	7/9	Wembley	D	0 – 0	
1980	19/11	Wembley	W	2 – 1	WCQ
1981	30/5	Basle	L	1 – 2	WCQ
1988	28/5	Lausanne	W	1 – 0	
1995	15/11	Wembley	W	3 – 1	
1996	8/6	Wembley	D	1 – 1	ECF
1998	25/3	Berne	D	1 – 1	

18, W 11, D 4, L 3, F 42, A 15

Tunisia

| 1990 | 2/6 | Tunis | D | 1 – 1 | |
| 1998 | 15/6 | Marseille | W | 2 – 0 | WCF |

2, W 1, D 1, L 0, F 3, A 1

Turkey

1984	14/11	Instanbul	W	8 – 0	WCQ
1985	16/10	Wembley	W	5 – 0	WCQ
1987	29/4	Izmir	D	0 – 0	ECQ
1987	14/10	Wembley	W	8 – 0	ECQ
1991	1/5	Izmir	W	1 – 0	ECQ
1991	16/10	Wembley	W	1 – 0	ECQ
1992	18/11	Wembley	W	4 – 0	ECQ
1993	31/3	Izmir	W	2 – 0	WCQ

8, W 7, D 1, L 0, F 29, A 0

USA

1950	29/6	Belo Horizonte	L	0 – 1	WCF
1953	8/6	New York	W	6 – 3	
1959	28/5	Los Angeles	W	8 – 1	
1964	27/5	New York	W	10 – 0	
1985	16/6	Los Angeles	W	5 – 0	
1993	9/6	Boston	L	0 – 2	
1994	7/9	Wembley	W	2 – 0	

7, W 5, D 0, L 2, F 31, A 7

v USSR (see also CIS)

1958	18/5	Moscow	D	1 – 1	
1958	8/6	Gothenburg	D	2 – 2	WCF
1958	17/6	Gothenburg	L	0 – 1	WCF
1958	22/10	Wembley	W	5 – 0	
1967	6/12	Wembley	D	2 – 2	
1968	8/6	Rome	W	2 – 0	ECF
1973	10/6	Moscow	W	2 – 1	
1984	2/6	Wembley	L	0 – 2	
1986	26/3	Tbilisi	W	1 – 0	
1988	18/6	Frankfurt	L	1 – 3	ECF
1991	21/5	Wembley	W	3 – 1	

P 11, W 5, D 3, L 3, F 19, A 13

v Uruguay

1953	31/5	Montevideo	L	1 – 2	
1954	26/6	Basle	L	2 – 4	WCF
1964	6/5	Wembley	W	2 – 1	
1966	11/7	Wembley	D	0 – 0	WCF
1969	8/6	Montevideo	W	2 – 1	
1977	15/6	Montevideo	D	0 – 0	
1984	13/6	Montevideo	L	0 – 2	
1990	22/5	Wembley	L	1 – 2	
1995	29/3	Wembley	D	0 – 0	

P 9, W 2, D 3, L 4, F 8, A 12

v Wales

1879	18/1	Kennington	W	2 – 1	
1880	15/3	Wrexham	W	3 – 2	
1881	26/2	Blackburn	L	0 – 1	
1882	13/3	Wrexham	L	3 – 5	
1883	3/2	Kennington	W	5 – 0	
1884	17/3	Wrexham	W	4 – 0	
1885	14/3	Blackburn	D	1 – 1	
1886	29/3	Wrexham	W	3 – 1	
1887	26/2	Kennington	W	4 – 0	
1888	4/2	Crewe	W	5 – 1	
1889	23/2	Stoke	W	4 – 1	
1890	15/3	Wrexham	W	3 – 1	
1891	7/5	Sunderland	W	4 – 1	
1892	5/3	Wrexham	W	2 – 0	
1893	13/3	Stoke	W	6 – 0	
1894	12/3	Wrexham	W	5 – 1	
1895	18/3	Kennington	D	1 – 1	
1896	16/3	Cardiff	W	9 – 1	
1897	29/3	Sheffield	W	4 – 0	
1898	28/3	Wrexham	W	3 – 0	
1899	20/3	Bristol	W	4 – 0	
1900	26/3	Cardiff	D	1 – 1	
1901	18/3	Newcastle	W	6 – 0	
1902	3/3	Wrexham	D	0 – 0	
1903	2/3	Portsmouth	W	2 – 0	
1904	29/2	Wrexham	D	2 – 2	
1905	27/3	Liverpool	W	3 – 1	
1906	19/3	Cardiff	W	1 – 0	
1907	18/3	Fulham	D	1 – 1	
1908	16/3	Wrexham	W	7 – 1	

1909	15/3	Nottingham	W	2 – 0		1964	18/11	Wembley	W	2 – 1	
1910	14/3	Cardiff	W	1 – 0		1965	2/10	Cardiff	D	0 – 0	
1911	13/3	Millwall	W	3 – 0		1966	16/11	Wembley	W	5 – 1	ECQ
1912	11/3	Wrexham	W	2 – 0		1967	21/10	Cardiff	W	3 – 0	ECQ
1913	17/3	Bristol	W	4 – 3		1969	7/5	Wembley	W	2 – 1	
1914	16/3	Cardiff	W	2 – 0		1970	18/4	Cardiff	D	1 – 1	
1920	15/3	Arsenal	L	1 – 2		1971	19/5	Wembley	D	0 – 0	
1921	14/3	Cardiff	D	0 – 0		1972	20/5	Cardiff	W	3 – 0	
1922	13/3	Liverpool	W	1 – 0		1972	15/11	Cardiff	W	1 – 0	WCQ
1923	5/3	Cardiff	D	2 – 2		1973	24/1	Wembley	D	1 – 1	WCQ
1924	3/3	Blackburn	L	1 – 2		1973	15/5	Wembley	W	3 – 0	
1925	28/2	Swansea	W	2 – 1		1974	11/5	Cardiff	W	2 – 0	
1926	1/3	Crystal Palace	L	1 – 3		1975	21/5	Wembley	D	2 – 2	
1927	12/2	Wrexham	D	3 – 3		1976	24/3	Wrexham	W	2 – 1	
1927	28/11	Burnley	L	1 – 2		1976	8/5	Cardiff	W	1 – 0	
1928	17/11	Swansea	W	3 – 2		1977	31/5	Wembley	L	0 – 1	
1929	20/11	Chelsea	W	6 – 0		1978	3/5	Cardiff	W	3 – 1	
1930	22/11	Wrexham	W	4 – 0		1979	23/5	Wembley	D	0 – 0	
1931	18/11	Liverpool	W	3 – 1		1980	17/5	Wrexham	L	1 – 4	
1932	16/11	Wrexham	D	0 – 0		1981	20/5	Wembley	D	0 – 0	
1933	15/11	Newcastle	L	1 – 2		1982	27/4	Cardiff	W	1 – 0	
1934	29/9	Cardiff	W	4 – 0		1983	23/2	Wembley	W	2 – 1	
1935	5/2	Wolverhampton	L	1 – 2		1984	2/5	Wrexham	L	0 – 1	
1936	17/10	Cardiff	L	1 – 2							
1937	17/11	Middlesbrough	W	2 – 1							

P 97, W 62, D 21, L 14, F 239, A 90

1938	22/10	Cardiff	L	2 – 4	
1946	13/11	Manchester	W	3 – 0	
1947	18/10	Cardiff	W	3 – 0	
1948	10/11	Aston Villa	W	1 – 0	
1949	15/10	Cardiff	W	4 – 1	WCQ

v Yugoslavia

1950	15/11	Sunderland	W	4 – 2	

1939	18/5	Belgrade	L	1 – 2	
1950	22/11	Highbury	D	2 – 2	
1951	20/10	Cardiff	D	1 – 1	
1954	16/5	Belgrade	L	0 – 1	
1952	12/11	Wembley	W	5 – 2	
1956	28/11	Wembley	W	3 – 0	
1953	10/10	Cardiff	W	4 – 1	WCQ
1958	11/5	Belgrade	L	0 – 5	
1954	10/11	Wembley	W	3 – 2	
1960	11/5	Wembley	D	3 – 3	
1955	22/10	Cardiff	L	1 – 2	
1965	9/5	Belgrade	D	1 – 1	
1956	14/11	Wembley	W	3 – 1	
1966	4/5	Wembley	W	2 – 0	
1957	19/10	Cardiff	W	4 – 0	
1968	5/6	Florence	L	0 – 1	ECF
1958	26/11	Aston Villa	D	2 – 2	
1972	11/10	Wembley	D	1 – 1	
1959	17/10	Cardiff	D	1 – 1	
1974	5/6	Belgrade	D	2 – 2	
1960	23/11	Wembley	W	5 – 1	
1986	12/11	Wembley	W	2 – 0	ECQ
1961	14/10	Cardiff	D	1 – 1	
1987	11/11	Belgrade	W	4 – 1	ECQ
1962	21/11	Wembley	W	4 – 0	
1989	13/12	Wembley	W	2 – 1	
1963	12/10	Cardiff	W	4 – 0	

P 14, W 5, D 5, L 4, F 23, A 20

22 ● SEMI-PROFESSIONAL INTERNATIONAL/FA REPRESENTATIVE MATCHES 1997–1998

FA XI 5   Northern Premier League 0

4 November 1997, Leigh RMI FC

FA XI: Stewart, Farley (Southport), Bradshaw (Halifax Town), Simpson (Northwich Victoria), Higgins (Barrow), Ryan (Southport), Proudlock (Gateshead), Healy (Morecambe), Tait (Northwich Victoria), Horsfield (Halifax Town), Walters (Northwich Victoria)

   Subs: Monk (Morecambe) for Bradshaw, Greygoose (Northwich Victoria) for Stewart, Vicary (Northwich Victoria) for Farley, Ceraolo (Morecambe) for Tait

   Scorers: Tait, Horsfield, Farley, Monk, Ceraolo

   Team Manager: John Owens

FA XI 2   Southern League 1

9 December 1997, Gloucester City FC

FA XI: Pennock (Yeovil Town), Banks, Victory (Cheltenham Town), Cousins (Yeovil Town), Webb, Yates (Kidderminster Harriers), Pitman (Hereford United), Howells, Eaton, Watkins (Cheltenham Town), Stott (Yeovil Town)

   Subs: Book (Cheltenham Town) for Pennock, Grayson (Hereford United) for Eaton

   Scorers: Stott + OG

   Team Manager: John Owens

FA XI 2   Isthmian League 0

10 December 1997, Kingstonian FC

FA XI: Mackenzie (Farnborough Town), Watts (Welling United), Sparks (Hayes), Hercules (Slough Town), Smith M., Perkins (Stevenage Borough), Betsy (Woking), Harlow (Farnborough Town), West (Woking), Randall (Hayes), Wingfield (Farnborough Town)

   Subs: Munday (Dover Athletic) for Watts, Meara (Hayes) for Mackenzie, Danzey (Woking) for Sparks, Stemp (Farnborough Town) for Hercules, Crawshaw (Stevenage Borough) for Randall

   Scorer: Perkins (2)

   Team Manager: John Owens

FA XI 1   British Students 2

3 February 1998, Durham City FC

FA XI: Cooksey (Hednesford Town), Jones (Barrow), Watson (Spennymoor United), Comyn (Hednesford Town), Ellender (Gainsborough Trinity), Bayles (Bishop Auckland), Farrey (Blyth Spartans), Bowey (Gateshead), Morton (Barrow), Shaw (Bishop Auckland), Calcutt (Emley)

   Subs: Farrelly (Barrow) for Cooksey, Lobb (Bishop Auckland) for Jones, Nicholson (Emley) for Farrey, Lee (Bishop Auckland) for Calcutt, Waller (Bishop Auckland) for Bowey

   Scorer: Morton

   Team Manager: John Owens

England 2   Holland 1

3 March 1998, Crawley Town FC

England: Stewart (Southport), Hooper (Kingstonian), Bradshaw (Halifax Town), Banks (Cheltenham Town), Smith M. (Stevenage Borough), Ryan (Southport), Howells (Cheltenham Town), Butterworth (Rushden & Diamonds), Grayson, Watkins (Cheltenham Town), Healy (Morecambe)

   Subs: Comyn (Hednesford Town) for Hooper, Victory (Cheltenham Town) for Bradshaw, Betsy (Woking) for Healy, Pickard (Yeovil Town) for Grayson, Cooksey (Hednesford Town) for Stewart

   Scorers: Grayson, Bradshaw

   Attendance: 1,561

   Team Manager: John Owens

23 ● FA CUP WINNERS 1872–1998

1872 & 1874–92	Kennington Oval	1895–1914	Crystal Palace
1873	Lillie Bridge, London	1915	Old Trafford, Manchester
1893	Fallowfield, Manchester	1920–22	Stamford Bridge, London
1894	Goodison Park, Liverpool	1923 to date	Wembley Stadium

Year	Winners		Runners–up	Result	
1872	Wanderers	v	Royal Engineers	1 – 0	
1873	Wanderers	v	Oxford University	2 – 0	
1874	Oxford University	v	Royal Engineers	2 – 0	
1875	Royal Engineers	v	Old Etonians	2 – 0	after 1 – 1 draw
1876	Wanderers	v	Old Etonians	3 – 0	after 0 – 0 draw
1877	Wanderers	v	Oxford University	2 – 0	after extra time
1878	Wanderers*	v	Royal Engineers	3 – 1	
1879	Old Etonians	v	Clapham Rovers	1 – 0	
1880	Clapham Rovers	v	Oxford University	1 – 0	
1881	Old Carhusians	v	Old Etonians	3 – 0	
1882	Old Etonians	v	Blackburn Rovers	1 – 0	
1883	Blackburn Olympic	v	Old Etonians	2 – 1	after extra time
1884	Blackburn Rovers	v	Queen's Park, Glasgow	2 – 1	
1885	Blackburn Rovers	v	Queen's Park, Glasgow	2 – 0	
1886	Blackburn Rovers†	v	West Bromwich Albion	2 – 0	after 0 – 0 draw
1887	Aston Villa	v	West Bromwich Albion	2 – 0	
1888	West Bromwich Albion	v	Preston North End	2 – 1	
1889	Preston North End	v	Wolverhampton Wanderers	3 – 0	
1890	Blackburn Rovers	v	Sheffield Wednesday	6 – 1	
1891	Blackburn Rovers	v	Notts County	3 – 1	
1892	West Bromwich Albion	v	Aston Villa	3 – 0	
1893	Wolverhampton Wanderers	v	Everton	1 – 0	
1894	Notts County	v	Bolton Wanderers	4 – 1	
1895	Aston Villa	v	West Bromwich Albion	1 – 0	
1896	Sheffield Wednesday	v	Wolverhampton Wanderers	2 – 1	
1897	Aston Villa	v	Everton	3 – 2	
1898	Nottingham Forest	v	Derby County	3 – 1	
1899	Sheffield United	v	Derby County	4 – 1	
1900	Bury	v	Southampton	4 – 0	
1901	Tottenham Hotspur	v	Sheffield United	3 – 1	after 2 – 2 draw
1902	Sheffield United	v	Southampton	2 – 1	after 1 – 1 draw
1903	Bury	v	Derby County	6 – 0	
1904	Manchester City	v	Bolton Wanderers	1 – 0	
1905	Aston Villa	v	Newcastle United	2 – 0	
1906	Everton	v	Newcastle United	1 – 0	
1907	Sheffield Wednesday	v	Everton	2 – 1	
1908	Wolverhampton Wanderers	v	Newcastle United	3 – 1	
1909	Manchester United	v	Bristol City	1 – 0	
1910	Newcastle United	v	Barnsley	2 – 0	after 1 – 1 draw
1911	Bradford City	v	Newcastle United	1 – 0	after 0 – 0 draw
1912	Barnsley	v	West Bromwich Albion	1 – 0	after 0 – 0 draw
1913	Aston Villa	v	Sunderland	1 – 0	
1914	Burnley	v	Liverpool	1 – 0	
1915	Sheffield United	v	Chelsea	3 – 0	
1920	Aston Villa	v	Huddersfield Town	1 – 0	after extra time

*Won outright but restored to The Association
†A special trophy was awarded for third consecutive win

Year	Winners		Runners–up	Result	
1921	Tottenham Hotspur	v	Wolverhampton Wanderers	1 – 0	
1922	Huddersfield Town	v	Preston North End	1 – 0	
1923	Bolton Wanderers	v	West Ham United	2 – 0	
1924	Newcastle United	v	Aston Villa	2 – 0	
1925	Sheffield United	v	Cardiff City	1 – 0	
1926	Bolton Wanderers	v	Manchester City	1 – 0	
1927	Cardiff City	v	Arsenal	1 – 0	
1928	Blackburn Rovers	v	Huddersfield Town	3 – 1	
1929	Bolton Wanderers	v	Portsmouth	2 – 0	
1930	Arsenal	v	Huddersfield Town	2 – 0	
1931	West Bromwich Albion	v	Birmingham City	2 – 1	
1932	Newcastle United	v	Arsenal	2 – 1	
1933	Everton	v	Manchester City	3 – 0	
1934	Manchester City	v	Portsmouth	2 – 1	
1935	Sheffield Wednesday	v	West Bromwich Albion	4 – 2	
1936	Arsenal	v	Sheffield United	1 – 0	
1937	Sunderland	v	Preston North End	3 – 1	
1938	Preston North End	v	Huddersfield Town	1 – 0	after extra time
1939	Portsmouth	v	Wolverhampton Wanderers	4 – 1	
1946	Derby County	v	Charlton Athletic	4 – 1	after extra time
1947	Charlton Athletic	v	Burnley	1 – 0	after extra time
1948	Manchester United	v	Blackpool	4 – 2	
1949	Wolverhampton Wanderers	v	Leicester City	3 – 1	
1950	Arsenal	v	Liverpool	2 – 0	
1951	Newcastle United	v	Blackpool	2 – 0	
1952	Newcastle United	v	Arsenal	1 – 0	
1953	Blackpool	v	Bolton Wanderers	4 – 3	
1954	West Bromwich Albion	v	Preston North End	3 – 2	
1955	Newcastle United	v	Manchester City	3 – 1	
1956	Manchester City	v	Birmingham City	3 – 1	
1957	Aston Villa	v	Manchester United	2 – 1	
1958	Bolton Wanderers	v	Manchester United	2 – 0	
1959	Nottingham Forest	v	Luton Town	2 – 1	
1960	Wolverhampton Wanderers	v	Blackburn Rovers	3 – 0	
1961	Tottenham Hotspur	v	Leicester City	2 – 0	
1962	Tottenham Hotspur	v	Burnley	3 – 1	
1963	Manchester United	v	Leicester City	3 – 1	
1964	West Ham United	v	Preston North End	3 – 2	
1965	Liverpool	v	Leeds United	2 – 1	after extra time
1966	Everton	v	Sheffield Wednesday	3 – 2	
1967	Tottenham Hotspur	v	Chelsea	2 – 1	
1968	West Bromwich Albion	v	Everton	1 – 0	after extra time
1969	Manchester City	v	Leicester City	1 – 0	
1970	Chelsea	v	Leeds United	2 – 1	after 2–2 draw both games extra time
1971	Arsenal	v	Liverpool	2 – 1	after extra time
1972	Leeds United	v	Arsenal	1 – 0	
1973	Sunderland	v	Leeds United	1 – 0	
1974	Liverpool	v	Newcastle United	3 – 0	
1975	West Ham United	v	Fulham	2 – 0	
1976	Southampton	v	Manchester United	1 – 0	
1977	Manchester United	v	Liverpool	2 – 1	
1978	Ipswich Town	v	Arsenal	1 – 0	
1979	Arsenal	v	Manchester United	3 – 2	
1980	West Ham United	v	Arsenal	1 – 0	
1981	Tottenham Hotspur	v	Manchester City	3 – 2	after 1–1 draw after extra time

Year	Winners		Runners–up	Result	
1982	Tottenham Hotspur	v	Queens Park Rangers	1 – 0	after 1–1 draw after extra time
1983	Manchester United	v	Brighton & Hove Albion	4 – 0	after 2–2 draw after extra time
1984	Everton	v	Watford	2 – 0	
1985	Manchester United	v	Everton	1 – 0	after extra time
1986	Liverpool	v	Everton	3 – 1	
1987	Coventry City	v	Tottenham Hotspur	3 – 2	after extra time
1988	Wimbledon	v	Liverpool	1 – 0	
1989	Liverpool	v	Everton	3 – 2	after extra time
1990	Manchester United	v	Crystal Palace	1 – 0	after 3–3 draw after extra time
1991	Tottenham Hotspur	v	Nottingham Forest	2 – 1	after extra time
1992	Liverpool	v	Sunderland	2 – 0	
1993	Arsenal	v	Sheffield Wednesday	2 – 1	after 1–1 draw both games extra time
1994	Manchester United	v	Chelsea	4 – 0	
1995	Everton	v	Manchester United	1 – 0	
1996	Manchester United	v	Liverpool	1 – 0	
1997	Chelsea	v	Middlesbrough	2 – 0	
1998	Arsenal	v	Newcastle United	2 – 0	

24 ● FA CUP – FINAL TIE 1998
Sponsored by Littlewoods

Arsenal 2   Newcastle United 0

Near the turn of the year Arsenal had been fifth in the Premiership table, a dozen points adrift of Manchester United, and had been held to a 0–0 draw at Highbury in the FA Cup third round by Port Vale who finished 19th in the First Division. Now on a sizzling afternoon at Wembley, Arsene Wenger's Arsenal completed a slightly improbable "Double" success, their first since the days of George and McLintock in 1971. Only Manchester United, two years ago, had achieved two "Doubles" in their history.

Dutch striker Dennis Bergkamp, chosen as the FWA's "Footballer of the Year" in the week of the final, had been ruled out of the Wembley showpiece with a hamstring injury. And the concern of some of the Highbury faithful had increased when Wenger's starting line-up included the relatively inexperienced Anelka and Wreh up front and excluded cult figure Ian Wright, Arsenal's top scorer of all time and a marksman in the 1990 and 1993 finals.

Two French midfielders had had a colossal influence on Arsenal's successful run-in. Patrick Vieira – "He comes from Sen-e-gal; he plays for Ars-e-nal" as the song went– and the pony-tailed Emmanuel Petit. It was the latter who engineered the lead that Arsenal clearly deserved on 23 minutes 27 seconds of the 117th FA Cup Final, chipping an astute pass over the top of the Newcastle defence. Marc Overmars, another Dutch star, unravelled himself from Pistone's unconvincing challenge to run on and bravely shoot through the advancing Given's legs before the inevitable collision. Newcastle, with Shearer largely isolated in attack, were hardly playing like a team who thought they could win the Cup and Anelka, Wreh and Man-of-the-Match Parlour all missed straightforward chances that would have buried them.

"1–0 to the Arsenal", has become an almost legendary scoreline and the Londoners had to fight to preserve it midway through the second half. Dabizas' header from a corner – Newcastle only managed two of those in the whole match – bounced on top of the angle

Arsenal's Anelka shoots into the corner to clinch the Cup.

of post and bar on 62 minutes and Shearer took advantage of a Keown slip to rifle a left-footer against the inside of a post two minutes later. The distance between success and failure can be measured in inches, as the England captain observed afterwards.

But Arsenal scored again in the 70th minute to clinch it. Parlour's clever through-ball went directly to Anelka, leaving the 19-year-old Frenchman with the searing pace to glide away from what was left of the Newcastle defence before shooting across Given and into the bottom left-hand corner. The red half of the stadium then erupted with the "Double" in sight. For Newcastle after a difficult season, there was the consolation of the Cup Winners' Cup.

Arsenal: Seaman, Dixon, Keown, Adams, Winterburn, Parlour, Vieira, Petit, Overmars, Wreh (Platt), Anelka.

Newcastle United: Given, Pistone, Dabizas, Howey, Pearce (Andersson), Barton (Watson), Lee, Batty, Speed, Ketsbaia (Barnes), Shearer.

Referee: P. Durkin (Dorset)

Attendance: 79,183

Arsenal – FA Cup winners 1998.

25 ● FA CUP 1997–1998
Sponsored by Littlewoods

Preliminary round – 30 August 1997

(Replays in italics)

			Result	Att
Atherton Collieries	v	Maine Road	1 – 2	78
Billingham Synthonia	v	Brandon United	1 – 1	140
Brandon United	*v*	*Billingham Synthonia*	*2 – 5*	*114*
Skelmersdale United	v	Pickering Town	3 – 2	131
Harrogate Railway	v	South Shields	2 – 3	107
Matlock Town	v	Curzon Ashton	3 – 1	205
Bedlington Terriers	v	Glapwell	6 – 1	130
Blackpool (Wren)Rovers	v	Burscough	1 – 4	115
Seaham Red Star	v	Ossett Town	1 – 1	50
Ossett Town	*v*	*Seaham Red Star*	*1 – 0*	*86*
Denaby United	v	West Auckland Town	3 – 1	108
Droylsden	v	Cheadle Town	4 – 1	230
Blidworth MW	v	Rossendale United	3 – 5	42
Buxton	v	Ilkeston Town	0 – 1	303
Tow Law Town	v	RTM Newcastle	1 – 2	100
Peterlee Newtown	v	Warrington Town	1 – 3	54
Pontefract Collieries	v	Ossett Albion	2 – 2	75
Ossett Albion	*v*	*Pontefract Collieries*	*0 – 3*	*99*
Arnold Town	v	Shildon	3 – 1	214
Billingham Town	v	Brodsworth	3 – 0	99
Maltby Main	v	Shotton Comrades	0 – 1	104
Kidsgrove Athletic	v	Whitley Bay	1 – 1	242
Whitley Bay	*v*	*Kidsgrove Athletic*	*3 – 3*	*179*
(Whitley Bay won 5–3 on kicks from the penalty mark)				
Netherfield	v	Chadderton	1 – 1	85
Chadderton	*v*	*Netherfield*	*1 – 2*	*104*
Chester-Le-Street Town	v	Ryhope CA	0 – 2	85
Congleton Town	v	Darwen	1 – 1	124
Darwen	*v*	*Congleton Town*	*4 – 3*	*88*
St Helens Town	v	Sheffield	3 – 1	110
Great Harwood Town	v	Stockton	2 – 1	87
Louth United	v	Glasshoughton Welfare	1 – 0	26
Belper Town	v	Glossop North End	2 – 2	192
Glossop North End	*v*	*Belper Town*	*1 – 2*	*190*
Bootle	v	Bradford (Park Avenue)	3 – 1	121
Parkgate	v	Nantwich Town	2 – 0	46
Eccleshill United	v	Thackley	1 – 1	164
Thackley	*v*	*Eccleshill United*	*0 – 2*	*161*
Evenwood Town	v	Durham City	0 – 3	262
Crook Town	v	Mossley	0 – 2	147
Gretna	v	Haslingden	4 – 2	68
Tadcaster Albion	v	Stocksbridge Park Steels	0 – 3	135
Liversedge	v	Willington	3 – 0	66
Morpeth Town	v	Horden CW	5 – 0	87
Atherton LR	v	Hucknall Town	0 – 1	117
Brigg Town	v	Eastwood Town	1 – 0	177
Oldham Town	v	Northallerton	4 – 2	72
Guisborough Town	v	Worksop Town	2 – 3	266

● 101

			Result	Att
Hebburn	v	Garforth Town	0 – 5	162
Borrowash Victoria	v	Jarrow Roofing Boldon CA	1 – 2	92
Castleton Gabriels	v	Clitheroe	0 – 1	120
Selby Town	v	Lincoln United	1 – 3	115
Flixton	v	Staveley MW	2 – 3	107
Hatfield Main	v	Dunston FB	2 – 3	68
Penrith	v	Trafford	3 – 0	139
Heanor Town	v	Salford City	1 – 0	100

(after abandoned match at Alfreton Town, 57 mins 1–2 – waterlogged pitch)

Yorkshire Amateur	v	Easington Colliery	1 – 4	59
Harrogate Town	v	Armthorpe Welfare	1 – 1	153
Armthorpe Welfare	*v*	*Harrogate Town*	*1 – 3*	*150*
Fakenham Town	v	Stourbridge	0 – 1	219
Eynesbury Rovers	v	Pershore Town	1 – 2	125
Stratford Town	v	Desborough Town	1 – 3	120
Dudley Town	v	Bridgnorth Town		

(walkover for Bridgnorth Town – Dudley Town withdrawn)

Banbury United	v	Rushall Olympic	3 – 2	143
Blakenall	v	Great Yarmouth Town	1 – 3	165
Stewarts & Lloyds	v	Soham Town Rangers	1 – 1	101

(at Soham Town Rangers)

Soham Town Rangers	*v*	*Stewarts & Lloyds*	*1 – 3*	*121*
Hinckley United	v	Wednesfield	2 – 0	281
Boston Town	v	Stapenhill	0 – 2	91
Brackley Town	v	Cogenhoe United	1 – 0	202
Sutton Coldfield Town	v	Stowmarket Town	1 – 3	139
Rocester	v	West Midlands Police	1 – 1	76
West Midlands Police	*v*	*Rocester*	*0 – 3*	*55*
Stafford Rangers	v	Ely City	1 – 1	554
Ely City	*v*	*Stafford Rangers*	*1 – 3*	*262*
Sandwell Borough	v	Spalding United	0 – 4	n/a
Raunds Town	v	Shifnal Town	6 – 0	100
Watton United	v	Lowestoft Town		

(walkover for Lowestoft Town – Watton United withdrawn)

Lye Town	v	Evesham United	2 – 1	232
Redditch United	v	Wellingborough Town	4 – 0	199
Racing Club Warwick	v	St Neots Town	3 – 1	161
Willenhall Town	v	Gorleston	4 – 1	135
Pelsall Villa	v	Barwell	2 – 3	83
Newmarket Town	v	Stamford	4 – 4	173
Stamford	*v*	*Newmarket Town*	*1 – 4*	*178*
Histon	v	Oldbury United	2 – 0	91
VS Rugby	v	Chasetown	1 – 0	344
Diss Town	v	Bloxwich Town	1 – 0	235
Stourport Swifts	v	Woodbridge Town	1 – 5	102
Northampton Spencer	v	Warboys Town	0 – 0	103
Warboys Town	*v*	*Northampton Spencer*	*2 – 3*	*107*
Wroxham	v	Paget Rangers	3 – 1	186
Long Buckby	v	Boldmere St Michaels	2 – 4	75
Littlehampton Town	v	Southend Manor	6 – 2	236
Folkestone Invicta	v	Marlow	3 – 4	428
Welwyn Garden City	v	East Thurrock United	2 – 3	48
Flackwell Heath	v	Barkingside	5 – 0	75
Grays Athletic	v	Langford	10 – 0	184
Ford United	v	Great Wakering Rovers	0 – 4	100
Pagham	v	Camberley Town	1 – 3	91
Chatham Town	v	Banstead Athletic	0 – 7	101
Horsham	v	Northwood	3 – 1	196

Croydon	v	Mile Oak	2 – 1	88
Tunbridge Wells	v	Chichester City	4 – 4	152
Chichester City	*v*	*Tunbridge Wells*	*4 – 1*	*150*
Corinthian-Casuals	v	Aveley	0 – 2	83
Leatherhead	v	Wealdstone	2 – 0	337
Langney Sports	v	Southall	2 – 1	166
Whitstable Town	v	Dorking	1 – 1	157
Dorking	*v*	*Whitstable Town*	*3 – 3*	*96*

(Dorking won 3–1 on kicks from the penalty mark)

Egham Town	v	Burnham	1 – 1	79
Burnham	*v*	*Egham Town*	*1 – 1*	*95*

(Burnham won 5–4 on kicks from the penalty mark)

Redhill	v	Ware	1 – 1	186
Ware	*v*	*Redhill*	*4 – 1*	*137*
Godalming & Guildford	v	Tonbridge	0 – 6	183
Worthing	v	Eastbourne Town	8 – 1	300
Epsom & Ewell	v	Canterbury City	0 – 1	45
Ringmer	v	Wick	0 – 1	110
Lewes	v	Tilbury	0 – 1	68
Wingate & Finchley	v	Corinthian	1 – 1	100
Corinthian	*v*	*Wingate & Finchley*	*0 – 2*	*102*
Leighton Town	v	Ashford Town	2 – 1	172
Hailsham Town	v	Metropolitan Police	0 – 4	180
Erith Town	v	Harlow Town	0 – 3	93
Wivenhoe Town	v	Chipstead	4 – 0	157
Croydon Athletic	v	Beaconsfield SYCOB	5 – 2	57
Sheppey United	v	Windsor & Eton	2 – 3	151
Hillingdon Borough	v	Stotfold	4 – 2	105
Tiptree United	v	Clapton	1 – 4	72
Hassocks	v	Barton Rovers	1 – 2	122
Milton Keynes	v	Viking Sports	1 – 1	72
Viking Sports	*v*	*Milton Keynes*	*1 – 0*	*85*
Kingsbury Town	v	Portfield	1 – 2	50
Witham Town	v	Deal Town	1 – 1	82
Deal Town	*v*	*Witham Town*	*3 – 0*	*232*
Halstead Town	v	Berkhamsted Town	0 – 3	190
Peacehaven & Telscombe	v	Potton United	0 – 3	105
Oakwood	v	Potters Bar Town	2 – 1	48
Romford	v	Hertford Town	2 – 0	226
Hythe United	v	Chalfont St Peter	3 – 2	72
Three Bridges	v	Whitehawk	1 – 2	65
Selsey	v	Wembley	0 – 3	140
Wootton Blue Cross	v	Hemel Hempstead	3 – 2	90
London Colney	v	Fisher Athletic	0 – 2	60
Royston Town	v	Shoreham	0 – 0	101
Shoreham	*v*	*Royston Town*	*2 – 1*	*136*
Maldon Town	v	Ruislip Manor	0 – 3	132
Slade Green	v	Erith & Belvedere	1 – 1	230
Erith & Belvedere	*v*	*Slade Green*	*5 – 3*	*246*
Hornchurch	v	Arundel	2 – 2	72
Arundel	*v*	*Hornchurch*	*4 – 3*	*120*
Arlesey Town	v	March Town United	2 – 1	118
Barking	v	Basildon United	3 – 1	121
Thamesmead Town	v	Saltdean United	3 – 3	90
Saltdean United	*v*	*Thamesmead Town*	*4 – 0*	*136*
Hanwell Town	v	Tring Town	3 – 1	36
Horsham YMCA	v	Dartford	2 – 4	129
Abingdon Town	v	Devizes Town	1 – 1	110

(Replays in italics)			Result	Att
Devizes Town	v	Abingdon Town	0 – 3	127
Bridgwater Town	v	Brislington	1 – 0	330
Paulton Rovers	v	Fareham Town	5 – 0	164
Cirencester Town	v	Tuffley Rovers	3 – 4	82
Cove	v	Brockenhurst	1 – 3	57
Bashley	v	Torrington	9 – 0	294
Chippenham Town	v	Eastleigh	0 – 0	124
Eastleigh	v	Chippenham Town	0 – 1	126
Westfields	v	Westbury United	2 – 1	81
Frome Town	v	Wokingham Town	0 – 5	116
Lymington	v	Endsleigh	6 – 0	95
Tiverton Town	v	Weymouth	2 – 0	785
St Blazey	v	Trowbridge Town	1 – 0	151
Wimborne Town	v	Falmouth Town	3 – 2	201
Odd Down	v	Backwell United	3 – 1	72
Fleet Town	v	Thame United	0 – 0	80
Thame United	v	Fleet Town	1 – 3	82
Elmore	v	Hungerford Town	4 – 5	79
Welton Rovers	v	Calne Town	1 – 5	101
Clevedon Town	v	Bemerton Heath Harlequins	4 – 0	201
Bournemouth	v	Gosport Borough	2 – 4	74
Bridport	v	Buckingham Town	1 – 2	134
Newport AFC	v	Maidenhead United	2 – 1	657
Didcot Town	v	Taunton Town	1 – 5	183
Glastonbury	v	Chard Town	0 – 2	73
Andover	v	Portsmouth Royal Navy	3 – 4	137
Barnstaple Town	v	Carterton Town	1 – 4	152
Waterlooville	v	Reading Town	2 – 0	197
Melksham Town	v	Yate Town	2 – 1	178
Minehead	v	Mangotsfield United	0 – 1	156

First round qualifying – 13 September 1997

Gateshead	v	Matlock Town	2 – 0	282
Billingham Synthonia	v	Maine Road	0 – 0	112
Maine Road	v	Billingham Synthonia	2 – 2	101
(Maine Road won 5–3 on kicks from the penalty mark)				
South Shields	v	Skelmersdale United	3 – 0	159
Witton Albion	v	Gainsborough Trinity	0 – 5	388
Halifax Town	v	Droylsden	4 – 1	799
Burscough	v	Bedlington Terriers	3 – 3	152
Bedlington Terriers	v	Burscough	1 – 2	80
Denaby United	v	Ossett Town	2 – 3	78
Leigh RMI	v	Accrington Stanley	1 – 0	343
Chorley	v	Pontefract Collieries	3 – 1	272
Ilkeston Town	v	Rossendale United	3 – 0	390
Warrington Town	v	RTM Newcastle	1 – 2	87
Radcliffe Borough	v	Bishop Auckland	1 – 3	257
Whitby Town	v	Netherfield	6 – 2	560
Billingham Town	v	Arnold Town	0 – 1	110
Whitley Bay	v	Shotton Comrades	0 – 0	186
Shotton Comrades	v	Whitley Bay	1 – 0	127
Winsford United	v	Leek Town	1 – 0	287
Hyde United	v	Louth United	3 – 0	478
Darwen	v	Ryhope CA	1 – 2	87
Great Harwood Town	v	St Helens Town	1 – 1	84
St Helens Town	v	Great Harwood Town	3 – 1	114

(Replays in italics)			Result	Att
Lancaster City	v	Consett	2 – 2	148
Consett	*v*	*Lancaster City*	*1 – 2*	*114*
Knowsley United	v	Durham City		
(Walkover for Durham City – Knowsley United withdrawn)				
Bootle	v	Belper Town	2 – 3	83
Eccleshill United	v	Parkgate	1 – 2	53
Workington	v	Emley	0 – 3	186
Frickley Athletic	v	Morpeth Town	3 – 3	109
Morpeth Town	*v*	*Frickley Athletic*	*4 – 1*	*74*
Gretna	v	Mossley	3 – 0	115
Liversedge	v	Stocksbridge Park Steels	3 – 3	130
Stocksbridge Park Steels	*v*	*Liversedge*	*2 – 3*	*168*
North Ferriby United	v	Barrow	2 – 1	274
Newcastle Town	v	Garforth Town	3 – 5	116
Brigg Town	v	Hucknall Town	3 – 0	171
Worksop Town	v	Oldham Town	4 – 2	386
Spennymoor United	v	Blyth Spartans	1 – 1	340
Blyth Spartans	*v*	*Spennymoor United*	*1 – 0*	*360*
Bamber Bridge	v	Dunston FB	1 – 1	182
Dunston FB	*v*	*Bamber Bridge*	*2 – 3*	*94*
Clitheroe	v	Jarrow Roofing Boldon CA	4 – 3	202
Staveley MW	v	Lincoln United	1 – 5	170
Marine	v	Ashton United	1 – 0	274
Guiseley	v	Alfreton Town	3 – 0	379
Heanor Town	v	Penrith	1 – 2	111
Harrogate Town	v	Easington Colliery	2 – 2	163
Easington Colliery	*v*	*Harrogate Town*	*4 – 1*	*33*
Ashington	v	Farsley Celtic	0 – 2	221
Telford United	v	Bedworth United	1 – 2	520
Pershore Town	v	Stourbridge	0 – 7	126
Bridgnorth Town	v	Desborough Town	1 – 1	92
Desborough Town	*v*	*Bridgnorth Town*	*1 – 3*	*101*
Bury Town	v	Nuneaton Borough	1 – 2	502
Kettering Town	v	Mirrlees Blackstone	1 – 0	768
Great Yarmouth Town	v	Banbury United	2 – 1	171
Hinckley United	v	Stewarts & Lloyds	5 – 0	213
Shepshed Dynamo	v	Cambridge City	0 – 3	227
Sudbury Wanderers	v	Stafford Rangers	3 – 0	186
Brackley Town	v	Stapenhill	4 – 0	202
Rocester	v	Stowmarket Town	3 – 2	89
Tamworth	v	Bromsgrove Rovers	1 – 2	725
Knypersley Victoria	v	Atherstone United	1 – 0	250
Raunds Town	v	Spalding United	2 – 4	136
Lye Town	v	Lowestoft Town	2 – 3	147
Holbeach United	v	Gresley Rovers	3 – 6	185
Rothwell Town	v	Corby Town	2 – 1	209
Racing Club Warwick	v	Redditch United	1 – 2	204
Barwell	v	Willenhall Town	1 – 2	127
Felixstowe Port & Town	v	Halesowen Town	2 – 5	253
Moor Green	v	Bilston Town	0 – 2	170
Histon	v	Newmarket Town	1 – 3	320
Diss Town	v	VS Rugby	0 – 1	312
Bourne Town	v	Kings Lynn	1 – 3	426
Solihull Borough	v	Burton Albion	2 – 0	323
Northampton Spencer	v	Woodbridge Town	1 – 1	98
Woodbridge Town	*v*	*Northampton Spencer*	*3 – 1*	*141*
Boldmere St Michaels	v	Wroxham	1 – 0	119
Halesowen Harriers	v	Grantham Town	0 – 1	142

(Replays in italics)			*Result*	*Att*
Whyteleafe	v	Crawley Town	3 – 2	420
Marlow	v	Littlehampton Town	2 – 2	195
Littlehampton Town	*v*	*Marlow*	*2 – 2*	*183*
(Marlow won 11–10 on kicks from the penalty mark)				
Flackwell Heath	v	East Thurrock United	1 – 0	80
Chertsey Town	v	Heybridge Swifts	1 – 1	217
Heybridge Swifts	*v*	*Chertsey Town*	*2 – 1*	*208*
St Leonards Stamcroft	v	Bishop's Stortford	1 – 0	408
Great Wakering Rovers	v	Grays Athletic	1 – 2	262
Banstead Athletic	v	Camberley Town	2 – 2	65
Camberley Town	*v*	*Banstead Athletic*	*2 – 1*	*70*
Brimsdown Rovers	v	Canvey Island	1 – 2	171
Hitchin Town	v	Bognor Regis Town	0 – 2	309
Croydon	v	Horsham	2 – 1	98
Aveley	v	Chichester City	2 – 1	85
Burnham Ramblers	v	Hastings Town	0 – 1	208
Sittingbourne	v	Molesey	5 – 0	404
Langney Sports	v	Leatherhead	2 – 1	270
Burnham	v	Dorking	1 – 3	25
Concord Rangers	v	Purfleet	0 – 1	122
Welling United	v	Leyton Pennant	3 – 0	444
Tonbridge	v	Ware	1 – 0	356
Canterbury City	v	Worthing	1 – 1	137
Worthing	*v*	*Canterbury City*	*4 – 1*	*246*
Cheshunt	v	Sutton United	0 – 4	243
Walton & Hersham	v	Hampton	2 – 0	233
Tilbury	v	Wick	3 – 1	69
Leighton Town	v	Wingate & Finchley	1 – 2	202
Baldock Town	v	Slough Town	0 – 0	290
Slough Town	*v*	*Baldock Town*	*5 – 0*	*259*
Uxbridge	v	Dover Athletic	0 – 2	270
Harlow Town	v	Metropolitan Police	0 – 2	397
Croydon Athletic	v	Wivenhoe Town	0 – 4	82
Bedford United	v	Kingstonian	0 – 5	430
Gravesend & Northfleet	v	Braintree Town	3 – 3	547
Braintree Town	*v*	*Gravesend & Northfleet*	*3 – 1*	*334*
Hillingdon Borough	v	Windsor & Eton	0 – 2	110
Barton Rovers	v	Clapton	1 – 0	94
Bedfont	v	Chesham United	2 – 4	185
Margate	v	Bracknell Town	5 – 0	248
Portfield	v	Viking Sports	2 – 1	52
Berkhamsted Town	v	Deal Town	1 – 1	101
Deal Town	*v*	*Berkhamsted Town*	*2 – 1*	*209*
Burgess Hill Town	v	Harrow Borough	1 – 3	307
Yeading	v	Chelmsford City	4 – 2	264
Oakwood	v	Potton United	0 – 1	59
Hythe United	v	Romford	4 – 7	203
Clacton Town	v	Stansted	2 – 7	60
Edgware Town	v	Aylesbury United	2 – 5	274
Wembley	v	Whitehawk	3 – 1	91
Fisher Athletic	v	Wootton Blue Cross	5 – 0	185
Harwich & Parkeston	v	Carshalton Athletic	1 – 1	232
Carshalton Athletic	*v*	*Harwich & Parkeston*	*4 – 0*	*191*
Tooting & Mitcham United	v	Billericay Town	1 – 2	214
Ruislip Manor	v	Shoreham	4 – 1	107
Arundel	v	Erith & Belvedere	1 – 4	104
Bedford Town	v	Dulwich Hamlet	1 – 1	497
Dulwich Hamlet	*v*	*Bedford Town*	*2 – 0*	*226*

Herne Bay	v	Dartford	1 – 2	411
Barking	v	Arlesey Town	4 – 1	85
Hanwell Town	v	Saltdean United	3 – 2	71
Staines Town	v	Bromley	3 – 1	180
Merthyr Tydfil	v	Brockenhurst	7 – 2	556
Bridgwater Town	v	Abingdon Town	1 – 1	319
Abingdon Town	*v*	*Bridgwater Town*	*1 – 2*	*83*
Tuffley Rovers	v	Paulton Rovers	1 – 3	65
Thatcham Town	v	Cheltenham Town	0 – 1	313
Worcester City	v	Lymington	3 – 2	673
Chippenham Town	v	Bashley	3 – 2	220
Wokingham Town	v	Westfields	1 – 1	185
Westfields	*v*	*Wokingham Town*	*1 – 3*	*100*
Yeovil Town	v	Witney Town	1 – 1	1704
Witney Town	*v*	*Yeovil Town*	*1 – 2*	*323*
Oxford City	v	Dorchester Town	1 – 1	247
Dorchester Town	*v*	*Oxford City*	*1 – 0*	*353*
St Blazey	v	Tiverton Town	0 – 2	314
Odd Down	v	Wimborne Town	1 – 4	88
Downton	v	Forest Green Rovers	0 – 4	123
Havant Town	v	Basingstoke Town	1 – 1	236
Basingstoke Town	*v*	*Havant Town*	*2 – 0*	*221*
Hungerford Town	v	Fleet Town	1 – 4	81
Clevedon Town	v	Calne Town	1 – 1	190
Calne Town	*v*	*Clevedon Town*	*2 – 1*	*82*
Bideford	v	Bath City	0 – 2	214
Salisbury City	v	Chard Town	3 – 0	274
Buckingham Town	v	Gosport Borough	1 – 1	147
Gosport Borough	*v*	*Buckingham Town*	*1 – 2*	*109*
Taunton Town	v	Newport	3 – 2	571
Weston-Super-Mare	v	Cinderford Town	0 – 0	244
Cinderford Town	*v*	*Weston-Super-Mare*	*0 – 1*	*203*
Gloucester City	v	Mangotsfield United	3 – 0	532
Carterton Town	v	Portsmouth Royal Navy	0 – 1	30
Melksham Town	v	Waterlooville	1 – 2	186
Newport (IW)	v	Aldershot Town	2 – 1	848

Second round qualifying – 27 September 1997

Gateshead	v	Gainsborough Trinity	1 – 4	369
South Shields	v	Maine Road	2 – 0	204
Halifax Town	v	Leigh RMI	4 – 0	1103
Burscough	v	Ossett Town	1 – 4	169
Chorley	v	Bishop Auckland	2 – 2	337
Bishop Auckland	*v*	*Chorley*	*2 – 3*	*135*
Ilkeston Town	v	RTM Newcastle	7 – 1	394
Whitby Town	v	Winsford United	1 – 4	582
Arnold Town	v	Shotton Comrades	2 – 0	227
Hyde United	v	Lancaster City	4 – 1	598
Ryhope CA	v	St Helens Town	2 – 1	68
Durham City	v	Emley	0 – 5	292
Belper Town	v	Parkgate	2 – 2	255
Parkgate	*v*	*Belper Town*	*0 – 2*	*145*
Morpeth Town	v	North Ferriby United	0 – 0	123
North Ferriby United	*v*	*Morpeth Town*	*1 – 0*	*154*
Gretna	v	Liversedge	3 – 1	90
Garforth Town	v	Blyth Spartans	0 – 1	346

Brigg Town	v	Worksop Town	1 – 1	314
Worksop Town	*v*	*Brigg Town*	*3 – 1*	*364*
Bamber Bridge	v	Marine	1 – 3	315
Clitheroe	v	Lincoln United	1 – 3	276
Guiseley	v	Farsley Celtic	0 – 0	574
Farsley Celtic	*v*	*Guiseley*	*1 – 4*	*324*
Penrith	v	Easington Colliery	6 – 3	125
Bedworth United	v	Nuneaton Borough	1 – 1	2342
Nuneaton Borough	*v*	*Bedworth United*	*6 – 1*	*1960*
Stourbridge	v	Bridgnorth Town	2 – 1	156
Kettering Town	v	Cambridge City	1 – 1	921
Cambridge City	*v*	*Kettering Town*	*2 – 4*	*498*
Hinckley United	v	Great Yarmouth Town	2 – 0	257
Sudbury Wanderers	v	Bromsgrove Rovers	1 – 1	227
Bromsgrove Rovers	*v*	*Sudbury Wanderers*	*2 – 0*	*409*
Brackley Town	v	Rocester	1 – 1	220
Rocester	*v*	*Brackley*	*2 – 1*	*120*
Knypersley Victoria	v	Gresley Rovers	3 – 1	280
Spalding United	v	Lowestoft Town	2 – 1	312
Rothwell Town	v	Halesowen Town	1 – 1	350
Halesowen Town	*v*	*Rothwell Town*	*4 – 1*	*489*
Redditch United	v	Willenhall Town	3 – 1	262
Bilston Town	v	Kings Lynn	1 – 2	196
Newmarket Town	v	VS Rugby	1 – 2	312
Solihull Borough	v	Grantham Town	2 – 1	234
Woodbridge Town	v	Boldmere St Michaels	4 – 2	136
Whyteleafe	v	Heybridge Swifts	0 – 2	200
Marlow	v	Flackwell Heath	2 – 3	407
St Leonards Stamcroft	v	Canvey Island	2 – 0	463
Grays Athletic	v	Camberley Town	1 – 2	159
Bognor Regis Town	v	Hastings Town	2 – 1	439
Croydon	v	Aveley	2 – 0	81
Sittingbourne	v	Purfleet	2 – 1	420
Langney Sports	v	Dorking	3 – 0	274
Welling United	v	Sutton United	2 – 2	704
Sutton United	*v*	*Welling United*	*2 – 1*	*502*
Tonbridge	v	Worthing	3 – 0	410
Walton & Hersham	v	Slough Town	0 – 0	519
Slough Town	*v*	*Walton & Hersham*	*0 – 0*	*377*
(Slough won 3–2 on kicks from the penalty mark)				
Tilbury	v	Wingate & Finchley	3 – 0	90
Dover Athletic	v	Kingstonian	0 – 4	938
Metropolitan Police	v	Wivenhoe Town	2 – 2	155
Wivenhoe Town	*v*	*Metropolitan Police*	*2 – 1*	*263*
Braintree Town	v	Chesham United	3 – 0	452
Windsor & Eton	v	Barton Rovers	2 – 5	120
Margate	v	Harrow Borough	4 – 0	302
Portfield	v	Deal Town	1 – 1	107
Deal Town	*v*	*Portfield*	*2 – 1*	*250*
Yeading	v	Stansted	3 – 0	95
Potton United	v	Romford	1 – 6	278
Aylesbury United	v	Carshalton Athletic	0 – 3	516
Wembley	v	Fisher Athletic	1 – 3	133
Billericay Town	v	Dulwich Hamlet	2 – 1	369
Ruislip Manor	v	Erith & Belvedere	0 – 0	170
Erith & Belvedere	*v*	*Ruislip Manor*	*3 – 0*	*172*
Dartford	v	Staines Town	1 – 2	352
Barking	v	Hanwell Town	3 – 0	121

(Replays in italics)   Result   Att

Merthyr Tydfil	v	Cheltenham Town	0 – 2	830
Bridgwater Town	v	Paulton Rovers	2 – 4	345
Worcester City	v	Yeovil Town	1 – 2	1201
Chippenham Town	v	Wokingham Town	1 – 1	308
Wokingham Town	*v*	*Chippenham Town*	*0 – 1*	*181*
Dorchester Town	v	Forest Green Rovers	1 – 0	652
Tiverton Town	v	Wimborne Town	11 – 1	608
Basingstoke Town	v	Bath City	1 – 1	488
Bath City	*v*	*Basingstoke Town*	*1 – 3*	*388*
Fleet Town	v	Calne Town	2 – 3	125
Salisbury City	v	Weston-Super-Mare	2 – 2	305
Weston-Super-Mare	*v*	*Salisbury City*	*2 – 2*	*210*

(Salisbury City 4–3 won on kicks from the penalty mark)

Buckingham Town	v	Taunton Town	0 – 2	160
Gloucester City	v	Newport (IW)	2 – 1	582
Portsmouth Royal Navy	v	Waterlooville	1 – 1	189
Waterlooville	*v*	*Portsmouth*	*7 – 0*	*145*

Third round qualifying – 11 October 1997

Gainsborough Trinity	v	South Shields	3 – 2	608
Halifax Town	v	Ossett Town	5 – 0	1060
Chorley	v	Ilkeston Town	1 – 3	477
Winsford United	v	Arnold Town	1 – 1	480
Arnold Town	*v*	*Winsford United*	*0 – 0*	*337*

(Winsford United won 6–5 on kicks from the penalty mark)

Hyde United	v	Ryhope CA	8 – 0	573
Emley	v	Belper Town	2 – 1	396
North Ferriby United	v	Gretna	2 – 0	254
Blyth Spartans	v	Worksop Town	4 – 0	596
Marine	v	Lincoln United	1 – 1	265
Lincoln United	*v*	*Marine*	*4 – 1*	*262*
Guiseley	v	Penrith	1 – 2	557
Nuneaton Borough	v	Stourbridge	4 – 1	1411
Kettering Town	v	Hinckley United	0 – 1	1002
Bromsgrove Rovers	v	Rocester	2 – 1	612
Knypersley Victoria	v	Spalding United	3 – 1	241
Halesowen Town	v	Redditch United	2 – 2	702
Redditch United	*v*	*Halesowen Town*	*0 – 3*	*512*
Kings Lynn	v	VS Rugby	4 – 3	1508
Solihull Borough	v	Woodbridge Town	6 – 0	241
Heybridge Swifts	v	Flackwell Heath	4 – 0	347
St Leonards Stamcroft	v	Camberley Town	1 – 3	440
Bognor Regis Town	v	Croydon	1 – 1	414
Croydon	*v*	*Bognor Regis Town*	*2 – 2*	*206*

(Bognor Regis Town won 3–1 on kicks from the penalty mark)

Sittingbourne	v	Langney Sports	2 – 1	498
Sutton United	v	Tonbridge	5 – 1	716
Slough Town	v	Tilbury	6 – 1	484
Kingstonian	v	Wivenhoe Town	1 – 0	529
Braintree Town	v	Barton Rovers	4 – 1	334
Margate	v	Deal Town	2 – 1	675
Yeading	v	Romford	0 – 2	235
Carshalton Athletic	v	Fisher Athletic	1 – 0	301
Billericay Town	v	Erith & Belvedere	4 – 1	388
Staines Town	v	Barking	3 – 1	188
Cheltenham Town	v	Paulton Rovers	5 – 0	827

Yeovil Town	v	Chippenham Town	4 – 0	1762
Dorchester Town	v	Tiverton Town	0 – 1	1174
Basingstoke Town	v	Calne Town	0 – 0	411
Calne Town	*v*	*Basingstoke Town*	*1 – 2*	*287*
Salisbury City	v	Taunton Town	3 – 0	403
Gloucester City	v	Waterlooville	2 – 0	558

Fourth round qualifying – 25 October 1997

Gainsborough Trinity	v	Halifax Town	2 – 1	1730
Runcorn	v	Lincoln United	1 – 2	555
Hinckley United	v	Colwyn Bay	1 – 2	939
Halesowen Town	v	Northwich Victoria	0 – 2	1206
Ilkeston Town	v	Hyde United	3 – 2	1232
Blyth Spartans	v	Kidderminster Harriers	2 – 1	656
Nuneaton Borough	v	Emley	2 – 3	1960
Winsford United	v	Penrith	2 – 0	611
Southport	v	North Ferriby United	2 – 0	1328
Stalybridge Celtic	v	Solihull Borough	3 – 3	576
Solihull Borough	*v*	*Stalybridge Celtic*	*4 – 3*	*402*
Knypersley Victoria	v	Boston United	0 – 1	575
Altrincham	v	Morecambe	0 – 2	1134
Billericay Town	v	Camberley Town	1 – 1	790
Camberley Town	*v*	*Billericay Town*	*0 – 1*	*599*
Tiverton Town	v	Sudbury Town	5 – 0	972
Staines Town	v	Margate	0 – 3	507
Basingstoke Town	v	Braintree Town	5 – 1	841
Bognor Regis Town	v	Farnborough Town	0 – 0	1124
Farnborough Town	*v*	*Bognor Regis Town*	*2 – 1*	*855*
Rushden & Diamonds	v	Boreham Wood	1 – 1	2107
Boreham Wood	*v*	*Rushden & Diamonds*	*1 – 0*	*704*
Yeovil Town	v	Hayes	1 – 1	2501
Hayes	*v*	*Yeovil Town*	*1 – 0*	*1132*
St Albans City	v	Hendon	1 – 2	708
Heybridge Swifts	v	Ashford Town	5 – 2	535
Cheltenham Town	v	Sutton United	1 – 0	1505
Bromsgrove Rovers	v	Romford	2 – 0	880
Kings Lynn	v	Salisbury City	5 – 0	1996
Gloucester City	v	Wisbech Town	1 – 1	912
Wisbech Town	*v*	*Gloucester City*	*3 – 2*	*1094*
Enfield	v	Carshalton Athletic	1 – 2	727
Slough Town	v	Kingstonian	2 – 1	1272
Sittingbourne	v	Hereford United	2 – 2	1011
Hereford United	*v*	*Sittingbourne*	*3 – 0*	*2054*

First round proper – 15 November 1997

Notts County	v	Colwyn Bay	2 – 0	3074
Darlington	v	Solihull Borough	1 – 1	2318
Solihull Borough	*v*	*Darlington*	*3 – 3*	*2131*
(Darlington won 4–2 on kicks from the penalty mark)				
Chesterfield	v	Northwich Victoria	1 – 0	5329
Hull City	v	Hednesford Town	0 – 2	6091
Hartlepool United	v	Macclesfield Town	2 – 4	3165
Chester City	v	Winsford United	2 – 1	3885
Rochdale	v	Wrexham	0 – 2	3956

(Replays in italics)			*Result*	*Att*
Morecambe	v	Emley	1 – 1	1496
Emley	*v*	*Morecambe*	*3 – 3*	*2402*
(Emley won 3–1 on kicks from the penalty mark)				
Ilkeston Town	v	Boston United	2 – 1	2504
Lincoln City	v	Gainsborough Trinity	1 – 1	6014
Gainsborough Trinity	*v*	*Lincoln City*	*2 – 3*	*5723*
Shrewsbury Town	v	Grimsby Town	1 – 1	3193
Grimsby Town	*v*	*Shrewsbury Town*	*4 – 0*	*3242*
Oldham Athletic	v	Mansfield Town	1 – 1	5253
Mansfield Town	*v*	*Oldham Athletic*	*0 – 1*	*4097*
Rotherham United	v	Burnley	3 – 3	5709
Burnley	*v*	*Rotherham United*	*0 – 3*	*3121*
Southport	v	York City	0 – 4	3952
Preston North End	v	Doncaster Rovers	3 – 2	7953
Carlisle United	v	Wigan Athletic	0 – 1	5182
Walsall	v	Lincoln United	2 – 0	3279
Blackpool	v	Blyth Spartans	4 – 3	4814
Scunthorpe United	v	Scarborough	2 – 1	3039
Swansea City	v	Peterborough United	1 – 4	2821
Hereford United	v	Brighton & Hove Albion	2 – 1	5787
Hayes	v	Boreham Wood	0 – 1	1343
Cheltenham Town	v	Tiverton Town	2 – 1	2781
Billericay Town	v	Wisbech Town	2 – 3	1947
Farnborough Town	v	Dagenham & Redbridge	0 – 1	1236
Hendon	v	Leyton Orient	2 – 2	2421
Leyton Orient	*v*	*Hendon*	*0 – 1*	*3361*
Brentford	v	Colchester United	2 – 2	2978
Colchester United	*v*	*Brentford*	*0 – 0*	*3626*
(Colchester United won 4–2 on kicks from the penalty mark)				
Bournemouth AFC	v	Heybridge Swifts	3 – 0	3385
Wycombe Wanderers	v	Basingstoke Town	2 – 2	3932
Basingstoke Town	*v*	*Wycombe Wanderers*	*2 – 2*	*5085*
(Basingstoke Town won 5–4 on kicks from the penalty mark)				
Woking	v	Southend United	0 – 2	5248
Luton Town	v	Torquay United	0 – 1	3446
Plymouth Argyle	v	Cambridge United	0 – 0	4793
Cambridge United	*v*	*Plymouth Argyle*	*3 – 2*	*3139*
Exeter City	v	Northampton Town	1 – 1	4605
Northampton Town	*v*	*Exeter City*	*2 – 1*	*5259*
Carshalton Athletic	v	Stevenage Borough	0 – 0	1405
Stevenage Borough	*v*	*Carshalton Athletic*	*5 – 0*	*2377*
Slough Town	v	Cardiff City	1 – 1	2262
Cardiff City	*v*	*Slough Town*	*3 – 2*	*2468*
Kings Lynn	v	Bromsgrove Rovers	1 – 0	2847
Bristol Rovers	v	Gillingham	2 – 2	4825
Gillingham	*v*	*Bristol Rovers*	*0 – 2*	*4459*
Margate	v	Fulham	1 – 2	5030
Barnet	v	Watford	1 – 2	4040
Bristol City	v	Millwall	1 – 0	8413

Second round proper – 6 December 1997

Scunthorpe United	v	Ilkeston Town	1 – 1	4187
Ilkeston Town	*v*	*Scunthorpe United*	*1 – 2*	*2109*
Lincoln City	v	Emley	2 – 2	3729
Emley	*v*	*Lincoln City*	*3 – 3*	*4891*
(Emley won 4–3 on kicks from the penalty mark)				

Rotherham United	v	Kings Lynn	6 – 0	5883
Chester City	v	Wrexham	0 – 2	5224
Macclesfield Town	v	Walsall	0 – 7	3566
Wigan Athletic	v	York City	2 – 1	4021
Oldham Athletic	v	Blackpool	2 – 1	6590
Grimsby Town	v	Chesterfield	2 – 2	4762
Chesterfield	*v*	*Grimsby Town*	*0 – 2*	*4553*
Hednesford Town	v	Darlington	0 – 1	1900
Preston North End	v	Notts County	2 – 2	7583
Notts County	*v*	*Preston North End*	*1 – 2*	*3052*
Peterborough United	v	Dagenham & Redbridge	3 – 2	5572
Cheltenham Town	v	Boreham Wood	1 – 1	3525
Boreham Wood	*v*	*Cheltenham Town*	*0 – 2*	*1615*
Cambridge United	v	Stevenage Borough	1 – 1	4847
Stevenage Borough	*v*	*Cambridge United*	*2 – 1*	*4886*
Torquay United	v	Watford	1 – 1	3416
Watford	*v*	*Torquay United*	*2 – 1*	*5848*
Cardiff City	v	Hendon	3 – 1	2672
Bournemouth AFC	v	Bristol City	3 – 1	5687
Fulham	v	Southend United	1 – 0	8537
Colchester United	v	Hereford United	1 – 1	3563
Hereford United	*v*	*Colchester United*	*1 – 1*	*3725*
(Hereford United won 5–4 on kicks from the penalty mark)				
Northampton Town	v	Basingstoke Town	1 – 1	588
Basingstoke Town	*v*	*Northampton Town*	*0 – 0*	*4933*
(Northampton Town won 4–3 on kicks from the penalty mark)				
Wisbech Town	v	Bristol Rovers	0 – 2	3537

Third round proper – 3 January 1998

Portsmouth	v	Aston Villa	2 – 2	16013
Aston Villa	*v*	*Portsmouth*	*1 – 0*	*25355*
Arsenal	v	Port Vale	0 – 0	37471
Port Vale	*v*	*Arsenal*	*1 – 1*	*14964*
(Arsenal won 4–3 on kicks from the penalty mark)				
Leicester City	v	Northampton Town	4 – 0	20608
Rotherham United	v	Sunderland	1 – 5	10843
Leeds United	v	Oxford United	4 – 0	21817
Sheffield United	v	Bury	1 – 1	14009
Bury	*v*	*Sheffield United*	*1 – 2*	*4920*
Everton	v	Newcastle United	0 – 1	20885
Crewe Alexandra	v	Birmingham City	1 – 2	4607
Liverpool	v	Coventry City	1 – 3	33888
Grimsby Town	v	Norwich City	3 – 0	8161
Queens Park Rangers	v	Middlesbrough	2 – 2	13379
Middlesbrough	*v*	*Queens Park Rangers*	*2 – 0*	*21817*
West Bromwich Albion	v	Stoke City	3 – 1	17598
Bristol Rovers	v	Ipswich Town	1 – 1	8610
Ipswich Town	*v*	*Bristol Rovers*	*1 – 0*	*11423*
Hereford United	v	Tranmere Rovers	0 – 3	7473
West Ham United	v	Emley	2 – 1	18629
Manchester City	v	Bradford City	2 – 0	23686
Swindon Town	v	Stevenage Borough	1 – 2	9407
Derby County	v	Southampton	2 – 0	27992
Tottenham Hotspur	v	Fulham	3 – 1	27909
Crystal Palace	v	Scunthorpe United	2 – 0	11624
Cardiff City	v	Oldham Athletic	1 – 0	6808

Watford	v	Sheffield Wednesday	1 – 1	18306
Sheffield Wednesday	*v*	*Watford*	*0 – 0*	*18707*
(Sheffield Wednesday won 5–3 on kicks from the penalty mark)				
Chelsea	v	Manchester United	3 – 5	34088
Wimbledon	v	Wrexham	0 – 0	6349
Wrexham	*v*	*Wimbledon*	*2 – 3*	*9538*
Cheltenham Town	v	Reading	1 – 1	6000
Reading	*v*	*Cheltenham Town*	*2 – 1*	*9686*
AFC Bournemouth	v	Huddersfield Town	0 – 1	7285
Preston North End	v	Stockport County	1 – 2	12180
Blackburn Rovers	v	Wigan Athletic	4 – 2	22402
Charlton Athletic	v	Nottingham Forest	4 – 1	13947
Darlington	v	Wolverhampton Wanderers	0 – 4	5018
Peterborough United	v	Walsall	0 – 2	12874
Barnsley	v	Bolton Wanderers	1 – 0	14978

Fourth round proper – 24 January 1998

Huddersfield Town	v	Wimbledon	0 – 1	14533
Manchester City	v	West Ham United	1 – 2	26495
Charlton Athletic	v	Wolverhampton Wanderers	1 – 1	15529
Wolverhampton Wanderers	*v*	*Charlton Athletic*	*3 – 0*	*20429*
Stevenage Borough	v	Newcastle United	1 – 1	8040
Newcastle United	*v*	*Stevenage Borough*	*2 – 1*	*36357*
Tottenham Hotspur	v	Barnsley	1 – 1	28722
Barnsley	*v*	*Tottenham Hotspur*	*3 – 1*	*18220*
Middlesbrough	v	Arsenal	1 – 2	28264
Coventry City	v	Derby County	2 – 0	22816
Leeds United	v	Grimsby Town	2 – 0	28775
Sheffield Wednesday	v	Blackburn Rovers	0 – 3	15940
Crystal Palace	v	Leicester City	3 – 0	15489
Birmingham City	v	Stockport County	2 – 1	15882
Manchester United	v	Walsall	5 – 1	54669
Ipswich Town	v	Sheffield United	1 – 1	14735
Sheffield United	*v*	*Ipswich Town*	*1 – 0*	*14144*
Cardiff City	v	Reading	1 – 1	10175
Reading	*v*	*Cardiff City*	*1 – 1*	*11808*
(Reading won 4–3 on kicks from the penalty mark)				
Aston Villa	v	West Bromwich Albion	4 – 0	39372
Tranmere Rovers	v	Sunderland	1 – 0	14055

Fifth round proper – 14 February 1998

Aston Villa	v	Coventry City	0 – 1	36979
West Ham United	v	Blackburn Rovers	2 – 2	25729
Blackburn Rovers	*v*	*West Ham United*	*1 – 1*	*21972*
(West Ham United won 5–4 on kicks from the penalty mark)				
Leeds United	v	Birmingham City	3 – 2	35071
Newcastle United	v	Tranmere Rovers	1 – 0	36522
Wimbledon	v	Wolverhampton Wanderers	1 – 1	15608
Wolverhampton Wanderers	*v*	*Wimbledon*	*2 – 1*	*25112*
Manchester United	v	Barnsley	1 – 1	54700
Barnsley	*v*	*Manchester United*	*3 – 2*	*18663*
Arsenal	v	Crystal Palace	0 – 0	37164
Crystal Palace	*v*	*Arsenal*	*1 – 2*	*15674*
Sheffield United	v	Reading	1 – 0	17845

Sixth round proper – 7 March 1998

			Result	Att
Arsenal	v	West Ham United	1 – 1	38077
West Ham United	*v*	*Arsenal*	*1 – 1*	*25859*
(Arsenal won 4–3 on kicks from the penalty mark)				
Coventry City	v	Sheffield United	1 – 1	23084
Sheffield United	*v*	*Coventry City*	*1 – 1*	*29034*
(Sheffield United won 3–1 on kicks from the penalty mark)				
Leeds United	v	Wolverhampton Wanderers	0 – 1	39902
Newcastle United	v	Barnsley	3 – 1	36504

Semi-finals – 5 April 1998

			Result	Att
Sheffield United	v	Newcastle United	0 – 1	53452
(at Manchester United FC)				
Wolverhampton Wanderers	v	Arsenal	0 – 1	39372
(at Aston Villa FC)				

26 ● FA TROPHY WINNERS 1970–1998

Year	Venue	Winners		Runners-up	Result
1970	Wembley	Macclesfield Town	v	Telford United	2 – 0
1971	Wembley	Telford United	v	Hillingdon Borough	3 – 2
1972	Wembley	Stafford Rangers	v	Barnet	3 – 0
1973	Wembley	Scarborough	v	Wigan Athletic	2 – 1*
1974	Wembley	Morecambe	v	Dartford	2 – 1
1975	Wembley	Matlock Town	v	Scarborough	4 – 0
1976	Wembley	Scarborough	v	Stafford Rangers	3 – 2*
1977	Wembley	Scarborough	v	Dagenham	2 – 1
1978	Wembley	Altrincham	v	Leatherhead	3 – 1
1979	Wembley	Stafford Rangers	v	Kettering Town	2 – 0
1980	Wembley	Dagenham	v	Mossley	2 – 1
1981	Wembley	Bishop's Stortford	v	Sutton United	1 – 0
1982	Wembley	Enfield	v	Altrincham	1 – 0*
1983	Wembley	Telford United	v	Northwich Victoria	2 – 1
1984	Wembley	Northwich Victoria	v	Bangor City	1 – 1
	Stoke	Northwich Victoria	v	Bangor City	2 – 1
1985	Wembley	Wealdstone	v	Boston United	2 – 1
1986	Wembley	Altrincham	v	Runcorn	1 – 0
1987	Wembley	Kidderminster Harriers	v	Burton Albion	0 – 0
	West Bromwich	Kidderminster Harriers	v	Burton Albion	2 – 1
1988	Wembley	Enfield	v	Telford United	0 – 0
	West Bromwich	Enfield	v	Telford United	3 – 2
1989	Wembley	Telford United	v	Macclesfield Town	1 – 0*
1990	Wembley	Barrow	v	Leek Town	3 – 0
1991	Wembley	Wycombe Wanderers	v	Kidderminster Harriers	2 – 1
1992	Wembley	Colchester United	v	Witton Albion	3 – 1
1993	Wembley	Wycombe Wanderers	v	Runcorn	4 – 1
1994	Wembley	Woking	v	Runcorn	2 – 1
1995	Wembley	Woking	v	Kidderminster Harriers	2 – 1*
1996	Wembley	Macclesfield Town	v	Northwich Victoria	3 – 1
1997	Wembley	Woking	v	Dagenham	1 – 0*
1998	Wembley	Cheltenham Town	v	Southport	1 – 0

* After extra time

27 ● WALKER'S FOURTH MEDAL

FA UMBRO TROPHY – FINAL TIE 1998

Cheltenham Town 1   Southport 0

Cheltenham's Trophy win in the blistering Wembley heat was a personal triumph for boss Steve Cotterill. The ex-Wimbledon and AFC Bournemouth striker, now 33, became the youngest to lead a side to Wembley victory with the exception of Roy McDonough, who was Colchester United's player-manager when they lifted the Trophy in 1992. Within weeks of his appointment he had led Cheltenham back to the Conference from the Dr. Marten's League; now in his first full season he had taken the "Robins" to the Third Round Proper of the FA Cup (losing in a replay to First Division Reading), second spot in the Conference behind Halifax – and their first FA Trophy.

In sweltering conditions and with both sides determined not to give an inch, it always looked likely that a single goal would decide the match. It finally arrived with eleven minutes left on the clock and two Cheltenham substitutes with "fresh legs" were involved in the breakthrough. Jimmy Smith, replacing the old campaigner Clive Walker, played his part in ensuring his 40-year-old team-mate would gain his fourth Trophy winners' medal in five years by earning a free-kick with a twisting run down the right flank. Russell Milton, another recent arrival on the pitch, curled a quick ball into the goalmouth and full-back Jamie Victory nudged it on for Jason Eaton to head in at the far post. In keeping with the slow tempo of the match, the ball seemed to take several seconds to hit the back of the net.

Southport had arguably shaded a first half in which their well-supported opponents found too many passes going astray and created just one good scoring chance. An intelligent flick by Eaton from Bloomer's pass upfield put Dale Watkins clear of the Southport defence in a central position and England semi-pro' cap Billy Stewart had to rush out and bravely smother the ball at his feet. Both players took a knock, with Watkins needing lengthy attention.

The Lancastrians had their half-chances throughout. Kevin Formby's firm left-footer was beaten down by Steve Book, son of the former Northampton Town 'keeper, and Brian Ross shot narrowly over the top after a clever move. Brian Butler, chosen later as Man-of-the-Match, was dispossessed

A goal attempt from an off-balance Jason Eaton.

right in front of goal and even 41-year-old defender (and player-manager) Paul Futcher weighed in with a mighty volley which unfortunately missed by a distance.

Cheltenham skipper Chris Banks received the Trophy from Roger Hunt, one of England's World Cup-winning stars from 1966. Gordon Banks, no relation to Chris, joined Hunt in presenting the England semi-professional squad with their caps in a pre-match ceremony on the touchline.

Cheltenham Town: Book, Duff, Freeman, Banks, Victory, Knight (Milton), Howells, Bloomer, Walker (Smith J.), Eaton, Watkins.

Southport: Stewart, Horner, Futcher, Ryan, Farley, Kielty, Butler, Gamble, Formby (Whittaker), Thompson (Bollard), Ross.

Referee: G. Willard (Sussex)

Attendance: 26,837

Cheltenham Town – FA Trophy winners 1998.

28 ● FA UMBRO TROPHY 1997–1998

First round qualifying – 18 October 1997

(Replays in italics)			Result	Att
Stafford Rangers	v	Hinckley United	1 – 1	514
Hinckley United	*v*	*Stafford Rangers*	*1 – 0*	*240*
Moor Green	v	Atherstone United	1 – 0	161
Buxton	v	Alfreton Town	0 – 1	234
Bedworth United	v	Stocksbridge Park Steels	3 – 1	174
Solihull Borough	v	Shepshed Dynamo	3 – 0	162
Lincoln United	v	Trafford	5 – 2	141
Tamworth	v	Congleton Town	5 – 1	489
Paget Rangers	v	Bilston Town	0 – 0	102
Bilston Town	*v*	*Paget Rangers*	*2 – 2*	*79*
(Bilston Town won 5–3 on kicks from the penalty mark)				
Witton Albion	v	Farsley Celtic	3 – 0	353
Radcliffe Borough	v	Dudley Town		
(walkover for Radcliffe Borough – Dudley Town withdrawn)				
Eastwood Town	v	Redditch United	1 – 1	140
Redditch United	*v*	*Eastwood Town*	*3 – 0*	*118*
Blakenall	v	Spennymoor United	2 – 3	195
Belper Town	v	Droylsden	2 – 2	267
Droylsden	*v*	*Belper Town*	*2 – 3*	*114*
Winsford United	v	Ilkeston Town	2 – 0	287
Flixton	v	Matlock Town	0 – 3	147
Netherfield	v	Whitby Town	1 – 1	161
Whitby Town	*v*	*Netherfield*	*3 – 3*	*481*
(Whitby Town won 4–3 on kicks from the penalty mark)				
Frickley Athletic	v	Leigh RMI	1 – 1	171
Leigh RMI	*v*	*Frickley Athletic*	*2 – 1*	*86*
Knowsley United	v	Great Harwood Town		
(walkover for Great Harwood Town – Knowsley United withdrawn)				
Sutton Coldfield Town	v	Gretna	2 – 1	131
Whitley Bay	v	Worksop Town	0 – 1	173
Wembley	v	Gravesend & Northfleet	2 – 6	160
Whyteleafe	v	Margate	1 – 5	125
Corby Town	v	Newport AFC	4 – 3	163
Yate Town	v	Molesey	1 – 3	115
Tonbridge	v	Newport (IW)	1 – 0	325
Oxford City	v	Cinderford Town	6 – 0	162
Havant Town	v	Hendon	2 – 2	222
Hendon	*v*	*Havant Town*	*2 – 1*	*137*
Trowbridge Town	v	Raunds Town	1 – 2	214
Bognor Regis Town	v	Thame United	4 – 0	326
Walton & Hersham	v	Staines Town	3 – 0	270
Aldershot Town	v	Croydon	5 – 1	1705
Waterlooville	v	Fisher Athletic	2 – 1	140
Crawley Town	v	Kingstonian	2 – 1	1587
Brackley Town	v	Worcester City	2 – 2	292
Worcester City	*v*	*Brackley Town*	*5 – 0*	*423*
Ashford Town	v	VS Rugby	2 – 1	397
Hampton	v	Wokingham Town	0 – 1	212
Evesham United	v	Rothwell Town	1 – 2	89
Billericay Town	v	Grays Athletic	3 – 2	478
Romford	v	Chertsey Town	2 – 0	336

			Result	Att
Harrow Borough	v	Weston-Super-Mare	1 – 1	182
Weston-Super-Mare	*v*	*Harrow Borough*	*1 – 2*	*225*
Hitchin Town	v	Erith & Belvedere	7 – 1	267
Basingstoke Town	v	Leatherhead	2 – 0	402
Leyton Pennant	v	Baldock Town	0 – 1	78
Cambridge City	v	Maidenhead United	2 – 1	216
Wisbech Town	v	Clevedon Town	4 – 3	502
Carshalton Athletic	v	Racing Club Warwick	2 – 0	233
Fleet Town	v	Abingdon Town	2 – 2	86
Abingdon Town	*v*	*Fleet Town*	*2 – 0*	*52*
Uxbridge	v	Weymouth	2 – 2	208
Weymouth	*v*	*Uxbridge*	*1 – 2*	*492*
Fareham Town	v	Witney Town	0 – 3	135

Second round qualifying – 8 November 1997

			Result	Att
Redditch United	v	Worksop Town	1 – 3	277
Winsford United	v	Spennymoor United	1 – 0	293
Hinckley United	v	Whitby Town	3 – 1	364
Radcliffe Borough	v	Leigh RMI	1 – 1	207
Leigh RMI	*v*	*Radcliffe Borough*	*1 – 0*	*201*
Stourbridge	v	Great Harwood Town	1 – 1	195
Great Harwood Town	*v*	*Stourbridge*	*3 – 1*	*81*
Witton Albion	v	Bilston Town	0 – 0	402
Bilston Town	*v*	*Witton Albion*	*2 – 2*	*156*
(Witton Albion won 6–5 on kicks from the penalty mark)				
Solihull Borough	v	Alfreton Town	9 – 1	188
Gainsborough Trinity	v	Bedworth United	3 – 0	387
Workington	v	Harrogate Town	1 – 1	166
Harrogate Town	*v*	*Workington*	*0 – 0*	*211*
(Harrogate Town won 5–4 on kicks from the penalty mark)				
Matlock Town	v	Sutton Coldfield Town	4 – 1	236
Lincoln United	v	Belper Town	1 – 2	189
Tamworth	v	Moor Green	4 – 3	602
Abingdon Town	v	Wokingham Town	2 – 0	179
Margate	v	Waterlooville	3 – 2	244
Billericay Town	v	Forest Green Rovers	4 – 0	426
Carshalton Athletic	v	Aldershot Town	0 – 0	890
Aldershot Town	*v*	*Carshalton Athletic*	*3 – 0*	*1652*
Cambridge City	v	Dartford	1 – 1	328
Dartford	*v*	*Cambridge City*	*0 – 1*	*260*
Crawley Town	v	Bishop's Stortford	1 – 2	1155
Berkhamsted Town	v	Worcester City	3 – 2	242
Baldock Town	v	Corby Town	1 – 2	155
Basingstoke Town	v	Witney Town	2 – 0	396
Tonbridge	v	Hastings Town	0 – 3	577
Uxbridge	v	Worthing	0 – 1	137
Bognor Regis Town	v	Chesham United	2 – 3	388
Oxford City	v	Wisbech Town	0 – 2	317
Ashford Town	v	Raunds Town	1 – 2	434
Cirencester Town	v	Gravesend & Northfleet	1 – 0	186
Bromley	v	Hendon	2 – 1	303
Hitchin Town	v	Barton Rovers	3 – 0	349
Romford	v	Rothwell Town	5 – 1	293
Harrow Borough	v	Molesey	5 – 0	219
Walton & Hersham	v	Bashley	0 – 0	257
Bashley	*v*	*Walton & Hersham*	*2 – 0*	*225*

Third round qualifying – 29 November 1997

			Result	Att
Marine	v	Grantham Town	1 – 1	255
Grantham Town	*v*	*Marine*	*1 – 0*	*326*
Bradford Park Avenue	v	Leigh RMI	1 – 1	127
Leigh RMI	*v*	*Bradford Park Avenue*	*1 – 0*	*120*
Tamworth	v	Lancaster City	0 – 1	618
Belper Town	v	Boston United	1 – 5	502
Bromsgrove Rovers	v	Worksop Town	1 – 2	517
Accrington Stanley	v	Runcorn	0 – 5	402
Solihull Borough	v	Emley	2 – 1	
Barrow	v	Hinckley United	4 – 1	1011
Great Harwood Town	v	Witton Albion	0 – 1	92
Matlock Town	v	Winsford United	1 – 1	231
Winsford United	*v*	*Matlock Town*	*0 – 0*	*168*
(Winsford won 5–3 on kicks from the penalty mark)				
Gainsborough Trinity	v	Bamber Bridge	1 – 0	429
Halesowen Town	v	Burton Albion	1 – 2	773
Harrogate Town	v	Blyth Spartans	0 – 3	301
Nuneaton Borough	v	Altrincham	0 – 2	903
Bromley	v	Purfleet	1 – 4	270
St Albans City	v	Bishop's Stortford	5 – 2	333
Harrow Borough	v	Bath City	1 – 3	305
Hitchin Town	v	Boreham Wood	0 – 2	321
Berkhamsted Town	v	Salisbury City	2 – 1	112
Wisbech Town	v	Raunds Town	2 – 2	680
Raunds Town	*v*	*Wisbech Town*	*3 – 2*	*148*
Dorchester Town	v	Worthing	3 – 0	626
Aylesbury United	v	Dulwich Hamlet	0 – 3	406
Bashley	v	Cirencester Town	4 – 1	223
Corby Town	v	Margate	2 – 2	168
Margate	*v*	*Corby Town*	*5 – 1*	*176*
Kings Lynn	v	Chelmsford City	1 – 4	1016
Basingstoke Town	v	Romford	4 – 0	592
Merthyr Tydfil	v	Cambridge City	2 – 2	469
Cambridge City	*v*	*Merthyr Tydfil*	*6 – 3*	*200*
Hastings Town	v	Heybridge Swifts	3 – 2	532
Chesham United	v	Sutton United	2 – 1	380
Yeading	v	St Leonards Stamcroft	2 – 0	120
Billericay Town	v	Aldershot Town	2 – 1	982
Sittingbourne	v	Abingdon Town	1 – 1	369
Abingdon Town	*v*	*Sittingbourne*	*1 – 2*	*88*

First round proper – 10 January 1998

			Result	Att
Barrow	v	Worksop Town	1 – 1	1199
Worksop Town	*v*	*Barrow*	*2 – 4*	*1044*
Grantham Town	v	Leigh RMI	1 – 1	560
Leigh RMI	*v*	*Grantham Town*	*0 – 0*	*171*
(Grantham Town won 4–3 on kicks from the penalty mark)				
Halifax Town	v	Blyth Spartans	2 – 1	1712
Lancaster City	v	Northwich Victoria	0 – 3	478
Hednesford Town	v	Gainsborough Trinity	2 – 1	876
Burton Albion	v	Witton Albion	2 – 1	735
Guiseley	v	Telford United	0 – 0	716

			Result	Att
Telford United	v	Guiseley	*3 – 2*	*557*
Morecambe	v	Solihull Borough	3 – 2	766
Hyde United	v	Boston United	2 – 1	792
Altrincham	v	Runcorn	3 – 2	555
Stalybridge Celtic	v	Gateshead	2 – 4	524
Bishop Auckland	v	Colwyn Bay	3 – 1	263
Southport	v	Winsford United	3 – 0	996
Gresley Rovers	v	Leek Town	4 – 4	638
Leek Town	v	*Gresley Rovers*	*3 – 1*	*324*
Ashton United	v	Chorley	0 – 0	439
Chorley	v	*Ashton United*	*0 – 2*	*430*
Kettering Town	v	Dorchester Town	1 – 0	1341
Welling United	v	Slough Town	1 – 1	663
Slough Town	v	*Welling United*	*2 – 1*	*560*
Dagenham & Redbridge	v	Billericay Town	1 – 0	1065
Bashley	v	Raunds Town	3 – 0	329
Hayes	v	Cambridge City	3 – 2	593
Kidderminster Harriers	v	Berkhamsted Town	4 – 1	1206
Bath City	v	Hastings Town	0 – 0	662
Hastings Town	v	*Bath City*	*0 – 1*	*481*
Stevenage Borough	v	Chesham United	2 – 2	2685
Chesham United	v	*Stevenage Borough*	*0 – 3*	*956*
Woking	v	Margate	0 – 1	2830
Rushden & Diamonds	v	Farnborough Town	3 – 2	2164
Enfield	v	Cheltenham Town	1 – 1	966
Cheltenham Town	v	*Enfield*	*5 – 1*	*1650*
Hereford United	v	Dulwich Hamlet	3 – 0	2101
Boreham Wood	v	Chelmsford City	2 – 1	407
Purfleet	v	Dover Athletic	0 – 1	333
Yeovil Town	v	Yeading	0 – 0	2016
Yeading	v	*Yeovil Town*	*1 – 0*	*286*
St Albans City	v	Sittingbourne	0 – 0	475
Sittingbourne	v	*St Albans City*	*0 – 1*	*450*
Basingstoke Town	v	Gloucester City	0 – 1	713

Second round proper – 31 January 1998

Altrincham	v	Morecambe	2 – 0	942
Bath City	v	Grantham Town	2 – 3	832
Barrow	v	St Albans City	2 – 1	1379
Hednesford Town	v	Leek Town	5 – 0	1073
Yeading	v	Southport	0 – 6	342
Hayes	v	Kidderminster Harriers	5 – 0	698
Halifax Town	v	Slough Town	1 – 1	1633
Slough Town	v	*Halifax Town*	*2 – 0*	*876*
Gloucester City	v	Burton Albion	1 – 1	963
Burton Albion	v	*Gloucester City*	*2 – 2*	*701*
(Gloucester City won 6–5 on kicks from the penalty mark)				
Bishop Auckland	v	Boreham Wood	1 – 4	369
Hereford United	v	Dover Athletic	0 – 2	2108
Margate	v	Bashley	1 – 2	550
Dagenham & Redbridge	v	Hyde United	0 – 5	989
Cheltenham Town	v	Rushden & Diamonds	3 – 1	2058
Telford United	v	Ashton United	0 – 1	626
Northwich Victoria	v	Kettering Town	4 – 0	1225
Gateshead	v	Stevenage Borough	1 – 2	902

● **121**

Third round proper – 21 February 1998

Grantham Town	v	Hednesford Town	2 – 1	2214
Hyde United	v	Dover Athletic	0 – 2	917
Stevenage Borough	v	Gloucester City	1 – 1	2835
Gloucester City	*v*	*Stevenage Borough*	*1 – 2*	*1540*
Slough Town	v	Boreham Wood	1 – 1	1221
Boreham Wood	*v*	*Slough Town*	*1 – 2*	*544*
Barrow	v	Northwich Victoria	1 – 0	2185
Altrincham	v	Southport	0 – 2	1196
Hayes	v	Bashley	2 – 0	671
Ashton United	v	Cheltenham Town	0 – 1	963

Fourth round proper – Saturday 14 March 1998

Dover Athletic	v	Barrow	1 – 1	2970
Barrow	*v*	*Dover Athletic*	*0 – 0*	*4217*
(Dover Athletic won 5–4 on kicks from the penalty mark)				
Stevenage Borough	v	Slough Town	0 – 1	3482
Cheltenham Town	v	Hayes	1 – 0	2385
Grantham Town	v	Southport	1 – 1	3695
Southport	*v*	*Grantham Town*	*3 – 1*	*1707*

Semi-finals – Ist Leg – Saturday 28 March 1998

Cheltenham Town	v	Dover Athletic	2 – 1	3011
Slough Town	v	Southport	0 – 1	2106

2nd Leg – Saturday 4 April 1998

Dover Athletic	v	Cheltenham Town	2 – 2	3240
(Cheltenham Town won 4–3 on aggregate)				
Southport	v	Slough Town	1 – 1	4895
(Southport won 2–1 on aggregate)				

29 ● FA VASE WINNERS 1976–1998

Year	Venue	Winners		Runners-up	Result
1975	Wembley	Hoddesdon Town	v	Epsom & Ewell	2 – 1
1976	Wembley	Billericay Town	v	Stamford	1 – 0*
1977	Wembley	Billericay Town	v	Sheffield	1 – 1*
	Nottingham	Billericay Town	v	Sheffield	2 – 1
1978	Wembley	Blue Star	v	Barton Rovers	2 – 1
1979	Wembley	Billericay Town	v	Almondsbury Greenway	4 – 1
1980	Wembley	Stamford	v	Guisborough Town	2 – 0
1981	Wembley	Whickham	v	Willenhall Town	3 – 2*
1982	Wembley	Forest Green Rovers	v	Rainworth Miners' Welfare	3 – 0
1983	Wembley	VS Rugby	v	Halesowen Town	1 – 0
1984	Wembley	Stansted	v	Stamford	3 – 2
1985	Wembley	Halesowen Town	v	Fleetwood Town	3 – 1
1986	Wembley	Halesowen Town	v	Southall	3 – 0
1987	Wembley	St Helens Town	v	Warrington Town	3 – 2
1988	Wembley	Colne Dynamoes	v	Emley	1 – 0*
1989	Wembley	Tamworth	v	Sudbury Town	1 – 1*
	Peterborough	Tamworth	v	Sudbury Town	3 – 0
1990	Wembley	Yeading	v	Bridlington Town	0 – 0*
	Leeds	Yeading	v	Bridlington Town	1 – 0
1991	Wembley	Guiseley	v	Gresley Rovers	4 – 4*
	Sheffield	Guiseley	v	Gresley Rovers	3 – 1
1992	Wembley	Wimborne Town	v	Guiseley	5 – 3
1993	Wembley	Bridlington Town	v	Tiverton Town	1 – 0
1994	Wembley	Diss Town	v	Taunton Town	2 – 1*
1995	Wembley	Arlesey Town	v	Oxford City	2 – 1
1996	Wembley	Brigg Town	v	Clitheroe	3 – 0
1997	Wembley	Whitby Town	v	North Ferriby United	3 – 0
1998	Wembley	Tiverton Town	v	Tow Law Town	1 – 0

*After extra time

30 ● TIVVY PROVE THEIR CLASS

FA CARLSBERG VASE – FINAL TIE 1998

Tiverton Town 1   Tow Law Town 0

Tiverton manager Martyn Rogers had already swept the club to a fourth Screwfix Direct League title – with an amazing record of 36 wins and two draws from 38 matches – and arguably the best team at their level of non-League football, started the 24th FA Carlsberg Vase final against Tow Law Town from the Arnott Insurance Northern League as clear favourites.

Rogers and six members of his Tivvy squad – Saunders, Everett, Daly, Hynds and Jason and Kevin Smith – had carried the pain of defeat in the 1993 Vase final to big-spending Bridlington Town for a long time and had made no secret of their ambition to make amends this time. But their County Durham opponents were determined to prove wrong a leading non-League manager's forecast that Tiverton would beat them in nine out of ten matches.

Tow Law were making their first visit to Wembley – a far cry from their little ground in Ironworks Road, purchased from the National Coal Board in 1966 and said to be the highest football ground

in England. The club which sold future England star Chris Waddle to Newcastle for £1,500 in 1980, and were due to finish the current league campaign in mid-table, had recently received some welcome assistance from the renowned footballing community in the North-East. They trained at Sunderland's new Stadium of Light and had a set of tracksuits and trainers delivered by none other than Kenny Dalglish.

Tow Law only has a population of 2,000, yet they sold twice that many tickets. But it was a substantially larger contingent from Devon which ultimately had a victory to cheer. Pete Varley, a trainee teacher in Exeter, had only been on the pitch for six minutes as a substitute when he cracked in Tiverton's match-winner with 80 minutes on the clock. A high kick into the Tow Law penalty box from the left touchline by Leonard rebounded off the back of a defender and sat up nicely for the alert Varley to hit a low right-footer into the bottom corner.

A match which had started brightly on a surprisingly warm day had a slower tempo after legs began to tire and Tow Law's frustration at the prospect of imminent defeat boiled over the last five minutes. Midfielder

Tow Law's Jarrod Suddick (left) was impressive in attack.

Nelson was shown the red card after appearing to punch Waters as they struggled to get to their feet after a full-bloodied tackle near the halfway line. But two Tow Law players had certainly looked the part in the Wembley sunshine – Jarrod Suddick, son of a former Newcastle and Blackpool forward, led the attack with skill and enterprise, and keeper Stuart Dawson bravely defied a Tiverton team with explosive attacking potential (154 goals in the league alone in the current season).

Tiverton Town: Edwards, Smith J., Tatterton, Saunders, Fallon, Conning, Daly, Leonard (Waters), Nancekivell (Rogers), Smith K. (Varley), Everett.

Tow Law Town: Dawson, Bailey, Moan, Hague, Darwent, Pickering, Johnson, Nelson, Robinson, Laidler (Bennett), Suddick.

Referee: M. Riley (West Riding)

Attendance: 13,193

Tiverton Town – FA Vase winners 1998.

31 ● FA CARLSBERG VASE 1997–1998

First round qualifying – 6 September 1997

Replays in italics			*Result*	*Att*
Easington Colliery	v	Norton & Stockton Ancients	1 – 0	61
Brandon United	v	Penrith	0 – 2	75
Glapwell	v	Hall Road Rangers	1 – 3	77
Oldham Town	v	Thackley	3 – 4	61
Burscough	v	Blackpool (Wren) Rovers	2 – 2	151
Blackpool (Wren) Rovers	*v*	*Burscough*	*0 – 2*	*90*
Long Eaton United	v	Harworth CI		
(walkover for Harworth CI – Long Eaton United withdrawn)				
Glossop North End	v	Vauxhall GM	2 – 4	128
Maltby Main	v	Arnold Town	1 – 2	77
Ramsbottom United	v	Chadderton	4 – 5	137
St Helens Town	v	Ossett Town	3 – 1	108
Pershore Town	v	Wellingborough Town	3 – 4	73
Shifnal Town	v	Wednesfield	0 – 7	88
Barrow Town	v	Meir KA	1 – 5	118
Stapenhill	v	Gornal Athletic	3 – 2	63
Fakenham Town	v	Holbeach United	2 – 0	227
Braintree Town	v	Brightlingsea United	6 – 1	192
Somersham Town	v	Warboys Town	1 – 6	115
Ipswich Wanderers	v	Lowestoft Town	3 – 0	140
Stansted	v	East Thurrock United	1 – 2	60
Biggleswade Town	v	Beaconsfield SYCOB	0 – 1	85
Chalfont St Peter	v	Ilford	4 – 2	50
Hertford Town	v	Flackwell Heath	0 – 3	55
Hornchurch	v	Wealdstone	4 – 5	154
Hanwell Town	v	Harlow Town	2 – 2	80
Harlow Town	*v*	*Hanwell Town*	*1 – 2*	*71*
Saltdean United	v	Three Bridges	2 – 5	43
Folkestone Invicta	v	East Preston	3 – 1	273
Pagham	v	Redhill	2 – 4	95
Erith Town	v	Farnham Town	3 – 5	64
Mile Oak	v	Lancing	1 – 2	42
Slade Green	v	Dorking	3 – 0	135
Christchurch	v	Sandhurst Town	0 – 2	90
Brockenhurst	v	Cowes Sports	1 – 2	60
Bodmin Town	v	Bishop Sutton		
(walkover for Bodmin Town – Bishop Sutton withdrawn)				
Odd Down	v	Torrington	1 – 0	99
Melksham Town	v	St Blazey	1 – 0	227

Second round qualifying – 4 October 1997

Easington Colliery	v	Penrith	2 – 1	29
Washington	v	RTM Newcastle	2 – 3	62
Shildon	v	West Allotment Celtic	1 – 4	139
Whickham	v	Stockton	0 – 2	40
Northallerton	v	Morpeth Town	3 – 2	118
Ryhope CA	v	Willington	1 – 3	36
Horden CW	v	Jarrow Roofing Boldon CA	1 – 2	38
Billingham Town	v	Evenwood Town	3 – 1	52
Tadcaster Albion	v	Pickering Town	1 – 0	105

Replays in italics			*Result*	*Att*
Marske United	v	Consett	1 – 1	267
Consett	*v*	*Marske United*	*0 – 3*	*162*
Shotton Comrades	v	Peterlee Newtown	0 – 3	93
Harrogate Railway	v	Ashington	0 – 5	63
South Shields	v	Crook Town	3 – 0	145
Eccleshill United	v	Leek CSOB	3 – 0	72
Douglas High School OB	v	Glasshoughton Welfare	2 – 3	114
Hatfield Main	v	Garforth Town	3 – 2	98
Yorkshire Amateur	v	Borrowash Victoria	0 – 3	92
Kidsgrove Athletic	v	Vauxhall GM	4 – 2	210
Poulton Victoria	v	Selby Town	4 – 1	75
Heanor Town	v	Atherton Collieries	3 – 0	126
East Manchester	v	Cheadle Town	2 – 2	94
Cheadle Town	*v*	*East Manchester*	*5 – 5*	*94*
(East Manchester won 3–2 on kicks from the penalty mark)				
Armthorpe Welfare	v	Pontefract Collieries	2 – 1	120
Hall Road Rangers	v	Bacup Borough	3 – 0	34
Liversedge	v	Bootle	0 – 2	74
Arnold Town	v	Maine Road	1 – 0	184
Burscough	v	Salford City	2 – 0	145
Louth United	v	Sheffield	0 – 1	51
Parkgate	v	Castleton Gabriels	0 – 2	55
Nettleham	v	St Helens Town	0 – 1	44
Skelmersdale United	v	Hallam	4 – 2	128
Brodsworth	v	Darwen	4 – 1	71
Harworth Cl	v	Blidworth MW	1 – 2	30
Holker Old Boys	v	Prescot Cables	0 – 2	45
Haslingden	v	Rossington Main	0 – 0	59
Rossington Main	*v*	*Haslingden*	*6 – 0*	*120*
Chadderton	v	Rainworth MW	2 – 0	142
Grimethorpe MW	v	Thackley	1 – 1	64
Thackley	*v*	*Grimethorpe MW*	*3 – 2*	*40*
Worsbro Bridge MW	v	Rossendale United	0 – 2	132
Ossett Albion	v	Staveley MW	2 – 3	82
Ford Sports Daventry	v	Oldbury United	2 – 1	73
Wellingborough Town	v	Birstall United	2 – 3	55
Oadby Town	v	Halesowen Harriers	3 – 2	195
Worcester Athletico	v	Dunkirk	2 – 1	29
St Andrews	v	Knypersley Victoria	0 – 2	50
Desborough Town	v	Banbury United	0 – 2	130
Stourport Swifts	v	Cradley Town	5 – 0	92
Sandwell Borough	v	Meir KA	3 – 3	56
Meir KA	*v*	*Sandwell Borough*	*2 – 5*	*90*
Chasetown	v	Shirebrook Town	2 – 1	76
Kings Heath	v	Gedling Town	1 – 0	37
Friar Lane OB	v	Willenhall Town	2 – 1	72
Stewarts & Lloyds	v	Bolehall Swifts	2 – 0	65
Pelsall Villa	v	Northampton Spencer	4 – 3	89
Tividale	v	Wednesfield	0 – 0	52
Wednesfield	*v*	*Tividale*	*1 – 0*	*80*
Coleshill Town	v	Newport Pagnell Town	1 – 3	75
Kimberley Town	v	Rocester	0 – 2	96
West Midlands Police	v	Sandiacre Town	1 – 2	53
Walsall Wood	v	Highgate United	2 – 1	59
Lye Town	v	Long Buckby	3 – 2	149
Stratford Town	v	Ibstock Welfare	1 – 0	100
Holwell Sports	v	Rushall Olympic	2 – 4	67
Bloxwich Town	v	Anstey Nomads	7 – 2	92

Replays in italics			Result	Att
Westfields	v	Stapenhill	1 – 4	61
Whitton United	v	Saffron Walden Town		
(walkover for Whitton United – Saffron Walden Town removed)				
Boston Town	v	Eynesbury Rovers	3 – 1	87
Mirrlees Blackstone	v	Clacton Town	5 – 1	65
Sawbridgeworth Town	v	Hadleigh United	2 – 2	52
Hadleigh United	*v*	*Sawbridgeworth Town*	*1 – 2*	*97*
Fakenham Town	v	March Town United	3 – 0	140
Stowmarket Town	v	Great Yarmouth Town	3 – 3	91
Great Yarmouth Town	*v*	*Stowmarket Town*	*4 – 3*	*141*
Soham Town Rangers	v	Warboys Town	0 – 1	115
Burnham Ramblers	v	Harwich & Parkeston	2 – 4	71
Maldon Town	v	Felixstowe Port & Town	2 – 1	102
Ely City	v	Thetford Town	2 – 1	107
Basildon United	v	Newmarket Town	0 – 0	62
Newmarket Town	*v*	*Basildon United*	*0 – 1*	*148*
Downham Town	v	St Neots Town	1 – 3	94
Stanway Rovers	v	Sudbury Town	0 – 3	166
Gorleston	v	Sudbury Wanderers	1 – 2	170
Watton United	v	Norwich United	0 – 3	52
Braintree Town	v	Swaffham Town	1 – 0	243
Bourne Town	v	Haverhill Rovers	2 – 1	80
Ipswich Wanderers	v	Tiptree United	1 – 2	100
Mildenhall Town	v	Cornard United	3 – 2	83
Needham Market	v	Witham Town	1 – 3	71
Yaxley	v	Great Wakering Rovers	0 – 3	85
Brimsdown Rovers	v	Milton Keynes	2 – 2	33
Milton Keynes	*v*	*Brimsdown Rovers*	*5 – 1*	*81*
East Thurrock United	v	Bowers United	1 – 4	75
Hanwell Town	v	Tring Town	1 – 2	46
Potters Bar Town	v	Potton United	3 – 0	80
Ware	v	Harpenden Town	3 – 2	97
Ford United	v	Bedford Town	2 – 1	197
Wootton Blue Cross	v	Tilbury	4 – 1	85
Brache Sparta	v	Chalfont St Peter	3 – 0	30
Edgware Town	v	Kingsbury Town	6 – 0	164
Harefield United	v	Wealdstone	1 – 4	201
London Colney	v	Langford	9 – 0	44
Aveley	v	Clapton	3 – 1	62
Viking Sports	v	Welwyn Garden City	3 – 4	65
Hillingdon Borough	v	Beaconsfield SYCOB	3 – 0	75
Shillington	v	Waltham Abbey	0 – 2	40
Wingate & Finchley	v	Amersham Town	2 – 3	61
Leighton Town	v	Southall	3 – 1	152
Hoddesdon Town	v	Cheshunt	4 – 3	130
Royston Town	v	Barkingside	2 – 2	89
Barkingside	*v*	*Royston Town*	*3 – 0*	*52*
Brook House	v	Haringey Borough	3 – 2	35
Ruislip Manor	v	Hemel Hempstead	2 – 3	133
Stotfold	v	Bedford United	2 – 0	77
Letchworth	v	Flackwell Heath	0 – 1	35
Godalming & Guildford	v	Ringmer	3 – 2	102
Ramsgate	v	Redhill	3 – 1	135
Bracknell Town	v	East Grinstead	0 – 2	111
Whitehawk	v	Slade Green	2 – 2	150
Slade Green	*v*	*Whitehawk*	*4 – 1*	*93*
(tie ordered to be replayed due to incorrect size of pitch)				
Whitehawk	*v*	*Slade Green*	*0 – 1*	*145*

Replays in italics   Result   Att

Portfield	v	Camberley Town	2 – 3	48
Arundel	v	Windsor & Eton	0 – 6	91
Bedfont	v	Oakwood	2 – 1	36
Hassocks	v	Littlehampton Town	1 – 2	117
Southwick	v	Eastbourne Town	2 – 4	86
Ashford Town (Middx)	v	Corinthian-Casuals	2 – 2	90
Corinthian-Casuals	*v*	*Ashford Town (Middx)*	*1 – 3*	*104*
Horsham	v	Beckenham Town		

(walkover for Horsham – Beckenham Town removed)

Langney Sports	v	Raynes Park Vale	1 – 0	153
Lancing	v	Faversham Town	0 – 2	69
Sheppey United	v	Ash United	4 – 3	107
Chatham Town	v	Selsey	2 – 1	63
Corinthian	v	Merstham	2 – 1	40
Deal Town	v	Thamesmead Town	2 – 1	131
Crowborough Athletic	v	Egham Town	0 – 4	47
Hailsham Town	v	Croydon Athletic	1 – 1	100
Croydon Athletic	*v*	*Hailsham Town*	*1 – 2*	*56*
Lewes	v	Chipstead	0 – 5	91
Three Bridges	v	Epsom & Ewell	1 – 3	56
Farnham Town	v	Chichester City	5 – 0	74
Canterbury City	v	Shoreham	3 – 5	89
Folkestone Invicta	v	Cobham	3 – 2	329
Tunbridge Wells	v	Hythe United	3 – 2	178
Horsham YMCA	v	Sidley United	2 – 2	60
Sidley United	*v*	*Horsham YMCA*	*1 – 1*	*135*

(Sidley United won 4–3 on kicks from the penalty mark)

Sandhurst Town	v	Cowes Sports	1 – 4	83
Didcot Town	v	North Leigh	1 – 3	42
Bicester Town	v	Stony Stratford Town	2 – 1	75
Calne Town	v	Andover	2 – 3	75
Downton	v	Gosport Borough	0 – 1	44
Totton	v	Cove	3 – 0	90
Romsey Town	v	Hungerford Town	0 – 1	72
Portsmouth Royal Navy	v	Newbury	2 – 4	39
Whitchurch United	v	Swindon Supermarine	0 – 5	72
Kintbury Rangers	v	BAT Sports	0 – 2	42
Bournemouth	v	Wantage Town	4 – 1	87
Eastleigh	v	Petersfield Town	4 – 0	69
First Tower United	v	Carterton Town	3 – 1	70

(tie ordered to be replayed due to ineligible player of First Tower United)

Carterton Town	*v*	*First Tower United*	*1 – 3*	*58*
Backwell United	v	Bridgwater Town	0 – 1	106
Devizes Town	v	Shortwood United	2 – 1	95
Hallen	v	Barnstaple Town	2 – 1	61
Paulton Rovers	v	Odd Down	2 – 1	100
Elmore	v	Warminster Town	4 – 1	45
Newquay	v	Chard Town	1 – 2	91
Bideford	v	Bridport	0 – 1	86
Westbury United	v	Dawlish Town	3 – 1	95
Tuffley Rovers	v	Fairford Town	1 – 2	40
Almondsbury Town	v	Endsleigh	0 – 2	54
Melksham Town	v	Ilfracombe Town	4 – 0	124
Keynsham Town	v	Wellington Town	2 – 0	76
Welton Rovers	v	Bodmin Town	1 – 3	126
Crediton United	v	Porthleven	2 – 6	85
Minehead	v	Frome Town	5 – 1	82
Brislington	v	Glastonbury	3 – 0	90

First round proper – 1 November 1997

			Result	Att
Willington	v	Stockton	1 – 4	61
Skelmersdale United	v	West Auckland Town	0 – 3	125
South Shields	v	Chadderton	2 – 3	150
East Manchester	v	Rossendale United	2 – 3	120
Tow Law Town	v	St Helens Town	2 – 1	168
Tadcaster Albion	v	Thackley	1 – 4	109
Prudhoe Town	v	Brodsworth	1 – 2	69
Poulton Victoria	v	Ashington	4 – 2	164
Prescot Cables	v	Sheffield	0 – 2	42
Murton	v	Rossington Main	3 – 1	29
Seaham Red Star	v	Hall Road Rangers	1 – 0	70
Jarrow Roofing Boldon CA	v	Bootle	2 – 0	41
Borrowash Victoria	v	Northallerton	1 – 0	75
Easington Colliery	v	Burscough	2 – 4	54
Glasshoughton Welfare	v	Billingham Town	1 – 2	82
Kidsgrove Athletic	v	RTM Newcastle	2 – 2	167
RTM Newcastle	*v*	*Kidsgrove Athletic*	*0 – 1*	*139*
Hebburn	v	Chester-Le-Street Town	2 – 2	87
Chester-le-Street Town	*v*	*Hebburn*	*2 – 0*	*73*
Armthorpe Welfare	v	West Allotment Celtic		
(abandoned 89 minutes, 1–1, due to an injury to an Armthorpe Welfare player)				
Armthorpe Welfare	*v*	*West Allotment Celtic*	*3 – 2*	*155*
Billingham Synthonia	v	Eccleshill United	5 – 1	151
Castleton Gabriels	v	Marske United	1 – 2	143
Hatfield Main	v	Nantwich Town	1 – 2	99
Peterlee Newtown	v	Heanor Town	4 – 2	80
Blidworth MW	v	Boston Town	0 – 8	37
Kings Heath	v	Wednesfield	2 – 2	61
Wednesfield	*v*	*Kings Heath*	*4 – 0*	*54*
Bridgnorth Town	v	Boldmere St Michaels	0 – 5	87
Stewarts & Lloyds	v	Rocester	0 – 3	84
Bloxwich Town	v	Rushall Olympic	2 – 0	112
Sandwell Borough	v	Staveley MW	0 – 4	63
Walsall Wood	v	Worcester Athletico	1 – 2	55
Stratford Town	v	Birstall United	0 – 2	95
Mirrlees Blackstone	v	Cogenhoe United	4 – 2	65
Banbury United	v	Oadby Town	1 – 2	196
Arnold Town	v	Stapenhill	4 – 2	123
Newcastle Town	v	Pelsall Villa	1 – 0	87
Knypersley Victoria	v	Sandiacre Town	3 – 0	85
Barwell	v	Ford Sports Daventry	2 – 0	128
Hucknall Town	v	Chasetown	2 – 0	202
Lye Town	v	Stourport Swifts	2 – 4	77
Newport Pagnell Town	v	Friar Lane OB	0 – 4	94
Flackwell Heath	v	Leighton Town	2 – 1	115
Harwich & Parkeston	v	Tring Town	3 – 1	150
London Colney	v	Brache Sparta	1 – 2	60
Braintree Town	v	Bury Town	3 – 0	293
Ely City	v	Wivenhoe Town	2 – 1	158
Concord Rangers	v	Great Yarmouth Town	1 – 0	128
Woodbridge Town	v	Southend Manor	5 – 1	140
Whitton United	v	Wealdstone	1 – 3	302
Wootton Blue Cross	v	Edgware Town	0 – 1	155
Ford United	v	Sudbury Wanderers	2 – 3	124
Norwich United	v	Welwyn Garden City	3 – 1	51
Aveley	v	St Neots Town	4 – 2	79

Replays in italics   *Result*   *Att*

Stotfold	v	Maldon Town	2 – 0	121
Histon	v	Witham Town	2 – 0	105
Amersham Town	v	Halstead Town	0 – 7	60
Hoddesdon Town	v	Bowers United	3 – 5	94
Fakenham Town	v	Potters Bar Town	1 – 2	201
Sudbury Town	v	Bourne Town	5 – 1	250
Milton Keynes	v	Great Wakering Rovers	0 – 3	80
Warboys Town	v	Basildon United	0 – 1	120
Hemel Hempstead	v	Barkingside	3 – 1	71
Hillingdon Borough	v	Ware	1 – 1	70
Ware	*v*	*Hillingdon Borough*	*2 – 4*	*59*
Tiptree United	v	Sawbridgeworth Town	0 – 1	59
Waltham Abbey	v	Mildenhall Town	2 – 1	93
East Grinstead Town	v	Folkestone Invicta	0 – 2	341
Thatcham Town	v	Reading Town	3 – 0	241
Bedfont	v	Faversham Town	1 – 2	40
Burnham	v	Egham Town	1 – 0	47
Langney Sports	v	Farnham Town	2 – 1	168
Sidley United	v	Brook House	0 – 2	191
Chatham Town	v	Hailsham Town	3 – 1	112
Ashford Town	v	Sheppey United	2 – 1	105
Metropolitan Police	v	North Leigh	3 – 1	60
Horsham	v	Ramsgate	0 – 1	210
Cowes Sports	v	Epsom & Ewell	5 – 2	124
Tunbridge Wells	v	Wick	2 – 4	149
Windsor & Eton	v	Shoreham	0 – 1	108
Corinthian	v	Slade Green	1 – 0	74
Deal Town	v	Godalming & Guildford	3 – 1	190
Bicester Town	v	Littlehampton Town	2 – 5	67
Abingdon United	v	Camberley Town	1 – 3	85
Eastbourne Town	v	Chipstead	1 – 4	152
Bodmin Town	v	Bournemouth	2 – 0	159
Chard Town	v	First Tower United	1 – 0	108
Chippenham Town	v	Devizes Town	1 – 1	181
Devizes Town	*v*	*Chippenham Town*	*0 – 4*	*159*
Melksham Town	v	Wimborne Town	4 – 6	192
Swindon Supermarine	v	Porthleven	1 – 1	106
Porthleven	*v*	*Swindon Supermarine*	*2 – 1*	*128*
Paulton Rovers	v	Minehead	4 – 0	94
BAT Sports	v	Hallen	3 – 2	77
Hungerford Town	v	Westbury United	2 – 1	84
Eastleigh	v	Bridport	1 – 2	127
Falmouth Town	v	Bridgwater Town	0 – 1	401
Brislington	v	Elmore	2 – 3	65
Bemerton Heath Harlequins	v	Totton	2 – 0	62
Endsleigh	v	Newbury AFC	2 – 2	72
Newbury AFC	*v*	*Endsleigh*	*0 – 1*	*59*
Fairford Town	v	Gosport Borough	2 – 3	82
Andover	v	Keynsham Town	5 – 0	163

Second round proper – 22 November 1997

Dunston Federation Brewery	v	Atherton LR	1 – 0	112
Seaham Red Star	v	Chadderton	2 – 1	73
Rossendale United	v	Tow Law Town	1 – 2	179
West Auckland Town	v	Curzon Ashton	1 – 0	80
Armthorpe Welfare	v	Denaby United	0 – 0	n/a

● **131**

Replays in italics			Result	Att
(after abandoned tie 70 mins due to fog, 1–1)				
Denaby United	v	Armthorpe Welfare	*1 – 0*	*110*
North Ferriby United	v	Murton	7 – 0	250
Peterlee Newtown	v	Brigg Town	1 – 3	73
Warrington Town	v	Poulton Victoria	0 – 1	105
Kidsgrove Athletic	v	Brodsworth	2 – 2	134
Brodsworth	*v*	*Kidsgrove Athletic*	*0 – 2*	*140*
Nantwich Town	v	Burscough	1 – 3	94
Stockton	v	Sheffield	3 – 1	78
Mossley	v	Jarrow Roofing Boldon CA	1 – 1	166
Jarrow Roofing Boldon CA	*v*	*Mossley*	*1 – 5*	*52*
Thackley	v	Borrowash Victoria	6 – 1	77
Chester-le-Street	v	Billingham Town	4 – 4	85
Billingham Town	*v*	*Chester-le-Street*	*6 – 4*	*58*
Clitheroe	v	Guisborough Town	5 – 0	180
Bedlington Terriers	v	Billingham Synthonia	5 – 0	222
Durham City	v	Marske United	0 – 1	216
Newcastle Town	v	Birstall United	0 – 1	138
Friar Lane OB	v	Wednesfield	1 – 0	97
Boldmere St Michaels	v	Arnold Town	0 – 0	112
Arnold Town	*v*	*Boldmere St Michaels*	*2 – 1*	*125*
Spalding United	v	Mirrlees Blackstone	2 – 0	221
Barwell	v	Boston Town	1 – 4	138
Knypersley Victoria	v	Stamford	0 – 1	134
Ely City	v	Worcester Athletico	1 – 0	161
Oadby Town	v	Norwich United	5 – 1	153
Staveley MW	v	Wroxham	1 – 3	175
Bloxwich Town	v	Diss Town	2 – 1	114
Rocester	v	Histon	2 – 2	107
Histon	*v*	*Rocester*	*1 – 0*	*204*
Hucknall Town	v	Stourport Swifts	2 – 1	240
Ashford Town (Middx)	v	Littlehampton Town	5 – 3	135
Deal Town	v	Great Wakering Rovers	2 – 2	217
Great Wakering Rovers	*v*	*Deal Town*	*2 – 1*	*180*
Shoreham	v	Sudbury Town	2 – 4	188
Basildon United	v	Edgware Town	3 – 2	101
Potters Bar Town	v	Whitstable Town	4 – 2	206
Faversham Town	v	Banstead Athletic	1 – 2	52
Braintree Town	v	Concord Rangers	8 – 1	310
Peacehaven & Telscombe	v	Chatham Town	1 – 0	151
Harwich & Parkeston	v	Folkestone Invicta	1 – 1	192
Folkestone Invicta	*v*	*Harwich & Parkeston*	*5 – 1*	*303*
Chipstead	v	Barking	2 – 1	102
Metropolitan Police	v	Tooting & Mitcham United	0 – 1	115
Hillingdon Borough	v	Brook House	1 – 6	100
Hemel Hempstead	v	Wick	3 – 2	91
Camberley Town	v	Corinthian	3 – 0	82
Brache Sparta	v	Halstead Town	5 – 1	60
(after abandoned tie 80 mins due to a waterlogged pitch, 2– 1)				
Sawbridgeworth Town	v	Stotfold	1 – 5	110
Burgess Hill Town	v	Canvey Island	2 – 1	513
Sudbury Wanderers	v	Flackwell Heath	4 – 0	162
Bowers United	v	Buckingham Town	3 – 0	82
Northwood	v	Woodbridge Town	0 – 2	177
Arlesey Town	v	Waltham Abbey	3 – 2	135

Replays in italics			*Result*	*Att*
Herne Bay	v	Langney Sports	2 – 0	244

(after abandoned tie 46 mins due to a floodlight failure, 1–1)

Aveley	v	Burnham	2 – 2	76
Burnham	*v*	*Aveley*	*0 – 2*	*47*
Ramsgate	v	Wealdstone	0 – 1	217
Wimborne Town	v	Gosport Borough	3 – 1	224
Elmore	v	Chard Town	2 – 4	74
Paulton Rovers	v	Porthleven	2 – 4	209
Chippenham Town	v	Andover	3 – 2	190
Tiverton Town	v	Mangotsfield United	5 – 1	552
Bridport	v	Bridgwater Town	3 – 0	194
Taunton Town	v	Hungerford Town	5 – 1	337
Thatcham Town	v	Marlow	2 – 0	196
BAT Sports	v	Bodmin Town	1 – 3	103
Lymington	v	Bemerton Heath Harlequins	0 – 0	112
Bemerton Heath Harlequins	*v*	*Lymington*	*1 – 2*	*120*
Endsleigh	v	Cowes Sports	0 – 2	111

Third round proper – 13 December 1997

Marske United	v	Bedlington Terriers	1 – 2	305
Stockton	v	Burscough	1 – 2	73
Mossley	v	West Auckland Town	0 – 2	205
Poulton Victoria	v	Kidsgrove Athletic	1 – 4	161
Tow Law Town	v	Dunston Federation Brewery	2 – 1	171
Billingham Town	v	Friar Lane OB	1 – 0	88
Arnold Town	v	North Ferriby United	1 – 3	199
Clitheroe	v	Boston Town	3 – 0	170
Oadby Town	v	Seaham Red Star	4 – 1	179
Brigg Town	v	Hucknall Town	1 – 2	199
Denaby United	v	Birstall United	0 – 1	85
Thackley	v	Stamford	2 – 3	175
Bloxwich Town	v	Spalding United	1 – 3	119
Braintree Town	v	Banstead Athletic	4 – 2	302
Hemel Hempstead	v	Taunton Town	2 – 3	175
Lymington	v	Woodbridge Town	2 – 0	131
Bodmin Town	v	Bowers United	5 – 3	179
Wimborne Town	v	Tiverton Town	0 – 4	622
Basildon United	v	Herne Bay	1 – 3	146
Cowes Sports	v	Chard Town	1 – 1	188
Chard Town	*v*	*Cowes Sports*	*0 – 0*	*180*

(Cowes Sports won 4–1 on kicks from the penalty mark)

Porthleven	v	Arlesey Town	3 – 2	275
Bridport	v	Potters Bar Town	0 – 4	261
Folkestone Invicta	v	Chipstead	2 – 1	367
Brook House	v	Histon	0 – 0	110
Histon	*v*	*Brook House*	*3 – 0*	*111*
Peacehaven & Telscombe	v	Sudbury Town	1 – 2	261
Aveley	v	Wroxham	1 – 2	103
Stotfold	v	Ashford Town (Middx)	2 – 1	187
Thatcham Town	v	Burgess Hill Town	0 – 3	252
Great Wakering Rovers	v	Wealdstone	2 – 1	344
Brache Sparta	v	Ely City	8 – 1	141
Chippenham Town	v	Tooting & Mitcham United	2 – 3	207
Camberley Town	v	Sudbury Wanderers	3 – 3	80
Sudbury Wanderers	*v*	*Camberley Town*	*3 – 1*	*122*

Fourth round proper – 17 January 1998

Taunton Town	v	Herne Bay	5 – 2	632
Sudbury Wanderers	v	Bedlington Terriers	3 – 0	481
Oadby Town	v	Tooting & Mitcham United	2 – 2	340
Tooting & Mitcham United	*v*	*Oadby Town*	*1 – 4*	*268*
Hucknall Town	v	Wroxham	2 – 1	502
Billingham Town	v	Bodmin Town	3 – 1	300
Tow Law Town	v	Histon	3 – 0	279
Kidsgrove Athletic	v	Brache Sparta	2 – 2	300
Brache Sparta	*v*	*Kidsgrove Athletic*	*0 – 3*	*327*
Braintree Town	v	Lymington	0 – 0	585
Lymington	*v*	*Braintree Town*	*2 – 1*	*441*
Stamford	v	Potters Bar Town	0 – 1	359
Cowes Sports	v	North Ferriby United	1 – 1	590
North Ferriby United	*v*	*Cowes Sports*	*3 – 1*	*412*
Sudbury Town	v	Burscough	1 – 0	598
Tiverton Town	v	West Auckland Town	9 – 0	936
Spalding United	v	Birstall United	2 – 1	389
Stotfold	v	Porthleven	1 – 2	645
Clitheroe	v	Burgess Hill Town	0 – 0	430
Burgess Hill Town	*v*	*Clitheroe*	*3 – 0*	*857*
Great Wakering Rovers	v	Folkestone Invicta	2 – 1	494

Fifth round proper – 7 February 1998

Tiverton Town	v	Oadby Town	2 – 1	1197
Sudbury Wanderers	v	Burgess Hill Town	1 – 0	479
Porthleven	v	Hucknall Town	1 – 0	1031
Sudbury Town	v	Tow Law Town	1 – 2	810
Kidsgrove Athletic	v	Lymington	3 – 2	540
Spalding United	v	Billingham Town	2 – 0	743
North Ferriby United	v	Taunton Town	0 – 2	466
Great Wakering Rovers	v	Potters Bar Town	0 – 1	659

Sixth round proper – 28 February 1998

Taunton Town	v	Porthleven	2 – 0	1804
Spalding United	v	Tiverton Town	1 – 2	2038
Sudbury Wanderers	v	Tow Law Town	1 – 1	881
Tow Law Town	*v*	*Sudbury Wanderers*	*2 – 0*	*797*
Kidsgrove Athletic	v	Potters Bar Town	2 – 0	935

Semi-finals first leg – 14 March 1998

Taunton Town	v	Tow Law Town	4 – 4	1569
Tiverton Town	v	Kidsgrove Athletic	2 – 0	1885

Second leg – 21 March 1998

Tow Law Town	v	Taunton Town	1 – 0	1819
Kidsgrove Athletic	v	Tiverton Town	2 – 1	1903

32 ● FA YOUTH CUP WINNERS 1953–1998

The FA Youth Cup Final is played on a two-leg basis but the 1978 final between Crystal Palace and Aston Villa was a single match. The only final which needed a replay was the 1983 contest between Norwich and Everton.

Year	Winners		Runners-up	Result
1953	Manchester United	v	Wolverhampton Wanderers	9 – 3
1954	Manchester United	v	Wolverhampton Wanderers	5 – 4
1955	Manchester United	v	West Bromwich Albion	7 – 1
1956	Manchester United	v	Chesterfield	4 – 3
1957	Manchester United	v	West Ham United	8 – 2
1958	Wolverhampton Wanderers	v	Chelsea	7 – 6
1959	Blackburn Rovers	v	West Ham United	2 – 1
1960	Chelsea	v	Preston North End	5 – 2
1961	Chelsea	v	Everton	5 – 3
1962	Newcastle United	v	Wolverhampton Wanderers	2 – 1
1963	West Ham United	v	Liverpool	6 – 5
1964	Manchester United	v	Swindon Town	5 – 2
1965	Everton	v	Arsenal	3 – 2
1966	Arsenal	v	Sunderland	5 – 3
1967	Sunderland	v	Birmingham City	2 – 0
1968	Burnley	v	Coventry City	3 – 2
1969	Sunderland	v	West Bromwich Albion	6 – 3
1970	Tottenham Hotspur	v	Coventry City	4 – 3
1971	Arsenal	v	Cardiff City	2 – 0
1972	Aston Villa	v	Liverpool	5 – 2
1973	Ipswich Town	v	Bristol City	4 – 1
1974	Tottenham Hotspur	v	Huddersfield Town	2 – 1
1975	Ipswich Town	v	West Ham United	5 – 1
1976	West Bromwich Albion	v	Wolverhampton Wanderers	5 – 0
1977	Crystal Palace	v	Everton	1 – 0
1978	Crystal Palace	v	Aston Villa	1 – 0
1979	Millwall	v	Manchester City	2 – 0
1980	Aston Villa	v	Manchester City	3 – 2
1981	West Ham United	v	Tottenham Hotspur	2 – 1
1982	Watford	v	Manchester United	7 – 6
1983	Norwich City	v	Everton	6 – 5*
1984	Everton	v	Stoke City	4 – 2
1985	Newcastle United	v	Watford	4 – 1
1986	Manchester City	v	Manchester United	3 – 1
1987	Coventry City	v	Charlton Athletic	2 – 1
1988	Arsenal	v	Doncaster Rovers	6 – 1
1989	Watford	v	Manchester City	2 – 1
1990	Tottenham Hotspur	v	Middlesbrough	3 – 2
1991	Millwall	v	Sheffield Wednesday	3 – 0
1992	Manchester United	v	Crystal Palace	6 – 3
1993	Leeds United	v	Manchester United	4 – 1
1994	Arsenal	v	Millwall	5 – 3
1995	Manchester United	v	Tottenham Hotspur	2 – 2†
1996	Liverpool	v	West Ham United	4 – 1
1997	Leeds United	v	Crystal Palace	3 – 1
1998	Everton	v	Blackburn Rovers	5 – 3

*aggregate score after replay
†won on penalty-kicks

33 ● THE TIMES FA YOUTH CUP 1997–1998

Preliminary round

(Replays in italics)			Result	Att
Lancaster City	v	Yorkshire Amateur	0 – 3	21
Wigan Athletic	v	Billingham Town	3 – 2	83
Guisborough Town	v	Hartlepool United	0 – 0	115
Hartlepool United	*v*	*Guisborough Town*	*3 – 2*	*160*
Farsley Celtic	v	Barrow		
(walkover for Farsley Celtic – Barrow withdrawn)				
Shotton Comrades	v	Carlisle United		
(walkover for Carlisle United – Shotton Comrades withdrawn)				
Stocksbridge Park Steels	v	Preston North End	1 – 3	111
Chester City	v	Runcorn	10 – 1	110
Scunthorpe United	v	Lincoln City	0 – 0	139
Lincoln City	*v*	*Scunthorpe United*	*1 – 2*	*77*
Louth United	v	Notts County	0 – 9	82
Hull City	v	Frickley Athletic	7 – 3	48
Nantwich Town	v	Stockport County	0 – 10	205
Southport	v	Mansfield Town	1 – 2	82
Warrington Town	v	Chadderton	2 – 2	45
Chadderton	*v*	*Warrington Town*	*2 – 2*	*31*
(Warrington won 5–3 on kicks from the penalty mark)				
Ilkeston Town	v	Morecambe	2 – 2	82
Morecambe	*v*	*Ilkeston Town*	*1 – 3*	*102*
Halifax Town	v	Denaby United	4 – 4	112
Denaby United	*v*	*Halifax Town*	*3 – 0*	*95*
Atherton LR	v	Leigh RMI	5 – 0	101
Doncaster Rovers	v	Ashton United	4 – 0	57
Curzon Ashton	v	Rochdale	0 – 9	80
Kidderminster Harriers	v	Chasetown	4 – 0	102
Birstall United	v	Lye Town	3 – 2	50
Redditch United	v	Bromsgrove Rovers	1 – 3	93
Pershore Town	v	Racing Club Warwick	2 – 2	52
Racing Club Warwick	*v*	*Pershore Town*	*1 – 2*	*53*
Ibstock Welfare	v	Halesowen Town	0 – 2	61
Bedworth United	v	Rothwell Town	4 – 2	56
Hinckley United	v	Banbury United	4 – 1	48
Gresley Rovers	v	Willenhall Town	7 – 0	95
Somersham Town	v	VS Rugby	3 – 0	78
Westfields	v	Histon	2 – 5	56
Eynesbury Rovers	v	Wednesfield	0 – 10	20
Cambridge United	v	Solihull Borough	8 – 1	94
Harlow Town	v	Sudbury Town	2 – 1	63
Gorleston	v	Wivenhoe Town	4 – 7	22
Basildon United	v	Fakenham Town	3 – 2	39
Felixstowe Port & Town	v	Ipswich Wanderers	0 – 2	85
Walton & Hersham	v	Royston Town	10 – 0	45
Chesham United	v	Bedfont	4 – 2	n/a
Ruislip Manor	v	Wembley	0 – 7	40
Barnet	v	Hillingdon Borough	4 – 1	116
Chelmsford City	v	Boreham Wood	5 – 2	42

(Replays in italics)			Result	Att
Kingsbury Town	v	Wingate & Finchley	0 – 4	40
Hayes	v	Bedford Town	2 – 3	51
Marlow	v	Hampton	4 – 2	59
Waltham Abbey	v	Cheshunt	2 – 3	89
Stevenage Borough	v	Arlesey Town	10 – 0	101
East Thurrock United	v	Purfleet	4 – 2	109
Leyton Sports	v	Concord Rangers	3 – 5	55
Hendon	v	Northwood	4 – 3	41
Tilbury	v	Stanway Rovers	1 – 1	50
Stanway Rovers	*v*	*Tilbury*	*2 – 1*	*79*
Harefield United	v	Dartford		
(walkover for Dartford – Harefield United withdrawn)				
Thamesmead Town	v	Baldock Town		
(walkover for Thamesmead Town – Baldock Town withdrawn)				
Welwyn Garden City	v	Yeading	3 – 3	38
Yeading	*v*	*Welwyn Garden City*	*5 – 0*	*60*
Corinthian	v	Tonbridge	1 – 3	56
Herne Bay	v	Ashford Town (Middx)	5 – 1	49
Carshalton Athletic	v	Camberley Town	0 – 3	64
Farnborough Town	v	Sittingbourne	0 – 6	54
Croydon	v	Faversham Town	5 – 1	35
Whitstable Town	v	Chipstead	1 – 5	66
Chatham Town	v	Kingstonian	0 – 1	n/a
Bromley	v	Hastings Town	3 – 2	59
Chichester City	v	Hythe United	6 – 2	22
Redhill	v	Dover Athletic	0 – 3	64
Ringmer	v	Folkestone Invicta	0 – 10	42
Eastbourne Town	v	Raynes Park Vale	7 – 0	35
Crawley Town	v	Portfield	1 – 0	75
Aldershot Town	v	Reading Town	1 – 0	61
Merstham	v	Basingstoke Town	2 – 1	n/a
Fisher Athletic	v	Leatherhead	3 – 0	n/a
Wokingham Town	v	Dorking	7 – 3	53
Egham Town	v	Tooting & Mitcham Utd	0 – 4	27
Carterton Town	v	Newbury AFC	2 – 3	65
Bashley	v	Romsey Town	2 – 3	44
Havant Town	v	Abingdon Town		
walkover for Abingdon Town – Havant Town withdrawn)				
Thame United	v	Weymouth	3 – 1	45
Oxford City	v	Eastleigh	3 – 1	56
Warminster Town	v	Salisbury City	1 – 1	80
Salisbury City	*v*	*Warminster Town*	*2 – 3*	*63*
Cinderford Town	v	Cheltenham Towne	2 – 3	138
Mangotsfield United	v	Yeovil Town	1 – 2	66
Forest Green Rovers	v	Gloucester City	0 – 0	113
Gloucester City	*v*	*Forest Green Rovers*	*2 – 1*	*54*
Yate Town	v	Cirencester Town	1 – 3	50

First round qualifying

Wigan Athletic	v	Darlington	2 – 1	94
Scarborough	v	Farsley Celtic	7 – 1	65
Hartlepool United	v	Harrogate Town	4 – 1	79
Yorkshire Amateur	v	Carlisle United	0 – 4	85
Chester City	v	Barnsley	2 – 1	67
Northwich Victoria	v	Notts County	0 – 5	109
Scunthorpe United	v	Marine	5 – 1	56

Preston North End	v	Sheffield Wednesday	1 – 0	158
Stockport County	v	Chesterfield	0 – 1	202
Stalybridge Celtic	v	Warrington Town	0 – 7	42
Mansfield Town	v	Worksop Town	7 – 2	128
Hull City	v	Cheadle Town	11 – 1	47
Denaby United	v	Brigg Town		
(walkover for Brigg Town – Denaby United withdrawn)				
Emley	v	Doncaster Rovers	1 – 3	93
Atherton LR	v	Bamber Bridge	0 – 2	58
Ilkeston Town	v	Rochdale	2 – 1	93
Kidderminster Harriers	v	Gornal Athletic	3 – 1	71
Northampton Spencer	v	Bromsgrove Rovers	0 – 2	35
Birstall United	v	Bilston Town	0 – 3	40
Walsall Wood	v	Burton Albion	0 – 5	50
Halesowen Town	v	Atherstone United	0 – 0	63
Atherstone United	*v*	*Halesowen Town*	*0 – 2*	*59*
Holwell Sports	v	Hinckley United	0 – 4	40
Bedworth United	v	Stourbridge	4 – 0	44
Pershore Town	v	Gresley Rovers	0 – 4	49
Histon	v	Tividale	7 – 2	43
Cradley Town	v	Cambridge United	0 – 5	71
Wednesfield	v	Cambridge City	0 – 2	20
Somersham Town	v	Tamworth	1 – 0	98
Wivenhoe Town	v	Maldon Town	3 – 3	41
Maldon Town	*v*	*Wivenhoe Town*	*0 – 4*	*22*
Great Wakering Rovers	v	Ipswich Wanderers	4 – 0	60
Basildon United	v	Kings Lynn	2 – 4	62
Harlow Town	v	Braintree Town	3 – 1	56
Chesham United	v	Hornchurch	0 – 2	47
Staines Town	v	Barnet	5 – 3	n/a
Wembley	v	Beaconsfield SYCOB	4 – 0	50
Walton & Hersham	v	Leighton Town	8 – 0	47
Wingate & Finchley	v	Romford	2 – 3	68
Hitchin Town	v	Marlow	5 – 1	30
Bedford Town	v	Hemel Hempstead	2 – 0	70
Chelmsford City	v	Cheshunt	5 – 1	n/a
East Thurrock United	v	Uxbridge	2 – 0	60
(ordered to be replayed as only 80 minutes played by referee)				
East Thurrock United	*v*	*Uxbridge*	*2 – 1*	*60*
Grays Athletic	v	Hendon	1 – 0	43
Concord Rangers	v	Hoddesdon Town	3 – 5	63
Stevenage Borough	v	Potters Bar Town	6 – 1	117
Dartford	v	Bishop's Stortford	1 – 0	65
St Albans City	v	Yeading	1 – 1	66
Yeading	*v*	*St Albans City*	*1 – 4*	*50*
Thamesmead Town	v	Erith & Belvedere	1 – 3	59
Stanway Rovers	v	Southend Manor	1 – 0	79
Herne Bay	v	Sutton United	1 – 2	49
Southwick	v	Sittingbourne	0 – 5	65
Camberley Town	v	Bracknell Town	3 – 1	67
Tonbridge	v	Welling United	0 – 5	66
Chipstead	v	Margate	5 – 1	57
Banstead Athletic	v	Bromley	1 – 2	56
Kingstonian	v	Burgess Hill Town	0 – 0	70
Burgess Hill Town	*v*	*Kingstonian*	*2 – 1*	*139*
Croydon	v	Horsham	2 – 1	35
Dover Athletic	v	Whitehawk	5 – 0	45
Horsham YMCA	v	Eastbourne Town	0 – 7	28

(Replays in italics)			Result	Att
Folkestone Invicta	v	Three Bridges	0 – 2	46
Chichester City	v	Crawley Town	1 – 3	39
Merstham	v	Whyteleafe	4 – 2	80
Maidenhead United	v	Wokingham Town	3 – 0	45
Fisher Athletic	v	Saltdean United	4 – 2	n/a
Aldershot Town	v	Tooting & Mitcham Utd	1 – 3	35
Romsey Town	v	Fareham Town	0 – 3	46
Thatcham Town	v	Thame United	4 – 2	51
Abingdon Town	v	Witney Town	7 – 2	48
Newbury AFC	v	Oxford City	1 – 3	48
Cheltenham Town	v	Odd Down	4 – 0	51
Paulton Rovers	v	Gloucester City	0 – 5	33
Yeovil Town	v	Chippenham Town	2 – 1	144
Warminster Town	v	Cirencester Town	0 – 14	86

Second round qualifying

Hartlepool United	v	Wigan Athletic	4 – 1	147
Scarborough	v	Carlisle United	3 – 2	n/a
Scunthorpe United	v	Chester City	1 – 2	122
Notts County	v	Preston North End	2 – 1	106
Mansfield Town	v	Chesterfield	2 – 1	295
Warrington Town	v	Hull City	0 – 8	53
Bamber Bridge	v	Brigg Town	4 – 0	52
Doncaster Rovers	v	Ilkeston Town	2 – 1	67
Bilston Town	v	Kidderminster Harriers	1 – 2	65
Bromsgrove Rovers	v	Burton Albion	1 – 1	36
Burton Albion	v	Bromsgrove Rovers	3 – 2	49
Bedworth United	v	Halesowen Town	2 – 1	39
Hinckley United	v	Gresley Rovers	5 – 0	64
Cambridge City	v	Histon	2 – 3	121
Cambridge United	v	Somersham Town	2 – 3	176
Kings Lynn	v	Wivenhoe Town	5 – 0	60
Great Wakering Rovers	v	Harlow Town	2 – 2	65
Harlow Town	v	Great Wakering Rovers	0 – 2	51
Wembley	v	Hornchurch	2 – 2	36
Hornchurch	v	Wembley	1 – 2	46
Staines Town	v	Walton & Hersham	0 – 0	96
Walton & Hersham	v	Staines Town	2 – 1	72
Bedford Town	v	Romford	3 – 1	53
Hitchin Town	v	Chelmsford City	2 – 4	60
Hoddesdon Town	v	East Thurrock United	5 – 1	53
Grays Athletic	v	Stevenage Borough	1 – 3	44
Erith & Belvedere	v	Dartford	3 – 1	104
St Albans City	v	Stanway Rovers	2 – 1	112
Camberley Town	v	Sutton United	1 – 1	60
Sutton United	v	Camberley Town	2 – 1	91
Sittingbourne	v	Welling United	1 – 1	146
Welling United	v	Sittingbourne	2 – 1	190
Burgess Hill Town	v	Chipstead	0 – 1	125
Bromley	v	Croydon	1 – 2	76
Three Bridges	v	Dover Athletic	1 – 0	39
Eastbourne Town	v	Crawley Town	0 – 2	62
Fisher Athletic	v	Merstham	2 – 2	50
Merstham	v	Fisher Athletic	2 – 2	n/a
Merstham won 5–4 on kicks from the penalty mark)				
Maidenhead United	v	Tooting & Mitcham United	1 – 3	37
Abingdon Town	v	Fareham Town	6 – 1	46

(Replays in italics)			Result	Att
Thatcham Town	v	Oxford City	1 – 3	65
Yeovil Town	v	Cheltenham Town	1 – 1	90
Cheltenham Town	*v*	*Yeovil Town*	*3 – 1*	*41*
Gloucester City	v	Cirencester Town	2 – 0	61

Third round qualifying

Scarborough	v	Hartlepool United	5 – 2	80
Notts County	v	Chester City	5 – 0	87
Hull City	v	Mansfield Town	2 – 0	95
Doncaster Rovers	v	Bamber Bridge	3 – 1	89
Burton Albion	v	Kidderminster Harriers	3 – 2	53
Hinckley United	v	Bedworth United	2 – 3	75
Somersham Town	v	Histon	2 – 2	115
Histon	*v*	*Somersham Town*	*6 – 2*	*111*
Great Wakering Rovers	v	Kings Lynn	3 – 2	53
Walton & Hersham	v	Wembley	3 – 3	49
Wembley	*v*	*Walton & Hersham*	*1 – 2*	*58*
Chelmsford City	v	Bedford Town	2 – 3	72
Stevenage Borough	v	Hoddesdon Town	5 – 0	118
St Albans City	v	Erith & Belvedere	0 – 2	94
Welling United	v	Sutton United	4 – 1	141
Croydon	v	Chipstead	0 – 1	118
Crawley Town	v	Three Bridges	1 – 0	240
Tooting & Mitcham United	v	Merstham	3 – 1	75
Oxford City	v	Abingdon Town	1 – 1	66
Abingdon Town	*v*	*Oxford City*	*1 – 1*	*77*
(Abingdon Town won 4–3 on kicks from the penalty mark)				
Gloucester City	v	Cheltenham Town	1 – 0	146

First round proper

Shrewsbury Town	v	Boldmere St Michaels	5 – 1	150
Rotherham United	v	Bury	0 – 1	168
Bradford City	v	Nuneaton Borough	9 – 0	90
Bolton Wanderers	v	Scarborough	1 – 2	410
Stoke City	v	Wolverhampton Wanderers	3 – 0	299
Burton Albion	v	Bedworth United	3 – 1	83
Burnley	v	Wrexham	2 – 0	336
Peterborough United	v	Doncaster Rovers	2 – 1	104
Grimsby Town	v	Leicester City	0 – 1	131
Walsall	v	Port Vale	4 – 4	143
Port Vale	*v*	*Walsall*	*1 – 2*	*108*
Derby County	v	Blackpool	0 – 2	118
Newcastle United	v	Hull City	0 – 1	174
Birmingham City	v	Crewe Alexandra	1 – 2	141
Huddersfield Town	v	York City	1 – 2	215
Aston Villa	v	Notts County	2 – 4	134
Enfield	v	Stevenage Borough	5 – 1	159
Torquay United	v	Leyton Orient	3 – 3	207
Leyton Orient	*v*	*Torquay United*	*0 – 4*	*88*
Reading	v	Oxford United	3 – 2	167
Erith & Belvedere	v	Tooting & Mitcham Utd	2 – 0	81
Crawley Town	v	Great Wakering Rovers	2 – 5	155
Welling United	v	Dulwich Hamlet	2 – 2	148

(Replays in italics)			Result	Att
ulwich Hamlet	v	*Welling United*	*0 – 1*	*118*
ournemouth AFC	v	Gillingham	0 – 3	102
xeter City	v	Colchester United	4 – 2	211
loucester City	v	Southampton	0 – 6	363
iston	v	Gravesend & Northfleet	3 – 2	111
hipstead	v	Chelsea	0 – 9	516
ymouth Argyle	v	Hereford United	4 – 2	265
oydon Athletic	v	Northampton Town	2 – 5	60
oking	v	Brighton & Hove Albion	3 – 3	185
righton & Hove Albion	*v*	*Woking*	*1 – 3*	*106*
ycombe Wanderers	v	Cardiff City	2 – 1	131
lham	v	Abingdon Town	3 – 1	96
vindon Town	v	Bristol Rovers	1 – 1	116
ristol Rovers	*v*	*Swindon Town*	*0 – 0*	*61*
(ristol Rovers won 10–9 on kicks from the penalty mark)				
vansea City	v	Bedford Town	3 – 2	143
alton & Hersham	v	Rushden & Diamonds	0 – 3	61

econd round proper

rton Albion	v	Nottingham Forest	0 – 5	196
ackpool	v	Everton	0 – 1	348
icester City	v	Liverpool	2 – 3	328
ry	v	Peterborough United	0 – 2	112
tts County	v	Walsall	2 – 1	124
adford City	v	Scarborough	2 – 1	212
rewsbury Town	v	Stoke City	1 – 2	176
effield United	v	Tranmere Rovers	3 – 3	152
anmere Rovers	*v*	*Sheffield United*	*5 – 3*	*315*
nderland	v	Crewe Alexandra	1 – 2	255
eds United	v	Oldham Athletic	3 – 2	833
rk City	v	Middlesbrough	0 – 1	114
est Bromwich Albion	v	Manchester City	1 – 1	144
anchester City	*v*	*West Bromwich Albion*	*3 – 2*	*153*
ll City	v	Burnley	1 – 0	135
ackburn Rovers	v	Manchester United	1 – 1	1257
anchester United	*v*	*Blackburn Rovers*	*2 – 3*	*3170*
shden & Diamonds	v	Charlton Athletic	1 – 6	217
uthampton	v	Histon	6 – 0	175
st Ham United	v	Millwall	2 – 0	605
rquay United	v	Bristol City	0 – 3	190
tford	v	Northampton Town	6 – 3	202
rwich City	v	Crystal Palace	0 – 0	130
rstal Palace	*v*	*Norwich City*	*2 – 1*	*77*
ield	v	Bristol Rovers	0 – 1	120
elsea	v	Wimbledon	2 – 2	172
mbledon	v	*Chelsea*	*1 – 3*	*103*
rtsmouth	v	Erith & Belvedere	5 – 0	136
wich Town	v	Great Wakering Rovers	4 – 0	180
ansea City	v	Brentford	2 – 2	159
ntford	*v*	*Swansea City*	*0 – 1*	*143*
ter City	v	Arsenal	1 – 1	1075
enal	*v*	*Exeter City*	*1 – 0*	*130*
eens Park Rangers	v	Southend United	3 – 2	73
ttenham Hotspur	v	Reading	1 – 0	126
ventry City	v	Luton Town	0 – 4	106
mouth Argyle	v	Fulham	0 – 3	189

			Result	Att
Wycombe Wanderers	v	Welling United	2 – 0	97
Woking	v	Gillingham	1 – 2	169

Third round proper

Watford	v	Fulham	2 – 0	280
Middlesbrough	v	Charlton Athletic	3 – 2	60
Liverpool	v	Queens Park Rangers	1 – 2	802
West Ham United	v	Blackburn Rovers	1 – 4	1587
Leeds United	v	Crystal Palace	3 – 1	1001
Everton	v	Stoke City	1 – 0	666
Tranmere Rovers	v	Chelsea	2 – 5	465
Portsmouth	v	Gillingham	2 – 0	131
Southampton	v	Nottingham Forest	3 – 0	214
Ipswich Town	v	Bradford City	2 – 1	197
Peterborough United	v	Wycombe Wanderers	2 – 0	168
Hull City	v	Bristol Rovers	3 – 1	161
Bristol City	v	Swansea City	2 – 0	312
Luton Town	v	Tottenham Hotspur	2 – 2	292
Tottenham Hotspur	*v*	*Luton Town*	*4 – 2*	*185*
Notts County	v	Arsenal	1 – 6	400
Crewe Alexandra	v	Manchester City	2 – 0	1574

Fourth round proper

Portsmouth	v	Chelsea	1 – 3	274
Middlesbrough	v	Leeds United	0 – 0	1069
Leeds United	*v*	*Middlesbrough*	*2 – 0*	*3418*
Hull City	v	Ipswich Town	1 – 1	752
Ipswich Town	*v*	*Hull City*	*1 – 0*	*459*
Queens Park Rangers	v	Blackburn Rovers	1 – 5	847
Arsenal	v	Bristol City	3 – 1	312
Southampton	v	Peterborough United	1 – 2	574
Watford	v	Everton	2 – 3	531
Crewe Alexandra	v	Tottenham Hotspur	1 – 0	2250

Fifth round proper

Everton	v	Ipswich Town	3 – 2	1210
Chelsea	v	Blackburn Rovers	1 – 1	1402
Blackburn Rovers	*v*	*Chelsea*	*2 – 0*	*1327*
Peterborough United	v	Crewe Alexandra	1 – 1	1394
Crewe Alexandra	*v*	*Peterborough United*	*1 – 3*	*2685*
Arsenal	v	Leeds United	0 – 1	852

Semi-finals

First Leg

Everton	v	Leeds United	2 – 1	6509

Second Leg

Leeds United	v	Everton	0 – 1	2245
(Everton won 3 1 on aggregate)				

			Result	*Att*
First Leg				
Blackburn Rovers	v	Peterborough United	1 – 0	3020
Second Leg				
Peterborough United	v	Blackburn Rovers	0 – 1	4216
(Blackburn Rovers won 2–0 on aggregate)				

Final

First Leg

Blackburn Rovers	v	Everton	1 – 3	9280

Second Leg

Everton	v	Blackburn Rovers	2 – 2	15258

34 ● FA COUNTY YOUTH CUP WINNERS 1945–1998

From 1945 to 1969 the FA County Youth Cup final was played over two legs. Since 1970 it has been one-match final and only twice (in 1988 and 1990) has a replay been required.

Year	Winners		Runners-up	Result
1945	Staffordshire	v	Wiltshire	3 – 2
1946	Berks & Bucks	v	Durham	4 – 3
1947	Durham	v	Essex	4 – 2
1948	Essex	v	Liverpool	5 – 3
1949	Liverpool	v	Middlesex	4 – 3
1950	Essex	v	Middlesex	4 – 3
1951	Middlesex	v	Leicestershire & Rutland	3 – 1
1952	Sussex	v	Liverpool	3 – 1
1953	Sheffield & Hallam	v	Hampshire	5 – 3
1954	Liverpool	v	Gloucestershire	4 – 1
1955	Bedfordshire	v	Sheffield & Hallam	2 – 0
1956	Middlesex	v	Staffordshire	3 – 2
1957	Hampshire	v	Cheshire	4 – 3
1958	Staffordshire	v	London	8 – 0
1959	Birmingham	v	London	7 – 5
1960	London	v	Birmingham	6 – 4
1961	Lancashire	v	Nottinghamshire	6 – 3
1962	Middlesex	v	Nottinghamshire	3 – 2
1963	Durham	v	Essex	3 – 2
1964	Sheffield & Hallam	v	Birmingham	1 – 0
1965	Northumberland	v	Middlesex	7 – 4
1966	Leics & Rutland	v	London	6 – 5
1967	Northamptonshire	v	Hertfordshire	5 – 4
1968	North Riding	v	Devon	7 – 4
1969	Northumberland	v	Sussex	1 – 0
1970	Hertfordshire	v	Cheshire	2 – 1
1971	Lancashire	v	Gloucestershire	2 – 0
1972	Middlesex	v	Liverpool	2 – 0
1973	Hertfordshire	v	Northumberland	3 – 0
1974	Nottinghamshire	v	London	2 – 0
1975	Durham	v	Bedfordshire	2 – 1
1976	Northamptonshire	v	Surrey	7 – 1
1977	Liverpool	v	Surrey	3 – 0
1978	Liverpool	v	Kent	3 – 1
1979	Hertfordshire	v	Liverpool	4 – 1
1980	Liverpool	v	Lancashire	2 – 0
1981	Lancashire	v	East Riding	3 – 1
1982	Devon	v	Kent	3 – 2
1983	London	v	Gloucestershire	3 – 0
1984	Cheshire	v	Manchester	2 – 1
1985	East Riding	v	Middlesex	2 – 1
1986	Hertfordshire	v	Manchester	4 – 0
1987	North Riding	v	Gloucestershire	3 – 1
1988	East Riding	v	Middlesex	1 – 1
	East Riding	*v*	*Middlesex*	5 – 3
1989	Liverpool	v	Hertfordshire	2 – 1
1990	Staffordshire	v	Hampshire	1 – 1

ar	Winners		Runners-up	Result
	Staffordshire	v	*Hampshire*	*2 – 1*
91	Lancashire	v	Surrey	6 – 0
92	Nottinghamshire	v	Surrey	1 – 0
93	Durham	v	Liverpool	4 – 0
94	West Riding	v	Sussex	3 – 1
95	Liverpool	v	Essex	3 – 2
96	Durham	v	Gloucestershire	1 – 0
97	Cambridgeshire	v	Lancashire	1 – 0
98	Northumberland	v	West Riding	2 – 1

ter extra time

35 ● FA COUNTY YOUTH CUP 1997–1998

First round

(Replays in italics)   *Results*

Sheffield & Hallamshire	v	Cumberland	3 – 2
Cheshire	v	Westmorland	6 – 0
Nottinghamshire	v	Liverpool	2 – 4
Derbyshire	v	Shropshire	3 – 4
Lincolnshire	v	Manchester	2 – 1
Middlesex	v	Worcestershire	1 – 4
Hertfordshire	v	Gloucestershire	1 – 2
Bedfordshire	v	Kent	1 – 3
Oxfordshire	v	Leicestershire & Rutland	1 – 3
Berks & Bucks	v	Sussex	1 – 3
Northamptonshire	v	Hampshire	2 – 1
Royal Navy	v	Somerset	2 – 8
Army	v	Wiltshire	1 – 3

19 Counties receiving byes to the Second round

Birmingham	Durham	Lancashire	Staffordshire
Cambridgeshire	East Riding	London	Suffolk
Cornwall	Essex	Norfolk	Surrey
Devon	Herefordshire	North Riding	West Riding
Dorset	Huntingdonshire	Northumberland	

Second round

Durham	v	Sheffield & Hallamshire	2 – 0
Northumberland	v	Cheshire	3 – 0
North Riding	v	Liverpool	2 – 0
Lancashire	v	Staffordshire	4 – 1
East Riding	v	Shropshire	4 – 3
West Riding	v	Lincolnshire	4 – 2
Cambridgeshire	v	Herefordshire	7 – 1
Huntingdonshire	v	Worcestershire	2 – 3
Birmingham	v	Gloucestershire	1 – 3
Norfolk	v	Kent	2 – 1
Suffolk	v	Leicestershire & Rutland	2 – 2
Leicestershire & Rutland	*v*	*Suffolk*	6 –
Essex	v	Sussex	0 – 4
Surrey	v	Dorset	6 – 1
London	v	Northamptonshire	2 –
Cornwall	v	Somerset	2 – 2
Somerset	*v*	*Cornwall*	1 –
Devon	v	Wiltshire	4 – 4
Wiltshire	*v*	*Devon*	4 –

*Cornwall won on penalty – kicks

Third round

Northumberland	v	Durham	2 – 0
North Riding	v	West Riding	1 – 5
Lancashire	v	East Riding	1 – 4
Sussex	v	Norfolk	2 – 0
Leicestershire & Rutland	v	Wiltshire	0 – 8
Worcestershire	v	Surrey	1 – 0
Cambridgeshire	v	Gloucestershire	0 – 2
Cornwall	v	London	1 – 0

Fourth round

Sussex	v	Worcestershire	2 – 0
Northumberland	v	Gloucestershire	4 – 2
West Riding	v	East Riding	2 – 1
Wiltshire	v	Cornwall	1 – 1
Cornwall	*v*	*Wiltshire*	*0 – 2*

Semi – finals

Northumberland	v	Wiltshire	3 – 2
West Riding	v	Sussex	2 – 1

Final – 25 April 1998

Northumberland (at Bradford City FC)	v	West Riding	2 – 1

36 ● YOUTH INTERNATIONAL MATCHES 1997–1998

Date	Venue				Result

Under-18

Date	Venue				Result
9.9.97	Rotherham	England	v	Yugoslavia	0 – 0*
11.10.97	Loznica	Yugoslavia	v	England	0 – 4*
27.10.97	Moscow	Russia	v	England	2 – 1*
14.11.97	Crewe	England	v	Russia	3 – 2*
12.2.98	Northwich	England	v	Israel	1 – 0
26.3.98	Stockport	England	v	France	3 – 0*
23.4.98	Rodez	France	v	England	1 – 0*
30.5.98	Clamecy	Cyprus	v	England	0 – 1
1.6.98	Clamecy	France	v	England	3 – 0

* UEFA Championship – Qualifying competition

Under-16

Date	Venue				Result
5.8.97	Vassa	Sweden	v	England	1 – 1[+]
6.8.97	Vassa	Faroe Islands	v	England	0 – 10[+]
8.8.97	Vassa	Denmark	v	England	1 – 2[+]
9.8.97	Vassa	Norway	v	England	2 – 3[+]
14.11.97	Warsaw	Poland	v	England	2 – 1
9.12.97	Lilleshall	England	v	N. Ireland	1 – 0
10.12.97	Lilleshall	England	v	N. Ireland	5 – 0
3.3.98	Rushden	England	v	Bosnia	3 – 1*
5.3.98	Kettering	England	v	Croatia	1 – 1*
7.3.98	Northampton	England	v	Slovakia	0 – 0*
6.4.98	Lilleshall	England	v	Norway	2 – 1
8.4.98	Lilleshall	England	v	Norway	0 – 2

* UEFA Championship – Qualifying competition
+ Nordic Championship (won by England)

	Yugoslavia	Yugoslavia	Russia	Russia	Israel	France	France	Cyprus	France
Under-18									
S. Simonsen (Tranmere Rovers)	1	1	1	1		1	1		
R. Cooper (Nottingham Forest)	2	2	2	4	8*	4	4		
M. Ball (Everton)	3	3	3	3		3	3		
W. Brown (Manchester United)	4	4				2	2		
J. Woodgate (Leeds United)	5	5	5	5		5	5		
M. Upson (Arsenal)	6	6	6	6		6	6		
G. Noel-Williams (Watford)	7								
K. Dixon (Leeds United)	8								
M. Owen (Liverpool)	9								
K. Nicholls (Charlton Athletic)	10	10	10	10					
L. Staton (Blackburn Rovers)	11								
C. Dudley (Notts County)	8*		11*		10				
R. Wellens (Manchester United)	11*								
T. Smith (Watford)	8**								
A. Ormerod (Middlesbrough)		7	7						
S. Johnson (Crewe Alexandra)		8	8	11		11	11		
D. Cadamarteri (Everton)		9		8		8	8		
L. Matthews (Leeds United)		11	9	9		9	9		
A. Campbell (Middlesbrough)		9*							
S. Haslam (Sheffield Wednesday)			4	2	6*			4	4
A. Hackworth (Leeds United)			11					9*	9
A. Griffin (Stoke City)			7*	7		7	7		
L. Morris (Sheffield United)			8*					10	10
R. Hulbert (Swindon Town)				7*				7	
D. Dunn (Blackburn Rovers)				10*	8				
R. Knight (Derby County)					1				
L. Young (Tottenham Hotspur)					2			2	2
P. Konchoskey (Charlton Athletic)					3				
N. Fenton (Manchester City)					4			6	6
M. Taylor (Blackburn Rovers)					5			5	5
D. Holden (Bolton Wanderers)					6				3
J. Piercy (Tottenham Hotspur)					7	8*		8	8
A. Smith (Leeds United)					9	9*			
P. Vernazza (Arsenal)					11	10	10		
D. Butterfield (Grimsby Town)					11*				
J. Greening (Manchester United)							8*		
R. Green (Norwich City)								1	1
G. Evans (Leeds United)								3	
P. Crouch (Tottenham Hotspur)								9	10*
J. Milligan (Everton)								11	11
K. Lunt (Crewe Alexandra)								7*	7
S. Taylor (Arsenal)									1*

*substitute

38 ● YOUTH INTERNATIONAL MATCHES 1947–1998

WYC = World Youth Championship
IYT = International Youth Tournament
* Qualifying Competition
† Professionals
§ Abandoned

v Algeria

†1984	22/4	Cannes	W	3 – 0	

v Argentina

†19815.10		Sydney	D	1 – 1	WYC

v Australia

†1981	8/10	Sydney	D	1 – 1	WYC
†1993	20/3	Sydney	W	2 – 1	WYC

v Austria

1949	19/4	Zeist	W	4 – 2	IYT
1952	17/4	Barcelona	D	5 – 5	IYT
1957	16/4	Barcelona	L	0 – 3	IYT
1958	4/3	Highbury	W	3 – 2	
1958	1/6	Graz	W	4 – 3	
1960	20/4	Vienna	L	0 – 1	IYT
†1964	1/4	Rotterdam	W	2 – 1	IYT
†1980	6/9	Pazin	L	0 – 1	
†1981	29/5	Bonn	W	7 – 0	IYT
†1981	3/9	Umag	W	3 – 0	
†1984	6/9	Izola	D	2 – 2	

v Belgium

1948	16/4	West Ham	W	3 – 1	IYT
1951	22/3	Cannes	D	1 – 1	IYT
1953	31/3	Brussels	W	2 – 0	IYT
§1956	7/11	Brussels	W	2 – 3	
1957	13/11	Sheffield	W	2 – 0	
†196515.4		Ludwigshafen	W	3 – 0	IYT
1969	11/3	West Ham	W	1 – 0	IYT*
†196926.3		Waregem	W	2 – 0	IYT
1972	13/5	Palma	D	0 – 0	IYT*
†1973	4/6	Viareggio	D	0 – 0	IYT
†1977	19/5	Lokeren	W	1 – 0	IYT
†1979	17/1	Brussels	W	4 – 0	
†1980	8/9	Labia	W	6 – 1	
†1983	13/4	Birmingham	D	1 – 1	
†1988	20/5	Chatel	D	0 – 0	
†1990	24/7	Nyiregyhaza	D	1 – 1	IYT
†1990	16/10	Sunderland	D	0 – 0	IYT*
†1991	16/10	Eernegem	L	0 – 1	IYT*
†1996	30/7	Besancon	W	3 – 2	IYT

v Brazil

†1986	29/3	Cannes	D	0 – 0	
†1986	13/5	Peking	L	1 – 2	
†1987	2/6	Niteroi	L	0 – 2	

v Bulgaria

1956	28/3	Salgotarjan	L	1 – 2	IYT
1960	16/4	Graz	L	0 – 1	IYT
1962	24/4	Ploesti	D	0 – 0	IYT
†1968	7/4	Nimes	D	0 – 0	IYT
†1969	26/3	Waregem	W	2 – 0	IYT
†1972	13/5	Palma	D	0 – 0	IYT
†1979	31/5	Vienna	L	0 – 1	IYT

v Cameroon

†1981	3/10	Sydney	W	2 – 0	WYC
†1985	1/6	Toulon	W	1 – 0	

v China

†1983	31/3	Cannes	W	5 – 1	
†1985	26/8	Baku	L	0 – 2	WYC
†1986	5/5	Peking	W	1 – 0	

v Cyprus

†1998	30/5	Clamecy	W	1 – 0	

v Czechoslovakia

1955	7/4	Lucca	L	0 – 1	IYT
†1966	21/5	Rijeka	L	2 – 3	IYT
†1969	20/5	Leipzig	W	3 – 1	IYT
1979	24/5	Bischofshofen	W	3 – 0	IYT
†1979	8/9	Pula	L	1 – 2	
†1982	11/4	Cannes	L	0 – 1	
†1983	20/5	Highbury	D	1 – 1	IYT
†1989	26/4	Bystrica	L	0 – 1	IYT*
†1989	14/11	Portsmouth	W	1 – 0	IYT*
†1990	25/4	Wembley	D	1 – 1	

v Denmark

†1955	1/10	Plymouth	W	9 – 2	
1956	20/5	Esbjerg	W	2 – 1	
†1979	31/10	Esbjerg	W	3 – 1	IYT*
1980	26/3	Coventry	W	4 – 0	IYT*
†1982	15/7	Stjordal	W	5 – 2	
†1983	16/7	Holbeck	L	0 – 1	
†1987	16/2	Manchester	W	2 – 1	
†1990	28/3	Wembley	D	0 – 0	

†1991	6/2	Oxford	L	1 – 5	
†1993	30/3	Stoke	W	4 – 2	
†1993	7/7	Nykobing	W	5 – 0	
†1995	22/2	Walsall	L	5 – 6	

v Egypt

†1981	11/10	Sydney	W	4 – 2	WYC
†1992	13/10	Bournemouth	W	2 – 1	

v Finland

†1975	19/5	Berne	D	1 – 1	IYT
1996	11/10	York	W	1 – 0	IYT*

v France

1957	24/3	Fontainebleau	W	1 – 0	
1958	22/3	Eastbourne	L	0 – 1	
†1966	23/5	Rijeka	L	1 – 2	IYT
†1967	11/5	Istanbul	W	2 – 0	IYT
†1968	25/1	Paris	L	0 – 1	
1978	8/2	C Palace	W	3 – 1	IYT*
1978	1/3	Paris	D	0 – 0	IYT*
†1979	2/6	Vienna	D	0 – 0	IYT
†1982	12/4	Cannes	L	0 – 1	
†1983	2/4	Cannes	L	0 – 2	
1984	1/3	Watford	W	4 – 0	
†1984	23/4	Cannes	L	1 – 2	
†1985	7/6	Toulon	L	1 – 3	
†1986	31/3	Cannes	L	1 – 2	
†1986	11/5	Peking	D	1 – 1	
†1988	22/5	Monthey	L	1 – 2	
†1988	15/11	Bradford	D	1 – 1	IYT*
†1989	11/10	Martigues	D	0 – 0	IYT*
†1990	22/5	Wembley	L	1 – 3	
†1992	7/10	Boulogne	L	0 – 2	
1993	18/7	Stoke	W	2 – 0	IYT
1993	27/10	Besançon	L	0 – 2	IYT*
1993	16/11	Yeovil	D	3 – 3	IYT*
1994	6/9	Reading	L	2 – 3	
1996	28/2	Meaux	D	1 – 1	
1998	26/3	Stockport	W	3 – 0	IYT*
1998	23/4	Rodez	L	0 – 1	IYT*
1998	1/6	Clamecy	L	0 – 3	

v East Germany

1958	7/4	Neunkirchen	W	1 – 0	IYT
1959	8/3	Zwickau	L	3 – 4	
1960	2/4	Portsmouth	D	1 – 1	
1965	25/4	Essen	L	2 – 3	IYT
1969	22/5	Magdeburg	L	0 – 4	IYT
1973	10/6	Florence	W	3 – 2	IYT
1984	25/5	Moscow	D	1 – 1	IYT
1988	21/5	Monthey		1 – 0	

v West Germany

1953	4/4	Boom	W	3 – 1	IYT
1954	15/4	Gelsenkirchen	D	2 – 2	IYT
1956	1/4	Sztalinvaros	W	2 – 1	IYT

1957	31/3	Oberhausen	W	4 – 1	
1958	12/3	Bolton	L	1 – 2	
1961	12/3	Flensberg	L	0 – 2	
†1962	31/3	Northampton	W	1 – 0	
†1967	14/2	Mönchengladbach	W	1 – 0	
†1972	22/5	Barcelona	W	2 – 0	IYT
†1975	25/1	Las Palmas	W	4 – 2	
†1976	14/11	Monte Carlo	D	1 – 1	
†1979	28/5	Salzburg	W	2 – 0	IYT
†1979	1/9	Pula	D	1 – 1	
†1983	5/9	Pazin	W	2 – 0	

v Ghana

1993	17/3	Sydney	L	1 – 2	WYC

v Greece

1957	18/4	Barcelona	L	2 – 3	IYT
1959	2/4	Dimitrovo	W	4 – 0	IYT
†1977	23/5	Beveren	D	1 – 1	IYT
†1983	28/6	Puspokladany		1 – 0	
†1988	26/10	Tranmere	W	5 – 0	IYT*
†1989	8/3	Xanthi	W	5 – 0	IYT*

v Holland

1948	17/4	Tottenham	W	3 – 2	IYT
1951	26/3	Cannes	W	2 – 1	IYT
†1954	21/11	Arnhem	L	2 – 3	
†1955	5/11	Norwich	W	3 – 1	
1957	2/3	Brentford	D	5 – 5	
1957	14/4	Barcelona	L	1 – 2	IYT
1957	2/10	Amsterdam	W	3 – 2	
1961	9/3	Utrecht	L	0 – 1	
†1962	31/1	Brighton	W	4 – 0	
†1962	22/4	Ploesti	L	0 – 3	IYT
1963	13/4	Wimbledon	W	5 – 0	IYT
1968	9/4	Nimes	W	1 – 0	IYT
†1974	13/2	West Brom	D	1 – 1	IYT*
†1974	27/2	The Hague	W	1 – 0	IYT*
†1980	23/5	Halle	W	1 – 0	IYT*
†1982	9/4	Cannes	W	1 – 0	
†1985	7/4	Cannes	L	1 – 3	
†1987	1/8	Wembley		3 – 1	
†1993	20/7	Walsall	W	4 – 0	IYT

v Hungary

1954	11/4	Düsseldorf	L	1 – 3	IYT
1956	31/3	Tatabanya	L	2 – 4	IYT
1956	23/10	Tottenham	W	2 – 1	
†1956	25/10	Sunderland	W	2 – 1	
†1965	21/4	Wuppertal	W	5 – 0	IYT
†1975	16/5	Olten	W	3 – 1	IYT
†1977	16/10	Las Palmas	W	3 – 0	IYT
†1979	5/9	Pula	W	2 – 0	
†1980	11/9	Pula	L	1 – 2	
†1981	7/9	Porec	W	4 – 0	
†1983	29/7	Debrecen	L	1 – 2	
†1983	3/9	Umag	W	3 – 2	
†1986	30/3	Cannes	W	2 – 0	

● 151

†1995	29/3	Budapest	W	1 – 0	IYT*
†1995	25/4	Walsall	L	0 – 2	IYT*

v Iceland

†1973	31/5	Viareggio	W	2 – 0	IYT
†1977	21/5	Turnhout	D	0 – 0	IYT
†1983		Reykjavik	W	3 – 0	IYT*
1983	19/9	Blackburn	W	4 – 0	IYT*
1983	12/10	Reykjavik	W	3 – 0	
†1983	1/11	Crystal palace	W	3 – 0	
†1984	16/10	Manchester	W	5 – 3	IYT*
†1985	11/9	Reykjavik	W	5 – 0	IYT*
†1990	12/9	Reykjavik	W	3 – 2	IYT*
†1991	12/9	Crystal Palace	W	2 – 1	IYT*

v Israel

†1962	20/5	Tel Aviv	W	3 – 1	
†1962	22/5	Haifa	L	1 – 2	
†1998	12/2	Northwich	W	1 – 0	

v Italy

1958	13/4	Luxembourg	L	0 – 1	IYT
1959	25/3	Sofia	L	1 – 3	IYT
1961	4/4	Braga	L	2 – 3	IYT
†1965	23/4	Marl-Huels	W	3 – 1	IYT
†1966	25/5	Rijeka	D	1 – 1	IYT
†1967	5/5	Izmir	W	1 – 0	IYT
†1973	14/2	Cava Dei Tirreni	L	0 – 1	
†1973	14/3	Highbury	W	1 – 0	
†1973	7/6	Viareggio	W	1 – 0	IYT
†1978	19/11	Monte Carlo	L	1 – 2	
†1979	28/2	Rome	W	1 – 0	IYT*
†1979	4/4	Birmingham	W	2 – 0	IYT*
†1983	22/5	Watford	D	1 – 1	IYT
†1984	20/4	Cannes	W	1 – 0	
†1985	5/4	Cannes	D	2 – 2	
†1996	25/7	Rombos	D	1 – 1	IYT

v Latvia

†1994	17/11	Reading	D	0 – 0	IYT*
†1995	16/11	Rushden	W	2 – 0	IYT*

v Luxembourg

1950	25/5	Vienna	L	1 – 2	IYT
1954	17/4	Bad Neuenahr	L	0 – 2	IYT
1957	2/2	West Ham	W	7 – 1	
1957	17/11	Luxembourg	W	3 – 0	
1958	9/4	Esch sur Alzette	W	5 – 0	IYT
†1984	29/5	Moscow	W	2 – 0	IYT

v Malta

†1969	18/5	Wolfen	W	6 – 0	IYT
†1979	26/5	Salzburg	W	3 – 0	IYT

v Mexico

†1984	18/4	Cannes	W	4 – 0	

†1985	5/6	Toulon	W	2 – 0	
†1985	29/8	Baku	L	0 – 1	WYC
†1991	27/3	Port of Spain	L	1 – 3	
†1993	14/3	Melbourne	D	0 – 0	WYC

v Northern Ireland

1948	15/5	Belfast	D	2 – 2	
1949	18/4	Haarlem	D	3 – 3	IYT
1949	14/5	Hull	W	4 – 2	
1950	6/5	Belfast	L	0 – 1	
1951	5/5	Liverpool	W	5 – 2	
1952	19/4	Belfast	L	0 – 2	
1953	11/4	Wolverhampton	D	0 – 0	
1954	10/4	Bruehl	W	5 – 0	IYT
1954	10/4	Newtownards	D	2 – 2	
1955	14/5	Watford	W	3 – 0	
1956	12/5	Belfast	D	0 – 1	
1957	11/5	Leyton	W	6 – 2	
1958	10/5	Bangor	L	2 – 4	
1959	9/5	Liverpool	W	5 – 0	
1960	14/5	Belfast	W	5 – 2	
1961	13/5	Manchester	W	2 – 0	
1962	12/5	Londonderry	L	1 – 2	
†1963	23/4	Wembley	W	4 – 0	IYT
1963	11/5	Oldham	D	1 – 1	
1964	25/1	Belfast	W	3 – 1	
1965	22/1	Birkenhead	L	2 – 3	
1966	26/2	Belfast	W	4 – 0	
1967	25/2	Stockport	W	3 – 0	
1968	23/2	Belfast	L	0 – 2	
1969	28/2	Birkenhead	L	0 – 2	
1970	28/2	Lurgan	L	1 – 3	
1971	6/3	Blackpool	D	1 – 1	IYT
1972	11/3	Chester	D	1 – 1	
1972	17/5	Sabadell	W	4 – 0	IYT
1973	24/3	Wellington	W	3 – 0	
1974	19/4	Birkenhead	L	1 – 2	
†1975	13/5	Kriens	W	3 – 0	IYT
†1980	16/5	Arnstadt	W	1 – 0	IYT
†1981	11/2	Walsall	W	1 – 0	IYT*
†1981	11/3	Belfast	W	3 – 0	IYT*
†1996	13/10	York	W	4 – 0	IYT*

v Norway

†1982	13/7	Levanger	L	1 – 4	
†1983	14/7	Korsor	W	1 – 0	
1992	24/7	Amberg	D	1 – 1	
†1994	24/7	Larvik	D	3 – 3	
†1994	26/7	Vikersund	W	3 – 2	

v Paraguay

†1985	24/8	Baku	D	2 – 2	WYC

v Poland

1960	18/4	Graz	W	4 – 2	IYT
†1964	26/3	Breda	D	1 – 1	IYT

†1971	26/5	Presov	D	0 – 0	IYT
†1972	20/5	Valencia	W	1 – 0	IYT
†1975	21/1	Las Palmas	D	1 – 1	
†1978	9/5	Chorzow	L	0 – 2	IYT
†1979	3/9	Porec	L	0 – 1	
†1980	25/5	Leipzig	W	2 – 1	IYT
†1982	17/7	Steinkver	W	3 – 2	
†1983	12/7	Stagelse	W	1 – 0	
†1990	15/5	Wembley	W	3 – 0	
†1992	20/7	Regensburg	W	6 – 1	IYT

v Portugal

1954	18/4	Bonn	L	0 – 2	IYT
1961	2/4	Lisbon	L	0 – 4	IYT
†1964	3/4	The Hague	W	4 – 0	IYT
†1971	30/5	Prague	W	3 – 0	IYT
†1978	13/11	Monte Carlo	W	2 – 0	
†1980	18/5	Rosslau	D	1 – 1	IYT
†1982	7/4	Cannes	W	3 – 0	
†1992	22/7	Schweinfurt	D	1 – 1	IYT
†1997	29/4	Bury	W	2 – 1	IYT*
†1997	13/5	Azores	L	0 – 3	IYT*

v Qatar

†1981	14/10	Sydney	L	1 – 2	WYC
†1983	4/4	Cannes	D	1 – 1	

v Republic of Ireland

1953	5/4	Leuven	W	2 – 0	IYT
1964	30/3	Middleburg	W	6 – 0	IYT
1968	7/2	Dublin	D	0 – 0	IYT*
1968	28/2	Portsmouth	W	4 – 1	IYT*
1970	14/1	Dublin	W	4 – 1	IYT*
1970	4/2	Luton	W	10 – 0	IYT*
1975	9/5	Brunnen	W	1 – 0	IYT
1985	26/2	Dublin	L	0 – 1	IYT*
1986	25/2	Leeds	W	2 – 0	IYT*
1988	17/2	Stoke	W	2 – 0	
1988	20/9	Dublin	W	2 – 0	
1996	27/7	Amneville	W	1 – 0	IYT

v Romania

1957	15/10	Tottenham	W	4 – 2	
1958	11/4	Luxembourg	W	1 – 0	IYT
1959	31/3	Pazardijc	L	1 – 2	IYT
1963	15/4	Highbury	W	3 – 0	IYT
1981	17/10	Adelaide	L	0 – 1	WYC
1993	7/9	Port Vale	D	1 – 1	IYT*
1993	13/10	Bucharest	D	1 – 1	IYT*

Russia

1997	27/10	Moscow	L	1 – 2	IYT*
1997	14/11	Crewe	W	3 – 2	IYT*

Saar

1954	13/4	Dortmund	D	1 – 0	IYT
1955	9/4	Prato	W	3 – 1	IYT

v Scotland

1947	25/10	Doncaster	W	4 – 2	
1948	30/10	Aberdeen	L	1 – 3	
1949	21/4	Utrecht	L	0 – 1	IYT
1950	4/2	Carlisle	W	7 – 1	
1951	3/2	Kilmarnock	W	6 – 1	
1952	15/3	Sunderland	W	3 – 1	
1953	7/2	Glasgow	W	4 – 3	
1954	6/2	Middlesbrough	W	2 – 1	
1955	5/3	Kilmarnock	L	3 – 4	
1956	3/3	Preston	D	2 – 2	
1957	9/3	Aberdeen	W	3 – 1	
1958	1/3	Hull	W	2 – 0	
1959	28/2	Aberdeen	D	1 – 1	
1960	27/2	Newcastle	D	1 – 1	
1961	25/2	Elgin	W	3 – 2	
1962	24/2	Peterborough	W	4 – 2	
†1963	19/4	White City	W	1 – 0	IYT
1963	18/5	Dumfries	W	3 – 1	
1964	22/2	Middlesbrough	D	1 – 1	
1965	27/2	Inverness	L	1 – 2	
1966	5/2	Hereford	W	5 – 3	
1967	4/2	Aberdeen	L	0 – 1	
†1967	1/3	Southampton	W	1 – 0	IYT*
†1967	15/3	Dundee	D	0 – 0	IYT*
1968	3/2	Walsall	L	0 – 5	
1969	1/2	Stranraer	D	1 – 1	
1970	31/1	Derby	L	1 – 2	
1971	30/1	Greenock	L	1 – 2	
1972	29/1	Bournemouth	W	2 – 0	
1973	20/1	Kilmarnock	W	3 – 2	
1974	26/1	Brighton	D	2 – 2	
†1981	27/5	Aachen	L	0 – 1	IYT
†1982	23/2	Glasgow	L	0 – 1	IYT*
†1982	23/3	Coventry	D	2 – 2	IYT*
†1983	15/5	Birmingham	W	4 – 2	IYT
1983	5/10	Middlesbrough	W	3 – 1	IYT
1983	19/10	Motherwell	W	4 – 0	
†1984	27/11	Fulham	L	0 – 1	IYT*
1985	8/4	Cannes	W	1 – 0	IYT*
†1986	25/3	Aberdeen	L	1 – 4	IYT*
†1996	19/3	Motherwell	W	3 – 0	IYT*
†1996	23/4	Yeovil	W	3 – 0	IYT*
†1997	18/2	Bury	W	4 – 1	

v Slovenia

†1994	13/11	High Wycombe	W	3 – 0	IYT*

v South Korea

†1993	7/3	Melbourne	D	1 – 1	WYC

v Spain

1952	15/4	Barcelona	L	1 – 4	IYT
1957	26/9	Birmingham	D	4 – 4	
1958	5/4	Saarbrücken	D	2 – 2	IYT
†1958	8/10	Madrid	W	4 – 2	
1961	30/3	Lisbon	D	0 – 0	IYT
†1964	27/2	Murcia	W	2 – 1	

†1964	5/4	Amsterdam	W	4 – 0	IYT
†1965	17/4	Heilbronn	D	0 – 0	IYT
†1966	30/3	Swindon	W	3 – 0	
†1967	7/5	Manisa	W	2 – 1	IYT
†1971	31/3	Pamplona	L	2 – 3	
†1971	20/4	Luton	D	1 – 1	
†1972	9/2	Alicante	D	0 – 0	
†1972	15/3	Sheffield	W	4 – 1	IYT*
†1975	25/2	Bristol	D	1 – 1	IYT*
†1975	18/3	Madrid	W	1 – 0	IYT*
†1976	12/11	Monte Carlo	W	3 – 0	
†1978	7/5	Bukowas	W	1 – 0	IYT
†1978	17/11	Monte Carlo	D	1 – 1	
†1981	25/5	Siegen	L	1 – 2	IYT
†1983	13/5	Stoke	W	1 – 0	IYT
†1990	29/7	Gyula	L	0 – 1	IYT
†1991	25/5	Wembley	D	1 – 1	
†1991	15/6	Faro	L	0 – 1	WYC
†1993	17/2	Alicante	D	1 – 1	
†1993	22/7	Walsall	W	5 – 1	IYT
†1996	23/7	Amneville	D	0 – 0	IYT

v Sweden

†1971	24/5	Poprad	W	1 – 0	IYT
†1981	5/9	Pazin	W	3 – 2	
†1984	10/9	Rovinj	D	1 – 1	
†1986	10/11	West Brom	D	3 – 3	
†1995	18/11	Kettering	W	6 – 2	IYT*

v Switzerland

1950	26/5	Stockerau	W	2 – 1	IYT
1951	27/3	Nice	W	3 – 1	IYT
1952	13/4	Barcelona	W	4 – 0	IYT
1955	11/4	Florence	D	0 – 0	IYT
1956	11/3	Schaffhausen	W	2 – 0	
1956	13/10	Brighton	D	2 – 2	
1958	26/5	Zurich	W	3 – 0	
†1960	8/10	Leyton	W	4 – 3	
1962	22/11	Coventry	W	1 – 0	
†1963	21/3	Bienne	W	7 – 1	
†1973	2/6	Forte Dei Marmi	W	2 – 0	IYT
†1975	11/5	Buochs	W	4 – 0	IYT
†1980	4/9	Rovinj	W	3 – 0	
†1982	6/9	Porec	W	2 – 0	
†1983	26/7	Hajduboszormeny	W	4 – 0	
†1983	1/9	Porec	W	4 – 2	
†1988	19/5	Sion	W	2 – 0	
†1992	17/11	Port Vale	W	7 – 2	

v Syria

| †1991 | 18/6 | Faro | D | 3 – 3 | WYC |

v Thailand

| †1986 | 7/5 | Peking | L | 1 – 2 | |

v Trinidad & Tobago

| †1991 | 25/3 | Port of Spain | W | 4 – 0 | |

v Turkey

1959	29/3	Dimitrovo	D	1 – 1	IYT
†1978	5/5	Wodzislaw	D	1 – 1	IYT
†1992	17/11	High Wycombe	W	2 – 1	
†1993	11/3	Melbourne	W	1 – 0	WYC
†1993	25/7	Nottingham	W	1 – 0	IYT

v Uruguay

†1977	9/10	Las Palmas	D	1 – 1	
†1987	10/6	Montevideo	D	2 – 2	
†1991	20/6	Faro	D	0 – 0	WYC

v USA

| †1993 | 9/3 | Melbourne | W | 1 – 0 | WYC |

v USSR

†1963	17/4	Tottenham	W	2 – 0	IYT
†1967	13/5	Istanbul	L	0 – 1	IYT
†1968	11/4	Nimes	D	1 – 1	IYT
†1971	28/5	Prague	D	1 – 1	IYT
†1978	10/10	Las Palmas	W	1 – 0	
†1982	4/9	Umag	W	1 – 0	
†1983	29/3	Cannes	D	0 – 0	
†1983	17/5	Aston Villa	L	0 – 2	IYT
1984	3/5	Ludwigsburg	L	0 – 2	
†1984	27/5	Moscow	D	1 – 1	IYT
†1984	8/9	Porec	W	1 – 0	
†1985	3/4	Cannes	W	2 – 1	
†1985	3/6	Toulon	L	0 – 2	
†1990	26/7	Debrecen	L	1 – 3	IYT

v Wales

1948	28/2	High Wycombe	W	4 – 3	
1948	15/4	London	W	4 – 0	
1949	26/2	Swansea	D	0 – 0	
1950	25/2	Worcester	W	1 – 0	
1951	17/2	Wrexham	D	1 – 1	
1952	23/2	Plymouth	W	6 – 0	
1953	21/2	Swansea	W	4 – 2	
1954	20/2	Derby	W	2 – 1	
1955	19/2	Milford Haven	W	7 – 2	
1956	18/2	Shrewsbury	W	5 – 1	
1957	9/2	Cardiff	W	7 – 1	
1958	15/2	Reading	W	8 – 2	
1959	14/2	Portmadoc	W	3 – 0	
1960	19/3	Canterbury	D	1 – 1	
1961	18/3	Newtown	W	4 – 0	
1962	17/3	Swindon	W	4 – 0	
1963	16/3	Haverfordwest	W	1 – 0	
1964	14/3	Leeds	W	2 – 1	
1965	20/3	Newport	D	2 – 2	
1966	19/3	Northampton	W	4 – 1	
1967	18/3	Cwmbran	D	3 – 3	
1968	16/3	Watford	L	2 – 3	
1969	15/3	Haverfordwest	W	3 – 1	
†1970	25/2	Newport	D	0 – 0	IYT*
†1970	18/3	Leyton	L	1 – 2	

1970	20/4	Reading	D	0 – 0	
1971	20/2	Aberystwyth	L	1 – 2	
1972	19/2	Swindon	W	4 – 0	
1973	24/2	Portmadoc	W	4 – 1	
1974	9/1	West Brom	W	1 – 0	IYT*
1974	2/3	Shrewsbury	W	2 – 1	
1974	13/3	Cardiff	L	0 – 1	IYT*
1976	11/2	Cardiff	W	1 – 0	IYT*
1976	3/3	Manchester	L	2 – 3	IYT*
1977	9/3	West Brom	W	1 – 0	IYT*
1977	23/3	Cardiff	D	1 – 1	IYT*
1991	30/4	Wrexham	W	1 – 0	IYT*
1991	22/5	Yeovil	W	3 – 0	IYT*

Yugoslavia

1953	2/4	Liège	D	1 – 1	IYT

1958	4/2	Chelsea	D	2 – 2	
1962	20/4	Ploesti	L	0 – 5	IYT
†1967	9/5	Izmir	D	1 – 1	IYT
†1971	22/5	Bardejor	W	1 – 0	IYT
†1972	17/5	Barcelona	W	1 – 0	IYT
†1976	16/11	Monte Carlo	L	0 – 3	
1978	15/11	Monte Carlo	D	1 – 1	
†1980	20/5	Altenberg	W	2 – 0	IYT
†1981	10/9	Pula	W	5 – 0	
†1982	9/9	Pula	W	1 – 0	
†1983	25/7	Debrecen	D	4 – 4	
†1983	8/9	Pula	D	2 – 2	
1984	5/5	Boblingen	W	1 – 0	
†1984	12/9	Buje	L	1 – 4	
†1997	9/9	Rotherham	D	0 – 0	IYT*
†1997	11/10	Loznica	W	4 – 0	IYT*

39 ● FA PREMIER LEAGUE AND FOOTBALL LEAGUE CHAMPIONS 1888–1998

FA Premier League Champions 1992–98

Season	Winners	Pts	Max	Season	Winners	Pts	Max
1992–93	Manchester United	84	126	1995–96	Manchester United	82	114
1993–94	Manchester United	92	126	1996–97	Manchester United	75	114
1994–95	Blackburn Rovers	89	126	1997–98	Arsenal	78	114

Football League Champions 1888–1992

First Division 1888–1992

Season	Winners	Pts	Max	Season	Winners	Pts	Max
1888–89	Preston North End	40	44	1926–27	Newcastle United	56	84
1889–90	Preston North End	33	44	1927–28	Everton	53	84
1890–91	Everton	29	44	1928–29	Sheffield Wednesday	52	84
1891–92	Sunderland	42	52	1929–30	Sheffield Wednesday	60	84
1892–93	Sunderland	48	60	1930–31	Arsenal	66	84
1893–94	Aston Villa	44	60	1931–32	Everton	56	84
1894–95	Sunderland	47	60	1932–33	Arsenal	58	84
1895–96	Aston Villa	45	60	1933–34	Arsenal	59	84
1896–97	Aston Villa	47	60	1934–35	Arsenal	58	84
1897–98	Sheffield United	42	60	1935–36	Sunderland	56	84
1898–99	Aston Villa	45	68	1936–37	Manchester City	57	84
1899–1900	Aston Villa	50	68	1937–38	Arsenal	52	84
1900–01	Liverpool	45	68	1938–39	Everton	59	84
1901–02	Sunderland	44	68	1946–47	Liverpool	57	84
1902–03	Sheffield Wednesday	42	68	1947–48	Arsenal	59	84
1903–04	Sheffield Wednesday	47	68	1948–49	Portsmouth	58	84
1904–05	Newcastle United	48	68	1949–50*	Portsmouth	53	84
1905–06	Liverpool	51	76	1950–51	Tottenham Hotspur	60	84
1906–07	Newcastle United	51	76	1951–52	Manchester United	57	84
1907–08	Manchester United	52	76	1952–53*	Arsenal	54	84
1908–09	Newcastle United	53	76	1953–54	Wolverhampton Wanderers	57	8
1909–10	Aston Villa	53	76	1954–55	Chelsea	52	84
1910–11	Manchester United	52	76	1955–56	Manchester United	60	84
1911–12	Blackburn Rovers	49	76	1956–57	Manchester United	64	8
1912–13	Sunderland	54	76	1957–58	Wolverhampton Wanderers	64	8
1913–14	Blackburn Rovers	51	76	1958–59	Wolverhampton Wanderers	61	8
1914–15	Everton	46	76	1959–60	Burnley	55	8
1919–20	West Bromwich Albion	60	84	1960–61	Tottenham Hotspur	66	8
1920–21	Burnley	59	84	1961–62	Ipswich Town	56	8
1921–22	Liverpool	57	84	1962–63	Everton	61	8
1922–23	Liverpool	60	84	1963–64	Liverpool	57	8
1923–24*	Huddersfield Town	57	84	1964–65*	Manchester United	61	8
1924–25	Huddersfield Town	58	84	1965–66	Liverpool	61	8
1925–26	Huddersfield Town	57	84	1966–67	Manchester United	60	8

* Won on goal average/difference   No competition 1915–19 and 1939–46

Season	Winners	Pts	Max	Season	Winners	Pts	Max
67–68	Manchester City	58	84	1980–81	Aston Villa	60	84
68–69	Leeds United	67	84	1981–82	Liverpool	87	126
69–70	Everton	66	84	1982–83	Liverpool	82	126
70–71	Arsenal	65	84	1983–84	Liverpool	80	126
71–72	Derby County	53	84	1984–85	Everton	90	126
72–73	Liverpool	60	84	1985–86	Liverpool	88	126
73–74	Leeds United	62	84	1986–87	Everton	86	126
74–75	Derby County	58	84	1987–88	Liverpool	90	120
75–76	Liverpool	60	84	1988–89*	Arsenal	76	114
76–77	Liverpool	57	84	1989–90	Liverpool	79	114
77–78	Nottingham Forest	64	84	1990–91	Arsenal	83	114
78–79	Liverpool	68	84	1991–92	Leeds United	82	126
79–80	Liverpool	60	84				

st Division 1992–1998 (Second Division 1892–1992)

Season	Winners	Pts	Max	Season	Winners	Pts	Max
92–93	Small Heath	36	44	1935–36	Manchester United	56	76
93–94	Liverpool	50	56	1936–37	Leicester City	56	76
94–95	Bury	48	60	1937–38	Aston Villa	57	76
95–96*	Liverpool	46	60	1938–39	Blackburn Rovers	55	84
96–97	Notts County	42	60	1946–47	Manchester City	62	84
97–98	Burnley	48	60	1947–48	Birmingham City	59	84
98–99	Manchester City	52	68	1948–49	Fulham	57	84
99–1900	Sheffield Wednesday	54	68	1949–50	Tottenham Hotspur	61	84
00–01	Grimsby Town	49	68	1950–51	Preston North End	57	84
01–02	West Bromwich Albion	55	68	1951–52	Sheffield Wednesday	53	84
02–03	Manchester City	54	68	1952–53	Sheffield United	60	84
03–04	Preston North End	50	68	1953–54*	Leicester City	56	84
04–05	Liverpool	58	68	1954–55*	Birmingham City	54	84
05–06	Bristol City	66	76	1955–56	Sheffield Wednesday	55	84
06–07	Nottingham Forest	60	76	1956–57	Leicester City	61	84
07–08	Bradford City	54	76	1957–58	West Ham United	57	84
08–09	Bolton Wanderers	52	76	1958–59	Sheffield Wednesday	62	84
09–10	Manchester City	54	76	1959–60	Aston Villa	59	84
0–11	West Bromwich Albion	53	76	1960–61	Ipswich Town	59	84
1–12	Derby County	54	76	1961–62	Liverpool	62	84
2–13	Preston North End	53	76	1962–63	Stoke City	53	84
3–14	Notts County	53	76	1963–64	Leeds United	63	84
4–15	Derby County	53	76	1964–65	Newcastle United	57	84
9–20	Tottenham Hotspur	70	76	1965–66	Manchester City	59	84
0–21	Birmingham	58	76	1966–67	Coventry City	59	84
1–22	Nottingham Forest	56	76	1967–68	Ipswich Town	59	84
2–23	Notts County	53	76	1968–69	Derby County	63	84
3–24	Leeds United	54	76	1969–70	Huddersfield Town	60	84
4–25	Leicester City	59	76	1970–71	Leicester City	59	84
5–26	Sheffield Wednesday	60	76	1971–72	Norwich City	57	84
6–27	Middlesbrough	62	76	1972–73	Burnley	62	84
7–28	Manchester City	59	76	1974–74	Middlesbrough	65	84
8–29	Middlesbrough	55	76	1974–75	Manchester United	61	84
9–30	Blackpool	58	76	1976–77	Sunderland	56	84
0–31	Everton	61	76	1976–77	Wolverhampton Wanderers	57	84
1–32	Wolverhampton Wanderers	56	76	1977–78	Bolton Wanderers	58	84
2–33	Stoke City	56	76	1978–79	Crystal Palace	57	84
3–34	Grimsby Town	59	76	1979–80	Leicester City	55	84
4–35	Brentford	61	76	1980–81	West Ham United	66	84

on on goal average/difference   No competition 1915–19 and 1939–46

Season	Winners	Pts	Max		Season	Winners	Pts	Max
1981–82	Luton Town	88	126		1990–91	Oldham Athletic	88	138
1982–83	Queens Park Rangers	85	126		1991–92	Ipswich Town	84	138
1983–84*	Chelsea	88	126		1992–93	Newcastle United	96	13
1984–85	Oxford United	84	126		1993–94	Crystal Palace	90	138
1985–86	Norwich City	84	126		1994–95	Middlesbrough	82	138
1986–87	Derby County	84	126		1995–96	Sunderland	83	13
1987–88	Millwall	82	132		1996–97	Bolton Wanderers	98	13
1988–89	Chelsea	99	138		1997–98	Nottingham Forest	94	13
1989–90	Leeds United	85	138					

Third Division (S) 1920–1958

Season	Winners	Pts	Max		Season	Winners	Pts	Max
1920–21	Crystal Palace	59	84		1936–37	Luton Town	58	8
1921–22*	Southampton	61	84		1937–38	Millwall	56	8
1922–23	Bristol City	59	84		1938–39	Newport County	55	8
1923–24	Portsmouth	59	84		1946–47	Cardiff City	66	8
1924–25	Swansea Town	57	84		1947–48	Queens Park Rangers	61	8
1925–26	Reading	57	84		1948–49	Swansea Town	62	8
1926–27	Bristol City	62	84		1949–50	Notts County	58	8
1927–28	Millwall	65	84		1950–51	Nottingham Forest	70	9
1928–29*	Charlton Athletic	54	84		1951–52	Plymouth Argyle	66	9
1929–30	Plymouth Argyle	68	84		1952–53	Bristol Rovers	64	9
1930–31	Notts County	59	84		1953–54	Ipswich Town	64	9
1931–32	Fulham	57	84		1954–55	Bristol City	70	9
1932–33	Brentford	62	84		1955–56	Leyton Orient	66	9
1933–34	Norwich City	61	84		1956–57*	Ipswich Town	59	9
1934–35	Charlton Athletic	61	84		1957–58	Brighton and Hove Albion	60	9
1935–36	Coventry City	57	84					

Third Division (N) 1921–1958

Season	Winners	Pts	Max		Season	Winners	Pts	Max
1921–22	Stockport County	56	76		1936–37	Stockport County	60	8
1922–23	Nelson	51	76		1937–38	Tranmere Rovers	56	8
1923–24	Wolverhampton Wanderers	63	84		1938–39	Barnsley	67	8
1924–25	Darlington	58	84		1946–47	Doncaster Rovers	72	8
1925–26	Grimsby Town	61	84		1947–48	Lincoln City	60	8
1926–27	Stoke City	63	84		1948–49	Hull City	65	8
1927–28	Bradford	63	84		1949–50	Doncaster Rovers	55	8
1928–29	Bradford City	63	84		1950–51	Rotherham United	71	9
1929–30	Port Vale	67	84		1951–52	Lincoln City	69	9
1930–31	Chesterfield	58	84		1952–53	Oldham Athletic	59	9
1931–32*	Lincoln City	57	80		1953–54	Port Vale	69	9
1932–33	Hull City	59	84		1954–55	Barnsley	65	
1933–34	Barnsley	62	84		1955–56	Grimsby Town	68	9
1934–35	Doncaster Rovers	57	84		1956–57	Derby County	63	9
1935–36	Chesterfield	60	84		1957–58	Scunthorpe United	66	9

Second Division 1992–1998 (Third Division 1958–1992)

Season	Winners	Pts	Max		Season	Winners	Pts	Max
1958–59	Plymouth Argyle	62	92		1966–67	Queens Park Rangers	67	
1959–60	Southampton	61	92		1967–68	Oxford United	57	
1960–61	Bury	68	92		1968–69*	Watford	64	
1961–62	Portsmouth	65	92		1969–70	Orient	62	
1962–63	Northampton Town	62	92		1970–71	Preston North End	61	
1963–64*	Coventry City	60	92		1971–72	Aston Villa	70	
1964–65	Carlisle United	60	92		1972–73	Bolton Wanderers	61	
1965–66	Hull City	69	92					

* *Won on goal average/difference*   *No competition 1915–19 and 1939–46*

Season	Winners	Pts	Max	Season	Winners	Pts	Max
1973–74	Oldham Athletic	62	92	1986–87	AFC Bournemouth	97	138
1974–75	Blackburn Rovers	60	92	1987–88	Sunderland	93	138
1975–76	Hereford United	63	92	1988–89	Wolverhampton Wanderers	92	138
1976–77	Mansfield Town	64	92	1989–90	Bristol Rovers	93	138
1977–78	Wrexham	61	92	1990–91	Cambridge United	86	138
1978–79	Shrewsbury Town	61	92	1991–92	Brentford	82	138
1979–80	Grimsby Town	62	92	1992–93	Stoke City	93	138
1980–81	Rotherham United	61	92	1993–94	Reading	89	138
1981–82*	Burnley	80	138	1994–95	Birmingham City	89	138
1982–83	Portsmouth	91	138	1995–96	Swindon Town	92	138
1983–84	Oxford United	95	138	1996–97	Bury	84	138
1984–85	Bradford City	94	138	1997–98	Watford	88	138
1985–86	Reading	94	138				

Third Division 1992–1998 (Fourth Division 1958–1992)

Season	Winners	Pts	Max	Season	Winners	Pts	Max
1958–59	Port Vale	64	92	1979–80	Huddersfield Town	66	92
1959–60	Walsall	65	92	1980–81	Southend United	67	92
1960–61	Peterborough United	66	92	1981–82	Sheffield United	96	138
1961–62	Millwall	56	88	1982–83	Wimbledon	98	138
1962–63	Brentford	62	92	1983–84	York City	101	138
1963–64*	Gillingham	60	92	1984–85	Chesterfield	91	138
1964–65	Brighton and Hove Albion	63	92	1985–86	Swindon Town	102	138
1965–66	Doncaster Rovers	59	92	1986–87	Northampton Town	99	138
1966–67	Stockport County	64	92	1987–88	Wolverhampton Wanderers	90	138
1967–68	Luton Town	66	92	1988–89	Rotherham United	82	138
1968–69	Doncaster Rovers	59	92	1989–90	Exeter City	89	138
1969–70	Chesterfield	64	92	1990–91	Darlington	83	138
1970–71	Notts County	69	92	1991–92	Burnley	83	126
1971–72	Grimsby Town	63	92	1992–93	Cardiff City	83	126
1972–73	Southport	62	92	1993–94	Shrewsbury Town	79	126
1973–74	Peterborough United	65	92	1994–95	Carlisle United	91	126
1974–75	Mansfield Town	68	92	1995–96	Preston North End	86	138
1975–76	Lincoln City	74	92	1996–97	Wigan Athletic	87	138
1976–77	Cambridge United	65	92	1997–98	Notts County	99	138
1977–78	Watford	71	92				
1978	Reading	65	92				

*Won on goal average/difference   No competition 1915–19 and 1939–46

40 ● GUNNERS CHAMPIONS

REVIEW OF THE LEAGUE SEASON 1997–98

Manchester United were so far ahead in the race for the Premiership title early in the year that all bets were declared off. Then Arsenal, under their enigmatic French Manager Arsene Wenger, put together such an impressive sequence of match-winning performances that they went into their 36th League fixture (out of 38) knowing that three points would secure the Championship. Everton, in desperate straits at the other end of the table, were the Gunners' opponents on 3 May and they were simply blown away – 4 – 0. And how fitting that inspirational skipper Tony Adams should weigh in with the fourth goal as half of North London had a party. Arsenal were champions for the eleventh time in history and Dutchman Dennis Bergkamp was "Footballer of the Year".

There were some illustrious names fighting for Premiership survival in the final weeks – Newcastle (missing the injured Shearer for more than half the season), Tottenham (helped by the improbable return of Klinsmann), Everton and Sheffield Wednesday. In the end it was the three promoted clubs who went straight back down. Crystal Palace looked in danger of being the first club to go through a League season without a single home win, but they managed to beat Derby and Sheffield Wednesday in the last three weeks. Barnsley won admirers for their attractive playing style, though the defence leaked goals to an alarming degree. Bolton would have escaped the drop if they had won at Chelsea on the last day (10 May, three days before the Blues' European final).

The three clubs which had been relegated from the Premiership in the previous season – Nottingham Forest, Middlesbrough and Sunderland – made all the running at the top of the Nationwide League First Division. Forest, with Dutchman Van Hooijdonk a prolific scorer, won the title by three points from Bryan Robson's team. Sunderland finished a point behind and had to take their chances in the play-offs. Despite a brave 5 – 2 win at Stoke in their last match, Manchester City suffered the ignominy of relegation to the Second Division for the first time. While Portsmouth looked doomed until Alan Ball returned to take over the reins late in the season, it was Stoke and Reading who went down with the Maine Road giants.

Watford and Bristol City had established such a lead by Christmas at the top of the Second Division that the rest had more or less resigned themselves to a fight for a play-off place. Graham Taylor's Watford won 2 – 1 in front of a 17,000 crowd at Fulham on 2 May to clinch the championship; a defeat against the big-spending play-off hopefuls would have let in the Bristol club.

Fulham, with players worth millions, made it into th[e] play-offs but only on goals scored. It was that clos[e] Chris Waddle's first foray into management was fair[ly] traumatic – after a long struggle they beat Plymout[h] 2 – 1 at Turf Moor on the last day and survived by tw[o] points. Meanwhile, poor Southend went down for th[e] second season running.

Notts County won the Third Division by a distanc[e] (17 points) and had their promotion confirmed i[n] March. Macclesfield, in their first season in the Leagu[e] were runners-up and Lincoln squeezed up in the thir[d] automatic spot after beating Brighton & Hove Albio[n] 2 – 1 at Sincil Bank in their last match. Albion's go[al] had come a minute from time; an equaliser would ha[ve] sent Colchester up instead. Doncaster Rovers lost the[ir] League status after 75 years, to be replaced [by] Conference champions Halifax Town.

NATIONWIDE LEAGUE PLAY – OFFS

Division 1

Semi-finals

| Ipswich Town v Charlton Athletic | 0 – 1 | 0 – |
| Sheffield United v Sunderland | 2 – 1 | 0 – |

Final

Charlton Athletic v Sunderland   4 – 4
(at Wembley)
Charlton Athletic won on penalty-kicks

Division 2

Semi-finals

| Fulham v Grimsby Town | 1 – 1 | 0 – |
| Bristol Rovers v Northampton Town | 3 – 1 | 0 – |

Final

Grimsby Town v Northampton Town 1 – 0
(at Wembley)

Division 3

Semi-finals

| Barnet v Colchester United | 1 – 0 | 1 – |
| Scarborough v Torquay United | 1 – 3 | 1 – |

Final

Colchester United v Torquay United 1 – 0
(at Wembley)

▲ Carling Premiership

| | P | Home | | | | | Away | | | | | GD | Pts |
		W	D	L	F	A	W	D	L	F	A		
Arsenal	38	15	2	2	43	10	8	7	4	25	23	35	78
Manchester United	38	13	4	2	42	9	10	4	5	31	17	47	77
Liverpool	38	13	2	4	42	16	5	9	5	26	26	26	65
Chelsea	38	13	2	4	37	4	7	1	11	34	29	28	63
Leeds United	38	9	5	5	31	21	8	3	8	26	25	11	59
Blackburn Rovers	38	11	4	4	40	26	5	6	8	17	26	5	58
Aston Villa	38	9	3	7	26	24	8	3	8	23	24	1	57
West Ham United	38	13	4	2	40	18	3	4	12	16	39	−1	56
Derby County	38	12	3	4	33	18	4	4	11	19	31	3	55
Leicester City	38	6	10	3	21	15	7	4	8	30	26	10	53
Coventry City	38	8	9	2	26	17	4	7	8	20	27	2	52
Southampton	38	10	1	8	28	23	4	5	10	22	32	−5	48
Newcastle United	38	8	5	6	22	20	3	6	10	13	24	−9	44
Tottenham Hotspur	38	7	8	4	23	22	4	3	12	21	34	−12	44
Wimbledon	38	5	6	8	18	25	5	8	6	16	21	−12	44
Sheffield Wednesday	38	9	5	5	30	26	3	3	13	22	41	−15	44
Everton	38	7	5	7	25	27	2	8	9	16	29	−15	40
Bolton Wanderers	38	7	8	4	25	22	2	5	12	16	39	−20	40
Barnsley	38	7	4	8	25	35	3	1	15	12	47	−45	35
Crystal Palace	38	2	5	12	15	39	6	4	9	22	32	−34	33

Nationwide League First Division

				Home					Away				
		P	W	D	L	F	A	W	D	L	F	A	Pts	G
1	Nottingham Forest	46	18	2	3	52	20	10	8	5	30	22	94	(82
2	Middlesbrough	46	17	4	2	51	12	10	6	7	26	29	91	(77
3	Sunderland	46	14	7	2	49	22	12	5	6	37	28	90	(86
4	Charlton Athletic	46	17	5	1	48	17	9	5	9	32	32	88	(80
5	Ipswich Town	46	14	5	4	47	20	9	9	5	30	23	83	(77
6	Sheffield United	46	16	5	2	44	20	3	12	8	25	34	74	(69
7	Birmingham City	46	10	8	5	27	15	9	9	5	33	20	74	(66
8	Stockport County	46	14	6	3	46	21	5	2	16	25	48	65	(71
9	Wolverhampton W.	46	13	6	4	42	25	5	5	13	15	28	65	(57
10	West Bromwich Albion	46	9	8	6	27	26	7	5	11	23	30	61	(54
11	Crewe Alexandra	46	10	2	11	30	34	8	3	12	28	31	59	(5
12	Oxford United	46	12	6	5	36	20	4	4	15	24	44	58	(6
13	Bradford City	46	10	9	4	26	23	4	6	13	20	36	57	(4
14	Tranmere Rovers	46	9	8	6	34	26	5	6	12	20	31	56	(5
15	Norwich City	46	9	8	6	32	27	5	5	13	20	42	55	(5
16	Huddersfield Town	46	9	5	9	28	28	5	6	12	22	44	53	(5
17	Bury	46	7	10	6	22	22	4	9	10	20	36	52	(4
18	Swindon Town	46	9	6	8	28	25	5	4	14	14	48	52	(4
19	Port Vale	46	7	6	10	25	24	6	4	13	31	42	49	(5
20	Portsmouth	46	8	6	9	28	30	5	4	14	23	33	49	(5
21	Queens Park Rangers	46	8	9	6	28	21	2	10	11	23	42	49	(5
22	Manchester City	46	6	6	11	28	26	6	6	11	28	31	48	(5
23	Stoke City	46	8	5	10	30	40	3	8	12	14	34	46	(4
24	Reading	46	8	4	11	27	31	3	5	15	12	47	42	(3

Nationwide League Second Division

		P	W	D	L	F	A	W	D	L	F	A	Pts	Gls
			Home					*Away*						
1	Watford	46	13	7	3	36	22	11	9	3	31	19	88	(67)
2	Bristol City	46	16	5	2	41	17	9	5	9	28	22	85	(69)
3	Grimsby Town	46	11	7	5	30	14	8	8	7	25	23	72	(55)*
4	Northampton Town	46	14	5	4	33	17	4	12	7	19	20	71	(52)
5	Bristol Rovers	46	13	2	8	43	33	7	8	8	27	31	70	(70)
6	Fulham	46	12	7	4	31	14	8	3	12	29	29	70	(60)
7	Wrexham	46	10	10	3	31	23	8	6	9	24	28	70	(55)
8	Gillingham	46	13	7	3	30	18	6	6	11	22	29	70	(52)
9	Bournemouth	46	11	8	4	28	15	7	4	12	29	37	66	(57)
10	Chesterfield	46	13	7	3	31	19	3	10	10	15	25	65	(46)
11	Wigan Athletic	46	12	5	6	41	31	5	6	12	23	35	62	(64)
12	Blackpool	46	13	6	4	35	24	4	5	14	24	43	62	(59)
13	Oldham Athletic	46	13	7	3	43	23	2	9	12	19	31	61	(62)
14	Wycombe Wanderers	46	10	10	3	32	20	4	8	11	19	33	60	(51)
15	Preston North End	46	10	6	7	29	26	5	8	10	27	30	59	(56)
16	York City	46	9	7	7	26	21	5	10	8	26	37	59	(52)
17	Luton Town	46	7	7	9	35	38	7	8	8	25	26	57	(60)
18	Millwall	46	7	8	8	23	23	7	5	11	20	31	55	(43)
19	Walsall	46	10	8	5	26	16	4	4	15	17	36	54	(43)
20	Burnley	46	10	9	4	34	23	3	4	16	21	42	52	(55)
21	Brentford	46	9	7	7	33	29	2	10	11	17	42	50	(50)
22	Plymouth Argyle	46	10	5	8	36	30	2	8	13	19	40	49	(55)
23	Carlisle United	46	8	5	10	27	28	4	3	16	30	45	44	(57)
24	Southend United	46	8	7	8	29	30	3	3	17	18	49	43	(47)

Nationwide League Third Division

			Home					Away						
		P	W	D	L	F	A	W	D	L	F	A	Pts	Gls
1	Notts County	46	14	7	2	41	20	15	5	3	41	23	99	(82)
2	Macclesfield Town	46	19	4	0	40	11	4	9	10	23	33	82	(63)
3	Lincoln City	46	11	7	5	32	24	9	8	6	28	27	75	(60)
4	Colchester United	46	14	5	4	41	24	7	6	10	31	36	74	(72)*
5	Torquay United	46	14	4	5	39	22	7	7	9	29	37	74	(68)
6	Scarborough	46	14	6	3	44	23	5	9	9	23	35	72	(67)
7	Barnet	46	10	8	5	35	22	9	5	9	26	29	70	(61)
8	Scunthorpe United	46	11	7	5	30	24	8	5	10	26	28	69	(56)
9	Rotherham United	46	10	9	4	41	30	6	10	7	26	31	67	(67)
10	Peterborough United	46	13	6	4	37	16	5	7	11	26	35	67	(63)
11	Leyton Orient	46	14	5	4	40	20	5	7	11	22	27	66	(62)†
12	Mansfield Town	46	11	9	3	42	26	5	8	10	22	29	65	(64)
13	Shrewsbury Town	46	12	3	8	35	28	4	10	9	26	34	61	(61)
14	Chester City	46	12	7	4	34	15	5	3	15	26	46	61	(60)
15	Exeter City	46	10	8	5	39	25	5	7	11	29	38	60	(68)
16	Cambridge United	46	11	8	4	39	27	3	10	10	24	30	60	(63)
17	Hartlepool United	46	10	12	1	40	22	2	11	10	21	31	59	(61)
18	Rochdale	46	15	3	5	43	15	2	4	17	13	40	58	(56)
19	Darlington	46	13	6	4	43	28	1	6	16	13	44	54	(56)
20	Swansea City	46	8	8	7	24	16	5	3	15	25	46	50	(49)
21	Cardiff City	46	5	13	5	27	22	4	10	9	21	30	50	(48)
22	Hull City	46	10	6	7	36	32	1	2	20	20	51	41	(56)
23	Brighton & Hove Albion	46	3	10	10	21	34	3	7	13	17	32	35	(38)
24	Doncaster Rovers	46	3	3	17	14	48	1	5	17	16	65	20	(30)

promoted via the play-offs
†*deducted three points*

42 ● LEAGUE CUP WINNERS 1961–1998

Two-legged finals until 1966, all finals after 1966 played at Wembley

Year	Winners		Runners-up	Result	
1961	Aston Villa	v	Rotherham United	3 – 2	(2 – 2, 3 – 0 after extra time)
1962	Norwich City	v	Rochdale	4 – 0	(3 – 0, 1 – 0)
1963	Birmingham City	v	Aston Villa	3 – 1	(3 – 1, 0 – 0)
1964	Leicester City	v	Stoke City	4 – 3	(1 – 1, 3 – 2)
1954	Chelsea	v	Leicester City	3 – 2	(3 – 2, 0 – 0)
1966	West Bromwich Albion	v	West Ham United	5 – 3	(1 – 2, 4 – 1)
1967	Queens Park Rangers	v	West Bromwich Albion	3 – 2	
1968	Leeds United	v	Arsenal	1 – 0	
1969	Swindon Town	v	Arsenal	3 – 1	after extra time
1970	Manchester City	v	West Bromwich Albion	2 – 1	after extra time
1971	Tottenham Hotspur	v	Aston Villa	2 – 0	
1972	Stoke City	v	Chelsea	2 – 1	
1973	Tottenham Hotspur	v	Norwich City	1 – 0	
1974	Wolverhampton Wanderers	v	Manchester City	2 – 1	
1975	Aston Villa	v	Norwich City	1 – 0	
1976	Manchester City	v	Newcastle United	2 – 1	
1977	Aston Villa	v	Everton	0 – 0	
	Aston Villa	v	Everton	1 – 1	after extra time
					replay at Hillsborough
	Aston Villa	v	Everton	3 – 2	after extra time;
					2nd replay at Old Trafford
1978	Nottingham Forest	v	Liverpool	0 – 0	after extra time
	Nottingham Forest	v	Liverpool	1 – 0	replay at Old Trafford
1979	Nottingham Forest	v	Southampton	3 – 2	
1980	Wolverhampton Wanderers	v	Nottingham Forest	1 – 0	
1981	Liverpool	v	West Ham United	1 – 1	after extra time
	Liverpool	v	West Ham United	2 – 1	replay at Villa Park

*s Milk Cup

Year	Winners		Runners-up	Result	
1982	Liverpool	v	Tottenham Hotspur	3 – 1	after extra time
1983	Liverpool	v	Manchester United	2 – 1	after extra time
1984	Liverpool	v	Everton	0 – 0	after extra time
	Liverpool	v	Everton	1 – 0	replay at Maine Road
1985	Norwich City	v	Sunderland	1 – 0	
1986	Oxford United	v	Queens Park Rangers	3 – 0	

*s Littlewoods Cup

Year	Winners		Runners-up	Result	
1987	Arsenal	v	Liverpool	2 – 1	
1988	Luton Town	v	Arsenal	3 – 2	
1989	Nottingham Forest	v	Luton Town	3 – 1	
1990	Nottingham Forest	v	Oldham Athletic	1 – 0	

*s Rumbelows Cup

Year	Winners		Runners-up	Result	
1991	Sheffield Wednesday	v	Manchester United	1 – 0	
1992	Manchester United	v	Nottingham Forest	1 – 0	

*s Coca-Cola Cup

Year	Winners		Runners-up	Result	
1993	Arsenal	v	Sheffield Wednesday	2 – 1	
1994	Aston Villa	v	Manchester United	3 – 1	
1995	Liverpool	v	Bolton Wanderers	2 – 1	
1996	Aston Villa	v	Leeds United	3 – 0	
1997	Leicester City	v	Middlesbrough	1 – 1	after extra time
	Leicester City	v	Middlesbrough	1 – 0	replay at Hillsbrough
					after extra time
1998	Chelsea	v	Middlesbrough	2 – 0	after extra time

43 ● COCA-COLA CUP 1997–1998

First Round (Two Legs)

Blackpool*	v	Manchester City	1 – 0	0 – 1
Bournemouth	v	Torquay United	0 – 1	1 – 1
Brentford	v	Shrewsbury Town	1 – 1	5 – 3
Brighton & Hove Albion	v	Leyton Orient	1 – 1	1 – 3
Bristol City	v	Bristol Rovers	0 – 0	2 – 1
Cambridge United	v	West Bromwich Albion	1 – 1	1 – 2
Cardiff City	v	Southend United	1 – 1	1 – 3
Charlton Athletic	v	Ipswich Town	0 – 1	1 – 3
Chester City	v	Carlisle United	1 – 2	0 – 3
Colchester United	v	Luton Town	0 – 1	1 – 1
Crewe Alexandra	v	Bury	2 – 3	3 – 3
Darlington	v	Notts County	1 – 1	1 – 2
Doncaster Rovers	v	Nottingham Forest	0 – 8	1 – 2
Gillingham	v	Birmingham City	0 – 1	0 – 3
Huddersfield Town	v	Bradford City	2 – 1	1 – 1
Lincoln City	v	Burnley	1 – 1	1 – 2
Macclesfield Town	v	Hull City	0 – 0	1 – 2
Mansfield Town	v	Stockport County	4 – 2	3 – 6
Northampton Town	v	Millwall*	2 – 1	1 – 2
Norwich City	v	Barnet	2 – 1	1 – 3
Oldham Athletic	v	Grimsby Town	1 – 0	0 – 5
Oxford United	v	Plymouth Argyle	2 – 0	5 – 3
Peterborough United	v	Portsmouth	2 – 2	2 – 1
Port Vale	v	York City	1 – 2	1 – 1
Queens Park Rangers	v	Wolverhampton Wanderers	0 – 2	2 – 1
Reading	v	Swansea City	2 – 0	1 – 1
Rochdale	v	Stoke City	1 – 3	1 – 1
Rotherham United	v	Preston North End	1 – 3	0 – 2
Scarborough	v	Scunthorpe United	0 – 2	1 – 2
Swindon Town	v	Watford	0 – 2	1 – 1
Tranmere Rovers	v	Hartlepool United	3 – 1	1 – 2
Walsall	v	Exeter City	2 – 0	1 – 0
Wigan Athletic	v	Chesterfield	1 – 2	0 – 1
Wrexham	v	Sheffield United	1 – 1	1 – 3
Wycombe Wanderers	v	Fulham	1 – 2	4 – 4

Second Round (Two Legs)

Birmingham City	v	Stockport County	4 – 1	1 – 2
Blackburn Rovers	v	Preston North End	6 – 0	1 – 1
Blackpool	v	Coventry City	1 – 0	1 – 3
Burnley	v	Stoke City	0 – 4	0 – 2
Chesterfield	v	Barnsley	1 – 2	1 – 4
Fulham	v	Wolverhampton Wanderers	0 – 1	0 – 1
Grimsby Town	v	Sheffield Wednesday	2 – 0	2 – 3
Huddersfield Town	v	West Ham United	1 – 0	0 – 3
Hull City	v	Crystal Palace	1 – 0	1 – 3
Ipswich Town	v	Torquay United	1 – 1	3 – 0
Leeds United	v	Bristol City	3 – 1	1 – 2
Leyton Orient	v	Bolton Wanderers	1 – 3	4 – 4
Luton Town	v	West Bromwich Albion	1 – 1	2 – 4
Middlesbrough	v	Barnet	1 – 0	2 – 0

Nottingham Forest	v	Walsall	0 – 1	2 – 2
Notts County	v	Tranmere Rovers	0 – 2	1 – 0
Oxford United	v	York City	4 – 1	2 – 1
Reading	v	Peterborough United	0 – 0	2 – 0
Scunthorpe United	v	Everton	0 – 1	0 – 5
Southampton	v	Brentford	3 – 1	2 – 0
Southend United	v	Derby County	0 – 1	0 – 5
Sunderland	v	Bury	2 – 1	2 – 1
Tottenham Hotspur	v	Carlisle United	3 – 2	2 – 0
Watford	v	Sheffield United	1 – 1	0 – 4
Wimbledon	v	Millwall	5 – 1	4 – 1

Third Round

Arsenal	v	Birmingham City	4 – 1
Barnsley	v	Southampton	1 – 2
Bolton Wanderers	v	Wimbledon	2 – 0
Chelsea*	v	Blackburn Rovers	1 – 1
Coventry City	v	Everton	4 – 1
Grimsby Town	v	Leicester City	3 – 1
Ipswich Town	v	Manchester United	2 – 0
Middlesbrough	v	Sunderland	2 – 0
Newcastle United	v	Hull City	2 – 0
Oxford United*	v	Tranmere Rovers	1 – 1
Reading	v	Wolverhampton Wanderers	4 – 2
Stoke City	v	Leeds United	1 – 3
Tottenham Hotspur	v	Derby County	1 – 2
Walsall	v	Sheffield United	2 – 1
West Bromwich Albion	v	Liverpool	0 – 2
West Ham United	v	Aston Villa	3 – 0

Fourth Round

Arsenal	v	Coventry City	1 – 0
Chelsea	v	Southampton	2 – 1
Derby County	v	Newcastle United	0 – 1
Leeds United	v	Reading	2 – 3
Liverpool	v	Grimsby Town	3 – 0
Middlesbrough	v	Bolton Wanderers	2 – 1
Oxford United	v	Ipswich Town	1 – 2
West Ham United	v	Walsall	4 – 1

Fifth Round

Ipswich Town	v	Chelsea*	2 – 2
Newcastle United	v	Liverpool	0 – 2
Reading	v	Middlesbrough	0 – 1
West Ham United	v	Arsenal	1 – 2

Semi – Finals (Two Legs)

| Arsenal | v | Chelsea | 2 – 1 | 1 – 3 |
| Liverpool | v | Middlesbrough | 2 – 1 | 0 – 2 |

Final

| Chelsea | v | Middlesbrough | 2 – 0 |

*won on penalty – kicks

44 ● CSI FA WOMEN'S CUP – FINAL TIE 1998

Arsenal 3 Croydon 2

Arsenal Ladies continued the fantastic year for the North London club when they won the CSI F.A. Women's Cup Final in a match which built up to a great climax at Millwall's New Den.

Their male counterparts had secured the F.A. Carling Premiership crown the day before, and the Arsenal Ladies had already won the F.A. Women's Premier League Cup against their opponents on the day Croydon WFC.

Both teams had a strong recent record in the F.A. Women's Cup which was sponsored for the first time by TV marketing company CSI and was in its fifth year under the control of The Football Association. Arsenal were winners in 1992–93 and 1994–95, and Croydon held the trophy aloft in 1995–96.

With both sides packed with international players, the match started at a fast pace in front of more than 2000 enthusiastic fans, and many more watching live on Sky TV.

Croydon took an early lead, Joanne Broadhurst stroking home a penalty on 10 minutes, after Tina Lindsey – who played in last year's final for Millwall Lionesses – had been brought down by Kirsty Pealling.

Arsenal soon struck back, when teenage England striker Rachel Yankey broke on the right and crossed for Marianne Spacey whose misfit flying volley looped over Croydon goalkeeper Louise Cooper for the equaliser on 17 minutes.

Both sides continued to create chances, the two Arsenal strikers combining well together, and Croydon's experienced midfield looking very solid but the scores remained level until half-time.

After the break, it was Arsenal who started more strongly, and after 51 minutes they re-took the lead. Rachel Yankey got on the end of a quick break, and rounded the goalkeeper to slot home.

Croydon, though, were far from beaten and equalised only three minutes later, Hope Powell firing home from close range after a misfit back-pass from Arsenal goalkeeper Sarah Read. Powell was captaining Croydon for

Croydon's Alex Cottier crosses in front of Rachel Yankey.

the last time, as she would hang up her boots at the end of the season following her appointment as the first ever full time National Coach for Women's Football.

But it was to prove no fairytale ending for Hope. Despite Croydon having perhaps the better chances in the final quarter, Arsenal secured an injury time winner through defender Kelly Few. After a foul by Sammy Britton on the edge of the area, Spacey sent in a stunning free kick, which Cooper tipped onto the bar, only for the ball to drop for Few to bundle it in.

Arsenal captain Sian Williams received the Cup from Chief Guest Delia Smith, and the Gunner Girls were further rewarded a couple of weeks later when they joined their double-winning counterparts on an open-top bus ride to celebrate their great season.

Arsenal: Reed, Pealling, Jerray-Silver, Slee, Harwood, White, Williams, Few, Spacey, Mapes (Daly), Yankey.

Croydon: Cooper, Fletcher, Cottier, Powell, Wylie, Darby, Britton, Bampton, Broadhurst, Davis, Proctor.

Referee: A.G. Wiley (Staffordshire)

Attendance: 2205

Arsenal Ladies – FA Women's Cup winners 1998.

45 ● CSI FA WOMEN'S CUP 1997–1998

Second round – 2 November 1997

(Replays in italics)   *Results*

Bangor City	v	Oldham Athletic	1 – 2
Garswood Saints	v	Droylsden	7 – 1
Preston North End	v	Darlington	14 – 1
Scunthorpe Ironesses	v	Stockport	1 – 4
Bury	v	Liverpool Feds	2 – 4
Chester City	v	Huddersfield Town	2 – 4
Blyth Spartans	v	Leeds United	6 – 3
Sheffield Wednesday	v	Doncaster Rovers	3 – 2
Newcastle Town	v	Newcastle	2 – 1
Hemsworth Town	v	Leeds City Vixens	1 – 5
Blackburn Rovers	v	Haslingden	6 – 1
Warrington Grange	v	Newsham PH	1 – 0
Milton Keynes Athletic	v	Derby County	1 – 6
Ipswich Town	v	Ilkeston Town	0 – 5
Coventry City	v	Mansfield Town	2 – 1
Loughborough Students	v	Highfield Rangers	4 – 4
Highfield Rangers	*v*	*Loughborough Students*	*2 – 1*
Gorleston	v	Birmingham City	0 – 2
Calverton MW	v	Arnold Town	0 – 1
Bloxwich Town	v	Shrewsbury Town	3 – 1
Wolverhampton Wanderers	v	Rushden Diamonds	14 – 0
Rea Valley Rovers	v	Aston Villa	0 – 8
Derby County	v	Canary Racers	1 – 5
Fulham	v	Teynham Gunners	7 – 1
Brighton & Hove Albion	v	Hampton	0 – 0
Hampton	*v*	*Brighton & Hove Albion*	*1 – 2*
Clapton	v	Tottenham Hotspur	0 – 4
London Women's	v	Leyton Orient	1 – 2
St Georges (Eltham)	v	Surbiton	1 – 1 (replay 0 – 3)
Langford	v	Chelmsford	1 – 1
Chelmsford	*v*	*Langford*	*0 – 4*
West Ham United	v	Risborough Rangers	3 – 1
Luton	v	Queens Park Rangers	0 – 1
Hendon	v	Hackney	5 – 5
Hackney	*v*	*Hendon*	*0 – 3*
Three Bridges	v	Chelsea	4 – 2
Welwyn Garden City	v	Whitehawk	1 – 10
Dulwich Hamlet	v	Wimbledon	0 – 16
Charlton	v	Abbey Rangers	1 – 1
Abbey Rangers	*v*	*Charlton*	*0 – 2*
Wembley Mill Hill	v	Gillingham Girls	7 – 1
Watford & Evergreen	v	Malling	3 – 0
Basingstoke Town	v	Reading Royals	0 – 8
Swindon Town	v	Cardiff County	0 – 2
Truro City	v	Swindon Spitfires	2 – 2
Swindon Spitfires	*v*	*Truro City*	*1 – 2*
Southampton Saints	v	Oxford United	3 – 1
Saltash Pilgrims	v	Portsmouth	2 – 5
Elmore Eagles	v	Barry Town	0 – 7
Binfield	v	Okeford United	1 – 0

Third round – 30 November 1997

Huddersfield Town	v	Leeds City Vixens	4 – 2
Liverpool Feds	v	Sheffield Wednesday	1 – 5
Blyth Spartans Kestrels	v	Garswood Saints	I – 3
Oldham Athletic	v	Preston North End	0 – 2
Warrington Grange	v	Newcastle Town	3 – 5
Stockport	v	Blackburn Rovers	4 – 2
Bloxwich Town	v	Highfield Rangers	6 – 1
Canary Racers	v	Arnold Town	6 – 0
Coventry City	v	Birmingham City	4 – 4
Birmingham City	*v*	*Coventry City*	*0 – 5*
Aston Villa	v	Wolverhampton Wanderers	1 – 0
Ilkeston Town	v	Derby County	6 – 0
Wembley Mill Hill	v	Whitehawk	1 – 4
Brighton & Hove Albion	v	Langford	3 – 3
Langford	*v*	*Brighton & Hove Albion*	*2 – 3*
Three Bridges	v	Watford & Evergreen	0 – 6
Queens Park Rangers	v	Wimbledon	3 – 4
Leyton Orient	v	Reading Royals	2 – 2
Reading Royals	*v*	*Leyton Orient*	*1 – 0*
Fulham	v	Tottenham Hotspur	4 – 7
West Ham United	v	Charlton	0 – 7
Hendon	v	St Georges (Eltham)	0 – 6
Truro City	v	Barry Town	0 – 4
Binfield	v	Southampton Saints	0 – 6
Cardiff County	v	Portsmouth	3 – 0

Fourth round – 11 January 1998

Huddersfield Town	v	Wimbledon	3 – 2
Bradford City	v	Aston Villa	5 – 1
Tranmere Rovers	v	Berkhamsted Town	4 – 2
Bloxwich Town	v	Ilkeston Town	0 – 2
Whitehawk	v	Coventry City	5 – 0
Cardiff County	v	Millwall Lionnesses	0 – 6
Tottenham Hotspur	v	Brighton & Hove Albion	2 – 1
Wembley	v	Croydon	0 – 10
Doncaster Belles	v	St Georges (Eltham)	10 – 0
Southampton Saints	v	Newcastle Town	2 – 1
Garswood Saints	v	Preston North End	4 – 1
Sheffield Wednesday	v	Watford & Evergreen	3 – 2
Everton	v	Liverpool	0 –1
Canary Racers	v	Arsenal	0 – 12
Charlton	v	Stockport	1 – 2
Reading Royals	v	Barry Town	0 – 2

Fifth round – 1 February 1998

Tranmere Rovers	v	Garswood Saints	1 – 2
Doncaster Belles	v	Huddersfield Town	6 – 0
Liverpool	v	Ilkeston Town	2 – 0
Croydon	v	Tottenham Hotspur	4 – 1
Millwall Lionesses	v	Whitehawk	2 – 0
Bradford City	v	Sheffield Wednesday	4 – 1
Barry Town	v	Stockport	2 – 1
Southampton Saints	v	Arsenal	0 – 1

Sixth round – 1 March 1998

Croydon	v	Bradford City	3 – 2
Garswood Saints	v	Barry Town	1 – 2
Doncaster Belles	v	Arsenal	1 – 2
Millwall Lionesses	v	Liverpool	2 – 2
Liverpool	*v*	*Millwall Lionesses*	*3 – 1*

(awarded to Millwall Lionesses as Liverpool played an ineligible player)

Semi-finals – 29 March 1998

Barry Town	v	Croydon	0 – 1
(at Forest Green Rovers FC)			
Arsenal	v	Millwall Lionesses	1 – 0
(at Kingstonian FC)			

National Division

	P	W	D	L	F	A	GD	Pts	
Everton	18	13	4	1	54	14	+40	43	
Arsenal	18	12	4	2	55	22	+33	40	
Doncaster Belles	18	12	2	4	54	18	+36	38	
Croydon	18	10	5	3	46	14	+32	35	
Millwall Lionesses	18	8	5	5	37	15	+22	29	
Liverpool	18	8	3	7	33	25	+8	27	Berkhamsted Town and
Tranmere Rovers	18	5	4	9	33	43	–10	19	Wembley relegated
Bradford City	18	3	3	12	39	52	–13	12	to Northern Division
Berkhamsted Town	18	3	2	13	22	64	–42	11	and Southern Division
Wembley	18	0	0	18	3	109	–106	0	respectively

Northern Division

	P	W	D	L	F	A	GD	Pts	
Ilkeston Town	18	17	0	1	68	6	+62	51	Ilkeston Town promoted
Garswood Saints	18	12	3	3	43	23	+20	39	to National Division
Aston Villa	18	10	2	6	38	23	+15	32	
Wolverhampton Wanderers	18	8	5	5	33	20	+13	29	
Blyth Spartans Kestrels	18	8	4	6	40	23	+17	28	
Sheffield Wednesday	18	8	3	7	39	40	–1	27	
Huddersfield Town	18	7	3	8	32	31	+1	24	
Coventry City	18	2	6	10	22	62	–40	12	Leeds United promoted
Arnold Town	18	2	4	12	11	36	–25	10	to Northern Division
Bloxwich Town	18	0	2	16	12	74	–62	2	

Southern Division

	P	W	D	L	F	A	GD	Pts	
Southampton Saints	18	12	6	0	50	14	+36	42	Southampton Saints
Brighton & Hove Albion	18	12	2	4	64	21	+43	38	promoted to National
Wimbledon	18	11	3	4	64	30	+34	36	Division
Langford	18	10	4	4	52	33	+19	34	
Whitehawk	18	9	4	5	69	30	+39	31	Reading Royals promoted
Barry Town	18	6	5	7	23	29	–6	23*	to Southern Division
Three Bridges	18	7	1	10	47	37	+10	22	
Ipswich Town	18	5	3	10	33	31	+2	18	
Leyton Orient	18	3	2	13	23	62	–39	11	
Rushden & Diamonds	18	0	0	18	10	148	–138	0	

The Management Committee awarded Barry Town three points for each of their three outstanding matches.

FA Women's Premier League Cup Final: Arsenal 0   Croydon 0
(at Barnet FC)   (Arsenal won 4–3 on penalty-kicks)

47 ● ENGLAND WOMEN'S CAPS 1997–1998

	Scotland	Germany	Holland	France	Germany	Italy	Norway	Holland
P. Cope (Millwall Lionesses)	1		1	1		1	1	1
M. Phillip (Millwall Lionesses)	2							
S. Britton (Croydon)	3	8	8	8	3	8	8	8
H. Powell (Croydon)	4	4	4	4	4	4	4	
M. Marley (Everton)	5	5		5	5	3*	2	2
G. Coultard (Doncaster Belles)	6	6	6	6	6	6	6	6
K. Burke (Everton)	7	7	7	7	7		7	7
P. Buckley (Millwall Lionesses)	8							
R.Yankey (Arsenal)	9	9	9	11*			11	11
K. Davis (Croydon)	10	10	10	10	10			
S. Smith (Tranmere Rovers)	11	11	11	11	11	11	3	3
S. Reed (Arsenal)	1*							
B. Easton (Everton)	2*	3	3	3	10*	8*		2*
D. Murphy (Millwall Lionesses)	3*	3*		5*	8	2	4*	4
F. White (Arsenal)	5*			2	2	5	5	5
K. Massey (Stockport)	8*			3*				
V. Exley (Doncaster Belles)	10*							
J. Lorton (Millwall Lionesses)	11*			6*				
R. Brown (Liverpool)		1		1*	1	1*		
J. Broadhurst (Croydon)		2	2			9		
T. Mapes (Arsenal)			5					
N. Daly (Arsenal)			9*					
M. Catterall (Liverpool)			9**	10*		10*		
C. Utley (Doncaster Belles)				2*		7		
M. Garside (Bradford City)				9	5*	10		
K. Smith (Seton Hall)					9		9	10
T. Proctor (Croydon)						3		
A. Cottier (Croydon)						9*		
K. Walker (Doncaster Belles)							10	9

*substitute

WOMEN'S INTERNATIONAL MATCHES 1997-98

Date	*Venue*				*Result*
23.8.97	Livingston	Scotland	v	England	0 – 4
25.9.97	Dessau	Germany	v	England	3 – 0*
30.10.97	West Ham	England	v	Holland	1 – 0*
15.2.98	Alencon	France	v	England	3 – 2
8.3.98	Millwall	England	v	Germany	0 – 1*
21.4.98	West Bromwich	England	v	Italy	1 – 2
14.5.98	Oldham	England	v	Norway	1 – 2*
23.5.98	Waalwijk	Holland	v	England	2 – 1*

*Women's World Cup – Qualifying Competition

Under – 18

| 10.11.97 | Oostduinkerk | Belgium | v | England | 1 – 2* |
| 11.11.97 | Oostduinkerk | France | v | England | 1 – 1* |

*UEFA Championship – Qualifying Competition

48 ● FA SUNDAY CUP WINNERS 1965–1998

Year	Venue	Winners		Runners-up	Result
1965		London	v	Staffordshire	6 – 2†
1966	Dudley	Unique United	v	Aldridge Fabrications	1 – 0
1967	Hendon	Carlton United	v	Stoke Works	2 – 0
1968	Cambridge	Drovers	v	Brook United	2 – 0
1969	Romford	Leigh Park	v	Loke United	3 – 1
1970	Corby	Vention United	v	Unique United	1 – 0
1971	Leamington	Beacontree Rovers	v	Saltley United	2 – 0
1972	Dudley	Newton Unity	v	Springfield Colts	4 – 0
1973	Spennymoor	Carlton United	v	Wear Valley	2 – 1*
1974	Birmingham	Newton Unity	v	Brentford East	3 – 0
1975	High Wycombe	Fareham Town Centipedes	v	Players Athletic Engineers	1 – 0
1976	Spennymoor	Brandon United	v	Evergreen	2 – 1
1977	Spennymoor	Langley Park RH	v	Newton Unity	2 – 0
1978	Nuneaton	Arras	v	Lion Rangers	2 – 2
	Bishop's Stortford	Arras	v	Lion Rangers	2 – 1
1979	Southport	Lobster	v	Carlton United	3 – 2
1980	Letchworth	Fantail	v	Twin Foxes	1 – 0
1981	Birkenhead	Fantail	v	Mackintosh	1 – 0
1982	Hitchin	Dingle Rail	v	Twin Foxes	2 – 1
1983	Walthamstow	Eagle	v	Lee Chapel North	2 – 1
1984	Runcorn	Lee Chapel North	v	Eagle	1 – 1
	Dagenham	Lee Chapel North	v	Eagle	4 – 3*
1985	Norwich	Hobbies	v	Avenue	1 – 1
	Birkenhead	Hobbies	v	Avenue	2 – 2
	Nuneaton	Hobbies	v	Avenue	2 – 1
1986	Birkenhead	Avenue	v	Glenn Sports	1 – 0
1987	Birmingham	Lodge Cottrell	v	Avenue	1 – 0*
1988	Newcastle	Nexday	v	Sunderland Humb Plains	2 – 0
1989	Stockport	Almithak	v	East Levenshulme	3 – 1
1990	West Bromwich	Humbledon Plains Farm	v	Marston Sports	2 – 1
1991	Wigan	Nicosia	v	Ouzavich	3 – 2*
1992	Reading	Theale	v	Marston Sports	3 – 2
1993	Chester	Seymour	v	Bedfont Sunday	1 – 0
1994	Woking	Ranelagh Sports	v	Hartlepool Lion Hotel	2 – 0
1995	Hull	St Joseph's (Luton)	v	B&A Scaffolding	2 – 1
1996	Northampton	St Joseph's (Luton)	v	Croxteth & Gilmoss RBL	2 – 1
1997	Mansfield	Marston Sports	v	Northwood	1 – 0
1998	Peterborough	Olympic Star	v	St. Joseph's (Luton)	1 – 1**

*after extra time
†two legs
**won on penalty kicks

49 ● FA SUNDAY CUP 1997–1998

(Replays in italics)   *Results*

Third round – 14 December 1997

Salerno	v	Queens Park	1 – 0
Bolton Woods	v	Rob Roy	2 – 0
Crown	v	Tanhouse Upholland Labour	2 – 1
Park Inn	v	Hartlepool Lion Hotel	0 – 3
A3	v	Sandon	1 – 3
Rovers Sports	v	East Bowling Unity	3 – 1
Eden Vale	v	Boulevard Mode Force	1 – 0
Lebeq Tavern	v	Marston Sports	1 – 3
St. Joseph's (Luton)	v	Lodge Cottrell	4 – 0
Forest Athletic	v	Clifton Albion	4 – 1
BRSC Aidan	v	Olympic Star	1 – 3
St. Joseph's (Sth Oxhey)	v	Pitsea	2 – 6
Warriors	v	Active Signs	5 – 6
Brookvale Athletic	v	Arras	4 – 0
Northfield Rangers	v	Morden Nomads	0 – 1
Heathfield	v	Coach & Horses	4 – 0

Fourth round – 11 January 1998

Hartlepool Lion Hotel	v	Olympic Star	0 – 1
Sandon	v	Bolton Woods	0 – 2
Crown	v	Eden Vale	2 – 5
Rovers Sports	v	Salerno	0 – 1
Pitsea	v	Heathfield	2 – 0
Marston Sports	v	Morden Nomads	0 – 0
Morden Nomads	*v*	*Marston Sports*	*1 – 4*
Brookvale Athletic	v	St. Joseph's (Luton)	1 – 3
Active Signs	v	Forest Athletic	2 – 4

Fifth round – 8 February 1998

Eden Vale	v	Salerno	2 – 1
Bolton Woods	v	Olympic Star	1 – 2
Marston Sports	v	St. Joseph's (Luton)	1 – 2
Forest Athletic	v	Pitsea	1 – 6

Semi-finals – 15 March 1998

Eden Vale	v	St. Joseph's (Luton)	1 – 2
Olympic Star	v	Pitsea	3 – 1

Final – 26 April 1998

Olympic Star	v	St. Joseph's (Luton)	1 – 1*
(at Peterborough United FC)			

*Olympic Star won on penalty-kicks

50 ● FA CHARITY SHIELD WINNERS
1908–1997

Year	Winners		Runners-up	Result
1908	Manchester United	v	Queens Park Rangers	1 – 1
	Manchester United	*v*	*Queens Park Rangers*	*4 – 0*
1909	Newcastle United	v	Northampton Town	2 – 0
1910	Brighton and Hove Albion	v	Aston Villa	1 – 0
1911	Manchester United	v	Swindon Town	8 – 4
1912	Blackburn Rovers	v	Queens Park Rangers	2 – 1
1913	Professionals	v	Amateurs	7 – 2
1914–18			not played	
1920	West Bromwich Albion	v	Tottenham Hotspur	2 – 0
1921	Tottenham Hotspur	v	Burnley	2 – 0
1922	Huddersfield Town	v	Liverpool	1 – 0
1923	Professionals	v	Amateurs	2 – 0
1924	Professionals	v	Amateurs	3 – 1
1925	Amateurs	v	Professionals	6 – 1
1926	Amateurs	v	Professionals	6 – 3
1927	Cardiff City	v	Corinthians	2 – 1
1928	Everton	v	Blackburn Rovers	2 – 1
1929	Professionals	v	Amateurs	3 – 0
1930	Arsenal	v	Sheffield Wednesday	2 – 1
1931	Arsenal	v	West Bromwich Albion	1 – 0
1932	Everton	v	Newcastle United	5 – 3
1933	Arsenal	v	Everton	3 – 0
1934	Arsenal	v	Manchester City	4 – 0
1935	Sheffield Wednesday	v	Arsenal	1 – 0
1936	Sunderland	v	Arsenal	2 – 1
1937	Manchester City	v	Sunderland	2 – 0
1938	Arsenal	v	Preston North End	2 – 1
1938–47			not played	
1948	Arsenal	v	Manchester United	4 – 3
1949	Portsmouth	v	Wolverhampton Wanderers	1 – 1*
1950	World Cup Team	v	Canadian Touring Team	4 – 2
1951	Tottenham Hotspur	v	Newcastle United	2 – 1
1952	Manchester United	v	Newcastle United	4 – 2
1953	Arsenal	v	Blackpool	3 – 1
1954	Wolverhampton Wanderers	v	West Bromwich Albion	4 – 4*
1955	Chelsea	v	Newcastle United	3 – 0
1956	Manchester United	v	Manchester City	1 – 0
1957	Manchester United	v	Aston Villa	4 – 0
1958	Bolton Wanderers	v	Wolverhampton Wanderers	4 – 1
1959	Wolverhampton Wanderers	v	Nottingham Forest	3 – 1
1960	Burnley	v	Wolverhampton Wanderers	2 – 2*
1961	Tottenham Hotspur	v	FA XI	3 – 2
1962	Tottenham Hotspur	v	Ipswich Town	5 – 1
1963	Everton	v	Manchester United	4 – 0
1964	Liverpool	v	West Ham United	2 – 2*
1965	Manchester United	v	Liverpool	2 – 2*
1966	Liverpool	v	Everton	1 – 0
1967	Manchester United	v	Tottenham Hotspur	3 – 3*
1968	Manchester City	v	West Bromwich Albion	6 – 1
1969	Leeds United	v	Manchester City	2 – 1

Year	Winners		Runners-up	Result
1970	Everton	v	Chelsea	2 – 1
1971	Leicester City	v	Liverpool	1 – 0
1972	Manchester City	v	Aston Villa	1 – 0
1973	Burnley	v	Manchester City	1 – 0
1974	Liverpool	v	Leeds United	1 – 1†
1975	Derby County	v	West Ham United	2 – 0
1976	Liverpool	v	Southampton	1 – 0
1977	Liverpool	v	Manchester United	0 – 0*
1978	Nottingham Forest	v	Ipswich Town	5 – 0
1979	Liverpool	v	Arsenal	3 – 1
1980	Liverpool	v	West Ham United	1 – 0
1981	Aston Villa	v	Tottenham Hotspur	2 – 2*
1982	Liverpool	v	Tottenham Hotspur	1 – 0
1983	Manchester United	v	Liverpool	2 – 0
1984	Everton	v	Liverpool	1 – 0
1985	Everton	v	Manchester United	2 – 0
1986	Everton	v	Liverpool	1 – 1*
1987	Everton	v	Coventry City	1 – 0
1988	Liverpool	v	Wimbledon	2 – 1
1989	Liverpool	v	Arsenal	1 – 0
1990	Liverpool	v	Manchester United	1 – 1*
1991	Arsenal	v	Tottenham Hotspur	0 – 0*
1992	Leeds United	v	Liverpool	4 – 3
1993	Manchester United	v	Arsenal	1 – 1†
1994	Manchester United	v	Blackburn Rovers	2 – 0
1995	Everton	v	Blackburn Rovers	1 – 0
1996	Manchester United	v	Newcastle United	4 – 0
1997	Manchester United	v	Chelsea	1 – 1†

*each club retained Shield for six months † won on penalty-kicks

51 ● THE FOOTBALL ASSOCIATION FIXTURE LIST 1998–1999

August 1998

8	Saturday	Start of FL season
9	Sunday	FA Charity Shield
11	Tuesday	UEFA Cup 2Q (1)
12	Wednesday	Champions League 2Q (1)
		Worthington Cup 1 (1)
13	Thursday	ECWC P (1)
15	Saturday	Start of FA Premier League season
19	Wednesday	Worthington Cup 1 (2)
25	Tuesday	UEFA Cup 2Q (2)
26	Wednesday	Champions League 2Q (2)
27	Thursday	ECWC P (2)
28	Friday	European Super Cup – Chelsea v Real Madrid – Monaco

September 1998

5	Saturday*	Sweden v England (EC)
		FA Cup P
		FA Youth Cup 1Q+
12	Saturday	FA Vase 1Q
13	Sunday	FA Women's Cup P
15	Tuesday	UEFA Cup 1 (1)
16	Wednesday	Champions League I (1)
		Worthington Cup 2 (1)
17	Thursday	ECWC 1 (1)
19	Saturday	FA Cup 1Q
23	Wednesday	Worthington Cup 2 (2)
26	Saturday	FA Youth Cup 2Q +
27	Sunday	FA Women's Cup 1
29	Tuesday	UEFA Cup 1 (2)
30	Wednesday	Champions League 1 (2)

October 1998

1	Thursday	ECWC 1 (2)
3	Saturday	FA Cup 2Q
10	Saturday*	England v Bulgaria (EC)
		FA Vase 2Q
		FA County Youth Cup I +
14	Wednesday	Luxembourg v England (EC)
17	Saturday	FA Cup 3Q
		FA Youth Cup 3Q+
20	Tuesday	UEFA Cup 2 (1)
21	Wednesday	Champions League 2 (1)
22	Thursday	ECWC 2 (1)
24	Saturday	FA Trophy 1
25	Sunday	FA Sunday Cup 1
28	Wednesday	Worthington Cup 3
31	Saturday	FA Cup 4Q

November 1998

1	Sunday	FA Women's Cup 2
3	Tuesday	UEFA Cup 2 (2)
4	Wednesday	Champions League 2 (2)
5	Thursday	ECWC 2 (2)
7	Saturday	FA Vase 1P
		FA Youth Cup 1P +
10	Tuesday	FA XI v Northern Premier League
11	Wednesday	Worthington Cup 4
14	Saturday	International (F)
		FA Cup 1P
		FA County Youth Cup 2+
18	Wednesday	International (F)
21	Saturday	FA Trophy 2
22	Sunday	FA Sunday Cup 2
24	Tuesday	UEFA Cup 3 (1)
25	Wednesday	Champions League 3 (1)
28	Saturday	FA Vase 2P
		FA Youth Cup 2P +

December 1998

2	Wednesday	Worthington Cup 5
5	Saturday	FA Cup 2P
6	Sunday	FA Women's Cup 3
8	Tuesday	FA XI v Southern League
		UEFA Cup 3 (2)
9	Wednesday	Champions League 3 (2)
		FA XI v Isthmian League
12	Saturday	FA Vase 3P
13	Sunday	FA Sunday Cup 3
19	Saturday	FA County Youth Cup 3 +

January 1999

2	Saturday	FA Cup 3P
5	Tuesday	FA XI v Combined Services
9	Saturday	International (not UEFA date)
		FA Vase 4P
		FA Youth Cup 3P+
10	Sunday	FA Women's Cup 4
13	Wednesday	International (not UEFA date)
16	Saturday	FA Trophy 3
17	Sunday	FA Sunday Cup 4
23	Saturday	FA Cup 4P
27	Wednesday	Worthington Cup SF (1)
30	Saturday	FA Vase 5P
		FA Youth Cup 4P+
		FA County Youth Cup 4 +

February 1999

2	Tuesday	FA XI v British Students
6	Saturday	International (not UEFA date)
		FA Trophy 4

7	Sunday	FA Women's Cup 5
10	Wednesday	International(F)
13	Saturday	FA Cup 5P
14	Sunday	FA Sunday Cup 5
17	Wednesday	Worthington Cup SF (2)
20	Saturday	FA Vase 6P
		FA Youth Cup 5P+
27	Saturday	FA Trophy 5

March 1999

2	Tuesday	Semi-Pro International
		UEFA Cup QF (1)
3	Wednesday	Champions League QF (1)
4	Thursday	ECWC QF (1)
6	Saturday	FA Cup 6P
7	Sunday	FA Women's Cup 6
13	Saturday	FA Vase SF (1)
		FA Youth Cup 6P+
		FA County Youth Cup SF+
16	Tuesday	UEFA Cup QF (2)
17	Wednesday	Champions League QF (2)
18	Thursday	ECWC QF (2)
20	Saturday	FA Vase SF (2)
21	Sunday	Worthington Cup Final
27	Saturday	England v Poland (EC)
		FA Trophy 6
28	Sunday	FA Sunday Cup SF
30	Tuesday	Semi-Pro International
31	Wednesday	International (F)

April 1999

4	Sunday	FA Women's Cup SF
6	Tuesday	UEFA Cup SF (1)
7	Wednesday	Champions League SF (1)
8	Thursday	ECWC SF (1)
10	Saturday	FA Trophy SF (1)
		FA Youth Cup SF+
11	Sunday	FA Cup SF
17	Saturday	FA Trophy SF (2)
20	Tuesday	UEFA Cup SF (2)
21	Wednesday	Champions League SF (2)
22	Thursday	ECWC SF (2)
24	Saturday	FA County Youth Cup Final (fixed date)
25	Sunday	FA Sunday Cup Final
28	Wednesday	International (F)

May 1999

3	Monday	FA Women's Cup Final
8	Saturday	End of Football League Season
12	Wednesday	UEFA Cup Final
15	Saturday	FA Trophy Final – Wembley Stadium
		FA Youth Cup Final+
16	Sunday	FA Vase Final – Wembley Stadium
		End of FA Premier League Season

16	Sunday	FL Play-offs SF (1)
19	Wednesday	European Cup Winners' Cup Final
		FL Play-offs SF (2)
22	Saturday	FA Cup Final – Wembley Stadium
26	Wednesday	European Champions League Final
27	Thursday	FA Cup Final (possible) Replay
29	Saturday	FL Play-offs Final Div 3
30	Sunday	FL Play-offs Final Div 2
31	Monday	FL Play-offs Final Div 1

June 1999

| 5 | Saturday | England v Sweden (EC) |
| 9 | Wednesday | Bulgaria v England (EC) |

⁺*closing date of round*
*no *FA Premier League games*
EC = European Championship

52 ● LEAGUE FIXTURES 1998–1999

Saturday, August 8 1998

Nationwide Football League Division 1

Barnsley v West Bromwich Albion ....
Bradford City v Stockport County..
Bristol City v Oxford United..
Bury v Huddersfield Town..
Crystal Palace v Bolton Wanderers..
Norwich City v Crewe Alexandra ....
Port Vale v Birmingham City..
Portsmouth v Watford ....
Sheffield United v Swindon Town..
Sunderland v Queens Park Rangers..
Wolverhampton Wanderers v Tranmere Rovers

Nationwide Football League Division 2

A.F.C. Bournemouth v Lincoln City ....
Burnley v Bristol Rovers..
Colchester United v Chesterfield ....
Gillingham v Walsall ....
Macclesfield Town v Fulham ....
Manchester City v Blackpool ....
Northampton Town v Stoke City ....
Oldham Athletic v Notts County..
Preston North End v York City..
Wigan Athletic v Millwall..
Wrexham v Reading ....
Wycombe Wanderers v Luton Town ....

Nationwide Football League Division 3

Brentford v Mansfield Town..
Carlisle United v Brighton & Hove Albion ....
Chester City v Leyton Orient ....
Darlington v Barnet..
Hartlepool United v Cardiff City..
Peterborough United v Halifax Town ....
Plymouth Argyle v Rochdale ....
Rotherham United v Hull City..
Scarborough v Southend United ....
Shrewsbury Town v Scunthorpe United ....
Swansea City v Exeter City ....
Torquay United v Cambridge United ....

Sunday, August 9 1998

Nationwide Football League Division 1

Grimsby Town v Ipswich Town 4:00..

Friday, August 14 1998

Nationwide Football League Division 2

Fulham v Manchester City..

Saturday, August 15 1998

FA Carling Premiership

Blackburn Rovers v Derby County..
Coventry City v Chelsea..
Everton v Aston Villa..
Manchester United v Leicester City..
Middlesbrough v Leeds United..
Newcastle United v Charlton Athletic..

Sheffield Wednesday v West Ham United ....
Wimbledon v Tottenham Hotspur..

Nationwide Football League Division 1

Bolton Wanderers v Grimsby Town..
Crewe Alexandra v Barnsley..
Huddersfield Town v Port Vale ....
Ipswich Town v Bury ....
Oxford United v Wolverhampton Wanderers..
Queens Park Rangers v Bristol City ....
Stockport County v Norwich City ....
Swindon Town v Sunderland ....
Tranmere Rovers v Portsmouth ....
Watford v Bradford City ....
West Bromwich Albion v Sheffield United ....

Nationwide Football League Division 2

Blackpool v Oldham Athletic ....
Bristol Rovers v Reading ....
Chesterfield v Burnley ....
Lincoln City v Wigan Athletic ....
Luton Town v Preston North End ....
Millwall v Wycombe Wanderers ....
Notts County v A.F.C. Bournemouth ....
Stoke City v Macclesfield Town ....
Walsall v Northampton Town ....
Wrexham v Colchester United ....
York City v Gillingham ....

Nationwide Football League Division 3

Barnet v Hartlepool United ....
Brighton & Hove Albion v Chester City ....
Cambridge United v Swansea City ....
Cardiff City v Peterborough United ....
Exeter City v Scarborough ....
Halifax Town v Brentford ....
Hull City v Darlington ....
Leyton Orient v Rotherham United ....
Mansfield Town v Plymouth Argyle ....
Rochdale v Torquay United ....
Scunthorpe United v Carlisle United ....
Southend United v Shrewsbury Town ....

Sunday, August 16 1998

FA Carling Premiership

Southampton v Liverpool 4:00 ....

Nationwide Football League Division 1

Birmingham City v Crystal Palace 1:00 ....

Monday, August 17 1998

FA Carling Premiership

Arsenal v Nottingham Forest 8:00 ....

Friday, August 21 1998

Nationwide Football League Division 1

Barnsley v Stockport County ....

Nationwide Football League Division 3

Shrewsbury Town v Cardiff City ....

Saturday, August 22 1998

FA Carling Premiership

Charlton Athletic v Southampton ....
Chelsea v Newcastle United ....
Derby County v Wimbledon ....
Leicester City v Everton ....
Liverpool v Arsenal ....
Nottingham Forest v Coventry City ....
Tottenham Hotspur v Sheffield Wednesday ....
West Ham United v Manchester United ....

Nationwide Football League Division 1

Bristol City v Watford ....
Bury v Crewe Alexandra ....
Crystal Palace v Oxford United ....
Grimsby Town v Huddersfield Town ....
Norwich City v Queens Park Rangers ....
Port Vale v West Bromwich Albion ....
Portsmouth v Ipswich Town ....
Sheffield United v Birmingham City ....
Sunderland v Tranmere Rovers ....
Wolverhampton Wanderers v Swindon Town ....

Nationwide Football League Division 2

A.F.C. Bournemouth v Millwall ....
Burnley v York City ....
Colchester United v Fulham ....
Gillingham v Bristol Rovers ....
Macclesfield Town v Lincoln City ....
Manchester City v Wrexham ....
Northampton Town v Notts County ....
Oldham Athletic v Chesterfield ....
Preston North End v Stoke City ....
Reading v Luton Town ....
Wigan Athletic v Blackpool ....
Wycombe Wanderers v Walsall ....

Nationwide Football League Division 3

Brentford v Brighton & Hove Albion ....
Carlisle United v Rochdale ....
Darlington v Halifax Town ....
Hartlepool United v Scunthorpe United ....
Peterborough United v Southend United ....
Plymouth Argyle v Barnet ....
Rotherham United v Cambridge United ....
Scarborough v Mansfield Town ....
Swansea City v Leyton Orient ....
Torquay United v Exeter City 12:00 ....

Sunday, August 23 1998

FA Carling Premiership

Aston Villa v Middlesbrough 4:00 ....

Nationwide Football League Division 1

Bradford City v Bolton Wanderers 1:00 ....

Nationwide Football League Division 3

Chester City v Hull City ....

Monday, August 24 1998

FA Carling Premiership

Leeds United v Blackburn Rovers 8:00 ....

Friday, August 28 1998

Nationwide Football League Division 1

Crewe Alexandra v Bradford City ....
Watford v Wolverhampton Wanderers ....

Nationwide Football League Division 3

Halifax Town v Shrewsbury Town ....

Saturday, August 29 1998

FA Carling Premiership

Arsenal v Charlton Athletic ....
Blackburn Rovers v Leicester City ....
Coventry City v West Ham United ....
Everton v Tottenham Hotspur ....
Middlesbrough v Derby County ....
Sheffield Wednesday v Aston Villa ....
Southampton v Nottingham Forest ....
Wimbledon v Leeds United ....

Nationwide Football League Division 1

Birmingham City v Barnsley ....
Bolton Wanderers v Sheffield United ....
Huddersfield Town v Portsmouth ....
Ipswich Town v Sunderland 6:00 ....
Oxford United v Grimsby Town ....
Queens Park Rangers v Bury ....
Stockport County v Crystal Palace ....
Swindon Town v Port Vale ....
Tranmere Rovers v Bristol City ....
West Bromwich Albion v Norwich City ....

Nationwide Football League Division 2

Blackpool v Gillingham ....
Bristol Rovers v Wigan Athletic ....
Chesterfield v Reading ....
Fulham v A.F.C. Bournemouth ....
Lincoln City v Preston North End ....
Luton Town v Colchester United ....
Millwall v Macclesfield Town ....
Notts County v Manchester City ....
Stoke City v Oldham Athletic ....
Walsall v Burnley ....
Wrexham v Northampton Town ....
York City v Wycombe Wanderers ....

Nationwide Football League Division 3

Barnet v Brentford ....
Brighton & Hove Albion v Torquay United ....
Cambridge United v Hartlepool United ....
Cardiff City v Rotherham United ....
Exeter City v Carlisle United ....
Hull City v Peterborough United ....
Leyton Orient v Scarborough ....
Mansfield Town v Swansea City ....
Rochdale v Darlington ....
Scunthorpe United v Plymouth Argyle ....
Southend United v Chester City ....

Sunday, August 30 1998

FA Carling Premiership

Newcastle United v Liverpool 4:00 ....

Monday, August 31 1998

Nationwide Football League Division 1

Barnsley v Oxford United ....
Bradford City v Birmingham City ....
Bristol City v Huddersfield Town ....
Bury v Swindon Town ....
Crystal Palace v Tranmere Rovers ....
Grimsby Town v West Bromwich Albion ....
Port Vale v Ipswich Town ....
Portsmouth v Queens Park Rangers ....
Sheffield United v Crewe Alexandra 8:00 ....
Sunderland v Watford ....
Wolverhampton Wanderers v Stockport County ....

Nationwide Football League Division 2

Colchester United v Stoke City ....
Macclesfield Town v Notts County ....
Northampton Town v Lincoln City ....
Preston North End v Chesterfield ....

Wigan Athletic v Luton Town ....
Wycombe Wanderers v Bristol Rovers ....

Nationwide Football League Division 3

Brentford v Rochdale ....
Darlington v Cardiff City ....
Hartlepool United v Hull City 12:00 ....
Peterborough United v Exeter City ....
Plymouth Argyle v Halifax Town ....
Rotherham United v Mansfield Town ....
Scarborough v Brighton & Hove Albion ....
Shrewsbury Town v Barnet ....
Swansea City v Scunthorpe United ....

Tuesday, September 1 1998

Nationwide Football League Division 1

Norwich City v Bolton Wanderers ....

Nationwide Football League Division 2

A.F.C. Bournemouth v Blackpool ....
Burnley v Millwall ....
Gillingham v Wrexham ....
Oldham Athletic v Fulham ....

Nationwide Football League Division 3

Carlisle United v Southend United ....
Chester City v Cambridge United 7:30 ....
Torquay United v Leyton Orient ....

Wednesday, September 2 1998

Nationwide Football League Division 2

Manchester City v Walsall ....
Reading v York City ....

Friday, September 4 1998

Nationwide Football League Division 1

Tranmere Rovers v Bradford City ....

Nationwide Football League Division 3

Halifax Town v Hartlepool United ....

Saturday, September 5 1998

Nationwide Football League Division 1

Birmingham City v Bury ....
Bolton Wanderers v Port Vale ....
Crewe Alexandra v Sunderland ....
Huddersfield Town v Sheffield United ....
Ipswich Town v Wolverhampton Wanderers ....
Queens Park Rangers v Barnsley ....
Stockport County v Grimsby Town ....
Swindon Town v Bristol City ....
Watford v Norwich City ....
West Bromwich Albion v Crystal Palace ....

Nationwide Football League Division 2

Blackpool v Northampton Town ....
Bristol Rovers v Preston North End ....
Chesterfield v Gillingham ....
Fulham v Wycombe Wanderers ....
Lincoln City v Oldham Athletic ....
Luton Town v Burnley ....
Millwall v Manchester City ....
Notts County v Wigan Athletic ....
Stoke City v A.F.C. Bournemouth ....
Walsall v Reading ....
Wrexham v Macclesfield Town ....
York City v Colchester United ....

Nationwide Football League Division 3

Barnet v Peterborough United ....
Brighton & Hove Albion v Swansea City ....

Cambridge United v Scarborough ....
Cardiff City v Plymouth Argyle 12:15 ....
Exeter City v Chester City ....
Hull City v Brentford ....
Leyton Orient v Carlisle United ....
Mansfield Town v Darlington ....
Rochdale v Shrewsbury Town ....
Scunthorpe United v Torquay United ....
Southend United v Rotherham United ....

Sunday, September 6 1998

Nationwide Football League Division 1

Oxford United v Portsmouth 1:00...

Tuesday, September 8 1998

FA Carling Premiership

Leeds United v Southampton ....
Nottingham Forest v Everton ....

Nationwide Football League Division 1

Barnsley v Norwich City ....
Birmingham City v Stockport County ....
Bury v Portsmouth ....
Crewe Alexandra v Crystal Palace ....
Huddersfield Town v Watford ....
Ipswich Town v Bradford City ....
Port Vale v Wolverhampton Wanderers ....
Queens Park Rangers v Tranmere Rovers ....
Sheffield United v Grimsby Town ....
Sunderland v Bristol City ....
West Bromwich Albion v Bolton Wanderers ....

Nationwide Football League Division 2

Blackpool v Notts County 7:30 ....
Bristol Rovers v Chesterfield ....
Fulham v Stoke City ....
Gillingham v Northampton Town ....
Manchester City v A.F.C. Bournemouth ....
Oldham Athletic v Macclesfield Town ....
Walsall v York City ....
Wigan Athletic v Colchester United ....
Wrexham v Luton Town 7:30 ....
Wycombe Wanderers v Preston North End ....

Nationwide Football League Division 3

Cardiff City v Barnet 7:30 ....
Carlisle United v Swansea City ....
Darlington v Hartlepool United 7:30 ....
Exeter City v Brighton & Hove Albion ....
Hull City v Rochdale 7:30 ....
Leyton Orient v Mansfield Town ....
Peterborough United v Chester City ....
Rotherham United v Plymouth Argyle ....
Scunthorpe United v Cambridge United 7:30 ....
Southend United v Halifax Town ....
Torquay United v Brentford ....

Wednesday, September 9 1998

FA Carling Premiership

Aston Villa v Newcastle United ....
Chelsea v Arsenal 8:00 ....
Derby County v Sheffield Wednesday ....
Leicester City v Middlesbrough ....
Liverpool v Coventry City ....
Manchester United v Charlton Athletic 8:00 ....
Tottenham Hotspur v Blackburn Rovers ....
West Ham United v Wimbledon ....

Nationwide Football League Division 1

Swindon Town v Oxford United ....

Nationwide Football League Division 2

Millwall v Lincoln City ....
Reading v Burnley ....

Nationwide Football League Division 3

Scarborough v Shrewsbury Town 7:30...

Friday, September 11 1998

Nationwide Football League Division 1

Tranmere Rovers v Huddersfield Town ....

Nationwide Football League Division 3

Halifax Town v Cardiff City ....

Saturday, September 12 1998

FA Carling Premiership

Aston Villa v Wimbledon ....
Charlton Athletic v Derby County ....
Chelsea v Nottingham Forest ....
Everton v Leeds United ....
Leicester City v Arsenal ....
Manchester United v Coventry City ....
Newcastle United v Southampton ....
Sheffield Wednesday v Blackburn Rovers ....
West Ham United v Liverpool ....

Nationwide Football League Division 1

Bolton Wanderers v Birmingham City ....
Bradford City v Sheffield United ....
Bristol City v West Bromwich Albion ....
Crystal Palace v Port Vale ....
Grimsby Town v Barnsley ....
Oxford United v Ipswich Town ....
Portsmouth v Swindon Town ....
Stockport County v Crewe Alexandra ....
Watford v Queens Park Rangers ....
Wolverhampton Wanderers v Sunderland ....

Nationwide Football League Division 2

A.F.C. Bournemouth v Wigan Athletic ....
Burnley v Wycombe Wanderers ....
Chesterfield v Walsall ....
Colchester United v Gillingham ....
Lincoln City v Blackpool ....
Luton Town v Bristol Rovers ....
Macclesfield Town v Manchester City ....
Northampton Town v Oldham Athletic ....
Notts County v Fulham ....
Preston North End v Reading ....
Stoke City v Millwall ....
York City v Wrexham ....

Nationwide Football League Division 3

Barnet v Hull City ....
Brentford v Rotherham United ....
Brighton & Hove Albion v Southend United ....
Cambridge United v Leyton Orient ....
Chester City v Torquay United ....
Hartlepool United v Exeter City ....
Mansfield Town v Carlisle United ....
Plymouth Argyle v Darlington ....
Rochdale v Scunthorpe United ....
Shrewsbury Town v Peterborough United ....
Swansea City v Scarborough ....

Sunday, September 13 1998

FA Carling Premiership

Tottenham Hotspur v Middlesbrough 4:00..

Nationwide Football League Division 1

Norwich City v Bury 1:00...

Friday, September 18 1998

Nationwide Football League Division 2

Walsall v Notts County ....

Saturday, September 19 1998

FA Carling Premiership

Coventry City v Newcastle United ....
Derby County v Leicester City ....
Leeds United v Aston Villa ....
Liverpool v Charlton Athletic ....
Middlesbrough v Everton ....
Nottingham Forest v West Ham United ....
Southampton v Tottenham Hotspur ....
Wimbledon v Sheffield Wednesday ....

Nationwide Football League Division 1

Barnsley v Crystal Palace ....
Birmingham City v Grimsby Town ....
Bury v Tranmere Rovers ....
Crewe Alexandra v Bolton Wanderers ....
Huddersfield Town v Wolverhampton Wanderers ....
Ipswich Town v Bristol City ....
Port Vale v Portsmouth ....
Queens Park Rangers v Stockport County ....
Sheffield United v Norwich City ....
Sunderland v Oxford United ....
Swindon Town v Watford ....

Nationwide Football League Division 2

Blackpool v Luton Town ....
Bristol Rovers v Lincoln City ....
Fulham v York City ....
Gillingham v Burnley ....
Manchester City v Chesterfield ....
Millwall v Northampton Town ....
Oldham Athletic v Preston North End ....
Reading v Colchester United ....
Wigan Athletic v Macclesfield Town ....
Wrexham v Stoke City ....
Wycombe Wanderers v A.F.C. Bournemouth ....

Nationwide Football League Division 3

Cardiff City v Rochdale ....
Carlisle United v Chester City ....
Darlington v Shrewsbury Town ....
Exeter City v Barnet ....
Hull City v Halifax Town ....
Leyton Orient v Brighton & Hove Albion ....
Peterborough United v Plymouth Argyle ....
Rotherham United v Hartlepool United ....
Scarborough v Brentford ....
Scunthorpe United v Mansfield Town ....
Southend United v Cambridge United ....
Torquay United v Swansea City ....

Sunday, September 20 1998

FA Carling Premiership

Arsenal v Manchester United 4:00...

Nationwide Football League Division 1

West Bromwich Albion v Bradford City 1:00 ....

Monday, September 21 1998

FA Carling Premiership

Blackburn Rovers v Chelsea 8:00...

Friday, September 25 1998

Nationwide Football League Division 1

Tranmere Rovers v Swindon Town ....

Saturday, September 26 1998

FA Carling Premiership

Aston Villa v Derby County ....
Charlton Athletic v Coventry City ....
Chelsea v Middlesbrough ....

verton v Blackburn Rovers ....
anchester United v Liverpool 11:15 ....
wcastle United v Nottingham Forest ....
effield Wednesday v Arsenal ....
ttenham Hotspur v Leeds United ....

ationwide Football League Division1

lton Wanderers v Huddersfield Town ....
adford City v Barnsley ....
istol City v Crewe Alexandra ....
imsby Town v Port Vale ....
orwich City v Birmingham City ....
xford United v Queens Park Rangers ....
rtsmouth v Sunderland ....
ockport County v West Bromwich Albion ....
atford v Ipswich Town ....
olverhampton Wanderers v Bury ....

ionwide Football League Division 2

.C. Bournemouth v Oldham Athletic ....
rnley v Wigan Athletic ....
esterfield v Wrexham ....
chester United v Wycombe Wanderers ....
coln City v Fulham ....
on Town v Walsall ....
cclesfield Town v Reading ....
rthampton Town v Manchester City ....
ts County v Millwall ....
ston North End v Gillingham ....
ke City v Blackpool ....
k City v Bristol Rovers ....

onwide Football League Division 3

net v Rotherham United ....
tford v Darlington ....
hton & Hove Albion v Scunthorpe United ....
bridge United v Exeter City ....
ster City v Cardiff City ....
fax Town v Torquay United ....
lepool United v Peterborough United ....
ssfield Town v Hull City ....
outh Argyle v Scarborough ....
dale v Leyton Orient ....
wsbury Town v Carlisle United ....
sea City v Southend United ....

day, September 27 1998

arling Premiership

ster City v Wimbledon 4:00 ....

onwide Football League Division 1

tal Palace v Sheffield United 1:00 ....

day, September 28 1998

arling Premiership

Ham United v Southampton 8:00 ....

day, September 29 1998

nwide Football League Division 1

en Wanderers v Swindon Town 8:00 ....
ord City v Port Vale ....
l City v Barnsley ....
sby Town v Crewe Alexandra ....
rich City v Sunderland ....
d United v West Bromwich Albion ....
outh v Birmingham City ....
port County v Huddersfield Town ....
ere Rovers v Ipswich Town ....
ord v Sheffield United ....
erhampton Wanderers v Queens Park Rangers ....

Wednesday, September 30 1998

Nationwide Football League Division 1

Crystal Palace v Bury ....

Saturday, October 3 1998

FA Carling Premiership

Blackburn Rovers v West Ham United ....
Coventry City v Aston Villa ....
Derby County v Tottenham Hotspur ....
Leeds United v Leicester City ....
Middlesbrough v Sheffield Wednesday ....
Nottingham Forest v Charlton Athletic ....
Southampton v Manchester United ....
Wimbledon v Everton ....

Nationwide Football League Division 1

Barnsley v Bolton Wanderers ....
Birmingham City v Tranmere Rovers ....
Bury v Bristol City ....
Crewe Alexandra v Wolverhampton Wanderers .....
Huddersfield Town v Oxford United ....
Ipswich Town v Crystal Palace ....
Port Vale v Norwich City ....
Queens Park Rangers v Grimsby Town ....
Sheffield United v Portsmouth ....
Sunderland v Bradford City ....
Swindon Town v Stockport County ....

Nationwide Football League Division 2

Blackpool v York City ....
Bristol Rovers v A.F.C. Bournemouth ....
Fulham v Luton Town ....
Gillingham v Macclesfield Town ....
Manchester City v Burnley ....
Millwall v Chesterfield ....
Oldham Athletic v Colchester United ....
Reading v Stoke City ....
Walsall v Preston North End ....
Wigan Athletic v Northampton Town ....
Wrexham v Lincoln City ....
Wycombe Wanderers v Notts County ....

Nationwide Football League Division 3

Cardiff City v Brighton & Hove Albion ....
Carlisle United v Barnet ....
Darlington v Swansea City ....
Exeter City v Mansfield Town ....
Hull City v Cambridge United ....
Leyton Orient v Hartlepool United ....
Peterborough United v Brentford ....
Rotherham United v Shrewsbury Town ....
Scarborough v Chester City ....
Scunthorpe United v Halifax Town ....
Southend United v Rochdale ....
Torquay United v Plymouth Argyle 12:00 ....

Sunday, October 4 1998

FA Carling Premiership

Arsenal v Newcastle United ....
Liverpool v Chelsea 4:00..

Nationwide Football League Division 1

West Bromwich Albion v Watford 1:00...................

Friday, October 9 1998

Nationwide Football League Division 2

Colchester United v Burnley ....

Nationwide Football League Division 3

Mansfield Town v Torquay United ....

Saturday, October 10 1998

Nationwide Football League Division 1

Bradford City v Bury ....
Bristol City v Portsmouth ....
Crewe Alexandra v West Bromwich Albion ....
Norwich City v Grimsby Town ....
Oxford United v Tranmere Rovers ....
Queens Park Rangers v Ipswich Town ....
Stockport County v Bolton Wanderers ....
Sunderland v Crystal Palace ....
Swindon Town v Huddersfield Town ....
Watford v Birmingham City ....
Wolverhampton Wanderers v Sheffield United ....

Nationwide Football League Division 2

Blackpool v Millwall ....
Fulham v Reading ....
Gillingham v Wycombe Wanderers ....
Macclesfield Town v A.F.C. Bournemouth ....
Manchester City v Preston North End ....
Northampton Town v Bristol Rovers ....
Notts County v Lincoln City ....
Oldham Athletic v Wigan Athletic ....
Wrexham v Walsall ....
York City v Luton Town ....

Nationwide Football League Division 3

Barnet v Chester City ....
Cambridge United v Brighton & Hove Albion ....
Carlisle United v Scarborough ....
Darlington v Peterborough United ....
Hartlepool United v Shrewsbury Town ....
Hull City v Cardiff City ....
Leyton Orient v Exeter City ....
Plymouth Argyle v Brentford ....
Rochdale v Halifax Town ....
Scunthorpe United v Southend United ....
Swansea City v Rotherham United ....

Sunday, October 11 1998

Nationwide Football League Division 1

Barnsley v Port Vale 1:00..

Monday, October 12 1998

Nationwide Football League Division 2

Stoke City v Chesterfield 8:00 ....

Friday, October 16 1998

Nationwide Football League Division 3

Halifax Town v Barnet ....

Saturday, October 17 1998

FA Carling Premiership

Arsenal v Southampton ....
Chelsea v Charlton Athletic ....
Everton v Liverpool ....
Manchester United v Wimbledon ....
Middlesbrough v Blackburn Rovers ....
Newcastle United v Derby County ....
Nottingham Forest v Leeds United ....
West Ham United v Aston Villa ....

Nationwide Football League Division 1

Birmingham City v Crewe Alexandra ....
Bolton Wanderers v Oxford United ....
Bury v Stockport County ....
Crystal Palace v Norwich City ....
Grimsby Town v Bradford City ....
Huddersfield Town v Queens Park Rangers ....
Ipswich Town v Swindon Town ....

Port Vale v Bristol City ....
Portsmouth v Wolverhampton Wanderers ....
Sheffield United v Barnsley ....
Tranmere Rovers v Watford ....

Nationwide Football League Division 2

A.F.C. Bournemouth v Northampton Town ....
Bristol Rovers v Wrexham ....
Burnley v Notts County ....
Chesterfield v York City ....
Lincoln City v Stoke City ....
Luton Town v Oldham Athletic ....
Millwall v Fulham ....
Preston North End v Colchester United ....
Reading v Gillingham ....
Walsall v Blackpool ....
Wigan Athletic v Manchester City ....
Wycombe Wanderers v Macclesfield Town ....

Nationwide Football League Division 3

Brentford v Hartlepool United ....
Brighton & Hove Albion v Mansfield Town ....
Cardiff City v Cambridge United ....
Chester City v Swansea City ....
Exeter City v Scunthorpe United ....
Peterborough United v Rochdale ....
Rotherham United v Darlington ....
Scarborough v Hull City ....
Shrewsbury Town v Plymouth Argyle ....
Southend United v Leyton Orient ....
Torquay United v Carlisle United ....

Sunday, October 18 1998

FA Carling Premiership

Coventry City v Sheffield Wednesday 4:00 ....

Nationwide Football League Division 1

West Bromwich Albion v Sunderland 1:00..

Monday, October 19 1998

FA Carling Premiership

Leicester City v Tottenham Hotspur 8:00 ....

Tuesday, October 20 1998

Nationwide Football League Division 1

Birmingham City v Swindon Town ....
Bolton Wanderers v Watford 8:00..
Bury v Oxford United ....
Crystal Palace v Wolverhampton Wanderers ....
Grimsby Town v Bristol City ....
Ipswich Town v Norwich City ....
Port Vale v Crewe Alexandra ....
Portsmouth v Bradford City ....
Sheffield United v Stockport County ....
Tranmere Rovers v Barnsley ....

Nationwide Football League Division 2

A.F.C. Bournemouth v Gillingham ....
Bristol Rovers v Stoke City ....
Burnley v Oldham Athletic ....
Chesterfield v Notts County ....
Lincoln City v Manchester City ....
Luton Town v Northampton Town ....
Preston North End v Macclesfield Town ....
Walsall v Colchester United ....
Wigan Athletic v Fulham ....
Wycombe Wanderers v Wrexham ....

Nationwide Football League Division 3

Brentford v Scunthorpe United ....
Brighton & Hove Albion v Plymouth Argyle ....
Cardiff City v Leyton Orient 7:30 ....
Chester City v Hartlepool United 7:30..

Sunday, October 25 1998

FA Carling Premiership

Blackburn Rovers v Arsenal 4:00 ....
Leeds United v Chelsea ....

Nationwide Football League Division 1

Queens Park Rangers v Birmingham City 1:00...

Saturday, October 31 1998

FA Carling Premiership

Chelsea v Aston Villa ....
Coventry City v Arsenal ....
Derby County v Leeds United ....
Everton v Manchester United ....
Leicester City v Liverpool ....
Newcastle United v West Ham United ....
Sheffield Wednesday v Southampton ....
Wimbledon v Blackburn Rovers ....

Nationwide Football League Division 1

Birmingham City v Huddersfield Town ....
Bradford City v Bristol City ....
Bury v Watford ....
Grimsby Town v Crystal Palace ....
Ipswich Town v West Bromwich Albion ....
Oxford United v Crewe Alexandra ....
Port Vale v Sheffield United ....
Portsmouth v Norwich City ....
Swindon Town v Queens Park Rangers ....
Tranmere Rovers v Stockport County ....
Wolverhampton Wanderers v Barnsley ....

Nationwide Football League Division 2

A.F.C. Bournemouth v Preston North End ....
Blackpool v Fulham ....
Bristol Rovers v Walsall ....
Burnley v Wrexham ....
Lincoln City v Gillingham ....
Luton Town v Chesterfield ....
Macclesfield Town v Northampton Town ....
Manchester City v Colchester United ....
Millwall v Oldham Athletic ....
Notts County v Stoke City ....
Wigan Athletic v York City ....
Wycombe Wanderers v Reading ....

Nationwide Football League Division 3

Barnet v Rochdale ....
Brentford v Carlisle United ....
Brighton & Hove Albion v Hartlepool United ....
Cardiff City v Exeter City ....
Chester City v Shrewsbury Town ....
Halifax Town v Swansea City ....
Leyton Orient v Scunthorpe United ....
Mansfield Town v Cambridge United ....
Peterborough United v Rotherham United ....
Plymouth Argyle v Hull City ....
Scarborough v Torquay United ....
Southend United v Darlington ....

Sunday, November 1 1998

FA Carling Premiership

Middlesbrough v Nottingham Forest 4:00...

Nationwide Football League Division 1

Bolton Wanderers v Sunderland 1:00...

Monday, November 2 1998

FA Carling Premiership

Tottenham Hotspur v Charlton Athletic 8:00...

Friday, November 6 1998

Nationwide Football League Division 2

Colchester United v Macclesfield Town ....

Saturday, November 7 1998

FA Carling Premiership

Arsenal v Everton
Aston Villa v Tottenham Hotspur ....
Blackburn Rovers v Coventry City ....
Charlton Athletic v Leicester City ....
Liverpool v Derby County
Nottingham Forest v Wimbledon ....
Southampton v Middlesbrough ....

Nationwide Football League Division 1

Barnsley v Bury
Bristol City v Wolverhampton Wanderers ....
Crewe Alexandra v Swindon Town ....
Crystal Palace v Portsmouth ....
Huddersfield Town v Ipswich Town ....
Norwich City v Bradford City ....
Queens Park Rangers v Bolton Wanderers ....
Sheffield United v Tranmere Rovers ....
Sunderland v Grimsby Town ....
Watford v Oxford United ....
West Bromwich Albion v Birmingham City 12:00 ....

Nationwide Football League Division 2

Chesterfield v Lincoln City ....
Fulham v Bristol Rovers ....
Gillingham v Wigan Athletic ....
Northampton Town v Wycombe Wanderers ....
Oldham Athletic v Manchester City ....
Preston North End v Burnley ....
Reading v A.F.C. Bournemouth ....
Stoke City v Luton Town ....
Walsall v Millwall ....
Wrexham v Blackpool ....
York City v Notts County ....

Nationwide Football League Division 3

Cambridge United v Barnet ....
Carlisle United v Halifax Town ....
Darlington v Brighton & Hove Albion ....
Exeter City v Southend United ....
Hartlepool United v Plymouth Argyle ....
Hull City v Leyton Orient ....
Rochdale v Mansfield Town ....
Rotherham United v Scarborough ....
Scunthorpe United v Chester City ....
Shrewsbury Town v Brentford ....
Swansea City v Peterborough United ....
Torquay United v Cardiff City ....

Sunday, November 8 1998

FA Carling Premiership

Leeds United v Sheffield Wednesday 4:00 ....
Manchester United v Newcastle United ....
West Ham United v Chelsea ....

Nationwide Football League Division 1

Stockport County v Port Vale 1:00 ....

Tuesday, November 10 1998

Nationwide Football League Division 2

Bristol Rovers v Blackpool ....
Burnley v Stoke City ....
Chesterfield v A.F.C. Bournemouth ....
Colchester United v Northampton Town ....
Gillingham v Oldham Athletic ....
Luton Town v Notts County ....
Preston North End v Millwall ....
Walsall v Lincoln City ....

Wrexham v Fulham 7:30 ....
Wycombe Wanderers v Manchester City ....
York City v Macclesfield Town ....

Nationwide Football League Division 3

Barnet v Scunthorpe United ....
Brentford v Southend United ....
Cardiff City v Scarborough 7:30 ....
Darlington v Carlisle United 7:30 ....
Halifax Town v Chester City ....
Hartlepool United v Mansfield Town 7:30 ....
Hull City v Brighton & Hove Albion 7:30 ....
Peterborough United v Cambridge United ....
Plymouth Argyle v Swansea City ....
Rochdale v Exeter City ....
Rotherham United v Torquay United ....
Shrewsbury Town v Leyton Orient ....

Wednesday, November 11 1998

Nationwide Football League Division 2

Reading v Wigan Athletic ....

Saturday, November 14 1998

FA Carling Premiership

Arsenal v Tottenham Hotspur ....
Charlton Athletic v Middlesbrough ....
Chelsea v Wimbledon ....
Liverpool v Leeds United ....
Manchester United v Blackburn Rovers ....
Newcastle United v Sheffield Wednesday ....
Southampton v Aston Villa ....
West Ham United v Leicester City ....

Nationwide Football League Division 1

Barnsley v Ipswich Town ....
Birmingham City v Oxford United ....
Bolton Wanderers v Tranmere Rovers ....
Bradford City v Swindon Town ....
Crewe Alexandra v Queens Park Rangers ....
Crystal Palace v Bristol City ....
Grimsby Town v Portsmouth ....
Norwich City v Wolverhampton Wanderers ....
Port Vale v Sunderland ....
Sheffield United v Bury ....
Stockport County v Watford ....
West Bromwich Albion v Huddersfield Town ....

Sunday, November 15 1998

FA Carling Premiership

Coventry City v Everton 4:00 ....

Monday, November 16 1998

FA Carling Premiership

Nottingham Forest v Derby County 8:00 ....

Friday, November 20 1998

Nationwide Football League Division 3

Mansfield Town v Barnet ....

Saturday, November 21 1998

FA Carling Premiership

Aston Villa v Liverpool ....
Blackburn Rovers v Southampton ....
Leeds United v Charlton Athletic ....
Leicester City v Chelsea ....
Middlesbrough v Coventry City ....
Sheffield Wednesday v Manchester United ....
Tottenham Hotspur v Nottingham Forest ....
Wimbledon v Arsenal ....

Nationwide Football League Division 1

istol City v Stockport County ....
ry v Grimsby Town ....
ddersfield Town v Bradford City ....
wich Town v Bolton Wanderers ....
ford United v Port Vale ....
rtsmouth v West Bromwich Albion ....
eens Park Rangers v Sheffield United ....
nderland v Barnsley ....
indon Town v Crystal Palace ....
anmere Rovers v Norwich City ....
atford v Crewe Alexandra ....

Nationwide Football League Division 2

F.C. Bournemouth v Burnley ....
ckpool v Preston North End ....
ham v Chesterfield ....
coln City v Luton Town ....
acclesfield Town v Walsall ....
nchester City v Gillingham ....
lwall v Bristol Rovers ....
rthampton Town v Reading ....
ts County v Colchester United ....
ham Athletic v Wrexham ....
ke City v York City ....
gan Athletic v Wycombe Wanderers ....

Nationwide Football League Division 3

ghton & Hove Albion v Halifax Town ....
mbridge United v Darlington ....
risle United v Rotherham United ....
ster City v Rochdale ....
er City v Shrewsbury Town ....
on Orient v Brentford ....
borough v Hartlepool United ....
nthorpe United v Hull City ....
hend United v Plymouth Argyle ....
quay United v Peterborough United ....

day, November 22 1998

arling Premiership

by County v West Ham United 4:00 ....

onwide Football League Division 1

verhampton Wanderers v Birmingham City 1:00 ....

nwide Football League Division 3

sea City v Cardiff City 12:00 ....

day, November 23 1998

arling Premiership

con v Newcastle United 8:00 ....

y, November 27 1998

nwide Football League Division 1

sley v Huddersfield Town ....

nwide Football League Division 3

ax Town v Mansfield Town ....

rday, November 28 1998

rling Premiership

ton Athletic v Everton ....
ea v Sheffield Wednesday ....
try City v Leicester City ....
hester United v Leeds United ....
astle United v Wimbledon ....
ngham Forest v Aston Villa ....
ampton v Derby County ....
Ham United v Tottenham Hotspur ....

Nationwide Football League Division 1

Birmingham City v Bristol City ....
Bolton Wanderers v Bury ....
Bradford City v Queens Park Rangers ....
Crewe Alexandra v Ipswich Town ....
Crystal Palace v Watford ....
Grimsby Town v Swindon Town ....
Port Vale v Tranmere Rovers ....
Sheffield United v Sunderland ....
Stockport County v Portsmouth ....

Nationwide Football League Division 2

Bristol Rovers v Oldham Athletic ....
Burnley v Blackpool ....
Chesterfield v Macclesfield Town ....
Colchester United v Millwall ....
Gillingham v Fulham ....
Luton Town v Manchester City ....
Preston North End v Wigan Athletic ....
Reading v Lincoln City ....
Walsall v A.F.C. Bournemouth ....
Wrexham v Notts County ....
Wycombe Wanderers v Stoke City ....
York City v Northampton Town ....

Nationwide Football League Division 3

Barnet v Torquay United ....
Brentford v Chester City ....
Cardiff City v Southend United ....
Darlington v Scarborough ....
Hartlepool United v Swansea City ....
Hull City v Carlisle United ....
Peterborough United v Scunthorpe United ....
Plymouth Argyle v Leyton Orient ....
Rochdale v Cambridge United ....
Rotherham United v Exeter City ....
Shrewsbury Town v Brighton & Hove Albion ....

Sunday, November 29 1998

FA Carling Premiership

Arsenal v Middlesbrough ....
Liverpool v Blackburn Rovers 4:00 ....

Nationwide Football League Division 1

Norwich City v Oxford United 1:00 ....
West Bromwich Albion v Wolverhampton Wanderers 1:00 ....

Saturday, December 5 1998

FA Carling Premiership

Aston Villa v Manchester United ....
Blackburn Rovers v Charlton Athletic ....
Derby County v Arsenal ....
Everton v Chelsea ....
Leeds United v West Ham United ....
Leicester City v Southampton ....
Tottenham Hotspur v Liverpool ....
Wimbledon v Coventry City ....

Nationwide Football League Division 1

Bristol City v Sheffield United ....
Bury v West Bromwich Albion ....
Huddersfield Town v Crystal Palace ....
Ipswich Town v Birmingham City ....
Oxford United v Bradford City ....
Portsmouth v Crewe Alexandra ....
Queens Park Rangers v Port Vale ....
Sunderland v Stockport County ....
Swindon Town v Norwich City ....
Tranmere Rovers v Grimsby Town ....
Watford v Barnsley ....
Wolverhampton Wanderers v Bolton Wanderers ....

Sunday, December 6 1998

FA Carling Premiership

Middlesbrough v Newcastle United 4:00 ....

Monday, December 7 1998

FA Carling Premiership

Sheffield Wednesday v Nottingham Forest 8:00 ....

Friday, December 11 1998

Nationwide Football League Division 1

Bury v Sheffield United ....

Nationwide Football League Division 3

Brighton & Hove Albion v Rotherham United
8:00 ....
Mansfield Town v Shrewsbury Town ....

Saturday, December 12 1998

FA Carling Premiership

Aston Villa v Arsenal ....
Blackburn Rovers v Newcastle United ....
Derby County v Chelsea ....
Everton v Southampton ....
Leicester City v Nottingham Forest ....
Middlesbrough v West Ham United ....
Sheffield Wednesday v Charlton Athletic ....
Tottenham Hotspur v Manchester United ....

Nationwide Football League Division 1

Bristol City v Crystal Palace ....
Huddersfield Town v West Bromwich Albion ....
Ipswich Town v Barnsley ....
Oxford United v Birmingham City ....
Queens Park Rangers v Crewe Alexandra ....
Sunderland v Port Vale ....
Swindon Town v Bradford City ....
Tranmere Rovers v Bolton Wanderers ....
Watford v Stockport County ....
Wolverhampton Wanderers v Norwich City ....

Nationwide Football League Division 2

A.F.C. Bournemouth v York City ....
Blackpool v Wycombe Wanderers ....
Fulham v Burnley ....
Lincoln City v Colchester United ....
Macclesfield Town v Luton Town ....
Manchester City v Bristol Rovers ....
Millwall v Reading ....
Northampton Town v Chesterfield ....
Notts County v Preston North End ....
Oldham Athletic v Walsall ....
Stoke City v Gillingham ....
Wigan Athletic v Wrexham ....

Nationwide Football League Division 3

Cambridge United v Plymouth Argyle ....
Carlisle United v Hartlepool United ....
Chester City v Darlington ....
Exeter City v Brentford ....
Leyton Orient v Peterborough United ....
Scarborough v Halifax Town ....
Scunthorpe United v Cardiff City ....
Southend United v Barnet ....
Swansea City v Rochdale ....
Torquay United v Hull City ....

Sunday, December 13 1998

FA Carling Premiership

Wimbledon v Liverpool 4:00 ....

Nationwide Football League Division 1

Portsmouth v Grimsby Town 1:00 ....

Monday, December 14 1998

FA Carling Premiership

Leeds United v Coventry City 8:00 ....

Wednesday, December 16 1998

FA Carling Premiership

Manchester United v Chelsea 8:00 ....

Friday, December 18 1998

Nationwide Football League Division 2

Bristol Rovers v Macclesfield Town ....
Colchester United v Blackpool ....

Nationwide Football League Division 3

Rotherham United v Chester City ....
Shrewsbury Town v Torquay United ....

Saturday, December 19 1998

FA Carling Premiership

Chelsea v Tottenham Hotspur ....
Coventry City v Derby County ....
Liverpool v Sheffield Wednesday ....
Manchester United v Middlesbrough ....
Newcastle United v Leicester City ....
Nottingham Forest v Blackburn Rovers ....
Southampton v Wimbledon ....
West Ham United v Everton ....

Nationwide Football League Division 1

Barnsley v Swindon Town ....
Birmingham City v Sunderland ....
Bolton Wanderers v Portsmouth ....
Bradford City v Wolverhampton Wanderers ....
Crewe Alexandra v Huddersfield Town ....
Crystal Palace v Queens Park Rangers ....
Grimsby Town v Watford ....
Norwich City v Bristol City ....
Port Vale v Bury ....
Stockport County v Oxford United ....
West Bromwich Albion v Tranmere Rovers ....

Nationwide Football League Division 2

Burnley v Northampton Town ....
Chesterfield v Wigan Athletic ....
Gillingham v Notts County ....
Luton Town v Millwall ....
Preston North End v Fulham ....
Reading v Oldham Athletic ....
Walsall v Stoke City ....
Wrexham v A.F.C. Bournemouth ....
Wycombe Wanderers v Lincoln City ....
York City v Manchester City ....

Nationwide Football League Division 3

Barnet v Leyton Orient ....
Brentford v Cambridge United ....
Cardiff City v Mansfield Town ....
Darlington v Scunthorpe United ....
Halifax Town v Exeter City ....
Hartlepool United v Southend United ....
Hull City v Swansea City ....
Peterborough United v Scarborough ....
Plymouth Argyle v Carlisle United ....
Rochdale v Brighton & Hove Albion ....

Sunday, December 20 1998

FA Carling Premiership

Arsenal v Leeds United 4:00 ....

ffield United v Ipswich Town 1:00 ....

nday, December 21 1998

Carling Premiership

arlton Athletic v Aston Villa 8:00 ....

urday, December 26 1998

Carling Premiership

nal v West Ham United 12:00 ....
kburn Rovers v Aston Villa 6:00 ....
entry City v Tottenham Hotspur ....
ton v Derby County ....
nchester United v Nottingham Forest ....
dlesbrough v Liverpool ....
castle United v Leeds United ....
field Wednesday v Leicester City ....
hampton v Chelsea ....
bledon v Charlton Athletic 12:00 ....

onwide Football League Division 1

ingham City v Sheffield United ....
on Wanderers v Bradford City ....
e Alexandra v Bury ....
dersfield Town v Grimsby Town ....
ich Town v Portsmouth ....
rd United v Crystal Palace ....
ns Park Rangers v Norwich City 12:00 ....
sport County v Barnsley ....
don Town v Wolverhampton Wanderers ....
mere Rovers v Sunderland ....
ord v Bristol City 12:00 ....
Bromwich Albion v Port Vale 1:00 ....

nwide Football League Division 2

pool v Wigan Athletic ....
ol Rovers v Gillingham ....
terfield v Oldham Athletic ....
m v Colchester United 12:00 ....
ln City v Macclesfield Town ....
n Town v Reading 12:00 ....
all v A.F.C. Bournemouth 12:00 ....
County v Northampton Town ....
City v Preston North End ....
all v Wycombe Wanderers ....
ham v Manchester City ....
City v Burnley ....

nwide Football League Division 3

t v Plymouth Argyle 1:30 ....
ton & Hove Albion v Brentford 12:00 ....
ridge United v Rotherham United ....
f City v Shrewsbury Town ....
City v Torquay United 11:00 ....
x Town v Darlington ....
City v Chester City ....
Orient v Swansea City 1:30 ....
field Town v Scarborough ....
dale v Carlisle United ....
horpe United v Hartlepool United ....
end United v Peterborough United ....

ay, December 28 1998

ling Premiership

Villa v Sheffield Wednesday ....
on Athletic v Arsenal ....
County v Middlesbrough ....
ter City v Blackburn Rovers ....
ool v Newcastle United ....
gham Forest v Southampton ....
ham Hotspur v Everton ....
am United v Coventry City ....

Barnsley v Queens Park Rangers ....
Bradford City v Tranmere Rovers ....
Bristol City v Swindon Town ....
Bury v Birmingham City ....
Crystal Palace v West Bromwich Albion ....
Grimsby Town v Stockport County ....
Port Vale v Bolton Wanderers ....
Portsmouth v Oxford United ....
Sheffield United v Huddersfield Town ....
Sunderland v Crewe Alexandra ....
Wolverhampton Wanderers v Ipswich Town 1:00 ....

Nationwide Football League Division 2

A.F.C. Bournemouth v Luton Town ....
Burnley v Lincoln City ....
Colchester United v Bristol Rovers ....
Macclesfield Town v Blackpool ....
Manchester City v Stoke City ....
Northampton Town v Fulham ....
Oldham Athletic v York City ....
Preston North End v Wrexham ....
Reading v Notts County ....
Wigan Athletic v Walsall ....
Wycombe Wanderers v Chesterfield ....

Nationwide Football League Division 3

Brentford v Cardiff City ....
Carlisle United v Cambridge United ....
Chester City v Mansfield Town ....
Darlington v Leyton Orient ....
Hartlepool United v Rochdale ....
Peterborough United v Brighton & Hove Albion ....
Plymouth Argyle v Exeter City ....
Rotherham United v Halifax Town 12:00 ....
Scarborough v Scunthorpe United ....
Shrewsbury Town v Hull City ....
Swansea City v Barnet ....
Torquay United v Southend United ....

Tuesday, December 29 1998

FA Carling Premiership

Chelsea v Manchester United 8:00 ....
Leeds United v Wimbledon ....

Nationwide Football League Division 1

Norwich City v Watford ....

Nationwide Football League Division 2

Gillingham v Millwall ....

Saturday, January 2 1999

Nationwide Football League Division 2

A.F.C. Bournemouth v Fulham ....
Burnley v Walsall ....
Colchester United v Luton Town ....
Gillingham v Blackpool ....
Macclesfield Town v Millwall ....
Manchester City v Notts County ....
Northampton Town v Wrexham ....
Oldham Athletic v Stoke City ....
Preston North End v Lincoln City ....
Reading v Chesterfield ....
Wigan Athletic v Bristol Rovers ....
Wycombe Wanderers v York City ....

Nationwide Football League Division 3

Brentford v Barnet ....
Carlisle United v Exeter City ....
Chester City v Southend United ....
Darlington v Rochdale ....
Hartlepool United v Cambridge United ....
Peterborough United v Hull City ....
Plymouth Argyle v Scunthorpe United ....

Rotherham United v Cardiff City ....
Scarborough v Leyton Orient ....
Shrewsbury Town v Halifax Town ....
Swansea City v Mansfield Town ....
Torquay United v Brighton & Hove Albion ....

Saturday, January 9 1999

FA Carling Premiership

Arsenal v Liverpool ....
Blackburn Rovers v Leeds United ....
Coventry City v Nottingham Forest ....
Everton v Leicester City ....
Manchester United v West Ham United ....
Middlesbrough v Aston Villa ....
Newcastle United v Chelsea ....
Sheffield Wednesday v Tottenham Hotspur ....
Southampton v Charlton Athletic ....
Wimbledon v Derby County ....

Nationwide Football League Division 1

Birmingham City v Port Vale ....
Bolton Wanderers v Crystal Palace ....
Crewe Alexandra v Norwich City ....
Huddersfield Town v Bury ....
Ipswich Town v Grimsby Town ....
Oxford United v Bristol City ....
Queens Park Rangers v Sunderland ....
Stockport County v Bradford City ....
Swindon Town v Sheffield United ....
Tranmere Rovers v Wolverhampton Wanderers ....
Watford v Portsmouth ....
West Bromwich Albion v Barnsley ....

Nationwide Football League Division 2

Blackpool v Manchester City ....
Bristol Rovers v Burnley ....
Chesterfield v Colchester United ....
Fulham v Macclesfield Town ....
Lincoln City v A.F.C. Bournemouth ....
Luton Town v Wycombe Wanderers ....
Millwall v Wigan Athletic ....
Notts County v Oldham Athletic ....
Reading v Wrexham ....
Stoke City v Northampton Town ....
Walsall v Gillingham ....
York City v Preston North End ....

Nationwide Football League Division 3

Barnet v Darlington ....
Brighton & Hove Albion v Carlisle United ....
Cambridge United v Torquay United ....
Cardiff City v Hartlepool United ....
Exeter City v Swansea City ....
Halifax Town v Peterborough United ....
Hull City v Rotherham United ....
Leyton Orient v Chester City ....
Mansfield Town v Brentford ....
Rochdale v Plymouth Argyle ....
Scunthorpe United v Shrewsbury Town ....
Southend United v Scarborough ....

Friday, January 15 1999

Nationwide Football League Division 2

Colchester United v Wrexham ....

Saturday, January 16 1999

FA Carling Premiership

Aston Villa v Everton ....
Charlton Athletic v Newcastle United ....
Chelsea v Coventry City ....
Derby County v Blackburn Rovers ....
Leeds United v Middlesbrough ....
Leicester City v Manchester United ....

Liverpool v Southampton ....
Nottingham Forest v Arsenal ....
Tottenham Hotspur v Wimbledon ....
West Ham United v Sheffield Wednesday ....

Nationwide Football League Division 1

Barnsley v Birmingham City ....
Bradford City v Crewe Alexandra ....
Bristol City v Tranmere Rovers ....
Bury v Queens Park Rangers ....
Crystal Palace v Stockport County ....
Grimsby Town v Oxford United ....
Norwich City v West Bromwich Albion ....
Port Vale v Swindon Town ....
Portsmouth v Huddersfield Town ....
Sheffield United v Bolton Wanderers ....
Sunderland v Ipswich Town ....
Wolverhampton Wanderers v Watford ....

Nationwide Football League Division 2

A.F.C. Bournemouth v Notts County ....
Burnley v Chesterfield ....
Gillingham v York City ....
Macclesfield Town v Stoke City ....
Manchester City v Fulham ....
Northampton Town v Walsall ....
Oldham Athletic v Blackpool ....
Preston North End v Luton Town ....
Reading v Bristol Rovers ....
Wigan Athletic v Lincoln City ....
Wycombe Wanderers v Millwall ....

Nationwide Football League Division 3

Brentford v Halifax Town ....
Carlisle United v Scunthorpe United ....
Chester City v Brighton & Hove Albion ....
Darlington v Hull City ....
Hartlepool United v Barnet ....
Peterborough United v Cardiff City ....
Plymouth Argyle v Mansfield Town ....
Rotherham United v Leyton Orient ....
Scarborough v Exeter City ....
Shrewsbury Town v Southend United ....
Swansea City v Cambridge United ....
Torquay United v Rochdale ....

Saturday, January 23 1999

Nationwide Football League Division 2

Blackpool v A.F.C. Bournemouth ....
Bristol Rovers v Wycombe Wanderers ....
Chesterfield v Preston North End ....
Fulham v Oldham Athletic ....
Lincoln City v Northampton Town ....
Luton Town v Wigan Athletic ....
Millwall v Burnley ....
Notts County v Macclesfield Town ....
Stoke City v Colchester United ....
Walsall v Manchester City ....
Wrexham v Gillingham ....
York City v Reading ....

Nationwide Football League Division 3 ....

Barnet v Shrewsbury Town ....
Brighton & Hove Albion v Scarborough ....
Cambridge United v Chester City ....
Cardiff City v Darlington ....
Exeter City v Peterborough United ....
Halifax Town v Plymouth Argyle ....
Hull City v Hartlepool United ....
Leyton Orient v Torquay United ....
Mansfield Town v Rotherham United ....
Rochdale v Brentford ....
Scunthorpe United v Swansea City ....
Southend United v Carlisle United ....

...Carling Premiership

...senal v Chelsea ....
...ackburn Rovers v Tottenham Hotspur ....
...arlton Athletic v Manchester United ....
...ventry City v Liverpool ....
...erton v Nottingham Forest ....
...ddlesbrough v Leicester City ....
...wcastle United v Aston Villa ....
...effield Wednesday v Derby County ....
...uthampton v Leeds United ....
...mbledon v West Ham United ....

...ionwide Football League Division 1

...rmingham City v Bradford City ....
...ton Wanderers v Norwich City ....
...we Alexandra v Sheffield United ....
...ddersfield Town v Bristol City ....
...wich Town v Port Vale ....
...ford United v Barnsley ....
...eens Park Rangers v Portsmouth ....
...ckport County v Wolverhampton Wanderers ....
...ndon Town v Bury ....
...nmere Rovers v Crystal Palace ....
...rford v Sunderland ....
...st Bromwich Albion v Grimsby Town ....

...onwide Football League Division 2

...kpool v Macclesfield Town ....
...ol Rovers v Colchester United ....
...sterfield v Wycombe Wanderers ....
...am v Northampton Town ....
...ln City v Burnley ....
...n Town v A.F.C. Bournemouth ....
...wall v Gillingham ....
...s County v Reading ....
...e City v Manchester City ....
...all v Wigan Athletic ....
...xham v Preston North End ....
...City v Oldham Athletic ....

...nwide Football League Division 3

...et v Swansea City ....
...ton & Hove Albion v Peterborough United ....
...bridge United v Carlisle United ....
...iff City v Brentford ....
...r City v Plymouth Argyle ....
...ax Town v Rotherham United ....
...City v Shrewsbury Town ....
...n Orient v Darlington ....
...field Town v Chester City ....
...dale v Hartlepool United ....
...thorpe United v Scarborough ....
...nend United v Torquay United ....

...y, February 5 1999

...nwide Football League Division 2

...ester United v York City ....

...nwide Football League Division 3

...sea City v Brighton & Hove Albion ....

...day, February 6 1999

...ling Premiership

...Villa v Blackburn Rovers ....
...ton Athletic v Wimbledon ....
...ea v Southampton ....
...County v Everton ....
...United v Newcastle United ....
...ter City v Sheffield Wednesday ....
...ool v Middlesbrough ....

Nottingham Forest v Manchester United ....
Tottenham Hotspur v Coventry City ....
West Ham United v Arsenal ....

Nationwide Football League Division 1

Barnsley v Crewe Alexandra ....
Bradford City v Watford ....
Bristol City v Queens Park Rangers ....
Bury v Ipswich Town ....
Crystal Palace v Birmingham City ....
Grimsby Town v Bolton Wanderers ....
Norwich City v Stockport County ....
Port Vale v Huddersfield Town ....
Portsmouth v Tranmere Rovers ....
Sheffield United v West Bromwich Albion ....
Sunderland v Swindon Town ....
Wolverhampton Wanderers v Oxford United ....

Nationwide Football League Division 2

A.F.C. Bournemouth v Stoke City ....
Burnley v Luton Town ....
Gillingham v Chesterfield ....
Macclesfield Town v Wrexham ....
Manchester City v Millwall ....
Northampton Town v Blackpool ....
Oldham Athletic v Lincoln City ....
Preston North End v Bristol Rovers ....
Reading v Walsall ....
Wigan Athletic v Notts County ....
Wycombe Wanderers v Fulham ....

Nationwide Football League Division 3

Brentford v Hull City ....
Carlisle United v Leyton Orient ....
Chester City v Exeter City ....
Darlington v Mansfield Town ....
Hartlepool United v Halifax Town ....
Peterborough United v Barnet ....
Plymouth Argyle v Cardiff City ....
Rotherham United v Southend United ....
Scarborough v Cambridge United ....
Shrewsbury Town v Rochdale ....
Torquay United v Scunthorpe United ....

Friday, February 12 1999

Nationwide Football League Division 2

Colchester United v Wigan Athletic ....

Saturday, February 13 1999

FA Carling Premiership

Aston Villa v Leeds United ....
Charlton Athletic v Liverpool ....
Chelsea v Blackburn Rovers ....
Everton v Middlesbrough ....
Leicester City v Derby County ....
Manchester United v Arsenal ....
Newcastle United v Coventry City ....
Sheffield Wednesday v Wimbledon ....
Tottenham Hotspur v Southampton ....
West Ham United v Nottingham Forest ....

Nationwide Football League Division 1

Bolton Wanderers v West Bromwich Albion ....
Bradford City v Ipswich Town ....
Bristol City v Sunderland ....
Crystal Palace v Crewe Alexandra ....
Grimsby Town v Sheffield United ....
Norwich City v Barnsley ....
Oxford United v Swindon Town ....
Portsmouth v Bury ....
Stockport County v Birmingham City ....
Tranmere Rovers v Queens Park Rangers ....
Watford v Huddersfield Town ....
Wolverhampton Wanderers v Port Vale ....

Nationwide Football League Division 2

A.F.C. Bournemouth v Manchester City ....
Burnley v Reading ....
Chesterfield v Bristol Rovers ....
Lincoln City v Millwall ....
Luton Town v Wrexham ....
Macclesfield Town v Oldham Athletic ....
Northampton Town v Gillingham ....
Notts County v Blackpool ....
Preston North End v Wycombe Wanderers ....
Stoke City v Fulham ....
York City v Walsall ....

Nationwide Football League Division 3

Barnet v Cardiff City ....
Brentford v Torquay United ....
Brighton & Hove Albion v Exeter City ....
Cambridge United v Scunthorpe United ....
Chester City v Peterborough United ....
Halifax Town v Southend United ....
Hartlepool United v Darlington ....
Mansfield Town v Leyton Orient ....
Plymouth Argyle v Rotherham United ....
Rochdale v Hull City ....
Shrewsbury Town v Scarborough ....
Swansea City v Carlisle United ....

Saturday, February 20 1999

FA Carling Premiership

Arsenal v Leicester City ....
Blackburn Rovers v Sheffield Wednesday ....
Coventry City v Manchester United ....
Derby County v Charlton Athletic ....
Leeds United v Everton ....
Liverpool v West Ham United ....
Middlesbrough v Tottenham Hotspur ....
Nottingham Forest v Chelsea ....
Southampton v Newcastle United ....
Wimbledon v Aston Villa ....

Nationwide Football League Division 1

Barnsley v Grimsby Town ....
Birmingham City v Bolton Wanderers ....
Bury v Norwich City ....
Crewe Alexandra v Stockport County ....
Huddersfield Town v Tranmere Rovers ....
Ipswich Town v Oxford United ....
Port Vale v Crystal Palace ....
Queens Park Rangers v Watford ....
Sheffield United v Bradford City ....
Sunderland v Wolverhampton Wanderers ....
Swindon Town v Portsmouth ....
West Bromwich Albion v Bristol City ....

Nationwide Football League Division 2

Blackpool v Lincoln City ....
Bristol Rovers v Luton Town ....
Fulham v Notts County ....
Gillingham v Colchester United ....
Manchester City v Macclesfield Town ....
Millwall v Stoke City ....
Oldham Athletic v Northampton Town ....
Reading v Preston North End ....
Walsall v Chesterfield ....
Wigan Athletic v A.F.C. Bournemouth ....
Wrexham v York City ....
Wycombe Wanderers v Burnley ....

Nationwide Football League Division 3

Cardiff City v Halifax Town ....
Carlisle United v Mansfield Town ....
Darlington v Plymouth Argyle ....
Exeter City v Hartlepool United ....
Hull City v Barnet ....
Leyton Orient v Cambridge United ....

Peterborough United v Shrewsbury Town ....
Rotherham United v Brentford ....
Scarborough v Swansea City ....
Scunthorpe United v Rochdale ....
Southend United v Brighton & Hove Albion ....
Torquay United v Chester City ....

Saturday, February 27 1999

FA Carling Premiership

Aston Villa v Coventry City ....
Charlton Athletic v Nottingham Forest ....
Chelsea v Liverpool ....
Everton v Wimbledon ....
Leicester City v Leeds United ....
Manchester United v Southampton ....
Newcastle United v Arsenal ....
Sheffield Wednesday v Middlesbrough ....
Tottenham Hotspur v Derby County ....
West Ham United v Blackburn Rovers ....

Nationwide Football League Division 1

Bolton Wanderers v Crewe Alexandra ....
Bradford City v West Bromwich Albion ....
Bristol City v Ipswich Town ....
Crystal Palace v Barnsley ....
Grimsby Town v Birmingham City ....
Norwich City v Sheffield United ....
Oxford United v Sunderland ....
Portsmouth v Port Vale ....
Stockport County v Queens Park Rangers ....
Tranmere Rovers v Bury ....
Watford v Swindon Town ....
Wolverhampton Wanderers v Huddersfield Town ....

Nationwide Football League Division 2

A.F.C. Bournemouth v Wycombe Wanderers ....
Burnley v Gillingham ....
Chesterfield v Manchester City ....
Colchester United v Reading ....
Lincoln City v Bristol Rovers ....
Luton Town v Blackpool ....
Macclesfield Town v Wigan Athletic ....
Northampton Town v Millwall ....
Notts County v Walsall ....
Preston North End v Oldham Athletic ....
Stoke City v Wrexham ....
York City v Fulham ....

Nationwide Football League Division 3

Barnet v Exeter City ....
Brentford v Scarborough ....
Brighton & Hove Albion v Leyton Orient ....
Cambridge United v Southend United ....
Chester City v Carlisle United ....
Halifax Town v Hull City ....
Hartlepool United v Rotherham United ....
Mansfield Town v Scunthorpe United ....
Plymouth Argyle v Peterborough United ....
Rochdale v Cardiff City ....
Shrewsbury Town v Darlington ....
Swansea City v Torquay United ....

Tuesday, March 2 1999

Nationwide Football League Division 1

Barnsley v Bradford City ....
Birmingham City v Norwich City ....
Bury v Wolverhampton Wanderers ....
Crewe Alexandra v Bristol City ....
Huddersfield Town v Bolton Wanderers ....
Ipswich Town v Watford ....
Port Vale v Grimsby Town ....
Sheffield United v Crystal Palace ....
Sunderland v Portsmouth ....
West Bromwich Albion v Stockport County ....

ionwide Football League Division 1

eens Park Rangers v Oxford United ....
indon Town v Tranmere Rovers ....

urday, March 6 1999

Carling Premiership

enal v Sheffield Wednesday ....
ckburn Rovers v Everton ....
ventry City v Charlton Athletic ....
by County v Aston Villa ....
ds United v Tottenham Hotspur ....
rpool v Manchester United ....
ddlesbrough v Chelsea ....
ttingham Forest v Newcastle United ....
thampton v West Ham United ....
nbledon v Leicester City ....

onwide Football League Division 1

asley v Bristol City ....
ningham City v Portsmouth ....
e v Crystal Palace ....
we Alexandra v Grimsby Town ....
ddersfield Town v Stockport County ....
ich Town v Tranmere Rovers ....
Vale v Bradford City ....
eens Park Rangers v Wolverhampton Wanderers ....
field United v Watford ....
erland v Norwich City ....
don Town v Bolton Wanderers ....
: Bromwich Albion v Oxford United ....

nwide Football League Division 2

pool v Stoke City ....
ol Rovers v York City ....
am v Lincoln City ....
agham v Preston North End ....
chester City v Northampton Town ....
all v Notts County ....
am Athletic v A.F.C. Bournemouth ....
ng v Macclesfield Town ....
all v Luton Town ....
n Athletic v Burnley ....
ham v Chesterfield ....
mbe Wanderers v Colchester United ....

nwide Football League Division 3

ff City v Chester City ....
le United v Shrewsbury Town ....
igton v Brentford ....
r City v Cambridge United ....
ity v Mansfield Town ....
n Orient v Rochdale ....
orough United v Hartlepool United ....
rham United v Barnet ....
rough v Plymouth Argyle ....
horpe United v Brighton & Hove Albion ....
end United v Swansea City ....
ay United v Halifax Town ....

ay, March 9 1999

wide Football League Division 1

a Wanderers v Barnsley 8:00 ....
rd City v Sunderland ....
City v Bury ....
Palace v Ipswich Town ....
by Town v Queens Park Rangers ....
ch City v Port Vale ....
d United v Huddersfield Town ....
nouth v Sheffield United ....
ort County v Swindon Town ....
ere Rovers v Birmingham City ....
rd v West Bromwich Albion ....
rhampton Wanderers v Crewe Alexandra ....

Nationwide Football League Division 2

A.F.C. Bournemouth v Bristol Rovers ....
Burnley v Manchester City ....
Chesterfield v Millwall ....
Colchester United v Oldham Athletic ....
Lincoln City v Wrexham ....
Luton Town v Fulham ....
Macclesfield Town v Gillingham ....
Northampton Town v Wigan Athletic ....
Notts County v Wycombe Wanderers ....
Preston North End v Walsall ....
York City v Blackpool ....

Nationwide Football League Division 3

Barnet v Carlisle United ....
Brentford v Peterborough United ....
Cambridge United v Hull City ....
Chester City v Scarborough 7:30 ....
Halifax Town v Scunthorpe United ....
Hartlepool United v Leyton Orient 7:30 ....
Mansfield Town v Exeter City ....
Plymouth Argyle v Torquay United ....
Rochdale v Southend United ....
Shrewsbury Town v Rotherham United ....
Swansea City v Darlington ....

Wednesday, March 10 1999

Nationwide Football League Division 2

Stoke City v Reading ....

Nationwide Football League Division 3

Brighton & Hove Albion v Cardiff City 8:00 ....

Friday, March 12 1999

Nationwide Football League Division 2

Bristol Rovers v Fulham ....

Saturday, March 13 1999

FA Carling Premiership

Chelsea v West Ham United ....
Coventry City v Blackburn Rovers ....
Derby County v Liverpool ....
Everton v Arsenal ....
Leicester City v Charlton Athletic ....
Middlesbrough v Southampton ....
Newcastle United v Manchester United ....
Sheffield Wednesday v Leeds United ....
Tottenham Hotspur v Aston Villa ....
Wimbledon v Nottingham Forest ....

Nationwide Football League Division 1

Birmingham City v West Bromwich Albion ....
Bolton Wanderers v Queens Park Rangers ....
Bradford City v Norwich City ....
Bury v Barnsley ....
Grimsby Town v Sunderland ....
Ipswich Town v Huddersfield Town ....
Oxford United v Watford ....
Port Vale v Stockport County ....
Portsmouth v Crystal Palace ....
Swindon Town v Crewe Alexandra ....
Tranmere Rovers v Sheffield United ....
Wolverhampton Wanderers v Bristol City ....

Nationwide Football League Division 2

A.F.C. Bournemouth v Reading ....
Blackpool v Wrexham ....
Burnley v Preston North End ....
Lincoln City v Chesterfield ....
Luton Town v Stoke City ....
Macclesfield Town v Colchester United ....
Manchester City v Oldham Athletic ....
Millwall v Walsall ....

Notts County v York City ....
Wigan Athletic v Gillingham ....
Wycombe Wanderers v Northampton Town ....

Nationwide Football League Division 3

Barnet v Cambridge United ....
Brentford v Shrewsbury Town ....
Brighton & Hove Albion v Darlington ....
Cardiff City v Torquay United ....
Chester City v Scunthorpe United ....
Halifax Town v Carlisle United ....
Leyton Orient v Hull City ....
Mansfield Town v Rochdale ....
Peterborough United v Swansea City ....
Plymouth Argyle v Hartlepool United ....
Scarborough v Rotherham United ....
Southend United v Exeter City ....

Saturday, March 20 1999

FA Carling Premiership

Arsenal v Coventry City ....
Aston Villa v Chelsea ....
Blackburn Rovers v Wimbledon ....
Charlton Athletic v Tottenham Hotspur ....
Leeds United v Derby County ....
Liverpool v Leicester City ....
Manchester United v Everton ....
Nottingham Forest v Middlesbrough ....
Southampton v Sheffield Wednesday ....
West Ham United v Newcastle United ....

Nationwide Football League Division 1

Barnsley v Wolverhampton Wanderers ....
Bristol City v Bradford City ....
Crewe Alexandra v Oxford United ....
Crystal Palace v Grimsby Town ....
Huddersfield Town v Birmingham City ....
Norwich City v Portsmouth ....
Queens Park Rangers v Swindon Town ....
Sheffield United v Port Vale ....
Stockport County v Tranmere Rovers ....
Sunderland v Bolton Wanderers ....
Watford v Bury ....
West Bromwich Albion v Ipswich Town ....

Nationwide Football League Division 2

Chesterfield v Luton Town ....
Colchester United v Manchester City ....
Fulham v Blackpool ....
Gillingham v Lincoln City ....
Northampton Town v Macclesfield Town ....
Oldham Athletic v Millwall ....
Preston North End v A.F.C. Bournemouth ....
Reading v Wycombe Wanderers ....
Stoke City v Notts County ....
Walsall v Bristol Rovers ....
Wrexham v Burnley ....
York City v Wigan Athletic ....

Nationwide Football League Division 3

Cambridge United v Mansfield Town ....
Carlisle United v Brentford ....
Darlington v Southend United ....
Exeter City v Cardiff City ....
Hartlepool United v Brighton & Hove Albion ....
Hull City v Plymouth Argyle ....
Rochdale v Barnet ....
Rotherham United v Peterborough United ....
Scunthorpe United v Leyton Orient ....
Shrewsbury Town v Chester City ....
Swansea City v Halifax Town ....
Torquay United v Scarborough ....

Friday, March 26 1999

Nationwide Football League Division 3

Halifax Town v Leyton Orient ....

Saturday, March 27 1999

Nationwide Football League Division 1

Birmingham City v Queens Park Rangers ....
Bolton Wanderers v Bristol City ....
Bury v Sunderland ....
Crystal Palace v Bradford City ....
Grimsby Town v Wolverhampton Wanderers ....
Huddersfield Town v Norwich City ....
Ipswich Town v Stockport County ....
Port Vale v Watford ....
Portsmouth v Barnsley ....
Sheffield United v Oxford United ....
Tranmere Rovers v Crewe Alexandra ....
West Bromwich Albion v Swindon Town ....

Nationwide Football League Division 2

A.F.C. Bournemouth v Colchester United ....
Bristol Rovers v Notts County ....
Burnley v Macclesfield Town ....
Chesterfield v Blackpool ....
Lincoln City v York City ....
Luton Town v Gillingham ....
Millwall v Wrexham ....
Preston North End v Northampton Town ....
Reading v Manchester City ....
Walsall v Fulham ....
Wigan Athletic v Stoke City ....
Wycombe Wanderers v Oldham Athletic ....

Nationwide Football League Division 3

Brentford v Swansea City ....
Brighton & Hove Albion v Barnet ....
Cardiff City v Carlisle United ....
Chester City v Plymouth Argyle ....
Exeter City v Darlington ....
Peterborough United v Mansfield Town ....
Rotherham United v Scunthorpe United ....
Scarborough v Rochdale ....
Shrewsbury Town v Cambridge United ....
Southend United v Hull City ....
Torquay United v Hartlepool United ....

Friday, April 2 1999

Nationwide Football League Division 2

Colchester United v Preston North End ....
Northampton Town v A.F.C. Bournemouth ....
Oldham Athletic v Luton Town 3:30 ....

Saturday, April 3 1999

FA Carling Premiership

Aston Villa v West Ham United ....
Blackburn Rovers v Middlesbrough ....
Charlton Athletic v Chelsea ....
Derby County v Newcastle United ....
Leeds United v Nottingham Forest ....
Liverpool v Everton ....
Sheffield Wednesday v Coventry City ....
Southampton v Arsenal ....
Tottenham Hotspur v Leicester City ....
Wimbledon v Manchester United ....

Nationwide Football League Division 1

Barnsley v Sheffield United ....
Bradford City v Grimsby Town ....
Bristol City v Port Vale ....
Crewe Alexandra v Birmingham City ....
Norwich City v Crystal Palace ....
Oxford United v Bolton Wanderers ....
Queens Park Rangers v Huddersfield Town ....
Stockport County v Bury ....
Sunderland v West Bromwich Albion ....
Swindon Town v Ipswich Town ....
Watford v Tranmere Rovers ....
Wolverhampton Wanderers v Portsmouth ....

Nationwide Football League Division2

Blackpool v Walsall ....
...lham v Millwall ....
...llingham v Reading ....
Macclesfield Town v Wycombe Wanderers ....
...anchester City v Wigan Athletic ....
...otts County v Burnley ....
...oke City v Lincoln City ....
...rexham v Bristol Rovers ....
...rk City v Chesterfield ....

Nationwide Football League Division 3

...rnet v Halifax Town ....
...mbridge United v Cardiff City ....
...rlisle United v Torquay United ....
...rlington v Rotherham United ....
...rtlepool United v Brentford ....
...ll City v Scarborough ....
...ton Orient v Southend United ....
...nsfield Town v Brighton & Hove Albion ....
...mouth Argyle v Shrewsbury Town ....
...chdale v Peterborough United ....
...nthorpe United v Exeter City ....
...ansea City v Chester City ....

...nday, April 5 1999

...Carling Premiership

...elsea v Leeds United ....
...entry City v Southampton ....
...ton v Sheffield Wednesday ....
...nchester United v Derby County ....
...ddlesbrough v Wimbledon ....
...wcastle United v Tottenham Hotspur ....
...tingham Forest v Liverpool ....
...t Ham United v Charlton Athletic ....

...onwide Football League Division 1

...mingham City v Watford ....
...on Wanderers v Stockport County ....
...v Bradford City ....
...tal Palace v Sunderland ....
...nsby Town v Norwich City ....
...ddersfield Town v Swindon Town ....
...ich Town v Queens Park Rangers ....
...t Vale v Barnsley ....
...nsmouth v Bristol City ....
...field United v Wolverhampton Wanderers ....
...mere Rovers v Oxford United ....
...t Bromwich Albion v Crewe Alexandra ....

...onwide Football League Division 2

...ol Rovers v Northampton Town ....
...ley v Colchester United ....
...terfield v Stoke City ....
...oln City v Notts County ....
...wall v Blackpool ....
...on North End v Manchester City ....
...ing v Fulham ....
...n Athletic v Oldham Athletic ....
...ombe Wanderers v Gillingham ....

...onwide Football League Division 3

...ford v Plymouth Argyle ....
...ff City v Hull City ....
...er City v Barnet ....
...r City v Leyton Orient ....
...ax Town v Rochdale ....
...borough United v Darlington ....
...erham United v Swansea City ....
...orough v Carlisle United ....
...wsbury Town v Hartlepool United ....
...end United v Scunthorpe United ....
...uay United v Mansfield Town ....

FA Carling Premiership

Arsenal v Blackburn Rovers ....
Leicester City v Aston Villa ....

Nationwide Football League Division 2

A.F.C. Bournemouth v Macclesfield Town ....
Luton Town v York City ....
Walsall v Wrexham ....

Nationwide Football League Division 3

Brighton & Hove Albion v Cambridge United 8:00 ....

Friday, April 9 1999

Nationwide Football League Division 3

Swansea City v Shrewsbury Town ....

Saturday, April 10 1999

FA Carling Premiership

Aston Villa v Southampton ....
Blackburn Rovers v Manchester United ....
Derby County v Nottingham Forest ....
Leeds United v Liverpool ....
Leicester City v West Ham United ....
Middlesbrough v Charlton Athletic ....
Sheffield Wednesday v Newcastle United ....
Tottenham Hotspur v Arsenal ....
Wimbledon v Chelsea ....

Nationwide Football League Division 1

Barnsley v Tranmere Rovers ....
Bradford City v Portsmouth ....
Bristol City v Grimsby Town ....
Crewe Alexandra v Port Vale ....
Norwich City v Ipswich Town ....
Oxford United v Bury ....
Queens Park Rangers v West Bromwich Albion ....
Stockport County v Sheffield United ....
Sunderland v Huddersfield Town ....
Swindon Town v Birmingham City ....
Watford v Bolton Wanderers ....
Wolverhampton Wanderers v Crystal Palace ....

Nationwide Football League Division 2

Blackpool v Reading ....
Colchester United v Walsall ....
Fulham v Wigan Athletic ....
Gillingham v A.F.C. Bournemouth ....
Macclesfield Town v Preston North End ....
Manchester City v Lincoln City ....
Northampton Town v Luton Town ....
Notts County v Chesterfield ....
Oldham Athletic v Burnley ....
Stoke City v Bristol Rovers ....
Wrexham v Wycombe Wanderers ....
York City v Millwall ....

Nationwide Football League Division 3

Barnet v Scarborough ....
Cambridge United v Halifax Town ....
Carlisle United v Peterborough United ....
Darlington v Torquay United ....
Hartlepool United v Chester City ....
Hull City v Exeter City ....
Leyton Orient v Cardiff City ....
Mansfield Town v Southend United ....
Plymouth Argyle v Brighton & Hove Albion ....
Rochdale v Rotherham United ....
Scunthorpe United v Brentford ....

Sunday, April 11 1999

FA Carling Premiership

Everton v Coventry City ....

Tuesday, April 13 1999

Nationwide Football League Division2

A.F.C. Bournemouth v Walsall ....
Blackpool v Burnley 7:30 ....
Fulham v Gillingham ....
Lincoln City v Reading ....
Macclesfield Town v Chesterfield ....
Northampton Town v York City ....
Notts County v Wrexham ....
Oldham Athletic v Bristol Rovers ....
Wigan Athletic v Preston North End ....

Nationwide Football League Division 3

Brighton & Hove Albion v Shrewsbury Town 8:00 ....
Cambridge United v Rochdale ....
Carlisle United v Hull City ....
Chester City v Brentford 7:30 ....
Exeter City v Rotherham United ....
Leyton Orient v Plymouth Argyle ....
Mansfield Town v Halifax Town ....
Scunthorpe United v Peterborough United 7:30 ....
Southend United v Cardiff City ....
Swansea City v Hartlepool United ....
Torquay United v Barnet ....

Wednesday, April 14 1999

Nationwide Football League Division 2

Manchester City v Luton Town ....
Millwall v Colchester United ....
Stoke City v Wycombe Wanderers ....

Nationwide Football League Division 3

Scarborough v Darlington 7:30 ....

Friday, April 16 1999

Nationwide Football League Division 2

Colchester United v Notts County ....

Saturday, April 17 1999

FA Carling Premiership

Arsenal v Wimbledon ....
Charlton Athletic v Leeds United ....
Chelsea v Leicester City ....
Coventry City v Middlesbrough ....
Liverpool v Aston Villa ....
Manchester United v Sheffield Wednesday ....
Newcastle United v Everton ....
Nottingham Forest v Tottenham Hotspur ....
Southampton v Blackburn Rovers ....
West Ham United v Derby County ....

Nationwide Football League Division 1

Barnsley v Sunderland ....
Birmingham City v Wolverhampton Wanderers ....
Bolton Wanderers v Ipswich Town ....
Bradford City v Huddersfield Town ....
Crewe Alexandra v Watford ....
Crystal Palace v Swindon Town ....
Grimsby Town v Bury ....
Norwich City v Tranmere Rovers ....
Port Vale v Oxford United ....
Sheffield United v Queens Park Rangers ....
Stockport County v Bristol City ....
West Bromwich Albion v Portsmouth ....

Nationwide Football League Division 2

Bristol Rovers v Millwall ....
Burnley v A.F.C. Bournemouth ....
Chesterfield v Fulham ....
Gillingham v Manchester City ....
Luton Town v Lincoln City ....
Preston North End v Blackpool ....
Reading v Northampton Town ....
Walsall v Macclesfield Town ....
Wrexham v Oldham Athletic ....
Wycombe Wanderers v Wigan Athletic ....
York City v Stoke City ....

Nationwide Football League Division 3

Barnet v Mansfield Town ....
Brentford v Leyton Orient ....
Darlington v Cambridge United ....
Halifax Town v Brighton & Hove Albion ....
Hartlepool United v Scarborough ....
Hull City v Scunthorpe United ....
Peterborough United v Torquay United ....
Plymouth Argyle v Southend United ....
Rochdale v Chester City ....
Rotherham United v Carlisle United ....
Shrewsbury Town v Exeter City ....

Sunday, April 18 1999

Nationwide Football League Division 3

Cardiff City v Swansea City 12:00 ....

Saturday, April 24 1999

FA Carling Premiership

Aston Villa v Nottingham Forest ....
Blackburn Rovers v Liverpool ....
Derby County v Southampton ....
Everton v Charlton Athletic ....
Leeds United v Manchester United ....
Leicester City v Coventry City ....
Middlesbrough v Arsenal ....
Sheffield Wednesday v Chelsea ....
Tottenham Hotspur v West Ham United ....
Wimbledon v Newcastle United ....

Nationwide Football League Division 1

Bristol City v Birmingham City ....
Bury v Bolton Wanderers ....
Huddersfield Town v Barnsley ....
Ipswich Town v Crewe Alexandra ....
Oxford United v Norwich City ....
Portsmouth v Stockport County ....
Queens Park Rangers v Bradford City ....
Sunderland v Sheffield United ....
Swindon Town v Grimsby Town ....
Tranmere Rovers v Port Vale ....
Watford v Crystal Palace ....

Nationwide Football League Division 2

A.F.C. Bournemouth v Chesterfield ....
Blackpool v Bristol Rovers ....
Fulham v Wrexham ....
Lincoln City v Walsall ....
Macclesfield Town v York City ....
Manchester City v Wycombe Wanderers ....
Millwall v Preston North End ....
Northampton Town v Colchester United ....
Notts County v Luton Town ....
Oldham Athletic v Gillingham ....
Stoke City v Burnley ....
Wigan Athletic v Reading ....

Nationwide Football League Division 3

Brighton & Hove Albion v Hull City ....
Cambridge United v Peterborough United ....
Carlisle United v Darlington ....

...hester City v Halifax Town ....
...eter City v Rochdale ....
...yton Orient v Shrewsbury Town ....
...ansfield Town v Hartlepool United ....
...arborough v Cardiff City ....
...unthorpe United v Barnet ....
...uthend United v Brentford ....
...ansea City v Plymouth Argyle ....
...rquay United v Rotherham United ....

...nday, April 25 1999

...ionwide Football League Division 1

...olverhampton Wanderers v West Bromwich Albion 1:00 ....

...turday, May 1 1999

...Carling Premiership

...enal v Derby County ....
...arlton Athletic v Blackburn Rovers ....
...elsea v Everton ....
...ventry City v Wimbledon ....
...erpool v Tottenham Hotspur ....
...anchester United v Aston Villa ....
...wcastle United v Middlesbrough ....
...ttingham Forest v Sheffield Wednesday ....
...thampton v Leicester City ....
...st Ham United v Leeds United ....

...onwide Football League Division 1

...nsley v Watford ....
...rmingham City v Ipswich Town ....
...on Wanderers v Wolverhampton Wanderers ....
...dford City v Oxford United ....
...we Alexandra v Portsmouth ....
...tal Palace v Huddersfield Town ....
...msby Town v Tranmere Rovers ....
...swich City v Swindon Town ....
...Vale v Queens Park Rangers ....
...field United v Bristol City ....
...ckport County v Sunderland ....
...t Bromwich Albion v Bury ....

...onwide Football League Division 2

...ol Rovers v Manchester City ....
...ley v Fulham ....
...sterfield v Northampton Town ....
...chester United v Lincoln City ....
...ngham v Stoke City ....
...on Town v Macclesfield Town ....
...ton North End v Notts County ....
...ding v Millwall ....
...all v Oldham Athletic ....
...xham v Wigan Athletic ....
...ombe Wanderers v Blackpool ....
... City v A.F.C. Bournemouth ....

...onwide Football League Division 3

...et v Southend United ....
...tford v Exeter City ....
...ff City v Scunthorpe United ....
...ington v Chester City ....
...ax Town v Scarborough ....
...l City v Torquay United ....
...borough United v Leyton Orient ....
...outh Argyle v Cambridge United ....
...dale v Swansea City ....
...erham United v Brighton & Hove Albion ....
...wsbury Town v Mansfield Town ....

Saturday, May 8 1999

FA Carling Premiership

Aston Villa v Charlton Athletic ....
Blackburn Rovers v Nottingham Forest ....
Derby County v Coventry City ....
Everton v West Ham United ....
Leeds United v Arsenal ....
Leicester City v Newcastle United ....
Middlesbrough v Manchester United ....
Sheffield Wednesday v Liverpool ....
Tottenham Hotspur v Chelsea ....
Wimbledon v Southampton ....

Nationwide Football League Division 2

A.F.C. Bournemouth v Wrexham ....
Blackpool v Colchester United ....
Fulham v Preston North End ....
Lincoln City v Wycombe Wanderers ....
Macclesfield Town v Bristol Rovers ....
Manchester City v York City ....
Millwall v Luton Town ....
Northampton Town v Burnley ....
Notts County v Gillingham ....
Oldham Athletic v Reading ....
Stoke City v Walsall ....
Wigan Athletic v Chesterfield ....

Nationwide Football League Division 3

Brighton & Hove Albion v Rochdale ....
Cambridge United v Brentford ....
Carlisle United v Plymouth Argyle ....
Chester City v Rotherham United ....
Exeter City v Halifax Town ....
Leyton Orient v Barnet ....
Mansfield Town v Cardiff City ....
Scarborough v Peterborough United ....
Scunthorpe United v Darlington ....
Southend United v Hartlepool United ....
Swansea City v Hull City ....
Torquay United v Shrewsbury Town ....

Sunday, May 9 1999

Nationwide Football League Division 1

Bristol City v Norwich City 1:30 ....
Bury v Port Vale 1:30 ....
Huddersfield Town v Crewe Alexandra 1:30 ....
Ipswich Town v Sheffield United 1:30 ....
Oxford United v Stockport County 1:30 ....
Portsmouth v Bolton Wanderers 1:30 ....
Queens Park Rangers v Crystal Palace 1:30 ....
Sunderland v Birmingham City 1:30 ....
Swindon Town v Barnsley 1:30 ....
Tranmere Rovers v West Bromwich Albion 1:30 ....
Watford v Grimsby Town 1:30 ....
Wolverhampton Wanderers v Bradford City 1:30 ....

Sunday, May 16 1999

FA Carling Premiership

Arsenal v Aston Villa 4:00 ....
Charlton Athletic v Sheffield Wednesday 4:00 ....
Chelsea v Derby County 4:00 ....
Coventry City v Leeds United 4:00 ....
Liverpool v Wimbledon 4:00 ....
Manchester United v Tottenham Hotspur 4:00 ....
Newcastle United v Blackburn Rovers 4:00 ....
Nottingham Forest v Leicester City 4:00 ....
Southampton v Everton 4:00 ....
West Ham United v Middlesbrough 4:00 ....